A SAMARITAN STATE
REVISITED

BEYOND BOUNDARIES: CANADIAN DEFENCE AND STRATEGIC STUDIES SERIES

Rob Huebert, Series Editor

ISSN 1716-2645 (Print) ISSN 1925-2919 (Online)

Canada's role in international military and strategic studies ranges from peacebuilding and Arctic sovereignty to unconventional warfare and domestic security. This series provides narratives and analyses of the Canadian military from both an historical and a contemporary perspective.

No. 1 · *The Generals: The Canadian Army's Senior Commanders in the Second World War*
J. L. Granatstein

No. 2 · *Art and Memorial: The Forgotten History of Canada's War Art*
Laura Brandon

No. 3 · *In the National Interest: Canadian Foreign Policy and the Department of Foreign Affairs and International Trade, 1909–2009*
Greg Donaghy and Michael K. Carroll

No. 4 · *Long Night of the Tankers: Hitler's War Against Caribbean Oil*
David J. Bercuson and Holger H. Herwig

No. 5 · *Fishing for a Solution: Canada's Fisheries Relations with the European Union, 1977–2013*
Donald Barry, Bob Applebaum, and Earl Wiseman

No. 6 · *From Kinshasa to Kandahar: Canada and Fragile States in Historical Perspective*
Michael K. Carroll and Greg Donaghy

No. 7 · *The Frontier of Patriotism: Alberta and the First World War*
Adriana A. Davies and Jeff Keshen

No. 8 · *China's Arctic Ambitions and What They Mean for Canada*
P. Whitney Lackenbauer, Adam Lajeunesse, James Manicom, and Frédéric Lasserre

No. 9 · *Scattering Chaff: Canadian Air Power and Censorship during the Kosovo War*
Bob Bergen

No. 10 · *A Samaritan State Revisited: Historical Perspectives on Canadian Foreign Aid*
Greg Donaghy and David Webster

UNIVERSITY OF CALGARY
Press

A SAMARITAN STATE
REVISITED

Historical Perspectives on Canadian Foreign Aid

Edited by **GREG DONAGHY** and **DAVID WEBSTER**

Beyond Boundaries:
Canadian Defence and Strategic Studies Series
ISSN 1716-2645 (Print) ISSN 1925-2919 (Online)

University of Calgary Press
2500 University Drive NW
Calgary, Alberta
Canada T2N 1N4
press.ucalgary.ca

LIBRARY AND ARCHIVES CANADA CATALOGUING IN PUBLICATION

Title: A samaritan state revisited : historical perspectives on Canadian foreign aid / edited by Greg Donaghy and David Webster.
Names: Donaghy, Greg, editor. | Webster, David, 1966- editor.
Series: Beyond boundaries series ; no. 10.
Description: Series statement: Beyond boundaries : Canadian defence and strategic studies series, 1716-2645 ; no. 10 | Includes bibliographical references and index.
Identifiers: Canadiana (print) 20190110317 | Canadiana (ebook) 20190110392 | ISBN 9781773850405 (softcover) | ISBN 9781773850412 (Open Access PDF) | ISBN 9781773850429 (PDF) | ISBN 9781773850436 (EPUB) | ISBN 9781773850443 (Kindle)
Subjects: LCSH: Economic assistance, Canadian—Developing countries—History.
Classification: LCC HC60 .S26 2019 | DDC 338.91/7101724—dc23

The University of Calgary Press acknowledges the support of the Government of Alberta through the Alberta Media Fund for our publications. We acknowledge the financial support of the Government of Canada. We acknowledge the financial support of the Canada Council for the Arts for our publishing program.

This book has been published with the help of a grant from the Canadian Federation for the Humanities and Social Sciences, through the Awards to Scholarly Publications Program, using funds provided by the Social Sciences and Humanities Research Council of Canada.

Printed and bound in Canada by Marquis
♻ This book is printed on Euroart Silk and Enviro paper

Front cover images: CIDA Photo Collection, Global Affairs Canada.
Back cover image: "Ville de Canada," by Elaine Brière. Image courtesy of the artist.

Copyediting by Peter Enman
Cover design, page design, and typesetting by Melina Cusano

CONTENTS

LIST OF ABBREVIATIONS

AECL	Atomic Energy of Canada Limited
CADEC	Christian Action for Development in the Caribbean
CALA	Canadian Association for Latin America
CBC	Canadian Broadcasting Corporation
CCC	Canadian Commercial Corporation
CCF	Cooperative Commonwealth Federation
CCIC	Canadian Council for International Cooperation
CIAT	Centro Internacional de Agricultura Tropical
CIDA	Canadian International Development Agency
CIDB	Canadian International Development Board
CIR	Canada-India Reactor
CMCP	Canadian Museum of Contemporary Photography
CSO	Civil Society Organization
CUSO	Canadian University Service Overseas
DEA	Department of External Affairs
DEAP	Development Education Animateur Programme
DFAIT	Department of Foreign Affairs and International Trade
DFATD	Department of Foreign Affairs, Trade and Development
EAO	External Aid Office
EDC	Export Development Corporation
ETAB	Economic and Technical Assistance Branch
FTA	Free Trade Agreements
GAC	Global Affairs Canada

GAFRN	Guelph African Famine Relief Network
GDP	Gross Domestic Product
GNI	Gross National Income
IAEA	International Atomic Energy Agency
ICIO	Interdepartmental Committee on International Organizations
ICRC	International Committee of the Red Cross
IDB	Inter-American Development Bank
IDPL	International Development Photo Library
IDRC	International Development Research Centre
IMF	International Monetary Fund
ITC	Industry, Trade and Commerce
KANUPP	Karachi Nuclear Power Plant
NAFTA	North American Free Trade Agreement
NATO	North Atlantic Treaty Organization
NDP	New Democratic Party
NGO	Non-governmental Organization
NPT	Non-proliferation Treaty
OAS	Organization of American States
ODA	Official Development Assistance
OECD	Organization for Economic Cooperation and Development
PPP	Public Participation Program
RAPP	Rajasthan Nuclear Power Project
SAP	Structural adjustment program
SPB	Special Programs Branch
TAA	Technical Assistance Administration (UN)
UNDP	United Nations Development Programme
UNESCO	United Nations Educational, Scientific and Cultural Organization
USAID	United States Agency for International Development
WID	Women in Development
WUSC	World University Service of Canada

ACKNOWLEDGEMENTS

This volume would not have been possible without the strong support of several organizations and many individuals. Global Affairs Canada encouraged the editors to pursue this project from an early date and generously helped fund a public symposium where contributors were able to showcase their research. This conference was only made possible by additional support from the history departments of both Carleton and Bishop's universities.

The editors also received substantial support and encouragement from a diverse group of people interested in the history of Canadian foreign aid and international history: Peter Boehm, Nicole Favreau, Mary Halloran, Geneviève Houle, Natasha Joukovskaia, Lilly Nicholls, Denis Robert, and Keith Spicer.

The success of our conference owed much to the efforts of the individuals who chaired its sessions: Deirdre Kent, Sandelle Scrimshaw, Anne-Marie Bourcier, Betty Plewes, David Stockwell, and Émile Gauvreau. They carried out their duties with good humour and panache, enlivening the academic proceedings with sharp observations and engaging reminisces from the field.

Professor Pierre Beaudet of the University of Ottawa stepped in at the last moment to fill an unexpected programming gap with a frank and iconoclastic account of Canadian aid in the Middle East. It is our loss that he was unable to take on the burden of writing a chapter for this book.

We offer a heartfelt thanks to our editorial collaborators at the University of Calgary Press, too. Over the last decade, we have relied on their expertise for several projects, and each time, they have responded with a demonstrable commitment to accessible and affordable academic excellence.

Finally, we are especially grateful for the exceptional support and enthusiasm offered by Professor Dominique Marshall, director of the Canadian Network on Humanitarian History. Dominique helped shape this collection from its very beginnings, and has become an ardent champion for the history of Canadian foreign aid. She brought with her three exceptional students from Carleton: Julie Van Drie, Tyler Owens, and Sean Eedy.

Introduction

David Webster and Greg Donaghy

Over the past two decades, Canadian international history has slipped its traditional North Atlantic moorings. Studies of Canada's postwar relationships with a waning United Kingdom or an ascendant United States have faded in popularity, replaced with a stream of publications on relations with the decolonized states of Asia, Africa, and the Caribbean, countries whose citizens increasingly comprise the population of contemporary Canada.[1]

The history of Canadian foreign aid, or official development assistance (ODA), however, remains a laggard. Reflecting the long-established tradition of Canadian missionary histories, the field favours their secular successors as they fled churches into the postwar volunteer sector, especially at the United Nations and the Canadian University Service Overseas (CUSO).[2] Although government aid agencies interacted with those groups, Ottawa's ODA efforts have received much less attention. Yet Canada's aid history was a complicated business, shaped by a broad range of forces, both internal and external. That history is only beginning to be written. This book seeks to enrich that story, while bringing Canada into global conversations on the history of development.[3]

Keith Spicer's pioneering study, *A Samaritan State? External Aid in Canada's Foreign Policy*, remains the touchstone, even as it passes its fiftieth anniversary.[4] Though a careful analyst, Spicer was a partisan in the debates he described and an advocate for doing aid differently. Other early histories of Canadian aid were prepared by stakeholders too. A classic example is the collection edited by Cranford Pratt in 1994, *Canadian International Development Assistance Policies: An Appraisal*, which already looked back to a lost golden age of Canadian aid.[5] David Morrison's *Aid and Ebb Tide* is the dominant institutional history of Canadian aid and of its major instrument from 1968 to 2013, the Canadian International Development Agency (CIDA). Part policy history, part administrative history, in the end, *Aid and Ebb Tide* is neither.[6] Its focus on public statements of high policy leaves little room for the mundane, yet important, task of describing exactly how Canadian aid was conceived, administered, and delivered.

In the fall of 2016, Global Affairs Canada and the history departments of Carleton and Bishop's universities hosted a symposium on the history of Canadian foreign aid. It seemed appropriate on the fiftieth anniversary of the publication of Spicer's *A Samaritan State?* to invite a new generation of historians and political scientists to reflect on the broad ideological and institutional origins of Canada's ODA in the 1950s, as well as specific themes in its evolution and professionalization after 1960. This volume is the result. Historians are beginning to look more carefully at Canada's aid history, a move that is part of a global turn to examine the evolution of development more seriously. In Canada, they are helped by improved access to archival sources, including voluminous project files detailing the history of Canadian overseas development assistance, which for many years were not easy to access. Non-governmental sources from private collections are also becoming more available.[7]

Studying Canadian aid history requires grappling with the common notion that Canada has acted as, in the title of both Spicer's volume and this one, a Samaritan state concerned mostly with doing good by helping the world's poorest. Spicer wrote with few illusions, rejecting his own title's implied premise. The image of selfless Samaritan, he argued, was myth that served no one. "Canada launched her development aid programme in 1950 with virtually no policy aim," he began, "beyond a lively anti-Communist instinct and an exhilarating vision of a free, multi-racial Commonwealth."[8]

In revisiting the concept of Canada as a "Samaritan state," this volume's contributors see Canadian government policy goals as much more important than pure altruism in shaping Canadian ODA. Defining the "national interest" is a tricky thing. Yet most authors here conclude that federal government perceptions of Canadian interests were the major influence on Canadian aid policy and practice. Talk of aid as altruism came later, aimed partly at building public support for aid by painting Canada as a "Samaritan" in the eyes of Canadians and the world. This image, built as much by non-governmental actors as by government, has certainly boosted Canada's global image, even as Canada's per capita aid figures often trailed those of other donors.

Policy papers, administrative reforms, and operational adjustments abounded and multiplied as the aid program grew from infancy into adulthood, at a time when, its early planners had hoped, it should be entering retirement. But aid shows no sign of ending. The need is clearly as great as ever, though its aims and means have shifted over the years. One of this book's questions is how clear and coherent these changing aims and strategies have been.

Authors find continuity in themes, but less coherence in implementation. In many ways donor and recipient interests dovetailed, allowing a proliferation of aid and aid structures. This was often offset, however, by an uneasy tension between the stress recipient governments placed on poverty reduction and industrialization, and the emphasis donor governments put on global stability. Should aid help the poorest—a Samaritan approach—or did it also aim to win allies for the West in the Global South, maintaining political, commercial, and cultural trade ties in a post-colonial age?

Canada joined many others in entering the field of development assistance in the late 1940s and 1950s. The venture built on postwar relief efforts in Europe, especially the massive multilateral mission by the United Nations Relief and Rehabilitation Administration (UNRRA) that carried the idea of orderly planning from war into peacetime.[9] Canada sent aid both multilaterally, through the United Nations and its agencies, as well as bilaterally to favoured countries, especially in the Asian Commonwealth. It pledged both technical assistance (experts, scholarships, and skills transfer) and capital aid (money for major development projects). From time to time, Ottawa increased the volume. Within the Colombo Plan, the Commonwealth's aid scheme for Asia, recipient governments drew up their own development plans and donors pitched in to projects of their choice, sometimes in exchange for the chance to "brand" them—a Canada dam here, a Canada bridge there. Aid was "tied" to Canadian products, serving as economic stimulus at home. If India needed tractors or Burma needed rail cars, and no Canadian company made them, then Canada would not give them as aid.

Still, Canada made plenty of things, and was willing to send them to Asia—at least to those parts that were non-communist and, most especially, Commonwealth members. During the 1950s, Canadian aid was heavily concentrated on India, Pakistan, and Ceylon (now Sri Lanka) in a way future governments seeking to focus aid on a small number of countries might envy. In the first fifteen years of Canada's aid program (1950–65), 95 per cent of Canadian assistance went to Asian Commonwealth member countries.[10] Amidst this activity, policy sometimes seemed a secondary consideration, which made aid administration and project selection more freewheeling and creative, and more open to recipient government priorities. Ottawa left the big picture to the United Nations, its aid programs distinct but conceived as part of a broader multilateral effort—not a bad summary of how Canadians saw their foreign relations as a whole.

Yet Canada's early aid program was still a complicated business, shaped, as the first three chapters in this collection demonstrate, by a range of unexplored internal and external factors. The focus of Jill Campbell-Miller's opening chapter on aid to India is not Ottawa but New Delhi. Her perspective reflects the pioneering work of US historian David Ekbladh on postwar modernization in the Global South, as well as her own extensive research in detailed Canadian project files. Campbell-Miller dismisses explanatory models that characterize the countries of the Global South as passive, neo-colonial recipients of Northern largesse. Rather, she sees foreign aid as global dialogue. Her closely argued account of the origins of Ottawa's commitment to the Colombo Plan explains how unprepared its officials and politicians were to venture into this novel field. India's colonial development experiences, which lingered into the 1950s, and its fierce postwar ambitions, she contends, did as much, if not more, than Ottawa to define Canadian aid to India.

Greg Donaghy's chapter traces how bureaucratic structures created to deliver Canadian capital and technical assistance left a lasting imprint on the shape of Canadian ODA. It amends the traditional view that the aid program was poorly conceived and chaotically managed. Administrative arrangements were an innovative experiment in keeping with the novelty of the aid program itself. Admittedly, dividing the aid mandate between the departments of External Affairs and Trade and Commerce during the 1950s generated interdepartmental rivalries. But at the same time, division created space to allow a unique organizational culture to flourish, especially under administrator R. G. "Nik" Cavell. The International Economic and Technical Cooperation Division, erected within Trade and Commerce in September 1951, skirted traditional notions of hierarchy, adopted a "can-do" ethos, and nurtured long-term expansionist ambitions. In a sense, the "organizational essence" that underpinned Canadian aid until the late 1980s was rooted in the imperfect bureaucracy of the 1950s.[11]

Equally important, and too often overlooked in the literature, Canada's aid program was formed through dialogue with the global community. This volume's third chapter, by David Webster, explores the UN career of Hugh Keenleyside to underscore this point. A Vancouver native with a PhD from the University of British Columbia, Keenleyside joined the Department of External Affairs in 1929, rose quickly, and became deputy minister of the Department of Mines and Resources in 1947. When he joined the UN's technical assistance work in 1950, he brought his faith in social democracy—especially its Canadian variant—government intervention, and economic modernization to bear on the UN's expanded aid program as it established its character in the 1950s. Simultaneously, Keenleyside's high-profile presence in New York legitimized UN aid operations in Ottawa, encouraging a Canadian aid program with a strong financial and political commitment to a global development model distinct from the one pursued by Washington.

By the late 1950s, Canada's aid program had broadened its focus beyond its South Asian origins. A growing volume of Ottawa's aid was directed through the United Nations, the World Bank, and other multilateral organizations. Requests for help from newly independent states in the Caribbean and Africa prompted the creation of more programs. Moreover, domestic pressure to respond to demands from French Canada for a foreign policy reflecting Canadian biculturalism spawned cultural, educational, and economic aid packages for francophone West Africa and Latin America. As diplomats in External Affairs established relations with the states emerging from European colonialism into independence, they grasped the implications of these changes for Canada's overall foreign policy and jockeyed for control over aid allocations with their rivals in Trade and Commerce. In 1960, Progressive Conservative prime minister John Diefenbaker moved all aid operations to a new External Aid Office (EAO). Under the leadership of senior diplomat Herb Moran, it reported directly to the secretary of state for external affairs.

Even as the EAO wrestled with its sprawling mandate, the intellectual climate shifted. Almost overnight, aid scattered in an ad hoc fashion over poorer parts of the globe became development assistance, a structured and often multilateral approach that marshalled technical and capital assistance, trade and financial policy, and coordinated donor support into a complex and long-term campaign for social change and economic growth. Few contemporary observers listed economic development in the Global South as an international priority after the Second World War, development economist Max Millikan observed in 1968. But now, he continued, it was "inconceivable that it would be left off anyone's list. The developed countries for their part are coming increasingly to view it both as in their national interest and as part of their world responsibility." Moreover, he continued, there was "growing recognition that development is a highly complex and multi-faceted process requiring simultaneous action on many fronts covered by many disciplines."[12]

The life stories of such early development economists as Benjamin Higgins, a Canadian who advised multiple countries on development strategies, illustrate how aid was professionalized and bureaucratized alongside the emergence of a new field of development economics.[13] The field promoted notions of government planning within capitalist economic structures, and built on previous colonial and post-colonial talk of modernization.[14] Planning meant increased control by both Southern governments over their people and Northern governments over economic directions.[15] In Eva-Maria Muschik's words, it was a shift from "the idea of helping countries help themselves to a more paternalist approach that focused on 'getting the work done' on behalf of aid recipients."[16] The crystallization of this "modernization theory" came with Walt Rostow's *Stages of Growth: A Non-Communist Manifesto*, which sketched alternative development trajectories, all based on Western models, championed as universally applicable with the correct injection of capital and expertise.

The transformation was driven in part by a shift in US policy: president John F. Kennedy's administration established the United States Agency for International Development (USAID) in November 1961, embraced modernization theory, and urged US allies to follow suit by expanding and professionalizing their own programs.[17] In May 1968, egged on by its reformist director-general, Maurice Strong, Liberal prime minister Pierre Trudeau transformed the EAO into CIDA. In forming the agency, Trudeau's government signalled its intention to become a major player in global aid, an ambition marked by a proliferating roster of recipient countries and a rising ODA budget. The launch of the International Development Research Centre (IDRC) in June 1970 underlined this determination to lead on aid policy and aid thinking.[18]

The evolving shape of Canadian aid administration echoed and amplified global trends, epitomized in the work of a UN-backed Commission on International Development chaired by former Liberal prime minister Lester B. Pearson. The result was *Partners in Development*, a major report launched in 1970 that re-imagined aid in ways better structured to the needs of developing countries and less tethered to the political twists and turns of donors. Famously, it set 0.7 per cent of GDP as the amount that wealthier states ought to spend on development assistance.

More important, Pearson's report recast aid as a cooperative endeavour between North and South, serving the interests of donor and recipient, and transcending the dichotomy between them. Northern interest in global stability was best served by aid that aimed to reduce poverty and spur industrialization—the goal of Southern governments. And, the report implied, vice versa. Governments and peoples on both sides of the North-South divide, in this vision, became "partners in development"—itself a concept being transformed into humanity's "mission statement" and a "global faith" for the later twentieth century.[19] CIDA too was supposed to mark a shift from "give away" aid to partnership.[20] Left unanswered was the question of whether development assistance also had neo-colonial dimensions that aimed to recast Southern societies in the image of Northern models.

Under Strong and his successor Paul Gérin-Lajoie, CIDA became almost a state within a state. The agency seemed to carry the potential for transformative change. Like the United Nations Development Programme (UNDP) and the Swedish International Development Agency (SIDA), both founded in 1965, it offered room for thinking about development differently. Its emergence reflected a shift in the anthropology of international development organizations, which became more bureaucratic, while simultaneously opening spaces for exploring the explosion of new work in agriculture, health, and other specialized fields.[21] CIDA hit the ground running. Its contribution to the Trudeau government's foreign policy review in 1969–70, a booklet simply titled *International Development,* insisted boldly that "for the first time in the history of the world, the accumulated wealth and technology of the affluent societies is sufficient to make possible the eradication of widespread endemic poverty."[22] It pledged to raise ODA; untie it from purchases made in Canada; target 80 per cent of aid to "countries of concentration"; and to deliver more funds through multilateral channels. It did not accomplish all these goals, but it did position CIDA as a voice calling for ODA to be driven first and foremost by humanitarian motives.

Yet aid often still aimed to serve the national interest. Ryan Touhey's chapter on Pakistan, India's near neighbour and bitter rival, pointedly asks what that aid meant for Canada. His grim answer: not much. To support Pakistani development and win political influence in Karachi, Ottawa spent some $230 million dollars on aid to Pakistan by 1965, making Canada the country's second largest donor. Increasingly sharp differences over Kashmir, nuclear non-proliferation, and the Cold War slowly woke Canadian policy makers up to the fact that fifteen years of aid purchased little influence. Trapped within the existing dynamic, Canadian diplomats in Pakistan and External Affairs squirmed uncomfortably as government-sponsored rioters targeted Canadian diplomatic premises in Karachi and Islamabad, but proved incapable of responding decisively. Only in 1971, following a war in South Asia that upset the geopolitical landscape, did Ottawa finally act, sharply reducing its stake in Pakistan.

Canadian aid often aimed to open doors for Canadian trade and investment, too. An example is provided in Stefano Tijerina's study of Canadian aid to Colombia from the 1950s to 1970s. Like Campbell-Miller, Tijerina is influenced by an American model, Emily Rosenberg's notion of the "promotional state," which marshals its political and economic resources to advance the interests of its domestic private sector corporate allies. Though Latin America was not a historic Canadian priority, as competition within the region's modernizing economy grew stronger, Tijerina argues, Ottawa

David Webster and Greg Donaghy

acted to preserve space for Canadian business to manoeuvre in the region. Diplomatic and trade support in the 1950s, evident in "goodwill" ministerial missions and arms sales, gave way in the 1960s and 1970s to "opportunistic" ODA, designed to safeguard Canada's market share in Colombia.

Tijerina's view is partly echoed in Asa McKercher's chapter on Pierre Trudeau's efforts to engage Latin America after his election in April 1968. Skeptical of Canada's postwar internationalism, Trudeau wanted policy rooted in Canada's economic interests, making trade and investment opportunities important factors determining aid allocations. But McKercher allows for other influences as well, noting the government's awareness of humanitarian need and its ideological enthusiasm for regional modernization and development. More important, in a chapter that focuses on aid to authoritarian Chile and revolutionary Cuba, McKercher explores the growing impact of Canadian civil society actors motivated by human rights concerns in shaping aid policies and allocations.

Measured as a percentage of GDP, Canadian aid under Trudeau reached 0.54 per cent in 1978, a number never again matched despite repeated government pledges to attain Pearson's target of 0.7 per cent.[23] If Canada's ODA had a pinnacle, this was it. Ironically, under Michel Dupuy, the veteran diplomat who replaced Paul Gérin-Lajoie as CIDA head in 1977, the agency's autonomy was slowly curbed as other departments harnessed its large budgets to broader foreign policy goals. Commercial considerations, in particular, increasingly came to the fore, even as CIDA reinforced its ties to Canada's growing community of non-governmental organizations (NGOs), which had long underpinned CIDA's public support.

Kevin Brushett delves more deeply into CIDA's public engagement work in the 1970s, an era he romanticizes as a "new golden age." His subject is Lewis Perinbam, a legendary "guerrilla bureaucrat," who ran CIDA's outreach programs for two decades. Born in Malaysia, educated in Scotland, and coming of age in Canada, Brushett's cosmopolitan Perinbam embodies the humane internationalist ideal.[24] Hired in 1969 to establish a division to engage Canadian NGOs, Perinbam transformed his original $5 million operation into CIDA's $323 million Special Branch Program over the next two decades, pragmatically branching out to engage business, industry, and youth. Elevated to CIDA vice-president, Perinbam proved innovative and effective in overcoming the inherent tensions between a government aid agency committed to the existing liberal economic order and more critical NGOs.

Domestic civic engagement, national identity, and public imagery were all part of Canada's development project right from the start. In Chapter 8, Ted Cogan sets the stage for a discussion of aid's symbolic character with an overview of the Canadian public's engagement with aid from 1950 to 1980, an era of sustained if episodic expansion. He flips the traditional lens on how civil society influenced aid policy—especially evident in this volume's chapters by McKercher and Laura Macdonald—on its head, asking instead how governments peddled foreign aid to their voters. Initially, he suggests, the array of complex economic and political forces behind the Colombo Plan made a clear narrative elusive. By the mid-1950s, however, Ottawa was promoting aid as a Canadian vocation, variously tied to the country's moral values, its shifting Commonwealth identify, or its internationalism. Yet popular support for aid waxed and waned with the country's economic fortunes, despite the increasingly sophisticated apparatus adopted by CIDA in the 1970s to enlist Canadian voters in its fight for development. "Expansion," Cogan concludes, "proved easier than consolidation."

Sonya de Laat's approach is more theoretical and more critical. Her chapter explores the evolution of CIDA's world-class photographic library, which began in the 1960s as an ad hoc collection of images used mostly to brief new employees on the agency's work and living conditions in the unfamiliar Global South. CIDA expanded its collecting activities in the 1970s, commissioning its own photographers to record material for public outreach and education activities. The International Development Photo Library (IDPL), as the collection was named in 1987, included 150,000 images by some of Canada's best photographers when it stopped collecting in 2010. De Laat tackles the IDPL, armed with a well-honed theoretical apparatus that locates the conventions of postwar development photography within their broader history of humanitarian images. CIDA employed a careful combination of negative and positive images, she argues, to cast Canada as "a caring and helpful nation." It was an image immune to political and policy changes, and one intended to bolster uncritical support for CIDA's work. "Samaritan" images were central to government aid messaging.

The effort was only partly successful. CIDA has, despite its best efforts, come under sustained attack for misdirected aid and grandiose projects.

Right-leaning critics denounced it as profligate and corrupt, while their left-leaning counterparts attacked its approach as neo-colonial.[25] Certainly, many aid projects have failed, and skepticism toward CIDA went hand in hand with increasing skepticism about the global aid industry.

While Ottawa's rhetorical commitment to aid rarely flagged, its resources did. Canada's aid to GDP ratio briefly recovered to 0.5 per cent in 1988, as Progressive Conservative prime minister Brian Mulroney's government signalled its intention to work closely with governments in the Global South. Mulroney re-oriented aid to focus on strengthening civil society, helping the poorest, and promoting "women in development," goals stressed during the tenure of CIDA president Margaret Catley-Carlson. Parliamentary support for this line shone through in the strong recommendations of a 1987 report by the House of Commons Committee on External Affairs and International Trade, *For Whose Benefit?* Dubbed the Winegard report after its chair, William Winegard, the report insisted that aid should serve "the needs of the poorest countries and people."[26] This expression of altruism as aid's purpose hardly reflected Canadian aid policy, but as funds disappeared, the theme became increasingly dominant and was formally entrenched in the Official Development Assistance Accountability Act of 2008.[27]

Winegard's strong support for Canadian foreign aid reflected the public reaction to the Ethiopian famine during the early 1980s. As Nassisse Solomon argues in her chapter on Canada's response to the African food crisis, the mid-1980s represent a singular moment in Canadian aid history. Like de Laat, Solomon explores aid imagery, especially the horrific images that emerged from famine-stricken Ethiopia in the fall of 1984. She is interested too in the political response from Mulroney's government and its successful effort to mobilize a broad coalition of Canadians in an immediate and widespread relief campaign. Solomon's Canada was indeed a "Samaritan State," at least until the hard facts in the Horn of Africa—brutal cold war politics, civil war and corruption, and aid's failure to show results—dampened popular enthusiasm. And finally, Solomon is interested in memory, wondering how the images of the 1980s inured later generations of Canadians to African distress, defining Ethiopia, and by extension the whole continent, as irredeemably broken.

FIGURE 0.1
Canadian Aid as Percentage of Gross National Income.

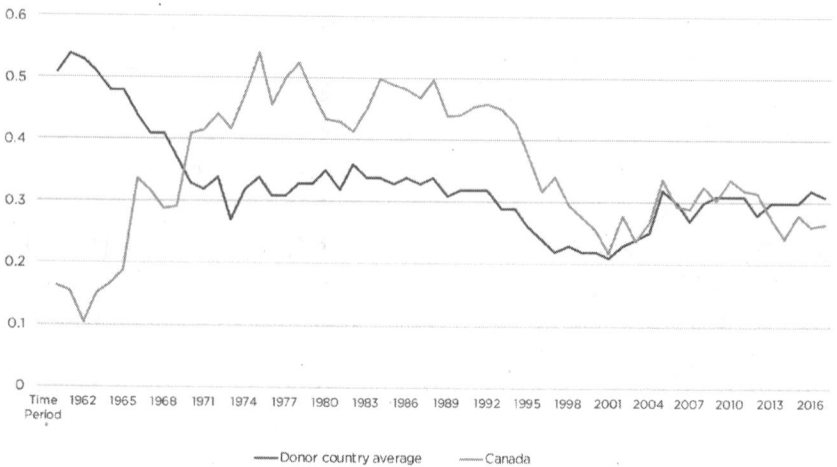

By the late 1980s, with the country's compassion exhausted, CIDA was vulnerable. In a Decima survey conducted in 1985, 50 per cent of respondents thought that aid was at the right level, whereas only 24 per cent wanted it to increase and 17 per cent judged it too high. Alarmingly, however, the highest level of respondents identified churches and NGOs rather than CIDA as making the major contribution to development.[28] There was not much political cost for governments that wanted to reduce Canada's involvement in international development.

Such a cutback began under Mulroney in 1989–92. Reductions in Canadian ODA reflected both a desire to trim deficits and the decreasing salience of aid as the Cold War sputtered to an end and the Global South ceased to be an arena of superpower contestation. Mulroney also aligned Canadian foreign policy more closely with Republican president Ronald Reagan's United States. Global trends after the Cold War made aid increasingly conditional on the neo-liberal structural adjustment programs championed by the international financial institutions (the World Bank and the International Monetary Fund) and major donor states. Under its president, Marcel Massé, CIDA embraced the free market "Washington consensus" that joined the largest international financial institutions and the US Treasury Department in pushing governments in the Global South to deregulate their economies. African, Asian, and Latin American governments were asked to reduce public spending and stress market-based policies. In a reflection of Canadian trade goals, CIDA prioritized more middle-income countries such as Indonesia and China as major recipients, while cutting out lower-income countries like Tanzania, once a favourite development partner.

Mulroney also began to dismantle the architecture of public engagement on which CIDA's popular support had rested. In 1992, the federal budget eliminated the National Advisory Committee on Development Education; the following year, he abolished CIDA's Public Participation Program.[29] The process accelerated under Liberal prime minister Jean Chrétien, was reflected in cuts to such groups as the Inter-Church Coalition on Africa, and culminated in the outright hostility toward many aid NGOs expressed by Conservative prime minister Stephen Harper's government. International development minister Bev Oda's elimination of funds to the NGO coalition KAIROS, and then to the Canadian Council for International Co-operation (an umbrella group gathering most Canadian aid NGOs), perfectly encapsulated the adversarial relationship between government and aid NGOs.[30] Hapless CIDA officials could not heal the breach, nor were they able to defend their own agency from calls to merge it with the much larger Department of Foreign Affairs and International Trade, a merger accomplished in 2013.

In our closing chapters, three veteran political scientists address in more detail these recent evolutions. Laura Macdonald, whose work has long been anchored in an activist commitment to justice in Latin America, ties Canadian aid to Ottawa's changing foreign policy priorities. As historic diffidence toward the region gave way to curiosity and interest in the 1960s, economic considerations, she argues, were clearly the most predominant and consistent influences on aid levels and policy. Yet, like McKercher, Macdonald is alive to other factors at play, especially a tradition of strong civil society linkages. Initially manifest in French-Canadian missionaries, secular North-South social networks flourished after 1970 as Canadian relations with South and Central America became highly politicized during the later years of the Cold War. While a search for economic advantage continued to shape Ottawa's aid policies in Latin America, especially under prime ministers Mulroney and Harper, sustained civil society engagement also mattered. This was true even as Harper's Conservative government merged CIDA with the foreign and trade department, and sharply reduced its traditional mechanisms for civil engagement.

CIDA's merger with the Department of Foreign Affairs and International Trade (DFAIT) is at the core of David Black's discussion of aid to Africa in the 1990s. Poverty and close ties with Canada (through the Commonwealth and La Francophonie) made sub-Saharan Africa CIDA's largest aid recipient, giving it an outsized role in buttressing CIDA's raison d'être, which was more fragile than ever. The challenges were threefold. Echoing many of our earlier chapters, Black underlines the continued uncertainty generated by the competing political, economic, and moral motives for Canadian aid. A failed experiment in decentralizing operations in the late 1980s, and Massé's embrace of neo-liberal economic policies, further eroded CIDA's sense of mission, rendering its "organizational essence" incoherent. When Chrétien's finance minister Paul Martin took the axe to its sub-Saharan African program in 1995, cutting it by 20.5 per cent over three years, he stripped CIDA of its vision for the future, leaving it defensive and risk averse. Unable to recover, CIDA was ripe for a takeover. In July 2013, Canadian aid operations were folded back into the Department of Foreign Affairs and International Trade. It was 1950 all over again.

Appropriately, our final chapter by Stephen Brown heads back to the future, revisiting Keith Spicer's *Samaritan State* in search of contemporary lessons. Two stand out. First, like Spicer and many more recent aid theorists, Brown is distrustful of aid's capacity to promote democracy and stability. Indeed, he goes even further, rejecting the power of aid's symbols and recipient country gratitude. The proof, he sharply points out, is scattered like litter across Afghanistan, Iraq, and Libya. Rather, and more modestly, Brown echoes Spicer's view that aid produces contact, engagement, and understanding, giving donors a tool to conduct more effective diplomacy and better contribute to international order.

Second, Brown embraces Spicer's preoccupation with policy coherence, insisting that there need be no contradiction between Canada's long-term interests in global order and the developing world's interest in poverty reduction. Trouble arises when the search for short-term donor

David Webster and Greg Donaghy

benefits—Canadian arms sales to Saudi Arabia or petroleum exports in an overheated world—trumps what we know to be in our long-term enlightened self-interest.

Development fashions have shifted considerably in the decades covered by this volume. Technical assistance gave way to megaprojects, which were eventually followed by waves of enthusiasm for the "basic needs" approach, for gender and development, and for sustainable development, all the way to the more recent UN-led Sustainable Development Goals and Canada's new stress on "feminist international development." Yet the basic theories around social change, modernization, and economic growth underlying the global development project have remained, leaving much of the ideological leadership with Northern actors.[31] Is ODA, then, destined to always remain a form of Northern economic dominance of the Global South? And has Canada acted in coercive, perhaps even imperialist, ways in doling out its meagre aid allotments?

Increasingly, the answer is in the affirmative. In his recent renewal of Cranford Pratt's "dominant class" thesis, for instance, political economist Jerome Klassen has argued that Canadian foreign policy, including aid, is driven by a capitalist model that has locked Canada into a US quest for global dominance.[32] In this view, Canada and its leading capitalists act along with Washington in co-imperialist ways toward the Global South. Todd Gordon offers another view of Canada as imperialist, but in ways that are not reliant on American leadership: Canada is an imperialist in its very own right.[33]

This book's chapters largely reject such deterministic models. They broadly accept the view that Canadian aid aimed to promote Ottawa's foreign policy goals, including the country's economic interests. Canada was clearly no Samaritan state. Yet the state hardly acted autonomously in shaping aid policy. Most chapters in this collection are rooted in detailed archival research, the valuable essence of the historical method, and explore both the broad motives and particularistic characteristics of aid operations. Most uncover meaningful limits on the Canadian state's autonomy to pursue imperialist objectives, including Southern resistance and preferences, the ideological choices of individual bureaucratic and political policy makers, corporate priorities, and the important role of civil society in advancing alternative views to influence state strategies. Indeed, Pratt already observed in the 1980s the beginning of a "counter-consensus" driven by non-governmental organizations.[34] That counter-consensus and the ways it interacts with government policies have developed considerably since then.

Together, the chapters in this volume offer a mixed view on the effectiveness and coherence of Canadian ODA over its seven-decade history. They note substantial shifts: aid, once "tied" entirely to the purchase of Canadian goods and services, is now untied and, in theory, more flexible and effective. Its implementation has slowly shifted toward centring Canadian NGOs in a more dynamic partnership between government aid strategies and NGO agents contracted to deliver it.

There are also considerable continuities, not all of them reflecting well on Canada. Trade motives were central at the start of Canadian ODA, with hopes that newly independent countries in Asia and later Africa might develop into more prosperous trade partners for Canada. Trade motives have not vanished; indeed, they made a comeback starting in the 1980s and culminating in a controversial push by the Harper government for coordination between Canadian aid and Canadian mining investments in the Global South. The early favour shown to non-communist countries as aid recipients during the Cold War is a thing of the past, but alignments between aid and strategic goals remain in today's "global war on terror." Canadian aid, too, flows disproportionately to countries with strong domestic lobbies in Canada, such as Haiti and the Ukraine.

On the brighter side, a renewed call to centre women in the "feminist international assistance policy" announced in 2017 by international development minister Marie-Claude Bibeau has promising echoes of CIDA's one-time stress on gender and development themes and civil society strengthening, though it is curiously uninformed by these historical forerunners and surprisingly under-resourced for such an ambitious program.[35] Canada has moved through new policies and new priorities in its ODA policy over the decades, with aid reviews perhaps even more common than foreign policy reviews, but coherence has long been lacking. Indeed, the repeated reviews and policy twists have themselves reduced coherence and thus effectiveness. The chapters in this book suggest that ODA has been formed in part from the dialogue between government and a civil society community engaged in development that the government has both sought to foster at times and undermine at others.

David Webster and Greg Donaghy

As a percentage of Gross National Income, Canadian ODA now stands at 0.26 per cent, less than half of its 1970s peak and well below the average for all donor states.[36] Ambitious positioning of Canada as global leader is undermined by the scant resources allocated. Still, Canadians see their country as generous and sympathetic, and Canadian governments have never ceased to be major players in global development debates. This book seeks to contribute to those debates by historicizing and nuancing Canadian involvement in development. Canada emerges neither as heroic do-gooder nor as imperialist exploiter. Rather, it occupies a more ambiguous position that has both reflected and shaped global trends in development thought and practice.

Notes

1   For a historiographical overview that laments the past focus on the North Atlantic and lists some of the newer literature, see David Meren, "The Tragedies of Canadian International History," *Canadian Historical Review* 96, no. 4 (Winter 2015): 534–66.

2   See, for instance, Ruth Compton Brouwer, "When Missions Became Development: Ironies of 'NGOization' in Mainstream Canadian Churches in the 1960s," *Canadian Historical Review* 91, no. 4 (Dec. 2010): 661–93.

3   For an overview of recent literature on development history, see Joseph Hodge, "Writing the History of Development (Part 1: The First Wave)," *Humanity* 6, no. 3 (2016): 429–63, http://humanityjournal.org/issue6-3/writing-the-history-of-development-part-1-the-first-wave/; and "Writing the History of Development (Part 2: Longer, Deeper, Wider)," *Humanity* 7, no. 1 (2016): 125–74, http://humanityjournal.org/issue7-1/writing-the-history-of-development-part-2-longer-deeper-wider/.

4   Keith Spicer, *A Samaritan State? External Aid in Canada's Foreign Policy* (Toronto: University of Toronto Press, 1966).

5   Cranford Pratt, ed., *Canadian International Development Assistance Policies: An Appraisal* (Montreal: McGill-Queen's University Press, 1994). Pratt lectured at Makerere University in Uganda in the mid-1950s and served as the first principal of the newly founded University of Dar es Salaam in Tanzania between 1960 and 1964.

6   David Morrison, *Aid and Ebb Tide: A History of CIDA and Canadian Development Assistance* (Waterloo, ON: Wilfrid Laurier University Press, 1998).

7   The Canadian Network on Humanitarian History has worked to make some of these records available. See aidhistory.ca for information on the network.

8   Spicer, *Samaritan State*, 3.

9   Jessica Reinisch, "Introduction: Relief in the Aftermath of War," *Journal of Contemporary History* 43, no. 3 (2008): 371–404; Reinisch, "'Auntie UNRRA' at the Crossroads," *Past and Present* 218, Issue supp. 8 (2013): 70–97; Suzanne Langlois, "'Neighbours Half the World Away': The National Film Board of Canada at Work for UNRRA (1944–47)," in *Canada and the United Nations: Legacies, Limits, Prospects,* ed. Colin McCullough and Robert Teigrob (Montreal: McGill-Queen's University Press, 2016), 44–81.

10   *A Report on Canada's External Aid Programmes 1965–66* (Ottawa: External Aid Office, 1966).

11   On "organizational essence," see David Black in this volume and Marie-Eve Desrosiers and Philippe Lagassé, "Canada and the Bureaucratic Politics of State Fragility." *Diplomacy and Statecraft* 20, no. 4 (2009): 659–78.

12   Max F. Millikan, "An Introductory Essay," in Richard N. Gardner and Max F. Millikan, eds., "The Global Partnership: International Agencies and Economic Development," *International Organization* 22, no. 1 (Winter 1968): 2, 6.

13   Benjamin Higgins, *All the Difference: A Development Economist's Quest* (Montreal: McGill-Queen's University Press, 1992); and *Economic Development* (New York: W. W. Norton, 1968).

14   See, for instance, Ruth Compton Brouwer, *Modern Women Modernizing Men: The Changing Missions of Three Professional Women in Asia and Africa, 1902–69* (Vancouver: University of British Columbia Press, 2002); Gilbert Rist, *The History of Development: From Western Origins to Global Faith,* 4th ed. (London: Zed Books, 2014); and Joseph Morgan Hodge, *Triumph of the Expert: Agrarian Doctrines of Development and the Legacies of British Colonialism* (Athens: Ohio University Press, 2007). On planning, see, for instance, Louis J. Walinsky, *The Planning and Execution of Economic Development* (New York: McGraw-Hill, 1963).

15   Arturo Escobar, "Planning," in Wolfgang Sachs, ed., *The Development Dictionary: A Guide to Knowledge as Power* (London: Zed Books, 1992).

16   Eva-Maria Muschik, "Managing the World: The United Nations, Decolonisation and the Strange Triumph of State Sovereignty in the 1950s and 1960s," *Journal of Global History* 12, no. 1 (March 2018): 122–44.

17   The voluminous literature on Kennedy-era modernization theory includes Michael Latham, *Modernization as Ideology: American Social Science and "Nation Building" in the Kennedy Era* (Chapel Hill: University of North Carolina Press, 2000); and David Ekbladh, *The Great American Mission: Modernization and the Construction of an American World Order, 1914 to the Present* (Princeton, NJ: Princeton University Press, 2010).

18   Bruce Muirhead and Ronald N. Harpelle, *IDRC: 40 Years of Ideas, Innovation, and Impact* (Waterloo, ON: Wilfrid Laurier University Press, 2010).

19   Nick Cullather, "Development? It's History," *Diplomatic History* 24, no. 4 (October 2000): 641–53; Rist, *History of Development.*

20   Morrison, *Aid and Ebb Tide,* 62.

21   On this approach to the study of international development organizations, see, among other sources, David Mosse, "The Anthropology of International Development," *Annual Review of Anthropology* 42 (2013): 227–46. On shifting definitions of development, see H. W. Arndt, *Economic Development: The History of an Ideal* (Chicago: University of Chicago Press, 1987); and Ariel Heryanto, "The Development of 'Development,'" *Indonesia* no. 46 (1988): 1–24, https://ecommons.cornell.edu/ bitstream/handle/1813/53891/INDO_46_0_1107010934_1_24.pdf?sequence=1. Recent work on new agrarian development and health care includes Corinne A. Pernet and Amalia Ribi Forclaz, "Revisiting the Food and Agriculture Organization (FAO): International Histories of Agriculture, Nutrition, and Development," *International History Review* (2018), https://doi.org/10.1080/07075332.2018.1460386; Sunil Amrith, *Decolonizing International Health: India and Southeast Asia, 1930–65* (London: Palgrave Macmillan, 2006); Madeleine Herren, "Towards a Global History of International Organizations," in *Networking the International System: Global Histories of International Organizations*, ed. Madeleine Herren (Heidelberg: Cham, 2014), 1–12; Marc Frey, Sönke Kunkel, and Corinna R. Unger, eds., *International Organizations and Development, 1945–1990* (London: Palgrave Macmillan, 2014). The best history of CIDA remains Morrison, *Aid and Ebb Tide.*

22   Department of External Affairs, *Foreign Policy for Canadians: International Development* (Ottawa: Queen's Printer, 1970), 7.

23   Ivan Head and Pierre Trudeau, *The Canadian Way: Shaping Canada's Foreign Policy, 1968–1984* (Toronto: McClelland and Stewart, 1995), 161; Cranford Pratt, "Canadian Development Assistance: A Profile," in Pratt, *Canadian International Development*, 5.

24   Cranford Pratt, *Middle Power Internationalism: The North-South Dimension* (Montreal: McGill-Queen's University Press, 1990).

25   William Easterly, *The Elusive Quest for Growth: Economists' Adventures and Misadventures in the Tropics* (Cambridge, MA: MIT Press, 2001); Dambisa Moyo, *Dead Aid: Why Aid Is Not Working and How There Is a Better Way for Africa* (New York: Farrar, Strauss and Giroux, 2009); Rist, *History of Development*; Sachs, *Development Dictionary.*

26   Cited in Pratt, *Canadian International Development*, 348.

27   See http://laws-lois.justice.gc.ca/eng/acts/O-2.8/FullText.html.

28   *Report to CIDA: Public Attitudes Toward International Development Assistance* (Ottawa: Minister of Supply and Services Canada, 1988), 10, 19.

29   François Legault, "Development Education in Canada, Then and Now," *Hunger Notes*, https://www.worldhunger.org/articles/us/deved/legault.htm.

30   "Declaration of the Voices-Voix Coalition," 2010, http://voices-voix.ca/en/about/ declaration.

31   Rist, *History of Development.*

32   Cranford Pratt, "Dominant Class Theory and Canadian Foreign Policy: The Case of the Counter-Consensus," *International Journal* 39, no. 1 (Winter 1983/1984): 99–135;

Jerome Klassen, *Joining Empire: The Political Economy of the New Canadian Foreign Policy* (Toronto: University of Toronto Press, 2014).

33   Todd Gordon, *Imperialist Canada* (Winnipeg: Arbeiter Ring, 2010); see also Todd Gordon and Jeffery R. Webber, *Blood of Extraction: Canadian Imperialism in Latin America* (Halifax: Fernwood, 2018).

34   Pratt, "Dominant Class Theory," 100.

35   Bibeau was minister of international development from 2015 to March 2019.

36   OECD figures, http://www.oecd.org/development/development-aid-rises-again-in-2016-but-flows-to-poorest-countries-dip.htm.

David Webster and Greg Donaghy

PART 1

ENTERING THE AID WORLD, 1950–1960

Today, foreign aid and official development assistance (ODA) are solid features of the landscape of international relations. Most developed countries—and a growing number of less developed countries—have a ministry or agency devoted to development assistance, surrounded by networks of advocates and civil society partners. The United Nations (UN) employs a top-level body devoted solely to humanitarian relief, with a budget of US$240 million, alongside a UN Development Programme with a budget of US$5 billion.[1] The Bill and Melinda Gates Foundation alone spends just over $3 billion annually on development assistance.[2] Contemporary foreign aid is big business.

All this marks a major departure from aid's tentative and low-budget beginnings. Vast sums flowed for European postwar reconstruction, and global governments would soon come to see the need for similar, if smaller, efforts in the Global South. Yet when the UN launched its program to deliver technical assistance to the world's most underdeveloped countries in 1946, it was entering largely uncharted territory. Canadian diplomats and cabinet ministers were understandably nervous about this new global challenge, but they signed on to the expanded UN program soon after its formation in 1949, as well as a larger Commonwealth aid program mandated to deliver both technical and capital assistance, the Colombo Plan, in early 1951. In New York and Ottawa questions abounded: What were the purposes of aid? Who would give it? Who would get it? How would it be distributed? Were strings attached? Understanding, debating, and gradually answering these questions would preoccupy the first generation of Canadian aid policy makers. Indeed, similar questions remain at the heart of contemporary considerations about aid.

The answers reached in the 1950s were worked out through dialogue and experience. Pioneering aid bureaucrats operated experimentally, with a wide degree of freedom of action. In 1950, there were few precedents or rules, no bureaucratic structures or standard operating procedures. Instead, as our first three chapters show, policy makers in Canada, at the UN, and in the Global South shaped their new work through discussion and a messy process of trial and error that we are only beginning to understand as the archival record is unearthed and absorbed.

The messy and innovative 1950s are described in three chapters that draw on newly accessed archival sources in Ottawa, New York, and New

Delhi. Chapter 1 examines the bilateral aid relationship between Canada and its major aid partner, India. India was the top recipient of Colombo Plan funds, and Canada in the early years was one of the plan's three largest donors, along with the United States and the United Kingdom.[3] Canada and India aimed in this period to develop a "special relationship," with aid cooperation a key pillar. As Jill Campbell-Miller explains, Indian priorities changed Canadian intentions and shaped the development of Canada's overall aid policy in this "golden" decade. Canada was not simply a donor setting the terms of its gift: its aid was affected by the recipient government, and that in turn shaped Canadian policy toward South and Southeast Asia as a whole.

The effects can be seen in Canada's emerging aid bureaucracy, outlined in Chapter 2. Similarly, the precise nature and form of Canada's aid owed much to its first three administrators, Tom Brook, Nik Cavell, and Orville Ault. Decisions about how Canadian aid was administered and who did that work shaped a bureaucratic culture—freewheeling, independent, and ambitious—that had long-term consequences for Canada's aid project in the decades that followed. The swashbuckling figure of R. G. "Nik" Cavell symbolized this decade of experimentation, as Cavell preached the gospel of aid in Canada and trotted around Asia trying to put it into practice. Cavell's stops in India (where he had previous experience in British imperial days) and elsewhere forced recipient priorities onto Ottawa's agenda.

In contrast to the first two chapters and their stress on the way Canadian aid policy was formed within the Commonwealth, Chapter 3 shows Canada moving within circles centred on the United Nations, another key arena for postwar Canadian foreign policy. Canada saw its goals increasingly well-served by the channel of UN technical assistance, directed by Canadian official Hugh Keenleyside. His forceful style and social democratic beliefs helped shape the UN's approach to technical assistance, giving it a working ideology distinct from that favoured by its dominant capitalist American and communist Soviet sponsors and one likely to appeal to Canadian sensitivities. As David Webster outlines, UN aid priorities would affect aspects of Canadian aid policy and reinforce public support for aid within Canadian civil society.

The 1950s were formative in many ways. Among those, as these chapters illustrate, was a dynamic interplay between donor and recipient that aimed to transform the relationship into one of partnership, not just giving and receiving. Even as Canadian aid was formed within UN and Commonwealth contexts, it was also affected by Southern calls for a different type of development. This in turn affected Canada's overall relations with the Global South.

Notes

1   See http://www.unocha.org/about-us/funding; http://www.undp.org/content/undp/en/home/funding/funding-channels.html.

2   See https://www.theguardian.com/global-development/2017/sep/13/bill-gates-foundation-dont-expect-pick-up-the-bill-for-sweeping-aid-cuts-trump.

3   Daniel Oakman, *Facing Asia: A History of the Colombo Plan* (Canberra: Pandanus Books, 2004), 82.

1

Encounter and Apprenticeship: The Colombo Plan and Canadian Aid in India, 1950–1960

Jill Campbell-Miller

"Canada launched her development aid programme in 1950 with virtually no policy aim beyond a lively anti-Communist instinct and an exhilarating vision of a free, multi-racial Commonwealth."[1] So reads the memorable first line of Keith Spicer's *A Samaritan State?: External Aid in Canada's Foreign Policy.* Fifty years after its publication, Spicer's work remains essential reading for anyone interested in Canada's early aid program. The worn bindings and marginal notes of copies in university libraries across Canada attest to its enduring importance.[2] Valuable though it is, after fifty years it is surely time to re-examine the early years of Canadian aid, especially the premise of this slightly cynical opening line. When Spicer published *A Samaritan State?* in 1966, the Canadian aid program was only fifteen years old. While Spicer questioned the motivations for giving aid, he was not cynical about the ideological project that underpinned this aid: development. As Stephen Brown argues in this volume, despite Spicer's realism, he "strongly believed in the value of the Canadian aid program."[3] For Spicer and his generation, the belief in aid for development was not just an entrenched part of Canadian foreign policy, it was a worldview that saw former colonies as primitive blank slates, ready to "take off" into a future of prosperity.[4]

When Spicer wrote his book, at the start of the UN "development decade," the idea of development itself had yet to undergo the persistent, and at times vicious, criticism by Marxists, postmodernists, retired development professionals, and others that lay in the decades ahead. Critics from dependency and postmodernist schools of thought describe aid as part of an ongoing project of Western hegemony, directing and controlling the lives of the powerless that it aims to help. Spicer, alongside many of his contemporaries, had yet to consider these critiques, believing that development in the "Third World" was both achievable and essential. Locked in the grip of what anthropologist and political scientist James C. Scott has termed "high modernism,"[5] academics and policy makers throughout the Global North and South believed that countries in the ever-expanding post-colonial world required support from richer countries to achieve technological "progress" and economic growth. Canada's decision to join the Colombo Plan for Co-operative Economic Development in 1951 was a relatively early expression of this belief, as were other efforts such as the UN Expanded Programme of Technical Assistance, as David Webster shows in Chapter 2.[6] When Canada and other Commonwealth members decided on a plan to "provide a frame-work within an international co-operative effort . . . to assist the countries of the area to raise their living standards," they created a program that invested in a certain vision of modernity.[7]

Spicer pokes fun at the broad policy aims that inspired Canada's early "development aid programme." But the Canadian government's commitment to and knowledge about aid in 1950 was even more tenuous than Spicer realized, in ways already hard to imagine by 1966. In his chapter, Webster describes the United Nations Technical Assistance Administration (TAA) under Hugh Keenleyside as very quickly adopting an explicit and sophisticated ideological basis for its development programming. The Colombo Plan administration evolved quite differently. In 1950, Canada had no experience with bilateral aid for development in the Global South, no administration to support such an effort, and few qualified personnel to manage such a program. Moreover, the Colombo Plan's originators believed it to be a temporary program. Simply put, while Canada committed to six years of Colombo Plan funding in 1951, it is only in retrospect that it can be said that Canada "launched her development aid program." The work of the program itself and the encounter with recipient governments

Jill Campbell-Miller

in those first struggling years transformed Canada into the donor country that Spicer recognized by the 1960s.

This was particularly true of Canada's aid relationship with India, where Canada directed approximately half of its Colombo Plan aid during this era. Elites in Prime Minister Jawaharlal Nehru's government believed just as fervently in the ethic of modernizing progress, and not because they were mindless agents of capitalist imperialism or colonial collaborators, as some critics have argued.[8] Instead, caught up in the complicated transition from colony to nation, and engaged in economic planning to spur growth, officials in India's government themselves helped to construct the high modernist worldview as it related to development. As India struggled to break free of the constraints imposed by its colonial economy, the government pursued rapid modernization of its industrial and agricultural sectors and reluctantly sought assistance to achieve this. Though Canada was a relatively minor donor from an Indian perspective, India provided a sort of apprenticeship to Canadian government and business about how to conduct aid programming overseas.[9] Both donor and recipient priorities drove the Colombo Plan, but it was India's economic plans that directed Canada's contributions. Canada built its own emerging bilateral aid program in a conversation with India and India's elites, and in some important ways remained the junior partner within the aid relationship in these early years.

High Modernism, Aid, and Its Critics

Aid programs such as the Colombo Plan were only one manifestation of high modernism. In Scott's view, the middle of the twentieth century witnessed a global peak in faith about the potential of industrial scientific and technical progress. During this era, governmental and non-governmental actors alike adopted an unquestioning adoration of technological solutions to all kinds of economic, social, and political problems. For Scott, high modernism was an ideology that permeated the consciousness of all those seeking to solve the major problems of their day.[10] The "problems" faced by the emerging post-colonial world appeared to lend themselves to technical solutions. The seemingly benighted of the world lacked electricity, "advanced" agricultural practices, and mechanized transportation infrastructure; development promised to resolve these deficiencies with dams, fertilizers, roads, and other markers of modernity.

While high modernist faith drove the expansion of aid programs during the 1950s and 1960s, by the 1970s the shine had begun to wear off among practitioners, theorists, and, as Ted Cogan explores in this volume, among the general public as well. Beginning in the late 1960s critics, first inspired by the dependency school of thought coming out of Latin America, began to publish excoriations of aid. These criticisms gained further prominence in the 1980s and 1990s, when postmodern academics, disenchanted former practitioners of development, and journalists continued to beat the drum against prevailing aid models. These critics viewed aid variously as an expression of a modern capitalist imperial system, meant to preserve a world order that deprived the Global South in order to enrich the North; as part of an insidious form of cultural and economic power crushing non-Western epistemological systems out of existence; or, more generously, as a misguided and incompetent enterprise that has done more harm than good.[11] They correctly argued that development projects squeezed out other forms of knowledge and other value systems in a totalizing quest to spur economic growth, at disproportionate cost to women, Indigenous peoples, and other marginalized groups.

However, the criticisms themselves were also totalizing. They tended to present categories of donor and recipient in easily identifiable categories—"imperial capitalist countries" versus the "Third World," "Western" hegemony versus "the local," or "the West" versus "the Rest."[12] Such categories may be useful tools of theoretical analysis, but history rarely yields such neat classifications. While the call to be conscious of class, race, gender, and other differentiating factors among those affected by the history of development and aid should be heeded, the importance of leaving room for aberrations and contradictions in the neat story of oppressor versus oppressed is also vital. More recently, neo-Marxist and postmodern scholars, though working from competing perspectives, have inspired more nuanced critiques of foreign aid, focusing on how it has been tied into transnational networks of power that integrate capitalism and militarism to further imperialistic aims.[13] However, they have tended to focus on either the pre–cold war or post–cold war eras.[14] Jerome Klassen has emphasized the ways in which Canadian post–cold war foreign policy has been captured by state and corporate elites, who, joining with a "transnational capitalist class," support the US-led effort to spread an "Empire of Capital."[15] This chapter borrows from these more complex ways of viewing the relationship between foreign aid and power, and emphasizes the ambiguity of the power dynamic within the Canada-India aid relationship. Moreover, it demonstrates the ways in which capitalist market-driven interests were built into Canadian aid programming from the very beginning.

1950: A New Beginning

In recent years, historians have become increasingly interested in the continuities between pre-war and postwar development. In the case of the United States and the United Kingdom, as well as other imperial powers, these connections are evident. As American historian David Ekbladh has shown, the experience of the Great Depression and the Second World War strongly influenced the shape of American postwar developmental aid.[16] For the newly independent countries emerging after 1945, labelled "underdeveloped" in the parlance of the era, the links to the colonial past are just as obvious, if not even more so. Those working on colonial development policies in the British government used the language of "developed" and "undeveloped" during the interwar years.[17] Former employees of Britain's Colonial Office were overrepresented among the first generation of "development experts" in donor agencies.[18]

In contrast, while firmly embedded in a British Commonwealth and settler colonial mindset that privileged Christian, "Anglo-Saxon" whiteness over other cultures, Canada did not have the same expansive history of external imperial ventures as Europe or the United States. Ottawa had few "colonial hands" within government from which to draw for its new development aid program.[19] When Foreign Minister Lester B. Pearson convinced the cabinet of Prime Minister Louis St. Laurent to join the Colombo Plan, Canada began something unprecedented in its history. Never before had Canada given aid to another government with the expressed purpose of helping to develop that country's economy, outside of a wartime or reconstruction environment.

The Second World War definitively shaped Canada's experience in delivering aid for both military and humanitarian purposes. In all, Canada provided approximately C$5 billion to the British war effort through Mutual Aid and other forms of assistance.[20] In addition, the Canadian government supplied C$154 million in aid to the UN Relief and Rehabilitation Administration, making it the third largest contributor after the United States and United Kingdom.[21] Canada even provided motor transport, locomotives, and wheat to India during the war, although the government supplied this through its Mutual Aid agreement with the United Kingdom.[22] As others have noted, economic self-interest played a substantial motivating force for the Canadian government, as this aid financed exports of military equipment, manufactured goods, and foodstuffs, driving Canadian prosperity and employment.[23]

While wartime and postwar aid may have positively contributed to the Canadian economy, it also represented a heavy burden on the federal budget, particularly after the country agreed to a C$1.25 billion loan to Britain in 1946.[24] Additionally, St. Laurent's cabinet tended toward fiscal conservatism and classical liberalism, and avoided measures that expanded government unless deemed absolutely necessary, politically or otherwise.[25] No wonder, then, that when Pakistan floated a vague idea for an undefined program of aid for South and Southeast Asia in the months leading up to the January 1950 Commonwealth foreign ministers' meeting in Colombo, the Department of External Affairs rejected it out of hand.[26] Pearson advised the Canadian high commissioner in London, Dana Wilgress, that "you should make it clear that the Canadian Government would not be prepared to encourage the establishment of a new Commonwealth organization for the promotion of economic development and investment."[27] Canadian officials were well aware of the pressures that the postwar economy placed on the government of the United Kingdom. To help fund the war effort it had borrowed massively from the sterling area, the currency system it shared with Commonwealth members, excluding Canada. Now Commonwealth governments, particularly India and Pakistan, desperately needed the UK government to release sterling to fund their own economic recovery, but the cash-strapped UK deferred these releases as much as possible.[28] Officials holding the Canadian chequebook saw danger, in the form of possible further financial commitments, written all over the proposal.

Their suspicions proved correct. During the meetings in Colombo, Sri Lanka's finance minister, Junius R. Jayewardene, and the outspoken

Australian foreign minister, Percy Spender, both put forward proposals for an economic development program in the region.[29] The so-called "Spender plan" would make it "easier for the United States to later participate in some kind of economic assistance plan for Asia," strengthen "the economies of the recipient countries" and help them "to combat the spread of communism," and supply "the sterling area as a whole with a flow of dollars."[30] The newly formed Consultative Committee, the body of officials tasked with overseeing the details of the proposal and later with its operation, fleshed out the scheme during a series of meetings over the course of 1950. Although it was a Commonwealth initiative, the Colombo Plan was really a series of bilateral aid agreements between donors and beneficiary governments.

Despite resistance from within cabinet, Pearson supported Canada's participation in the plan for diplomatic, humanitarian, and strategic reasons.[31] As Pearson advised his most skeptical colleague, Finance Minister Douglas Abbott, the commitment was temporary in nature, because the plan was only to cover a six-year period before sources of private investment would be found, at which point "a much larger programme of economic development could be undertaken without further inter-governmental finance."[32] Abbott felt that Pearson had committed Canada to the plan in Colombo without properly consulting the rest of cabinet. He also believed that the UK was getting too good a deal, not "contributing to the Plan in any real sense." This referred to the UK's intention to simply release sterling to its former colonies—something it needed to do in any case—as its initial major Colombo Plan contribution.[33] Though Abbott's cabinet colleagues largely shared his fiscal conservatism, an increasingly fraught cold war environment made the plan attractive as 1950 progressed. In early 1951, Canada signed onto the plan with an initial C$25 million commitment for the first operational year.

Canada's first large-scale aid commitment to the Global South was made with some hesitation, and was meant to be temporary. Lacking other forms of experience, wartime practices shaped the form that postwar development aid took. In theory, the Department of External Affairs took charge of policy and diplomatic matters related to aid, and the Department of Trade and Commerce assumed responsibility for the actual administrative work,

FIGURE 1.1
Indian prime minister Jawaharlal Nehru and Canadian fisheries minister James Sinclair chat at the inaugural conference of the Colombo Plan Consultative Committee in New Delhi on 13 October 1953. (Source: Editorial Associates/LAC e999920078-u)

following the interdepartmental practices established by the Mutual Aid Board.[34] In reality, their responsibilities frequently overlapped.

In 1946, the government established the Canadian Commercial Corporation (CCC) to support European reconstruction efforts. After 1950, the CCC also began procuring goods for the Colombo Plan.[35] The emphasis on obtaining Canadian goods and services for Canadian Colombo Plan aid flowed naturally out of wartime conditions. By the time Prime Minister Stephen Harper's Conservative government committed to "untie" aid in 2008, the use of tied aid had been roundly discredited as bad policy for decades.[36] In the immediate postwar era, though, the notion that Canadian aid would be used to purchase Canadian materiel was simply a matter of course. C. D. Howe's Department of Trade and Commerce became the home of the Colombo Plan administration, headed by Nik Cavell. As Greg Donaghy shows in chapter 2 of this volume, in the eyes of decision makers Cavell's background in Britain's colonial forces and as a businessperson with direct experience in Asia made him fit for the role. Though Canada may not have had the equivalent of a colonial office, the country's strong Commonwealth connections made such "expertise" available.

The close association between Canadian exports and the aid program meant that the practical application of aid was viewed as a logistical problem, primarily composed of managing the transfer of Canadian goods and services overseas. The underlying issue of "underdevelopment" was not a major preoccupation for officials during the early years of the Canadian aid program. As Donaghy illustrates, Cavell and his colleagues knew that aid was more a political than an economic exercise. Speeches and media releases on the Colombo Plan were characterized by a mix of vague expressions of goodwill and an unflinching faith in modernity, emphasizing, for example, the importance of developments in "science, engineering, medicine, and mathematics," the "friendly and constructive cooperation of the Colombo Plan," and the "magic quality" of electricity.[37] In practice, though, officials gave little thought to if and how the program actually impacted these problems. One of the few internal assessments of the purpose of Colombo Plan aid among officials did not come until a full five years into the program, when it was recorded in the minutes of the Colombo Plan Group, the interdepartmental committee overseeing aid matters, that "our main motive in extending aid, within our means, was to help Asian members of the Plan develop along the lines which we ourselves had, without attaching to our assistance any considerations of an ideological nature."[38] Outside of technical preparation, such as feasibility studies, or occasional diplomatic despatches analyzing "lessons learned," Canadian officials rarely connected individual projects to larger developmental goals. Thinking about the problems of and solutions to underdevelopment was left to those actually faced with economic challenges—the recipient countries themselves.

India and the Development Continuum

In India, the concept of economic development, and what was required to create it, emerged from a continuum of previously held ideas that paradoxically arose from both the colonial government and the anti-colonial forces that upended it. A strong component of the independence movement in India had been driven by a sense of economic injustice, as articulated by the "drain theory" championed by economic nationalists since the nineteenth century. It argued that British colonialism impeded the development of indigenous industry by siphoning off India's wealth.[39] Mohandas Gandhi's idealism may have envisioned an ascetic nation of spinners, but politicians such as Jawaharlal Nehru believed in modernity. A variety of economic planning initiatives, focused on building domestic industries, sprang up during the interwar period, developed by the Indian National Congress (INC) under the guidance of Nehru, the business community, and the government of United Provinces.[40] While little came of these early efforts, historian Nariaki Nakazato argues that substantive economic planning policy measures accelerated within the colonial administration during the Second World War, supported by the Bombay (now Mumbai) industrial elite. When Nehru assumed leadership as prime minister and as chair of the National Planning Commission at India's independence, he took over a process already under way in the colonial government.[41] Economic self-sufficiency was, in Nehru's mind, the only path to long-term political independence. His government's Second Five Year Plan reflected these views, and set out

> to rebuild rural India, to lay the foundations of industrial progress, and to secure to the greatest extent feasible opportunities for weaker and under-privileged sections of our people and the balanced development of all parts of the country. For a country whose economic development was long retarded these are difficult tasks but . . . they are well within our capacity to achieve.[42]

While Canada began delivering aid with little experience or knowledge about economic development planning in the Global South, officials and politicians in India had already been engaged in, or at the very least aware of, such processes for years.

The Colombo Plan

In the 1953 progress report of the Colombo Plan, a document that the Consultative Committee produced annually, St. Laurent's government outlined its modest aid philosophy: "In providing aid to these countries, Canada recognises that they are generally in the best position to know their own needs and it is therefore left to their initiative to propose projects for Canadian aid."[43] This relaxed attitude characterized Ottawa's approach to the early years of Colombo Plan funding. Of course, recipients did not have an entirely free hand in choosing these projects. The Canadian government had preferences about what type of aid it wanted to fund, based on the principles of enlightened economic self-interest that had guided earlier aid efforts in wartime and reconstruction Europe:[44] For Ottawa; the ideal Colombo Plan project would use Canadian goods, expertise, and have a large public profile. Typically, for instance, when the deputy high commissioner for India, P. K. Banerjee, met with officials at External Affairs to discuss funding in early 1951, he was told that India should select projects "which would bear a distinctive Canadian stamp."[45]

In addition, projects should advance "further economic development (e.g. public utilities such as electric power stations)" rather than simply be "ordinary commercial enterprises."[46] Projects would be judged on the basis of specifics, such as their timeline and urgency, but also by how well they "fit into the over-all plans for development."[47] Maintaining the aid program as specifically *Canadian* was an important consideration for Cavell and other officials in Ottawa, and guided their approach to setting up the norms under which the program operated. Cavell insisted that Canada's approach to aid was unique because it did not expect political ownership over the economic development projects it assisted. Opposing the imposition of an World Bank–style contract that would ensure management by outside engineers on the Umtru dam in Assam, India, for example, Cavell explained that "I have always tried to give them the impression that we had no desire to coerce them or impose any particular point of view upon them, but wished only to assist them as best we could in our own Canadian way."[48] During the 1950s, Canadian industry fuelled the country's own economic growth by using the bountiful natural resources provided by lands taken from Indigenous communities, whether it was through mining, hydroelectric projects, or expanding agricultural production. Canadian officials felt that the expertise gained by Canadian industries, universities, and governments within Canada was relevant abroad.

India, and other Asian countries participating in the Colombo Plan, wanted fertilizers, minerals, capital equipment for multipurpose dams that would provide both irrigation and electricity, transmission lines, mines,

FIGURE 1.2
Canadian Colombo Plan Projects and Programs, Fiscal Year 1951/52 to Fiscal Year 1960/61.

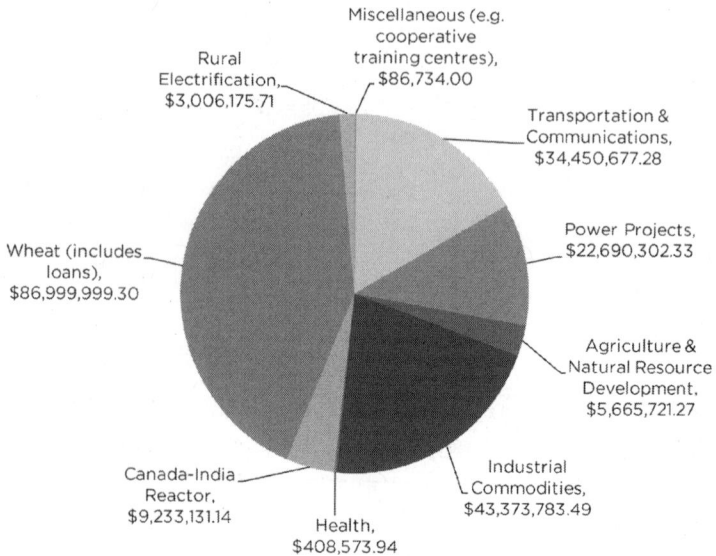

and transportation and communication infrastructure. While in the short term many of the goods to achieve these ends had to be imported, governments desired economic self-sufficiency. To attain this, they wanted to explore for oil and minerals, and build factories that supplied capital-intensive industries, such as cement and steel plants, with less of an emphasis on those that produced consumer goods. It is not difficult to see, then, how Canadian objectives for aid could easily be paired with India's developmental goals (see Figure 1.2). Canada had an interest in showpiece projects such as electricity generating facilities, while recipient countries had an interest in projects that would further the industrial capacity of their economies.

The colonial development and planning mentality that predated Indian independence helped inform the government's early post-independence initiatives. Many of the same Indian Civil Service functionaries who had served the colonial regime continued on with the government. Political

scientist Albert H. Hanson describes the First Five Year Plan, published in 1952, as not so much a "plan" as a collection of projects already under development.[49] Indeed, the first major project funded by Canada actually predated independence. The Mayurakshi project, a dam that Canada funded in West Bengal between 1953 and 1955 and eventually took the name "The Canada Dam," dated back as far as 1927.[50] Early aid efforts blurred the line between colonial and post-colonial. "In one Asian country," Spicer wrote of the lingering colonial attitudes he encountered on a visit to the region, "a local Canadian aid administrator expressed the view that some consultants—not necessarily Canadians—only 'drank gin, copied the old British Army reports, and recommended extensions of their own contracts.'"[51]

The other major component of Colombo Plan funding was in the form of technical assistance, or technical cooperation as it was also known. Although technical assistance did not cost nearly as much as capital-intensive

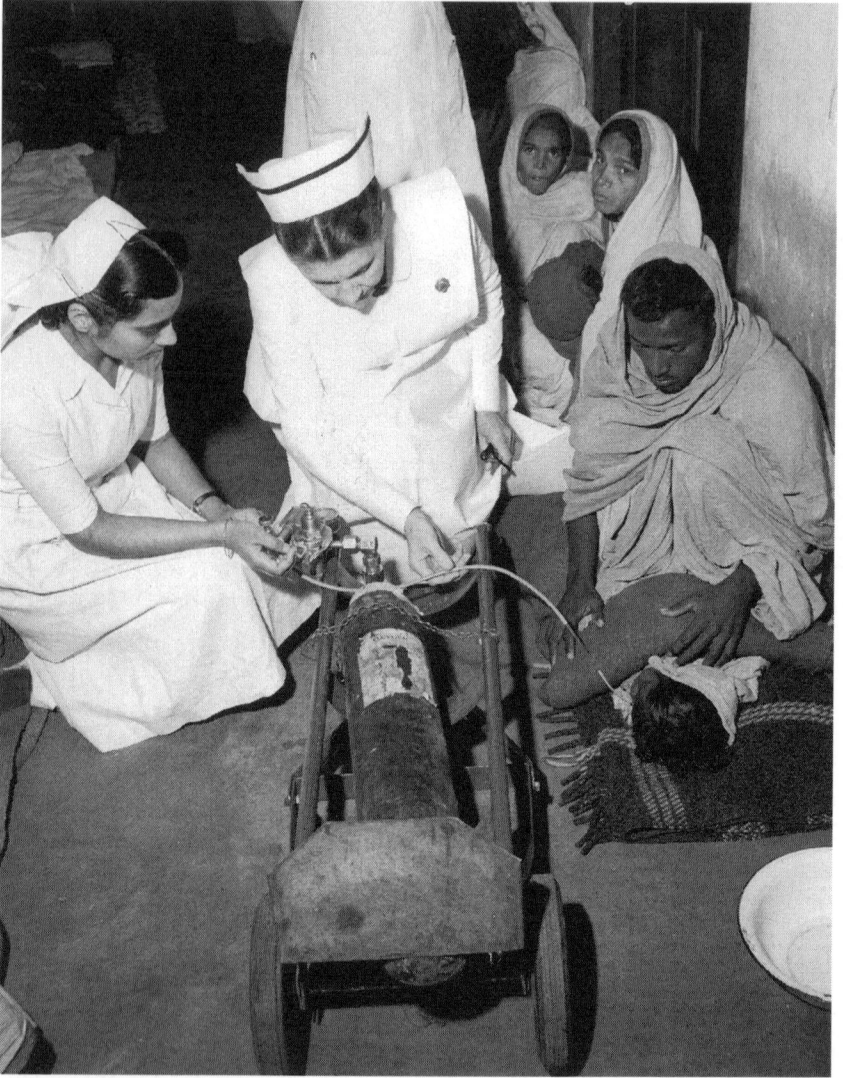

An unidentified Indian student nurse gives oxygen to an ill Indian child under the supervision of Canadian nurse Kay Feisel, an educator at the Nurses' Training School of the Patna Medical College Hospital. (Source: Richard Harrington/National Film Board/LAC e999920076-u)

projects such as hydroelectric dams, it did require a great deal of effort and planning.[52] It also represented the greatest part of the cross-cultural exchange that occurred between Canada and India under the Colombo Plan. Technical assistance relied on Canadian institutions receiving Colombo Plan trainees, or Canadian "experts" going abroad to do in-country training. Canada provided training in the fields of public health and medicine, agriculture and fisheries, cooperatives, education, engineering, business, and other practical fields. Citizens of India received training in these subjects as well as public administration and finance, mining, accounting, law, and geology.[53] By 1960, 106 Indian nationals had come to Canada for training and 43 Canadians had been sent to India as experts.[54] The priorities of both donor and recipient are obvious in the statistics about technical cooperation listed by the tenth annual report of the Colombo Plan: "Over the past ten years some 19 per cent of Colombo Plan trainees coming to Canada have studied various branches of engineering, another 14 per cent have been engaged in some aspect of training in agriculture and 13 per cent have taken training in some branch of medical or health services."[55] Canada also trained a number of Indian engineers on the operation of the Canada-India reactor.

Encountering India

The Canadian and Indian governments broadly agreed about the purposes of the Colombo Plan and the types of projects suited to it. Though the Canadian government generally followed India's lead by responding to its developmental plans, Canada's role as donor necessarily gave it a place of privilege within the aid relationship. Canada was privileged but not always powerful, because while Canada and India shared a broad understanding about the purpose of the Colombo Plan, they did not always agree on the specifics. The early history of Canadian aid is littered with examples of negotiation, compromise, and push-back from Indian officials who did not believe that their role as recipient automatically made them subordinate.

India made this position clear right away. Canada's first contribution to the Colombo Plan in 1951 came in the form of a C$10 million grant of wheat.[56] Food aid did not necessarily fit with Canada's aid preferences, but it was easy to deliver, plentiful, and supported by the public. Further, it could be justified as an economic development tool by Canada through the use of counterpart funds, the practice of generating revenue by selling commodities locally and then designating the profits for Colombo Plan projects.[57] Initially, India happily accepted wheat, as it displaced the need to spend precious foreign exchange on basic commodities. The government was so eager to have the grain, in fact, that in March 1952, India asked to have the entire 1952–53 Colombo Plan program delivered as wheat, as had been the case during the hastily planned first year.[58] Canada demurred, as this did not fit with its overall goals, and encouraged Indian officials to make requests for capital equipment. The Indian government made its opinions on the issue known as the spring and summer progressed, quietly declining to ask for capital equipment. When Canada tried to force the issue by unilaterally announcing that it would only spend C$5 million on wheat, Indian officials pushed back. Paresh Chandra Bhattacharyya, the head of Colombo Plan programming in New Delhi and future governor of the Reserve Bank of India, complained not just about the lack of wheat but also about Canada's failure to listen to India, ignoring "the advice and needs as presented by the Indian government."[59] Though India failed to raise the $5 million allotment, the Canadian government also made no progress on planning for the 1952–53 program until the fiscal year was over, setting them a year behind. Even without Bhattacharyya's letter, officials in India made their message clear: they were not in a hurry to accept Canadian aid if it did not fit with their own priorities.

As the years passed, India grew even more confident in asserting its aid priorities. Sometimes the government made its interests known through delay and obfuscation. Other times it used pressure tactics; for instance, Nehru's government used diplomatic needling to convince a reluctant Ottawa to sign onto the World Bank Aid India Consortium in 1958. In other cases, New Delhi simply used direct negotiation, as during discussions about the final agreement for the Canada-India reactor, which Canada only uneasily signed in 1956 after it became clear that the deal would not move forward unless they made concessions to India over fuel management.[60] While Canada was always in control of the aid it granted to India, it could not be said that it was always in control of the aid relationship.

Canadian and Indian officials and employees also clashed with each other at the project level. Minor problems included delays in communication, or miscommunication, hardly surprising given the distance between governments and the comparatively slow and expensive communication systems used at the time. More significant problems included project delays, budget overruns, problems with and mistrust between Canadian and recipient government personnel, and a sense among local officials that they were being pushed out of decision-making processes, either by their own central government, or by Canadian consultants, or both.

Entrenched colonial assumptions coloured reports by Canadian staff, both in government and the private sector, often portraying local personnel as untrustworthy, slow, and inept. At the Mayurakshi project, for instance, Canadian engineering consultants and mission officials were quite suspicious of the local administrator, a Mr. R. Banerjee, with, as it turned out, justifiable reason. When a local Canadian mission official, C. E. McGaughey, asked to see some of the tree-cutting activity necessary for the project, he was warned off by Banerjee due to "extra-ordinarily belligerent bears" in the area. McGaughey walked through the site anyway, drily noting that he found "no sign of tree cutting operations, or incidentally, of bears."[61]

The distrust and dismissiveness shown by McGaughey toward Banerjee was not isolated to the sometimes troubled Mayurakshi project, however. In 1958 John Teakles, a mission official in New Delhi, reported on the stalled Calcutta Milk Scheme that Canada supported alongside the United States, the Netherlands, and New Zealand.[62] Project delays were clearly due to Canadian content requirements. "No formal request has been received from India to date," admitted Canadian officials privately, "since there has been considerable difficulty in determining exactly what equipment Canada could provide within this allocation."[63] Ottawa eventually agreed to provide coal-fired boilers, but by then, Canada no longer made them![64] Typically, though, Teakles unfairly concluded that the fault lay with local officials, due to their "disturbing propensity for sudden changes in plans."[65]

The Colombo Plan understandably presented many challenges, and no doubt many of these challenges originated within India, but Canadian officials rarely admitted fault for contributing to problems even when their efforts clearly fell short. Canadian staff erred seriously during the installation of the Canada-India reactor in Trombay. Though the reactor is infamous today for enabling India's 1974 "peaceful nuclear explosion," at the time it was better known within government circles for its cost overruns and construction delays. This, in part, forced Atomic Energy of Canada Limited (AECL) to fire the Canadian project manager overseeing its construction. Incredibly, given the sensitive nature of the project, an AECL representative confessed to Canadian High Commissioner Chester Ronning that the former manager lacked "sufficient training and experience" and that the company had not investigated his background thoroughly enough.[66]

Impact on Canadian Business

Pearson initially promised Abbott that sources of private investment would displace governmental aid. Not surprisingly, given the state of India's economy during the 1950s, this did not come to pass. However, the Colombo Plan was a major factor in bringing Canadian business to India, and South Asia in general, at least in the field of engineering consultancy. The Colombo Plan provided a direct incentive for companies to expand into India, since the Canadian government paid them to do so. For example, the Montreal Engineering Company first went to South Asia as a result of the Colombo Plan, undertaking work on the Umtru and Kundah hydroelectric projects in India and an extension of the Inginiyagala hydroelectric plant in Sri Lanka during the 1950s and 1960s.[67] During the 1960s, the company worked directly for the Department of Atomic Energy in India as consultants for the Rajasthan nuclear power project (RAPP-1), and also for the Canadian General Electric Company which built the KANUPP nuclear plant in Pakistan.[68] In 1969, W. J. Smith, the vice-president of the Montreal Engineering Company, wrote Maurice Strong, head of the Canadian International Development Agency, to highlight the role that Canadian aid had played in bringing that firm into South Asia, and India in particular:

> This work has resulted in this Company having a large staff with extensive experience on Indian projects, including some twenty-five supervising engineers, twenty resident engineers (electrical, mechanical and civil), as well as the Chief Engineers and management personnel. . . . Throughout all this work, we have gained a good understanding of the problems of India and a real feeling of desire to help in the development of the country as much as we can through the medium

of engineering. We have trained many Indian engineers in our Company, both on the projects mentioned as well as other Colombo Plan trainees and, since early 1967, have been running a branch office in Bombay, developing Indian engineering talent there in the nuclear power design field.[69]

While more work remains to be done on this aspect of Canadian aid history, it is certainly the case that the Colombo Plan was an important factor in giving international experience to certain major Canadian companies.

Conclusion

On the eve of the UN's development decade of the 1960s, new multilateral initiatives drew Canada away from the independent Commonwealth path that it had followed during the 1950s. These initiatives included the World Bank–led Aid India Consortium in 1958, the establishment of the International Development Association and the Organization for Economic Co-operation and Development in 1960, and the creation of the World Food Programme in 1961. Aid was going global.

Despite Progressive Conservative prime minister John Diefenbaker's attempts to keep the Commonwealth at the core of Canadian policy after 1957, it was already fading in importance. The Colombo Plan's declining value was reflected in the government's decision in 1960 to transfer administrative responsibility for aid from Trade and Commerce to a new independent agency with a global outlook, the External Aid Office (EAO). Under Herb Moran and his successor, Maurice Strong, the EAO was eventually transformed into the Canadian International Development Agency, whose modern and global ethos submerged the old Colombo Plan. As Spicer wrote wistfully on the anniversary of Canada's twentieth year in the plan in 1970, it "no longer excites among Canada's official philanthropists the sense of pioneering wonder that challenged their ministerial predecessors at the inaugural meeting in January 1950."

Yet the plan's influence over Canada's bilateral aid program had been immense. The architecture of Canadian official development assistance was originally constructed to support the modest aims of the Colombo Plan. Of the Colombo Plan recipients, India had the greatest impact on Canada.

India's economic trajectory was marked by a curious mix of its colonial experience and the desire to reject that history. Its economic planning initiatives focused on heavy industry, transportation, and natural resource development, areas where Canadian business had particular expertise. For its part, the Canadian government, on the heels of giving aid during and after the Second World War, saw no contradiction between helping out and helping themselves. It preferred to focus on large capital assistance projects that used Canadian knowledge and highlighted Canadian beneficence. As the 1968 Colombo Plan annual report explained, "Canadian assistance to Colombo Plan recipients has reflected the capacity of Canada to respond to the needs of recipient countries and in particular there has been a concentration in those fields where Canadian technological experience, gained in many cases through the development of Canada itself, has been of special value." These types of projects suited the shared focus on industrialization and economic self-sufficiency that marked the economic planning efforts of India. And this approach was largely welcomed by both donor and recipient, though tensions and problems existed at both the bilateral and project level. Though colonial and racist attitudes may have given Canadian officials an illusion of control, their Indian colleagues never submitted easily to donor priorities that conflicted with their own objectives.

The bilateral aid program that the Colombo Plan created focused on economic growth to the exclusion of almost any other consideration. It was a conception of development that flourished in an era of high modernism, when an absolute faith in technological progress encouraged the belief that "man-made" problems had "man-made" solutions. Though modernism still remains a pervasive worldview, its reputation has sustained some serious damage. As development theorists have shown, its patriarchal and elitist logic failed, or refused, to see that such "progress" frequently disproportionately harmed women, minorities, and other oppressed groups. Yet this mentality was not necessarily a product of a "First World" imposing its vision on a subservient "Third World." The aid relationship between Canada and India demonstrates that it was a shared collaboration of elites. When it came to issues of economic development in a post-colonial context, Canada had little experience in such matters and took its lead from India itself. Though Canada, as donor, maintained control over its aid disbursements, India's government frequently challenged and negotiated with Ottawa, forcing Canada to tailor aid to Indian needs. The "exhilarating" vision of an anti-Communist, multi-racial Commonwealth that inspired the Colombo Plan may have indeed been a shallow one. However, in cooperation with, and often following the lead of, beneficiaries such as India, Canada built an aid program that provided a foundation for later and larger efforts.

Notes

1   Keith Spicer, *A Samaritan State?: External Aid in Canada's Foreign Policy* (Toronto: University of Toronto Press, 1966), 3. The author would like to extend thanks to the Social Sciences Research Council and the Shastri Indo-Canadian Institute for their assistance in funding the research for this piece.

2   The same can be said for what can arguably be considered its companion work, David R. Morrison's *Aid and Ebb Tide: A History of CIDA and Canadian Development Assistance* (Waterloo, ON: Wilfrid Laurier University Press, 1998).

3   See Chapter 13.

4   The phrase "take off," of course, was popularized by Walt W. Rostow in *The Stages of Economic Growth: A Non-Communist Manifesto* (Cambridge: Cambridge University Press, 1960).

5   James C. Scott, *Seeing Like a State: How Certain Schemes to Improve the Human Condition have Failed* (New Haven, CT: Yale University Press, 1998), 4.

6   The year that many scholars commonly associate with the Colombo Plan is 1950, because the initial idea emerged from the first Commonwealth foreign ministers' meeting in January of that year. Though cabinet members continued to express reservations about the program until late in the year, by December most were resigned to commitment. However, Canada did not publicly commit to the Colombo Plan until February 1951, and the government made the fiscal year of 1951–52 the first full year of the program's operation. For an overview of this timeline, see John Hilliker and Donald Barry, *Canada's Department of External Affairs*, vol. 2: *Coming of Age, 1946–68* (Montreal: McGill-Queen's University Press, 1995), 83–85.

7   Consultative Committee, *The Colombo Plan for Co-operative Economic Development in South and South-East Asia, Progress Report* (New Delhi: October 1953), 3.

8   See, for example, James Petras and Henry Veltmeyer, "Age of Reverse-Aid: Neoliberalism as a Catalyst of Regression," *Development and Change* 33, no. 2 (2002): 281–93. Petras and Veltmeyer are inspired by earlier critiques of the imperialist nature of aid developed by Teresa Hayter, *Aid as Imperialism* (Baltimore: Penguin, 1971) and Harry Magdoff, *The Age of Imperialism: The Economics of U.S. Foreign Policy* (New York: New York University Press, 1969), 117.

9   The same could be argued, though to a lesser degree, of its relationship with Pakistan, which was also a significant recipient of Canadian aid during these years.

10 Scott, *Seeing Like a State*, 4.

11 Classic examples include Hayter, *Aid as Imperialism*; James Ferguson, *The Anti-Politics Machine: Depoliticization and Bureaucratic Power in Lesotho* (Minneapolis: University of Minnesota Press, 1994); William Easterly, *The White Man's Burden: Why the West's Efforts to Aid the Rest Have Done So Much Ill and So Little Good* (New York: Penguin, 2006). For a helpful overview of some of the key thinkers in dependency theory, see M. A. Mohamed Salih, "Samir Amin," Roberto Sánchez-Rodríguez , "Fernando Henrique Cardoso," and Michael Watts, "Andre Gunder Frank," in David Simon, ed., *Fifty Key Thinkers on Development* (New York: Routledge, 2005), 20–25, 61–67, and 90–96 respectively. Reflection of the type of Marxist and dependency theory–inspired critiques of Canadian aid made by many academics and practitioners in the 1970s and 1980s can be found in Robert Carty and Virginia Smith, and Latin America Working Group, *Perpetuating Poverty: The Political Economy of Canadian Foreign Aid* (Toronto: Between the Lines, 1981); for an overview of post-modern critiques of development, see Wolfgang Sachs, ed., *The Development Dictionary: A Guide to Knowledge as Power* (London: Zed Books, 2010).

12 Terms used variously by Teresa Hayter in *Aid as Imperialism*; Arturo Escobar in *Encountering Development: The Making and Unmaking of the Third World* (Princeton, NJ: Princeton University Press, 2012, originally published 1995); and Easterly in *White Man's Burden*.

13 The difference between the two centres mainly on the role of the state in imperialism. Though Michael Hardt and Antonio Negri's influential *Empire* (Cambridge, MA: Harvard University Press, 2000) did not contemplate foreign aid, its approach predicted a turn away from state-focused critiques and a turn toward a decentralized view of imperial power with implications for critics of foreign aid. For a neo-Marxist approach, see Mark Duffield, *Global Governance and the New Wars: The Merging of Development and Security*, 2nd ed. (London: Zed Books, 2014).

14 For example, the chapters in Mark Duffield and Vernon Hewitt's *Empire, Development and Colonialism: The Past in the Present* (Suffolk, UK: Boydell and Brewer, 2009).

15 Jerome Klassen, *Joining Empire: The Political Economy of the New Canadian Foreign Policy* (Toronto: University of Toronto Press, 2014), 6, 62. Michael Bueckert argued in 2015 that the merger of CIDA with the former Department of Foreign Affairs and International Trade represented a shift away from the autonomy that had allowed CIDA to resist attempts to fully integrate capitalist class interests into foreign aid policy. "CIDA and the Capitalist State: Shifting Structures of Representation Under the Harper Government," *Studies in Political Economy* 96, no. 1 (2015): 3–22. In this way, the newly merged structure, if not its programming, harkens back to the early Colombo Plan efforts. See also Jill Campbell-Miller, "'Leveraging the Synergies' or a Return to the Past?" The Decision to Do Away with CIDA," 4 April 2013, Activehistory.ca, http://activehistory.ca/2013/04/leveraging-the-synergies-or-a-return-to-the-past-the-decision-to-do-away-with-cida/.

16   David Ekbladh, *The Great American Mission: Modernization and the Construction of an American World Order* (Princeton, NJ: Princeton University Press, 2010), 40–113; Michael Adas, a historian of technology, articulates a similar theme in *Dominance by Design: Technological Imperatives and America's Civilizing Mission* (Cambridge, MA: Harvard University Press, 2006).

17   Stephen Constantine, *The Making of British Colonial Development Policy, 1914–1940* (London: Frank Cass, 1984), 9.

18   Joseph Hodge, *The Triumph of the Expert: Agrarian Doctrines of Development and the Legacies of British Colonialism* (Athens: Ohio University Press, 2007), 207–53.

19   For more on how race thinking affected Canada's international relationships, see Laura Madokoro, Francine McKenzie, and David Meren, eds., *The Dominion of Race: Rethinking Canada's International History* (Vancouver: University of British Columbia Press, 2017).

20   Hector Mackenzie, "Sinews of War and Peace: The Politics of Economic Aid to Britain, 1939–1945," *International Journal* 54, no. 4 (Autumn 1999): 649.

21   Robert Bryce details the rather complicated mechanisms by which Canada provided this aid to India in Robert B. Bryce, *Canada and the Cost of World War II: The International Operations of Canada's Department of Finance*, ed. Matthew J. Bellamy (Montreal: McGill-Queen's University Press, 2005), 170–72.

22   Bryce, *Canada and the Cost*, 262.

23   Hector Mackenzie, "The Path to Temptation: The Negotiation of Canada's Reconstruction Loan to Britain in 1946," *Historical Papers/Communications historiques* 17, no. 1 (1982): 196; Hector Mackenzie, "Sinews of War and Peace: The Politics of Economic Aid to Britain, 1939–1945," *International Journal* 54, no. 4 (Autumn 1999): 648–49; Susan Armstrong-Reid and David Murray, *Armies of Peace: Canada and the UNRRA Years* (Toronto: University of Toronto Press, 2008), 29.

24   Mackenzie, "The Path to Temptation," 218.

25   Greg Donaghy, *Grit: The Life and Politics of Paul Martin Sr.* (Vancouver: University of British Columbia Press, 2015), 101–2.

26   Secretary of State for External Affairs (SSEA) to Canadian High Commissioner, telegram, 20 December 1949, Douglas LePan Papers, vol. 2, file 11, Library and Archives Canada (LAC).

27   Ibid.

28   The same telegram noted that the problems faced by underdeveloped countries in the Commonwealth were partly as a result of dollar deficits in the sterling area, but also "arises, in large measure, from the overall deficits of certain members of the sterling area. These deficits are being financed by the United Kingdom at the cost of a great strain on her economy." See also B. R. Tomlinson, "The Weapons of the Weakened: British Power, Sterling Balances, and the Origins of the Colombo Plan," in *The Transformation of the International Order of Asia: Decolonization, the Cold War, and the Colombo Plan*, ed. Shigeru Akita, Gerold Krozewski, and Shoichi Watanabe (London: Routledge, 2015), 34–49.

29 Ademola Adeleke, "Ties Without Strings? The Colombo Plan and the Geopolitics of International Aid, 1950–1980" (PhD diss., University of Toronto, 1996), 31.

30 Canadian Delegation to SSEA, Minutes, 17 January 1950, L. B. Pearson Papers, vol. 22, file Commonwealth Foreign Ministers Conference – 1950 – Colombo Conference, LAC.

31 Pearson outlines these in a letter to Douglas Abbot dated 17 January 1951 in Douglas LePan Papers, vol. 2, file 13, LAC.

32 Ibid.

33 Arnold Heeney to Pearson, 11 January 1951, Douglas LePan Papers, vol. 2, file 13, LAC.

34 Bryce, Canada and the Cost, 152.

35 Armstrong-Reid and Murray, Armies of Peace, 78. After 1968, the CCC also became the point of supply for the Canadian International Development Agency. Canadian Commercial Corporation, "Our history in foreign aid delivery," http://www.ccc.ca/en/partners/sourcing-supply-for-stabilization-and-reconstruction/our-history-in-foreign-aid-delivery.

36 The OECD's Development Assistance Committee (DAC) led this initiative. Organization for Economic Cooperation and Development, "Untying Aid: The Right to Choose," http://www.oecd.org/dac/untied-aid/untyingaidtherighttochoose.htm.

37 These quotations are from the notes of a speech given by Canadian diplomat George Hampson at the opening of the Mayurakshi Dam, one of the major dam projects that Canada contributed to during the 1950s in India. "Notes for a Speech by Mr. George Hampson, Messanjore [sic], West Bengal, December 16, 1956," 14 December 1956, RG 25, file 11038-1-2A-40, LAC.

38 "Colombo Plan – Second Meeting, October 24th," 25 October 1956, RG 19, vol. 3868, file 8321-03, LAC.

39 J. V. Naik, "Forerunners of Dadabhai Naoroji's Drain Theory," Economic and Political Weekly 36, nos. 46/47 (2001): 4428–32.

40 Nariaki Nakazato, "The Transfer of Economic Power in India: Indian Big Business, the British Raj and Development Planning, 1930–1948," in The Unfinished Agenda: Nation-Building in South Asia, ed. Mushirul Hasan and Nariaki Nakazato (New Delhi: Manohar, 2001), 247; A. H. Hanson, The Process of Planning: A Study of India's Five-Year Plans, 1950–1964 (London: Oxford University Press, 1966), 35–36.

41 Nakazato, "The Transfer," 265–70.

42 National Planning Commission, Second Five Year Plan (New Delhi, 1956), xiii–xiv.

43 Colombo Plan Consultative Committee, Second Annual Report of the Consultative Committee, The Colombo Plan for Co-operative Economic Development in South and South-East Asia (New Delhi: October 1953), 77.

44 Armstrong-Reid and Murray, Armies of Peace, 39.

45 A. F. W. Plumptre for SSEA, 29 March 1951, reprinted in Greg Donaghy, ed., Documents on Canadian External Relations (DCER), vol. 17:1951 (Ottawa: Canadian Government Publishing, 1996), 567.

46 A. F. W. Plumptre, "Colombo Plan Aid to Pakistan and India," 27 March 1951, reprinted in *DCER* 17:1951, 566.

47 USSEA to High Commissioner of India, 23 July 1951, reprinted in *DCER* 17:1951, 578.

48 Nik Cavell to A. E. Ritchie, 7 May 1954, RG 25, vol. 6579, file 11038-1-2B-40, LAC.

49 Hanson, *Process of Planning*, 89.

50 R. R. Saksena to A. D. P. Heeney, and attached letter No. D.9830-BII/51, 18 March 1952, RG 25, vol. 6577, file 11038-1-40, LAC.

51 Note 5 in Spicer, *A Samaritan State?*, 128.

52 For example, in India between 1950 and 1968 the cost of technical assistance accounted for just 1.07 per cent of the total aid funding it received from Canada. Central Secretariat Library (New Delhi), Ministry of Finance, *External Assistance, 1967–68* (New Delhi: Government of India, 1968), 30.

53 This summary is based on the Colombo Plan Consultative Committee's annual progress reports for the period under review.

54 Consultative Committee, *The Tenth Annual Report of the Consultative Committee of The Colombo Plan for Co-operative Economic Development in South and South-East Asia. Commemorative Issue to mark the Tenth Anniversary of the Colombo Plan* (Kuala Lumpur: November 1961), 190.

55 Consultative Committee, *Tenth Annual Report of the Consultative Committee of The Colombo Plan*, 216.

56 Consultative Committee, *Progress Report*, 78.

57 This is what External Affairs explained to a somewhat doubtful auditor general, Watson Sellar, when called upon by the Auditor General's Office to explain how food aid could be considered aid for economic development. See R. A. MacKay to Watson Sellar, 5 January 1954, RG 25, vol. 6578, file 11038-1-40, LAC.

58 High Commissioner for Canada in India to SSEA, Letter No. 430, 20 March 1952, RG 25, vol. 6577, file 11038-1-40, LAC.

59 P. C. Bhattacharyya to R. R. Saksena, 10 October 1952, RG 25, vol. 6577, file 11038-1-40, LAC.

60 For more information, see Jill Campbell-Miller, "The Mind of Modernity: Canadian Bilateral Foreign Assistance to India, 1950-60" (PhD diss., University of Waterloo, 2014), 191–203.

61 High Commissioner for Canada in India to SSEA, Letter No. 1540, and attached "Memorandum for the High Commissioner," 16 November 1955, RG 25, vol. 6579, file 11038-1-2A-40, LAC.

62 High Commission for Canada in India to the Under-Secretary of State for External Affairs (USSEA), 8 March 1955, RG 25, vol. 7343, file 11038-1-14-40, LAC.

63 D. F. Alger to R. W. Rosenthal, 8 November 1957, RG 25, vol. 7343, file 11038-1-14-40, LAC.

64 Note for File 11038-2-12-40, 1 May 1959, RG 25, vol. 7343, file 11038-1-14-40, LAC.

65 High Commission for Canada in India to USSEA, 8 March 1958, RG 25, vol. 7343, file 11038-1-14-40, LAC.

66 High Commissioner for Canada in New Delhi to USSEA, Letter No. 353, 28 April 1958, RG 25, vol. 5414, file 11038-1-13-40, LAC.

67 Jack Sexton, *Monenco: The First 75 Years* (Montreal: Monenco, 1982), 145–48. It is not surprising that C. D. Howe was a former professor and long-time friend of Denis Stairs, President of the Montreal Engineering Company and the consultant who travelled to Assam to evaluate the feasibility of the Umtru project. Sexton, *Monenco*, 22–23; Nik Cavell to Denis Stairs, 16 November 1953, RG 25, vol. 6579, file 11038-1-2B-40, LAC.

68 Sexton, *Monenco*, 179–85.

69 W. J. Smith to Maurice Strong, 29 May 1969, RG 74, acc. 1980-81-102, box 59, pt. 2, LAC.

2

"Reasonably Well-Organized": A History of Early Aid Administration

Greg Donaghy

The early history of Canada's foreign aid already has its hero: Herb Moran. Born in Peterborough, Ontario in 1908, Moran practised corporate law during the 1930s, before heading to war in 1940. After serving with distinction in Italy and Northwestern Europe, he joined External Affairs in 1946 as head of its Economic Division, becoming assistant undersecretary in 1949, ambassador to Turkey in 1952, and high commissioner to Pakistan in October 1957. A blunt, no-nonsense diplomat with a head for detail, Moran returned to Ottawa in the summer of 1960, when he was tapped to head Canada's brand new External Aid Office. The product of a recent short and lopsided rivalry between the departments of External Affairs and Trade and Commerce, the External Aid Office gathered Canada's sprawling foreign aid programs into one centralized unit, reporting directly to the secretary of state for external affairs.

As so often happens, the victors write the history. Moran's admirers, Keith Spicer and David Morrison among them, celebrate his appointment as finally bringing professional order to the amateur chaos that had marked Canada's aid program since 1950. The program's recent past, an emerging generation of aid officers proclaimed, was chronically disorganized, demoralized, aimless and unreflective, "a career backwater" populated by "misfits."[1] Inaccurate and unfair, this judgment minimized and obscured a decade of aid history, leaving later scholars largely ignorant of Canada's early aid administrators, their ambitions, their challenges, and their setbacks. This chapter is a brief introduction to the men before Moran: the hapless T. J. Brook; R. G. "Nik" Cavell, who dominated Canada's aid program from 1951 to 1957; and Orville Ault, who led it from 1957 until 1960. A close look at their bureaucratic remnants suggests that they were much better administrators than their successors allowed. Cavell, in particular, was a strong leader, whose pragmatism, profile, and institutional ambitions foreshadowed the unruly tactics that Lewis Perinbam, profiled in chapter 7, adopted a quarter century later.

Ottawa's postwar liberal internationalism, especially evident in its strong support for the UN, drew Canada into the aid business even before the Second World War had ended. Through the mid-1940s, Ottawa supplied technical advice and a small number of experts on an ad hoc basis to many UN specialized agencies, which usually recruited help directly through appropriate federal government departments. That casual approach changed at the end of the decade. In May 1949, Prime Minister Louis St. Laurent's Liberal cabinet endorsed UN plans for an expanded technical assistance program, estimated to top $30 million, and agreed to participate in a funding conference the following spring.[2] Soon after, in January and May 1950, Commonwealth foreign ministers gathered in Colombo, Sri Lanka, and then Sydney, Australia, to develop their own plans for a program of capital and technical assistance. In June 1950, cabinet approved a contribution of $850,000 to the UN's expanded assistance program, sending another $400,000 to the program developed by the Commonwealth Consultative Committee on South and Southeast Asia.[3] Amid concerns in both the PMO and UN headquarters about potential conflict and duplication, Ottawa officials began to consider how to coordinate Canadian technical assistance.

In early November 1950, the deputy undersecretary of external affairs, Escott Reid, summoned representatives from fifteen departments to consider the issue. A subcommittee under George Heasman, the veteran director of the Trade Commission Service, met twice over the next week, ultimately deciding to divide the field into two. Since foreign aid impinged so closely on foreign affairs, it was readily agreed that the diplomats would remain in charge of policy, formally receiving and replying to all requests for help. Trade and Commerce, with its close contacts with domestic industrial and engineering concerns, would administer the program through a director and staff housed within the trade department.[4]

Though officials were certainly aware of the dangers involved in dividing jurisdiction, the unorthodox arrangement reflected the exciting novelty surrounding foreign aid. For deputy external affairs minister Arnold Heeney, whose views were shaped by a long stint as PCO clerk, foreign aid represented a modern and increasingly "interdepartmental" policy-making environment, where "no hard and fast logical case could be made that the operation should be the responsibility of any one Minister."[5] In keeping with that expansive ethos, the terms of the deal were generous. The new director, styled "the executive officer," was to handle all publicity, contracts, and staffing. He was "generally free" to correspond with external agencies and foreign governments. An interdepartmental group on technical assistance, chaired by External Affairs, would coordinate policy, but its members were promised access to the deputy ministers on the supervising Interdepartmental Committee on International Organizations (ICIO).[6] At its last meeting of the year, cabinet approved the arrangement. Canada, along with the Netherlands, France, and the United States, became one of just four countries with an office dedicated to technical assistance.[7]

Initially, at least, making the interdepartmental arrangement work proved virtually impossible. From the start, External Affairs harboured "serious reservations" about the first head of the new Technical Assistance Service, T. J. Brook, a former trade commissioner who had worked in India in the late 1930s. In contrast to local observers at the British high commission, who judged him "most energetic," "extremely efficient," and "fully alive" to Indian needs, Canadian diplomats doubted that Brook could ever overcome his prosaic trade commissioner roots.[8] "I do not believe," wrote Robert Ford, the tart-tongued chief of UN Division, "that experience in the Department of Trade and Commerce will adequately fill in the background which it is important he should have or emphasize sufficiently the main principles which should guide the work of the unit."[9]

The diplomats soon had all the evidence they needed to substantiate their prejudice against Brook. In early January, Trade and Commerce floated a draft press release announcing his appointment but omitting any reference to UN programs and referring to Asians by the dated and racially charged term "Asiatics."[10] When External Affairs vetoed the release, Brook leaked it, prompting UN Division to rethink its attitude toward interdepartmental cooperation. "We are now thinking of the interdepartmental group as a very much more active supervisory body than we had at first envisaged," diplomat John Holmes wrote Heeney. "With this change in approach, I think we should consider the group as the instrument of External Affairs influence." Holmes abandoned plans to lend Brook a diplomatic advisory officer, instead assigning one of his staff, Jack Thurrott, to keep "a close watch on the unit."[11]

Through the spring of 1951, Brook and his Trade and Commerce colleagues began to flesh out the technical assistance program. Meanwhile, Thurrott and Holmes, who belittled his staff as "five girls," focused on "fixing and limiting" his autonomy.[12] This was no easy task, for Brook insisted on his right to deal directly with foreign agencies when policy was not at issue. For instance, when Hugh Keenleyside, head of the UN's technical assistance program, asked for Canadian civil servant Irene Baird to help with a UN program, Brook secured her release directly from her deputy minister and the Civil Service Commission, only informing External Affairs as she boarded the train for New York.[13] Similarly, Brook sent both UN Division and Canada's mission in New York into paroxysms of rage when he arranged to see UN technical assistance expert Howard Daniel alone.[14] This kind of thing went on all the time, Thurrott complained in June, in this instance, incited by an "especially objectionable" case where Brook had allowed a woman clerk to accept a UN fellow "in her own name."[15] Clearly, Heeney warned the minister, L. B. Pearson, "Mr. Brook is not competent."[16]

Indeed, the "brains trust" in External Affairs had begun to cast about for Brook's replacement in late February 1951, soon after cabinet approved an initial $25 million contribution to a new Commonwealth scheme for capital assistance, the Colombo Plan. Managing this new and vastly larger venture would require a more experienced man, one who could perhaps also take over the existing technical assistance program. Wynne Plumptre, head of the Economic Division at External Affairs, nominated Nik Cavell in early March.[17]

Captain George Reginald Cavell was an unusual sort of civil servant in drab postwar Ottawa. Born in Hampshire, England in 1894, young George ran away from theological school, eventually joining the Indian Army—Calvary Branch, he claimed—in 1913. A charismatic and gifted storyteller, he saw active service along the Burma-Chinese border, in the Moplah Rebellion, and on the North-West frontier. There, as he coolly noted for awe-struck Canadian journalists decades later, he "played with the tribes and watched my colleagues get murdered."[18] Following the First World War, Cavell remained in India until the mid-1920s, working as a land settlements officer in the Punjab, a military horse breeder, a magistrate, and a plague prevention officer—"hellish gruesome that one!"[19] After an unsuccessful spell as a farmer and journalist in South Africa, he joined the private sector, running branches of the American multinational, Automatic Electric, in China, Japan, and, beginning in 1934, Canada.

Life in Canada transformed Cavell. The world war against Nazi totalitarianism and the postwar confrontation with Soviet communism sharpened his liberal and Canadian instincts. "If freedom and the sanctity of human personality are to be preserved in the world," he proclaimed, "it is from its last citadel—this North American Continent—that the work will have to be done."[20] That view was doubtless reinforced by his closest Canadian connections. Significantly, he was among the handful of notable progressives who gathered at the Chateau Laurier in July 1940 to press Mackenzie King's government to total war and a postwar future of "more human welfare, freedom and security."[21] During and after the war, he became a fixture in the liberal-nationalist Canadian Institute of International Affairs and its domestic counterpart, the Canadian Institute of Public Affairs (the Couchiching Institute), becoming chairman of both by the late 1940s and a prolific speaker on global affairs.

At the same time, he drew close to the young Liberals around Brooke Claxton, the rising cabinet minister and Montreal reformer, whom he advised on Liberal Party policy and political advertising. His best friend was W. H. Herbert, a senior Liberal Party organizer and strong Canadian cultural nationalist, with whom he joined forces in the postwar cultural agency, the Canada Foundation. "The fostering of our basic cultures here in Canada is one of the most useful things any of us can do," Cavell declared. "We are in the process of building a nation composed of people of widely differing racial backgrounds and the only hope for us is to knit it all together into something which we can call Canadian."[22]

By the mid-1940s, Cavell had shed his military rank and adopted a variation of his mother's maiden name, Nicolini, as his own. "R. G. Cavell," he explained to Herbert, "was a horrible English fellow, who had all the faults and more, usually attributed to those insular Islanders. . . . this English fellow was reincarnated. In his reincarnation, the Gods gave him a better fate: he was born a Canadian and took the simple name of Nik Cavell."[23]

Increasingly disenchanted with his corporate life and his American directors, Cavell (and his Liberal backers) had been searching for the right government job since 1944.[24] Plumptre and External Affairs embraced Cavell as an accomplished businessman with extensive experience in South Asia and a sound grasp of international affairs, championing him as just the kind of "really strong man" that Ottawa needed to give "initiative" to its technical and capital assistance programs. He was expected to match donor needs with Canadian capacity, generate public support for aid, and reinforce the fragile political consensus among ministers. Nurtured on the imperial adventures of Rudyard Kipling and G. A. Henty, Canada's decision makers were perhaps seduced too by the whiff of exotic romance about Cavell, whose CV listed "tribal diplomatic and espionage work" among his accomplishments.[25] Cavell delighted Ottawa audiences by claiming that Gandhi had even called him a "whiskey-swilling swashbuckler."[26]

Cavell was known too in the Department of Trade and Commerce. He knew C. D. Howe, the powerful Liberal minister, and Fred Bull, his deputy, as well as several senior officials. His liberal views on international trade, the need for expanded Canadian markets, and "more effective coordination between government and business" echoed those of Ottawa economic policy makers.[27] Pearson and Howe cleared the appointment in June, Brook was released in July, and Cavell took over the enlarged International Economic and Technical Cooperation Division in September. The unit would administer both Canada's technical assistance and its Colombo Plan capital assistance programs under the general supervision of two interdepartmental committees: one for technical assistance and a more senior one for capital aid, soon known as the "Colombo Group." "It is a clear case," the *Ottawa Citizen* gushed, "of fate at the throttle of the train of human events."[28]

Cavell's personal history made him an ideal appointment. As an apparently authentic product of colonial India, he helped slot Canada's new development role in Asia into the familiar British Empire, or increasingly Commonwealth, framework through which postwar Canada liked to

FIGURE 2.1
The whiff of romance
surrounding Nik
Cavell is reflected in
this caricature from
the menu of one of
the countless service
club lunches that he
routinely addressed to
promote the Colombo
Plan. (Source: Greg
Donaghy/Richard
Bingham)

approach Pacific affairs. Though that continent throbbed with the promise of revolutionary upset, Cavell himself was reassuring evidence that Canada's development project represented a secure status quo. In the person of Cavell, as in the Colombo Plan itself, racialized tensions between the white North and the Global South were temporarily resolved within a vague and comforting sense of "Britishness."[29] Yet, simultaneously, as Cogan's chapter in this collection makes clear, postwar governments in Canada linked Colombo Plan aid to the country's growing identity as a global "middle power." Cavell's self-professed Canadianism thus also reinforced and personified the tie between Ottawa's aid efforts and postwar manifestations of Canadian national identity. Moreover, Cavell's entrepreneurial roots and transnational business background signalled that Colombo Plan aid would remain closely associated with the Canadian state's search for new markets abroad, a characteristic of Emily Rosenberg's "promotional state" that had emerged in both the United States and Canada in the first half of the twentieth century.[30]

Cavell's style and "impish" personality drove the interdepartmental aid program forward.[31] He was confident, well-liked, and not easily intimidated. To the obvious consternation of Bull, the Civil Service Commission, and the Treasury Board, he began by successfully demanding a salary of $12,000 annually, the same as his minister's.[32] He styled himself "Administrator," a more original title than "Director," and one that deliberately echoed the commanding role played by his pioneering US counterpart, Economic Cooperation Administrator Paul Hoffman.[33] Like Brook, he issued a press release on his appointment, again ignoring, diplomat Escott Reid noted archly, the UN entirely.[34] "Like the great movie actress [Greta Garbo]," Cavell told friends of his singular style, "I like to be alone."[35]

Cavell's views on aid reflected the prevailing liberal-internationalist orthodoxy in postwar Ottawa. He accepted humanitarian justifications for Canadian aid as obvious and "unanswerable," or beyond debate.[36] He was doubtful, however, of its economic and developmental significance. Despite his colourful personality, he remained a practical businessman, who was inclined to dismiss Western aid as "stop gaps."[37] Though doubtless aware of emerging debates about the best forms of foreign aid—he was good friends with the early American development theorist Wilfred Malenbaum from MIT—Cavell mostly placed his faith in the invisible hand of Adam Smith's liberal capitalism. "Whilst our aid programme to South-East Asia is valuable in putting some kind of floor, no matter how thin, under their living," he wrote deputy trade minister Bull, "I think we are all agreed that it will not really do much towards the rehabilitation of so many millions. . . . In the last analysis, the only way they can really rehabilitate themselves and raise the standards of living of their people is to get into the flow of world trade."[38] At best, the Colombo Plan and other aid programs helped "survey the problem," clearing the way for the forces of "Finance and Industry" to usher Asia into "the orbit of our prosperity."[39] Meanwhile, Cavell cautioned his former Bay Street cronies in Toronto's financial hub, Asia would not be a viable market for Canadian exports or welcome Canadian direct investment for years to come.[40]

Aid for Cavell was essentially political (though obviously there might be small ancillary trade and development benefits). The cold war confrontation of the 1950s between Western liberalism and Communist totalitarianism, he argued, was simply the latest manifestation of a timeless struggle between freedom and tyranny. In Cavell's stark view, the context in Asia pitted newly independent India, with its British democratic traditions,

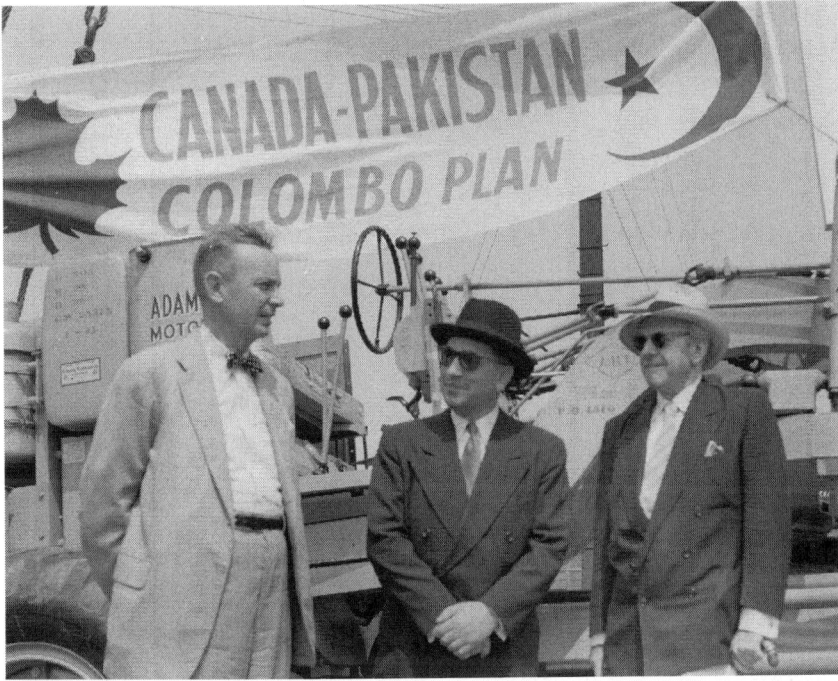

FIGURE 2.2
Cavell was a genius at promotion. Pakistani High Commissioner M. O. Ali Baig, Deputy Under-Secretary R. M. MacDonnell, and Nik Cavell are shown in front of a heavy grader being shipped to Pakistan for the Warsak Hydro-Electric and Irrigation Project. (Source: Editorial Associates, LAC e008303260)

against communist China, with other Asian nations waiting on the side-lines for a winner to emerge. Aid was clearly a weapon in Canada's cold war arsenal. Aid, Cavell campaigned on behalf of the St. Laurent government, was largely intended to give Asians "confidence in their government and thus offer them an attractive alternative to following China behind the Iron Curtain and into the slavery of the Communist state."[41] In private, he was franker. "The whole emphasis of the West is wrong," he wrote in 1955. "It is, of course, right and proper that we should try to raise their living standards, but did you ever hear of their minor revolutions from Iran to West Bengal which had poverty and hunger as its motif? You never did. What these people shout about is a place in the sun, recognition as a people, recognition as nations, the right to run their own show their own way—that is what worries them more than their terrible poverty."[42] Consequently, Cavell placed enormous emphasis on person-to-person contacts over both the character of Canadian aid and its administrative needs. He routinely left Ottawa in mid-February for a three- or four-month swing through Asia, directly engaging the continent's leading industrial, financial, and political figures in joint exercises defining the next year's aid allocation. "Above all," he explained to his Canadian interlocutors, "we must convince these people that we are concerned about them, that we want them to be prosperous, that we want them to remain free and sovereign states. . . . That means that we must really get to know them and understand their difficulties. We must forget the silly idea that they are mysterious inscrutable beings; they are people just as we are people, with the same hopes and fears and aspirations."[43]

Cavell was hardly a perfect fit. His annual Asian tour, with its outspoken critiques of American foreign policy, European missionaries, and the monarchy, dismayed Canadian diplomats, who often assigned one of their own to clean up his messes. "In his own inimitable manner," diplomat Ed Ritchie complained, "Nik will undoubtedly cover a great deal of ground and see a vast number of people but someone else will have to collect and evaluate the hard factual material needed."[44]

Administrative detail left Cavell cold. Characteristically, the woeful filing system that he found on his arrival in Trade and Commerce—"this is quite the most urgent job"—remained broken five years on. "We have all had trouble of one kind or another in locating reports," complained his deputy. "We have never had a proper system of filing."[45] Similarly, Finlay Sims, the comptroller-secretary at Trade and Commerce, regularly took Cavell to task for his unit's lax financial controls.[46]

More problematic, Cavell resented the "obstruction and ignorance" he encountered in Ottawa, and the interdepartmental structure that supervised his work.[47] As he ramped up his operation through 1952, the small staff in External Affairs struggled to keep up with the flood of paperwork, especially with regard to technical assistance. Ritchie's Economic Division, which inherited aid responsibilities from UN Division early that year, firmly resisted all efforts to reform and simplify the system. Since Colombo Plan funds formally rested with External Affairs, which also chaired the interdepartmental advisory committees and was responsible for missions abroad, he explained, it would be "impossible for us to contract entirely out of even the routine parts of the technical assistance operation."[48]

Ritchie also rejected requests from Canadian diplomatic missions themselves that they be allowed to deal directly with Trade and Commerce. Even pressure from Max Wershof, legal advisor and assistant undersecretary, and undersecretary Jules Léger failed to render Ritchie more accommodating. The standoff irked Cavell, especially when his staff too readily turned to External Affairs for policy advice. "I am in charge of Colombo Plan operations," he complained. "A problem arises which is really for my decision . . . [and] I am not even asked about it!"[49]

Yet Cavell's accomplishments were not inconsiderable, and he deserves more credit for successfully managing the many administrative challenges that he faced. Not least, despite the unsatisfactory administrative arrangements with External Affairs, he maintained good relations with the genial Ritchie and his successor, Louis Couillard. His outbursts—"blowing off steam"—passed quickly, replaced by a cheerful can-do attitude that set the tone for the entire program.[50] For instance, he breezily dismissed one squabble with External Affairs by explaining that "my only objective is to get the work done expeditiously, and within that objective I do not care very much who does what or how."[51] Ignoring External's strictures, he frequently wrote to missions and trade commissioners informally, boasting that he had "a reply before External or anyone else has even got around to preparing a first draft."[52]

Cavell built his organization almost from the ground up. Though critics complained of staff turnover and Cavell's ad hoc approach, in fact, he arrived with a coherent and ambitious staffing plan that included a field coordinator posted to Colombo, with responsibility for the region. As the aid program mushroomed in the early 1950s, the division's establishment grew from just six staff in 1950–51 to twelve in 1951–52 to nineteen by 1954, doubling again by March 1958. While junior administrators moved rapidly from portfolio to portfolio, competent senior staff remained in place. Robert W. Rosenthal became Cavell's assistant administrator, responsible for staffing and personnel issues, a role he occupied from 1952 until the end of the decade. From 1952 to 1954, John MacDonald headed the division's Technical Co-operation Service; he was succeeded by D. W. Bartlett, who also remained until late in the decade. Both men were supported throughout by assistant chief J. T. Hobart, one of a team of "conscientious and able" staff.[53] Arrangements were equally steady on the capital assistance front, run by Frank Pratt, a knowledgeable engineer, who remained until 1960. By the fall of 1954, Cavell was largely content with his domestic arrangements, assuring senior managers in Trade and Commerce that his outfit was "reasonably well-organized."[54]

There was only one significant organizational gap: abroad. But Cavell was making progress even there, a field that External Affairs jealously safeguarded as its own. In early 1954, he campaigned to post "semi-technical" officers to India, Pakistan, and Sri Lanka, where they would manage relations with recipient governments, help refine project proposals, and support local Canadian experts.[55] This was a large step for External Affairs to take. Eventually, however, the two departments agreed to appoint David Mills to Pakistan in 1955 on an experimental basis as arguably Canada's first foreign aid field officer.[56] Other appointments would surely follow. "As I see it," Bartlett wrote Mills, "eventually our people should occupy the about the same position vis-à-vis Ottawa and the rest of the Mission as Commercial Secretaries do at present."[57] In other words, aid seemed on its way to becoming an autonomous branch of Trade and Commerce.

As Jill Campbell-Miller points out in chapter 1, there were any number of complications in delivering capital and technical assistance in the early 1950s. But on the whole, both the interdepartmental process and Cavell's unit muddled along, delivering where it mattered. Canada's technical assistance program grew steadily through the decade. In 1951–52, it welcomed 64 trainees into Canada, a number that climbed to 192 in 1954 and 313 in 1956. The program usually sent just over 30 Canadian experts abroad each year, and helped recruit between 80 and 100 Canadians annually for UN aid programs.[58]

Canada's capital assistance program gathered momentum too. After a disappointing start in 1951–52 and 1952–53, it settled into a predictable routine that pushed available Canadian aid out the door. Typically, Cavell toured Asia early in the year, troubleshooting existing projects, soliciting new ones, and encouraging the most likely. Recipient countries presented detailed project proposals in the spring, when Ottawa specified what kinds of aid Canada could supply, favouring capital goods, commodities, and, finally, wheat. The early backlog of uncommitted funds disappeared by 1954 as donor and recipients—a group that steadily moved beyond India, Pakistan, and Sri Lanka to embrace Indonesia, Burma, and other parts of Southeast Asia—grasped what was needed and what was available.

Though effective enough, Cavell's structure did not long survive his departure in late 1957, when he left Ottawa to take up a new role as high commissioner in Sri Lanka. His reassignment coincided with a dramatic surge in Canada's aid program, leading to renewed and increasingly bitter interdepartmental rivalry. Beginning in the spring of 1957, Louis St. Laurent's government and its Progressive Conservative successor under John Diefenbaker began expanding foreign aid expenditures and programs. Pressure from other international donors, especially the United States, the stepped-up pace of decolonization, and domestic considerations prompted the increase. In March 1957, cabinet set aside $10 million for the newly independent island nations of the British West Indies. Within two years, ministers had bumped the Colombo Plan up from $35 million to $50 million, added a concessional program to subsidize Canadian wheat sales, and increased contributions to UN and World Bank multilateral programming.

The implications of this growth were not lost on External Affairs, which set up a dedicated unit, Economic Division II, to handle the growing volume of work in October 1958. By early 1960, diplomat Geoffrey Bruce estimated, Canada was spending $75–80 million annually on aid. "It is perhaps no exaggeration to say," he ventured, "that the formulation and implementation of this Canadian economic aid programme comprise one of the most important and influential elements in Canadian foreign policy."[59] Clearly, the diplomats in External Affairs coveted this juicy bureaucratic prize.

Cavell's replacement, Orville Ault, was no less aware of the stakes at play. Initially trained as a rural teacher in eastern Ontario, he returned to Queen's University for his BA degree during the 1920s, ultimately attaining a doctorate in psychology at Edinburgh University in 1934. He loved Scotland and embraced its values. "There was little deviation from what was routine, what was honest, what was wholesome," he later recalled.[60] An expert adult educator, he served during the Second World War with the Canadian Army Overseas as its director of education, setting up the "Khaki University," a widely admired educational service intended to boost troop morale and speed their transition to civilian life. Retiring as a lieutenant colonel,

Ault rose steadily through the ranks of the postwar Civil Service Commission, eventually heading its recruitment and training divisions, and taking on UN technical assistant roles in Israel and Ghana during the 1950s. Like Cavell, he was well connected. A partisan Progressive Conservative, he had served overseas in 1945 with Diefenbaker's powerful trade minister, Gordon Churchill, whom he considered a friend.

Ault hit the ground running. On the margins of the Montreal Commonwealth trade conference in September, Churchill had encouraged Ault to develop plans to reorganize Canadian foreign aid. Ault's appreciation of aid was arguably narrow, favouring educational exchanges over capital development, but there was no denying his ambitious bureaucratic vision. Given the growing volume and breadth of Canadian bilateral and multilateral aid, he urged the minister to create one single agency, a Bureau of Technical and Economic Aid, to manage all aid. Headed by a commanding director general, it would report through the deputy trade minister directly to the minister. A deputy minister–level External Aid Committee and a small cabinet committee would provide limited oversight and guidance.[61] Ault's future shimmered brightly. Soon after his formal appointment in December, the International Economic and Technical Cooperation Division was elevated into the Economic and Technical Assistance Branch (ETAB), a larger and more independent operating unit.

Over the next eighteen months, however, Ault's plans suffered a series of unhappy reverses. First, as word of his reforming work spread, External Affairs responded in December 1958 with a plan to transform the "Colombo Group" into a formal Interdepartmental Committee on External Aid Policy with more frequent meetings and representation from the Privy Council Office, an ally of the department. Backed by Wynne Plumptre of Finance, with whom Economic Division II consulted in advance, diplomats Doug LePan and George Glazebrook swept aside Ault's efforts to keep the discussions "exploratory," and struck the new committee at a group meeting on 23 December.[62] "Plodding" and "shy" by his own account, with few friends in official Ottawa, whose liberalism he fiercely resented, Ault was ill equipped for a bureaucratic showdown as the committee exerted tighter control over his program. The diplomats were "demanding" and "contentious," recalled Ault, making his role progressively more difficult. "The conflicting and sometimes confusing attitudes among those who were by choice or by appointment associated with Canada's aid programme," he recorded in his memoirs, "made progress slow and requests [sat] on desks for weeks."[63]

Initially unfazed by the prospect of closer outside oversight, Ault moved ahead with his reform plans in the new year, revising and elaborating on his early ideas. These were strongly supported by deputy trade minister John English, an experienced trade commissioner with a long-standing interest in aid programming, and Churchill. Ault and English reviewed their plans with Norman Robertson, deputy minister of external affairs, and Doug LePan, now an assistant deputy minister at Finance, in early March without encountering serious opposition.[64] Thus encouraged, Ault appointed D. W. Bartlett to head a new division, Programme Planning, whose forecasting function represented the first step in his developing campaign for a comprehensive stand-alone aid agency.[65] But as the new unit settled in, trouble struck for a second time: English was stricken by illness in the early summer of 1959, dying early in the new year. His replacement, first on an acting basis and then full-time, was James Roberts. A hard-nosed Toronto businessman recruited by Diefenbaker's government to tackle Canada's perennial trade deficit, Roberts was focused exclusively on exports and was utterly uninterested in aid. Ault's reforms stalled.

There was one final indignity to come. In early 1960, Economic Division II began to hatch its own reorganization plans. Though inspired by concerns about coherence and administrative efficiency similar to Ault's, they were much less well conceived. Initially, D. R. Taylor, the division's head, simply proposed to relocate the government's entire aid apparatus into External Affairs.[66] Anticipating stiff opposition from Trade and Commerce, he subsequently recommended grouping senior staff from External, Trade and Commerce, and Finance into External Affairs to oversee aid policy, leaving ETAB to administer aid under a junior official, turning the clock back to 1951.[67] Finally, Taylor and Ed Ritchie, the assistant undersecretary responsible for economic affairs, adopted a scheme not unlike Ault's; it proposed creating an entirely independent aid agency under a director general, a deputy minister–level position reporting to the secretary of state for external affairs.[68] In mid-May, backed by foreign minister Howard Green, Ritchie sold the concept to the deputy minister of finance, Ken Taylor, and Roberts, who was only too happy to rid himself of the aid portfolio. Ault, who was not even informed of the meeting, was brusquely pushed out of his job.

The establishment of the External Aid Office, Canada's first stand-alone aid agency, in November 1960 under Herb Moran signalled a new era in the administration of Canada's foreign aid program. Yet, key legacies of the 1950s and the program's first three administrators persisted, helping to shape the culture surrounding Canadian ODA long into the future. Most important, the decision to divide jurisdiction between the departments of External Affairs and Trade and Commerce opened vital space for aid bureaucrats to develop their own distinctive culture. The relative lack of hierarchy and a "can-do" ethos, and the often informal administrative procedures adopted by Brook, Cavell, and Ault, set off the tiny International Economic and Technical Cooperation Division as unique and different. Its early singularity was further reflected in the ambitions for an independent overseas service that were nurtured by both Cavell and Ault, and widely shared among their staff. Indeed, this brief survey of aid administration suggests an operation that was more motivated, ambitious, and capable than credited in the literature.

Both bureaucratic division and emerging corporate aid culture reinforced (and were reinforced by) the outsized role occupied by Cavell, a part inherited to a lesser extent by Ault. Unlike most civil servants of the decade, aid administrators were expected to be part bureaucrat, part overseas salesman, and part domestic publicist. They enjoyed a high profile and were often seen to singlehandedly embody their program. Ambitious and comfortable operating on both the bureaucratic and political level, Cavell, especially, pioneered a personality-driven leadership style that became a defining feature of later Canadian aid administrations.

Finally, this split jurisdiction and distinctive aid culture complicated efforts to manage the naturally competing interests of the program's founding departments, External Affairs, Finance, and Trade and Commerce. Administrative divisions and different cultures generated an ingrained sense of interdepartmental rivalry that hampered aid distribution in the 1950s and beyond, defining the program's relations with External Affairs and other government departments into the next century.

Notes

1   Keith Spicer, *A Samaritan State? External Aid in Canada's Foreign Policy* (Toronto: University of Toronto Press, 1966), 102–5. The charges are repeated in David Morrison, *Aid and Ebb Tide: A History of CIDA* (Waterloo, ON: Wilfrid Laurier University Press, 1998), 30–33. The Spicer-Morrison view is echoed in Jill Campbell-Miller, "The Mind of Modernity: Canadian Bilateral Foreign Assistance to India, 1950–60" (PhD diss., University of Waterloo, 2014), 8, 282.

2   Memorandum from Secretary of State for External Affairs (SSEA) to Cabinet, 20 December 1949, reprinted in Hector Mackenzie, ed., *Documents on Canadian External Relations (DCER),* vol. 15: *1949* (Ottawa: Canada Communications Group, 1995), 405–6.

3   Extract from Cabinet Conclusions, 12 June 1950, reprinted in Greg Donaghy, ed., *DCER,* vol. 16: *1950* (Ottawa: Canada Communications Group, 1995), 623–24, and 1226–27.

4   Draft Report of the Interdepartmental Committee on International Organization (ICCO), Document No 1, 22 November 1950, RG 74, acc. 80/1-103, vol. 1, file 36-1-1, LAC.

5   Minutes of the ICIO, 30 November 1950, RG 74, acc. 80/1-103, vol. 1, file 36-1-1, LAC.

6   See minutes of the subcommittee meetings on November 6 and 10, RG 74, acc. 80/1-103, vol. 1, file 36-1-1, LAC.

7   External Affairs Circular Document, A3/15, 11 January 1951, RG 74, acc. 80/1-103, vol. 1, file 36-1-1, LAC.

8   J. Thompson, British High Commission, Ottawa, to A.C.B. Symon, Commonwealth Relations Office, 29 June 1951, FO 371/93055, National Archives, United Kingdom.

9   R. A. D. Ford to Under-Secretary of State for External Affairs (USSEA), 13 December 1950, RG 25, vol. 6442, file 5475-DU-8-40, LAC.

10   J. W. Holmes to USSEA, 8 January 1952, RG 25, vol. 6442, file 5475-DU-8-40, LAC. On "Asiatics," see Stefan Huebner, *Pan-Asian Sports and the Emergence of Modern Asia, 1913–1974* (Singapore: NUS Press, 2016), 105.

11   J. W. Holmes to USSEA, 12 January 1952, RG 25, vol. 6442, file 5475-DU-8-40, LAC.

12   J. H. Thurrott to J. W. Holmes, 17 March 1951, RG 26, vol. 6442, file 5475-DU-8-40, LAC.

13   Brook to J. H. Thurrott, 17 May 1951, RG 25, vol. 6442, file 5475-DU-8-40, LAC.

14   A/Permanent Representative in New York to SSEA, tel. 481, 19 May 1951; SSEA to A/PRNY, tel. 367, 21 May 1951; A/PRNY to SSEA, tel. 485, 22 May 1951, RG 25, vol. 6442, file 5475-DU-8-40, LAC.

15   J. H. Thurrott to Escott Reid, 13 June 1951, RG 26, vol. 6442, file 5475-DU-8-40, LAC.

16   A. D. P. Heeney, Memorandum for the Minister, 10 May 1951, RG 25, vol. 6442, file 5475-DU-8-40, LAC.

17 A. F. W. Plumptre to M. W. Mackenzie, 2 March 1951, RG 32, vol. 426, file: Cavell, LAC.

18 Phyllis Wilson, "Cavell Canada's Colombo Plan Director," *Ottawa Citizen*, 3 November 1951.

19 Cavell to Walter Herbert, 30 January 1951, Herbert Papers, vol. 12, file: Cavell, LAC.

20 Cavell to H. M. Millichamp, 28 November 1949, Herbert Papers, vol. 12, file: Cavell, LAC.

21 Hugh Keenleyside, *Hammer the Golden Day*, vol. 2: *On the Bridge of Time* (Toronto: McClelland and Stewart, 1982), 49.

22 Cavell to Walter Herbert, 5 September 1952, Herbert Papers, vol. 12, file: Cavell, LAC.

23 Cavell to Walter Herbert, 5 June 1961, Herbert Papers, vol. 12, file: Cavell, LAC.

24 See correspondence on Brooke Claxton Papers, vol. 26, file: Cavell, LAC.

25 A. D. P. Heeney to Fred Bull, 28 June 1951, RG 25, vol. 4306, file 11336-6-40, LAC.

26 "'Mahatma Gandhi,' Speech by Nik Cavell on the occasion of the celebration of the anniversary of Mahatma Gandhi's Birthday," 2 October 1952, in Canada Foundation Papers, vol. 12, nominal file: Nik Cavell, LAC.

27 Cavell to Walter Reinke, 23 November 1948, Canada Foundation Papers, vol. 12, nominal file: Nik Cavell, LAC; "Markets Abroad Urged for Canada," *Montreal Gazette*, 1 April 1948.

28 Phyllis Wilson, "Cavell Canada's Colombo Plan Director," *Ottawa Citizen*, 3 November 1951.

29 Historians have long implicitly theorized a link between Canadian foreign policy and identity, and the British Empire. Carl Berger's *The Sense Of Power: Studies in the Ideas of Canadian Imperialism* (Toronto: University of Toronto Press, 1970) made the prewar connection. José Eduardo Igartua, *The Other Quiet Revolution: National Identities in English Canada, 1945–71* (Vancouver: University of British Columbia Press, 2006) makes the postwar connection on the left; C. P. Champion, *The Strange Demise of British Canada: The Liberals and Canadian Nationalism, 1964–68* (Montreal: McGill-Queen's University Press, 2010) does so on the right. Most recently, see Laura Madokoro, Francine McKenzie, and David Meren, eds., *Dominion of Race: Rethinking Canada's International History* (Vancouver: University of British Columbia Press, 2017), especially Dan Gorman, "Race, the Commonwealth, and the United Nations: From Imperialism to Internationalism in Canada, 1940 to 1960," 139–59.

30 Emily S. Rosenberg, *Spreading the American Dream: American Economic and Cultural Expansion, 1890–1945* (New York: Hill and Wang, 1982). Rosenberg's promotional state takes form in Canada in the same timeframe of the 1890s. See O. Mary Hill, *Canada's Salesmen to the World: The Department of Trade and Commerce, 1892–1939* (Montreal: McGill-Queen's University Press, 1977).

31 A. E. Ritchie to Gerry Stoner, 14 January 1955, Ritchie Papers, vol. 12, LAC.

32 See the correspondence on RG 25, vol. 4344, file 11407-40, LAC.

33 Cavell to A. F. W. Plumptre, 21 August 1951, RG 25, vol. 4344, file 11407-40, LAC.

34   Escott Reid's marginal note, dated 11 January 1952, on Department of Trade and Commerce Press Release, 27/51, 6 September 1951, RG 25, vol. 4344, file 11407-40, LAC.

35   Cavell to Herbert, 20 August 1951, Herbert Papers, vol. 12, file: Cavell, LAC.

36   Nik Cavell, "Technical Assistance and the Colombo Plan," an address to a joint meeting of the Canadian Importers' and Traders' Association, the Canadian Exporters' Association, and the Canadian Institute of International Affairs, 5 October 1951, reprinted in Canada, Department of External Affairs, *Statements and Speeches* 51/38.

37   Cavell, "Asia and the Free World," an address to the Canadian Exporters' Association, 24 September 1953, reprinted in *Statements and Speeches* 53/38.

38   Cavell to Fred Bull, 17 November 1953, RG 74, acc. 80-1/103, box 4, file 36-1-11, LAC.

39   Cavell, "Technical Assistance and the Colombo Plan," *Statements and Speeches* 51/38.

40   Cavell to Harold Fry, 4 May 1955, RG 74, acc. 80-1/103, box 4, file 36-1-11, LAC.

41   Cavell, "Asia and the Free World," an address to the Canadian Exporters' Association, 24 September 1953, reprinted in *Statements and Speeches* 53/38..

42   Cavell to Ned Corbett, 20 August 1954, RG 74, acc. 80-1/103, box 4, file 36-1-11, LAC.

43   Cavell, "Asia and the Free World."

44   A. E. Ritchie to Escott Reid, 13 February 1953, Ritchie Papers, vol. 12, LAC.

45   Rosenthal to Cavell, 8 February 1956, RG 74, acc. 80-1/103, box 1, file T-36-1666, LAC.

46   See, for example, Robert Rosenthal to Finlay Sims, 26 April 1954, RG 74, acc. 80-1/103, vol. 1, file 36-1-1, LAC.

47   Cavell to Escott Reid, 11 June 1964, Reid Papers, vol. 31, file 77, LAC.

48   Ritchie to Cavell, 11 February 1953, RG 74, acc. 90-1/103, box 1, file 36-1-1, LAC.

49   Cavell to Escott Reid, 11 June 1964, Reid Papers, vol. 31, file 77; Cavell to J. T. Hobart, 20 April 1955, RG 74, acc. 80-1/103, box 1, file T-36-1-1, LAC.

50   Ritchie's marginalia on Cavell to Ritchie, 12 December 1952, RG 25, vol. 6442, file 5475-DU-8-40, LAC.

51   Cavell to Ritchie, 14 February 1953, RG 74, acc. 80-1/103, vol. 1, file T-36-1-1, LAC.

52   Cavell marginalia on J. T. Hobart to C. Drolet, 29 September 1955, RG 74, acc. 80-1/103, vol. 1, file T-36-1-1, LAC.

53   The assessments of Hobart and Pratt are from Allan S. McGill, *My Life As I Remember It* (Abbotsford: Granville Island Publishing, 2004), 170–71.

54   Cavell to Finlay Sim, 16 September 1954, and Cavell to Ritchie, 5 November 1954, RG 74, acc. 80-1/103, box 1, file T-36-1-1, LAC.

55   Minutes of the Colombo Group Meeting, 23 February 1954, RG 74, acc. 80-1/103, vol. 1, file T-36-3323, LAC.

56   Dave Bartlett to Stenographers, TCS Staff, 16 August 1956, RG 74, acc. 80-1/130, vol. 1, file T-36-3323, LAC.

57 Dave Bartlett to W. D. Mills, 28 November 1957, RG 74, acc. 80-1/103, vol. 1, file T-36-3323, LAC.

58 Statistics drawn from Canada, Department of Trade and Commerce, *Annual Reports, 1950–1958* (Ottawa: Queen's Printer, 1951–59).

59 Geoffrey Bruce to A. E. Ritchie, 19 January 1960, RG 25, vol. 5567, file 12822-40, LAC.

60 Orville Ault, *My Way* (Ottawa: privately published, 1991), 39.

61 Orville Ault, Memorandum for the Hon. Gordon Churchill, [Fall 1958], Churchill Papers, vol. 25, file: Colombo Plan Administration, LAC.

62 John English to Norman Robertson, 5 December 1958; Ault to Doug LePan, 19 December 1958; Keith Goldschlag to Mr. LePan and attachment, 22 December 1958; and Minutes of the Colombo Group, 30 December 1958, on RG 25, vol. 4297, file 11038-6-C-40, LAC.

63 Ault, *My Way*, 40, 113, 114.

64 John English to Orville Ault, 10 March 1959, RG 74, acc. 80-1/103, box 1, file T-36-1-1, LAC.

65 Ault to Economic and Technical Assistance Branch, 23 March 1959, RG 74, acc. 80-1/103, box 1, file T-36-1-1, LAC.

66 D. R. Taylor, Memorandum: Administration of Canadian Aid Programmes, 8 April 1960, RG 25, vol. 4297, file 11038-6C-40, LAC.

67 D. R. Taylor, Memorandum for A. E. Ritchie, 13 April 1960, RG 25, vol. 4297, file 11038-6C-40, LAC.

68 E. A. Ritchie, Memorandum for the Minister, 13 May 1960, and attachment, RG 26, vol. 4297, file 11038-6C-40, LAC.

3

Developing the World in Canada's Image: Hugh Keenleyside and Technical Assistance

David Webster

Canada entered the world of international development aid not with a bang but with a whine.

The occasion was a cabinet meeting in November 1950 to grant what the Department of External Affairs thought was a routine matter: approval of the first report of the Colombo Plan, a Commonwealth scheme to aid economic development in South and Southeast Asia. Lester Pearson, the external affairs minister, was in New York for UN meetings. Robert Mayhew, minister of fisheries and previously Canadian delegate to Commonwealth conferences where the Colombo Plan was hashed out, was also absent. So was Brooke Claxton, the minister of defence and a prominent booster of the idea of Canadian aid to Asia. Cabinet did not wave through the report. Instead, "the attitude was icy," reported Wynne Plumptre, head of the Economic Division of External Affairs. "The red herrings hatched in the Department of Finance reared their heads. Further, and most disappointing, the Prime Minister [Louis St. Laurent] himself gave no support—rather the reverse."[1]

Finance minister Douglas Abbott carried the day with his argument that aid to Asia was doomed to fail. He implied that there were two problems, population growth and military spending by Asian governments, that would more than consume the limited amounts of aid that Canada could provide. Cabinet declined to approve Canadian participation that day, though it did not object to other Commonwealth governments going ahead.[2] Only in early 1951 did Canada finally and reluctantly sign on to the Colombo Plan, which became the face of Canadian development aid, embraced by leaders of all three major political parties and a vast array of groups outside government. Its centrality in Canada-India relations is described in Jill Campbell-Miller's chapter in this volume.

Canada's embrace of the early idea of development aid was not pioneering, idealistic, and enthusiastic. Rather, it was contentious, hesitant, and grounded in the cold war clash between the communist Soviet Union and the American-led Western alliance.[3] Ministers were not sold on the idea of aid, and many thought that development work was the proper domain of the United Nations. Indeed, UN aid provided Canada with a global development mission and helped shape the multilateral character of Canadian development assistance. In particular, St. Laurent and his ministers wondered if it would be wiser to channel all aid through the United Nations. Thus, before cabinet approved the Colombo Plan, the order was given to consult "UN officials concerned with technical assistance" before committing to an aid scheme involving only the Asian Commonwealth.[4] This was mainly a sign of preference for efficiency and for working through the UN, but it was also a demand from St. Laurent to consult a former Canadian civil service mandarin who was serving as director-general of the United Nations Technical Assistance Administration (TAA): Hugh Keenleyside.

Technical assistance was a scheme for wealthier and more technically advanced countries to send experts to less developed countries, where they would share their knowledge and skills—their "know-how" and "show-how," in the American terminology.[5] It also offered fellowships for people from the Global South to study in the industrialized North, and funded equipment needed to implement technical advice. It is normally traced back to US president Harry S. Truman's 1949 inaugural address. "Point Four" of Truman's foreign policy agenda was to launch "a bold new program for making the benefits of our scientific advances and industrial progress available for the improvement and growth of underdeveloped areas." While

David Webster

material resources were finite, Truman said, "our imponderable resources in technical knowledge are constantly growing and are inexhaustible."[6]

But technical assistance was not only Truman's Point Four; it was also Point Six of UN Secretary-General Trygve Lie's program for achieving peace through the United Nations.[7] The origins of technical assistance were not just American: they were multilateral, rooted in the United Nations, and heavily shaped by middle-ranking powers, like Canada.

Keenleyside's years at the TAA serve as the thread weaving together Canadian involvement in technical assistance—the only channel outside the Colombo Plan in which Canada assisted in economic development during the 1950s. They show multilateral technical assistance emerging as a vital aspect of Canada's overseas development policy. The amounts were less than those that would flow to capital assistance for infrastructure (especially in India, Pakistan, and Sri Lanka) through the Colombo Plan. Politically, however, UN technical assistance loomed large on Canadian policy makers' aid horizons. Keenleyside's leadership of the TAA heightened existing Canadian preference for multilateral channels, while positioning Canada as a leading proponent of the UN's technical assistance system.

Hugh Keenleyside and the Origins of Technical Assistance

Born in 1898 in Toronto, Keenleyside grew up in Vancouver, the child of devout Christian parents: he attended four church services each Sunday as a child. After completing a PhD in history at the University of British Columbia in 1923, he began teaching history in the United States, sometimes drawing on his research expertise to comment on US domestic politics. Keenleyside impressed American progressive politicians with speeches that used the case of publicly owned railways in Canada as proof that public ownership did not inevitably lead to economic disaster. Along with Lester Pearson, he was one of two men to win appointment in the first competitive examination for the Department of External Affairs in 1928. He soon took charge of opening Canada's first embassy in Japan. The posting earned him a reputation for "meticulous reporting of Far Eastern affairs" from Canada's only diplomatic outpost outside Europe and North America.[8] It also solidified his left-leaning politics. Touring Canada during the

Great Depression, Keenleyside wrote that he "came to the view that while there were more violent crimes [,] there was none so shameful as poverty."[9]

Keenleyside returned to Ottawa in 1936, eventually rising to the rank of assistant undersecretary in 1941, and established himself as a pro-Asian voice in Ottawa. Soon after his return, he was calling for a liberal stance on migration from China and Japan, in contrast to the predominant view, in British Columbia especially, that migration from Asia should be banned.[10] He was a progressive outlier in the Ottawa civil service, especially after he opposed deportations of Japanese-Canadians from the west coast during the Second World War. This was probably the reason for what Prime Minister Mackenzie King described as "considerable prejudice against him on the part of some Members of Parliament."[11] Perhaps in a bid to remove him from Ottawa, he was made ambassador to Mexico from 1944 to 1947, winning plaudits for his focus on "mutual-interest business matters" rather than the cocktail circuit.[12]

On his return from Mexico, Keenleyside became deputy minister of mines and resources, where he implemented numerous reforms and reorganized the government department that dealt with one of Ottawa's longest list of responsibilities: northern regional development, forestry, national parks, immigration policy, Indigenous people, and running the Northwest Territories. As commissioner of the Northwest Territories, he led what historian Shelagh Grant described as a "distinct departure from the former laisser-faire approach to economic development" in the North. Education spending soared by 575 per cent during his tenure, for instance, thirteen times the national average.[13] His activist approach to the North, Canada's less-developed periphery, was reformist and interventionist in administration, modernizing in economic development policy, and paternalistic toward Indigenous peoples. He was a leading figure in pushing through a modernizing, technocratic approach to the Northwest Territories that would be echoed soon afterward by the CCF government of Saskatchewan.[14] He would carry the same leadership style into his UN work.

Again he stood on the fringes in an increasingly anti-communist Ottawa: as deputy minister, he was no keener to take action against the communist-controlled International Seamen's Union than he had been on uprooting Japanese-Canadians. The powerful "minister of everything" C. D. Howe even called him a communist at one cabinet meeting.[15] The

FIGURE 3.1
Hugh Keenleyside,
October 1954. (Source:
UN Photo 337064)

chance to take on UN work in warmer climates with fewer checks on his freedom of action was probably welcome. In 1950, Keenleyside agreed to head a UN technical assistance mission to Bolivia, after obtaining the consent of his minister and Prime Minister St. Laurent for three months' leave to take part in what Resources and Development Minister Robert Winters called a "pioneering" mission.[16]

The technical assistance mission to Bolivia studied the pattern of the landlocked South American country's economy and asked why its natural resources had not led to much prosperity for its people. Its staff of twenty-two included five Americans and experts from Canada, France, Mexico, the Netherlands, South Africa, and Switzerland, who deployed to Bolivia for a four-month survey. This was very much a group of experts offering universal lessons to a specific locale about which they knew little. Offered the post, Keenleyside began by getting an atlas and starting to learn about "a country of whose history I had only an indifferent knowledge and of whose current social and economic circumstances I knew even less." The mission's model was to be a team of multinational experts, each with their own specialty but living together in one hotel with a common dining room table and a common lounge used for weekly check-in sessions.[17]

Oddly, the UN's technical assistance mission to Bolivia operated with limited awareness of the country's development history and highly stratified society, where a small elite dominated and Indigenous people were marginalized. Bolivian governments stressed nationalism and economic development. Tin exports buoyed an export-oriented economy, spurring strong mining unions and left-wing political movements. The UN responded to Bolivian requests for technical aid by sending two officials in 1949 for conversations in La Paz. They arrived just as a revolution broke out (the government survived, but would be toppled in 1952). When the opposition National Revolutionary Movement (MNR) finished second in subsequent national elections, the president resigned in favour of Vice-President Mamerto Urriolagoitia, described by American diplomats as a "resolute" and "honest" figure "around which a stronger future Bolivian state can be built."[18]

The 1949 uprising meant that "the conditions for rendering technical assistance did not seem very propitious," one UN memorandum recorded drily.[19] Still, the revolution leant "particular urgency" to the need for experts "whose judgments will command respect because of their own competence and because of the moral prestige of the United Nations."[20] Bolivian demands and UN wishes dovetailed in some aspects, but each had its own goals. The UN's technical assistance stressed economic modernization, the application of expertise, continued alignment with US intentions for South America, and political stability. It was far from the demands expressed by popular movements that were on the rise in Bolivia.

The Keenleyside mission that followed these early UN steps into Bolivia would set the stamp on the UN's overall pattern of technical assistance and lead to Keenleyside becoming the director-general of the TAA immediately afterward. In a remarkable report that largely ignored the social changes taking place in Bolivia, it recommended that the country accept foreign advisors and appoint them to decision-making roles in the Bolivian civil

FIGURE 3.2
Hugh Keenleyside signs a technical assistance agreement with Colombia, while UN Secretary-General Trygve Lie (right) looks on. (Source: UN Photo 335071)

service. Without such a "bold and dramatic step," the report went, Bolivia would face centuries more underdevelopment. But foreign experts, the mission concluded, would make it "possible to telescope into a single generation or less the economic and social advance that will otherwise involve a slow progression over many decades."[21] Obviously, there would be fears of foreign control if foreign advisors were to staff Bolivian government offices. To defuse that, Keenleyside pointed to the multilateral character of the advisors: "The fact that they would come from a number of countries and would serve in a sense under U.N. auspices would, we believed, counteract charges that the programme was just a continuance of the old colonial system."[22] Multilateralism was made into virtue. Images of Bolivian poverty, meanwhile, served to underpin the campaign for change.

The notion of "telescoping" development indicated one of the main appeals of technical assistance: the hope that it could deliver fast results. The other major selling point was that technical assistance was cheap: officials from both Indonesia and the United States, for example, said it could

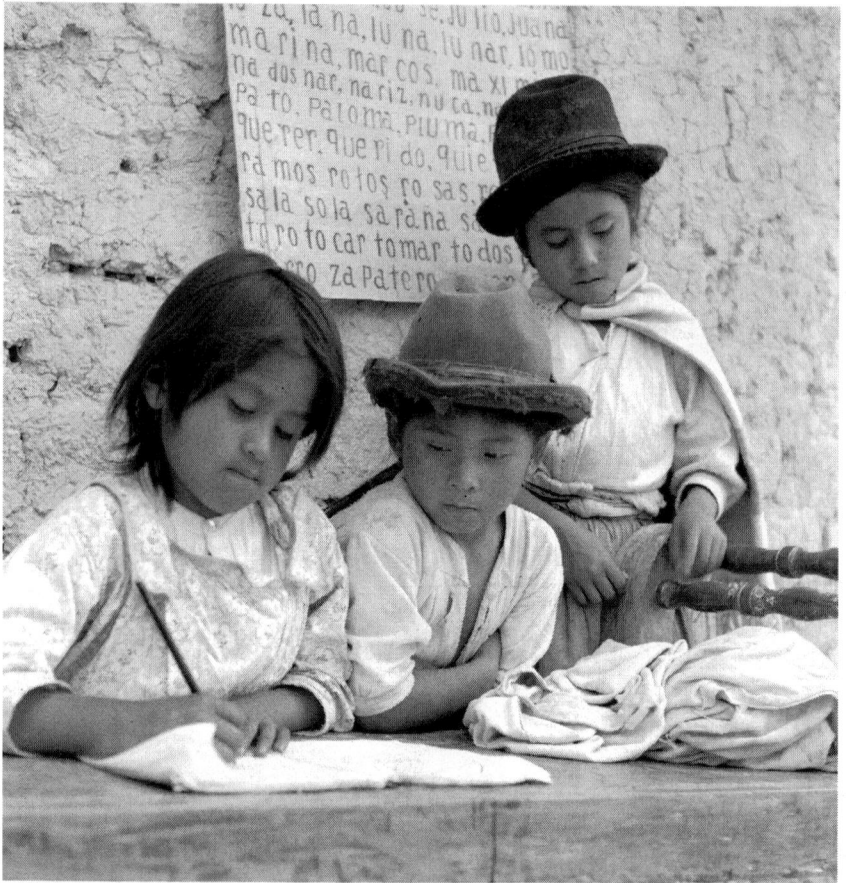

FIGURE 3.3
Three Bolivian children are shown studying outdoors while awaiting the completion of a new school building in this UN photo promoting its technical assistance activities in the South American country in 1950. (Source: UN Photo 75191)

deliver a "hundredfold" return.[23] Put in a dollar's worth of expertise, the theory ran, and receive a hundred dollars' worth of development in return.

The Bolivia mission report was billed as the consensus of the entire mission staff. Yet Keenleyside's travel diaries make it very clear that the idea of handing decision-making powers to foreign nationals attached to the Bolivian civil service—the question that raised issues for some of "colonial control"—was very much Keenleyside's own idea.[24] He formed it early in the mission, pitching it at a dinner party hosted by Bolivia's third largest mining magnate soon after his arrival in La Paz, before he had even left the capital city, and while the streets outside were under martial law imposed over fears of a left-wing revolution. His leadership style forced an issue of foreign tutelage over a less developed country in a way that others at the UN shied away from. Keenleyside hammered his staff until they all agreed to recommend a plan that employed these powerful foreign experts, under the innocuous term "administrative assistants." He knew the idea would be a tough sell. "But," he wrote, "I'm not going to be satisfied with—though I may have to accept—anything less fundamental. I'm not going to waste four months on a report that could have been written in Lake Success—and that would produce no really useful results."

In a meeting with two right-wing party leaders whom he considered "idiotic," Keenleyside noted that "both swallowed the foreign control idea without gagging." So too did president Urriolagoitia. With the Bolivian government onside, Keenleyside flew to New York and Geneva to win the support of the UN. "Some of the people at the top are frightened of my suggestions although those at the operating levels are all enthusiastic in their support," he wrote. But he would not be dissuaded, lobbying hard and delivering an ultimatum that his recommendation for "effective administrators" would not change in the final report, come what may.[25] Keenleyside won the fight at the UN and returned to Bolivia to finish the mission's report.

The final document reflected his preferences. It charted a clear course for Bolivia based on technical expertise to keep the country on its existing trajectory and reliance on mineral exports, ignoring opposition demands for a more people-centred agrarian development path. Though this is nowhere noted in UN accounts, the opposition MNR and the trade unions stridently opposed UN plans. The UN and the Urriolagoitia government had "imposed ignominiously upon us a foreign mission which came to govern us with extraordinary powers to place the Bolivian economy at the entire disposition of imperialist military plans," one labour-oriented newspaper wrote.[26]

The MNR won the 1952 election, prompting a military coup, then an MNR-led protest movement that finally brought the party to power. Although it briefly froze the admission of new advisors and nationalized tin mines, a step that Keenleyside's mission had called "wholly impractical under present conditions," the MNR government soon saw value in the UN presence. The UN was able to negotiate an agreement to provide "technical consultants" to the new regime. UN planning and publicity continued unchanged, in keeping with claims that technical assistance was apolitical. A UN paper two years later stressed "continuity in the composition of the mission," with UN advisors acting as "a stable and trusted element in the agencies where they served. . . . It does not seem exaggerated to ascribe the consistency and relative moderation of the Government policies, in part at last, to the stabilizing influence of the Mission."[27]

UN advice guided the revolutionary government toward becoming a modernizing technocratic administration. As UN Technical Assistance Resident Representative Margaret Anstee recalled, the MNR had few options if it wanted outside help, since the World Bank and Washington opposed it completely. Thus the MNR proved willing to welcome "senior people who would not just be advisors but who would have line functions in very high positions in key ministries."[28] At all levels, UN officials interpenetrated the Bolivian government—"part of the national team, not as outsiders at all," in Anstee's words.[29]

Bolivia became one of the UN's largest technical assistance fields of operation. By 1956, it was by far the largest TAA project in Latin America, receiving more than double the funds spent on second-place Colombia. The UN's ability to ease a revolutionary government into modernizing paths was, to Keenleyside and other UN officials, a sign of technical assistance's utility.

Keenleyside's Bolivia experience, meanwhile, won him the post of first director-general of the new Technical Assistance Administration. Prime Minister St. Laurent agreed that Canada had a "great" interest in technical assistance, and a Canadian ended up with a senior UN job in a field in which Canada would become highly active.[30]

Press reports in Canada cheered Keenleyside's appointment. The *Montreal Star* hailed him as a "brutally frank . . . no-nonsense executive" well equipped to tackle "the largest peacetime operation the United Nations has attempted."[31] His "reputation for energy" would be important to the great new work of international technical aid, wrote the *Winnipeg Free Press*.[32] In his regular broadcast from the UN, CBC radio reporter Peter Stursberg raved about the opportunities opening up: "It's a great story—this technical aid—a story that cannot be told too often—particularly at this time when there seems to be nothing happening here except the squabbles in the Security Council."[33] It also provided a modest boost to Canada's self-image at a time when the UN was central enough in Canadian foreign policy that UN staff appointments made headlines. Technical assistance offered a gleam of hope at a time when things looked bleak at the UN.

As the Cold War took hold and the UN was unable to do much on peace and security, technical assistance provided it with a mission and a new lease on life. As director-general of the TAA, Keenleyside preferred a low profile to the front lines. Only a refusal to shake hands with former Nazi economist and then advisor to the Indonesian government, Hjalmar Schacht, on a visit to Indonesia put his name on the front pages. Keenleyside's leadership style was operational and managerial, seeking to enhance TAA status and budgets within the UN system and to position the UN as the major actor in international aid. In this, he reflected the preferences and style of other UN officials. The TAA was, in Keenleyside's words, a "busy shop" doing a great deal more operational work than most of the UN Secretariat.[34] It had a clear vision: to help less developed countries create and implement national development plans. These plans would be inspired not by American liberalism but by European and Commonwealth social democratic thought.

Keenleyside's politics, which he described as Labour Cooperative in the British mould, fit well within this TAA social-democratic milieu. Keenleyside had worked for Prime Minister Mackenzie King, but he did not believe that King was the best man for the job. He preferred M. J. Coldwell, leader of the Cooperative Commonwealth Federation (CCF), forerunner to today's New Democratic Party.[35] To help run the TAA, Keenleyside brought in George Cadbury, the head of the Economic Advisory Planning Board in Tommy Douglas's CCF government of Saskatchewan, to be his director of operations. He named Frank Scott, the McGill law professor, poet, and former national president of the CCF, as UN technical assistance chief in Burma. In 1958, he even hired retired CCF leader Coldwell to head up a community evaluation mission to India, and he was later instrumental in arranging a UNDP resident representative post for Woodrow Lloyd, the outgoing CCF premier of Saskatchewan.[36]

Canada and UN Technical Assistance

Canada was never, of course, governed by the CCF. But Liberal and Progressive Conservative governments of the 1950s certainly embraced the UN's technical assistance work.[37] Canada always gave more money to UN technical assistance than it did through the Colombo Plan's technical assistance scheme. The efficiency and centralized nature of the TAA appealed to those in Ottawa who liked things tidy. Canada initially lacked the cash and the interest to follow the United States, France, and others into creating a large bilateral aid program. More impact might come within multilateral channels such as UN technical assistance. UN figures, too, preferred to have funds flow through their coffers, not bilaterally. Keenleyside and others at the UN thought that the TAA's processes ran much more smoothly than the clunky and inefficient aid administration run by Nik Cavell in Ottawa, the subject of Greg Donaghy's chapter. TAA officials regretted that Canada maintained its own technical assistance bureaucracy rather than simply writing a cheque to the UN. Still, Canada's support for the TAA bolstered multilateral technical assistance even as the United States preferred to put most of its technical assistance cash into its own large bilateral program.

The TAA was always short of funds and periodically under attack in the US Congress, often suspicious of foreign aid and of the United Nations more generally. It looked to Canada for both cash and a vote of confidence in UN technical assistance. Thus Keenleyside undertook a Canada-wide speaking tour in 1953 to build public support for the UN and international development.[38] This is the sort of initiative that boosted public awareness and public support for overseas aid. Keenleyside would continue this effort to shape public opinion in several more trips north in subsequent years. He warned an audience at McGill University in 1955, for instance, that "no peace can be deemed secure so long as over half the population of the world is ignorant, diseased, hungry and oppressed."[39] Calls from churches, trade unions, and non-governmental organizations for Canada to increase its aid abounded in the 1950s.

This created a public constituency for aid and a public commitment to the idea of aid, a theme discussed in Ted Cogan's chapter in this volume. "We have been conscious that Canadians, as individuals—and this has been clearly reflected in the press from one end of the country to the

FIGURE 3.4
Technical Assistance Pledges, 1956.

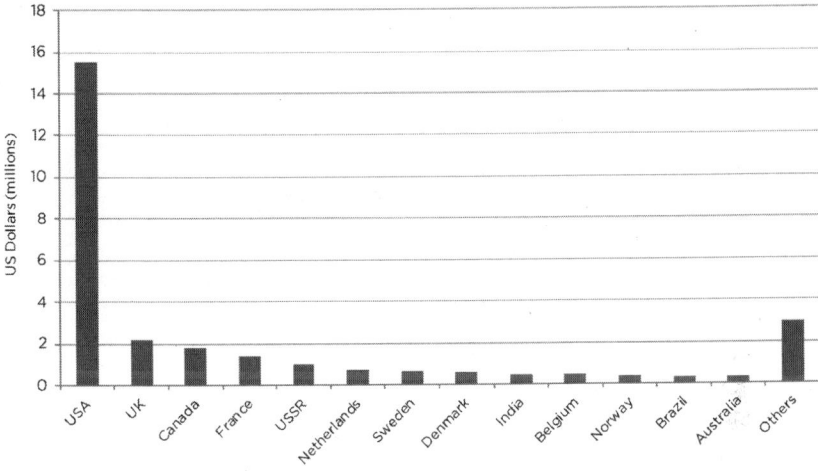

FIGURE 3.5
Annual Pledges, 1952–57.

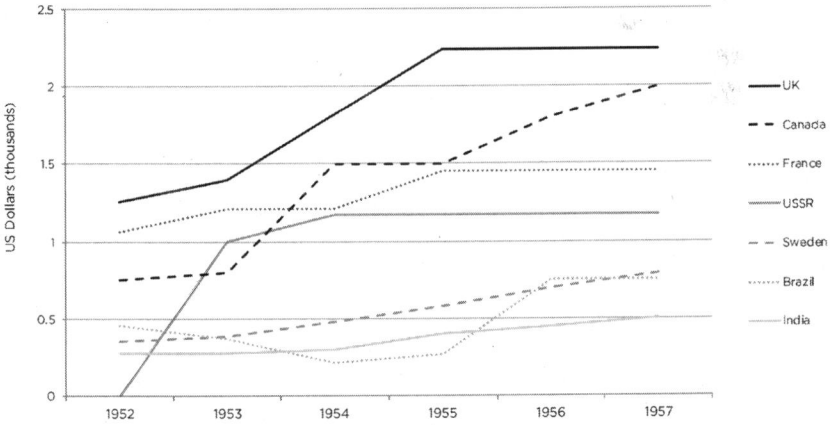

other—wish to contribute to the success of this plan," Pearson said after a parliamentary foreign affairs debate.[40] An increasing volume of letters from the public reached Ottawa in support of foreign aid and calling for more funds. Correspondents ranged from the Ministerial Association in Almonte, Ontario, to the Canadian Congress of Labour (which wanted aid quadrupled).[41] The chief Colombo Plan administrator in Canada reported that he was "deluged" with requests for information.[42] Australian advocates of increased aid looked jealously to Canada's higher public support for aid.[43] Keenleyside noted growing support in Canada for aid in general too. He thought "our people are ahead of the Government in this matter."[44] Keenleyside did not of course shift Canadian public opinion on his own, but the presence and advocacy of one of the best-informed Canadians active in the aid field probably contributed to an atmosphere of growing public support for overseas development aid.

Keenleyside moved smoothly from public speeches to private lobbying. He appealed to Pearson to come to New York and deliver a speech that "like the shot fired at Lexington, would be heard round the world."[45] Six weeks later, Keenleyside followed up with a plea for more money, saying Congress might cut US funding, and that more money from Canada, Britain, Australia, France, and the Netherlands was vital. Canada, he wrote, was the most important of those countries because it could influence US views. After all: "Americans looked upon Canadians as being hard-headed, sensible and practical people." Meanwhile, Canada could afford, he thought, "a somewhat spectacular gesture."[46] Not too spectacular, but somewhat spectacular.

Keenleyside's lobbying paid off. In 1956, Canada overtook France to become the third-largest contributor to UN technical assistance, after the US and the UK, taking first place among contributors in per capita terms.[47]

Canada also ranked high among the countries sending out technical advisors. A comprehensive list of UN experts from 1954 gives a snapshot. The TAA at that point had roughly 400 experts in the field. Seventy of them held US citizenship. Britain followed closely with 63—at least a couple of these actually being residents of Canada—and France stood third. Canada, the Netherlands, and Sweden led a large number of other countries.[48]

In all this, it is evident that Canada was playing a different role from the bigger powers, in common with some other "like-minded countries"

FIGURE 3.6
UN TAA Experts by Nationality, 1954.

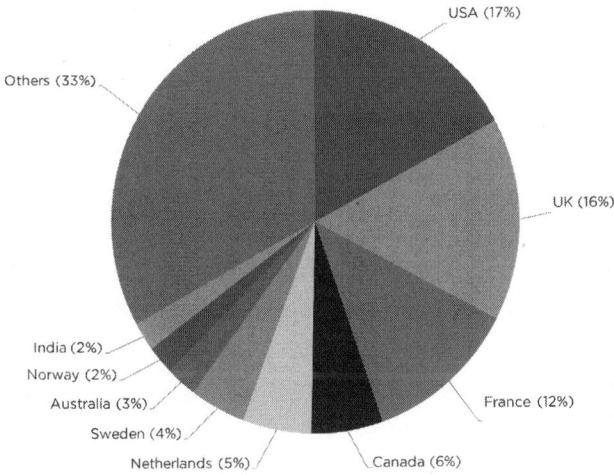

in northern Europe. This alignment was clear by the 1970s,[49] but it can be traced to the 1950s. Technical assistance paved the way.

Development Diplomacy

While technical assistance aimed to promote economic development as its primary goal, it also had diplomatic objectives. The UN secretariat called technical assistance "a new form of diplomacy."[50] Canadian officials felt just the same: a technical expert "is in fact an ambassador of our country," to quote the standard recruitment letter from the Technical Cooperation Service in the Department of Trade And Commerce.[51] It all evoked the missionary days, when so many Canadians crossed an ocean to change other societies. Keenleyside's standard letter of welcome to experts billed technical assistance as a "great crusade for human progress" guided by "high purposes." Technical assistance, he wrote, was "based upon the assumption that it is possible and practical to transfer knowledge and techniques from one area to another for the purpose of advancing the economic and social development of the people of the world."[52] The religious language was not accidental. Writing much later, Keenleyside felt that the best advisors were "infused with some measure of the true missionary spirit."[53] Development work was the new missionary work, and technical advisors were guided by similar fervour to improve other societies.[54] Technical advisors, like missionaries, travelled with helpful intent. Yet, like missionaries, they often ended up as "beneficent imperialists," spreading a model of cultural change based on their own national experiences and overly reliant on a simplistic ideology of technological transfer.[55]

The thousands of technical advisors who travelled on multiple looping journeys to advise the governments of less developed countries were not simply itinerant experts who flew in, advised, and then departed. They were also diplomats. In the case of Canada and many other countries, they could be a more important channel for contacts and connections than the government's own official diplomats. In this, they took over a niche once occupied by Christian missionaries, whose own work was undergoing "NGO-ization"—a process examined by Ruth Compton Brouwer.[56] They were in effect acting as diplomats carrying out a form of what Mary Young and Susan Henders describe as Canadian "other diplomacy."[57]

Technical assistance diplomacy was one of the ties that bound less developed countries to the industrialized West. When the governments of newly independent states in non-communist Asia began to seek economic development and to replace their colonial economies with "national economies" in the 1950s, they almost all opted for the tool of "development planning." That meant taking back control of the national economy from former colonial rulers, but it also meant continued international links. First, the more developed countries of the North provided possible models, potential "paths to modernity." Second, they could offer the technical experts and the technical expertise that new states felt they needed. Third, development required capital, and many countries sought that through raw material exports, meaning they had to remain integrated into the global economy.

UN technical assistance favoured middle-sized countries seen as having good potential for the sort of economic development the UN was looking for—which, again, tended to be social-democratic. The 1954 snapshot

FIGURE 3.7
UN TAA Experts by Country Placements, 1954.

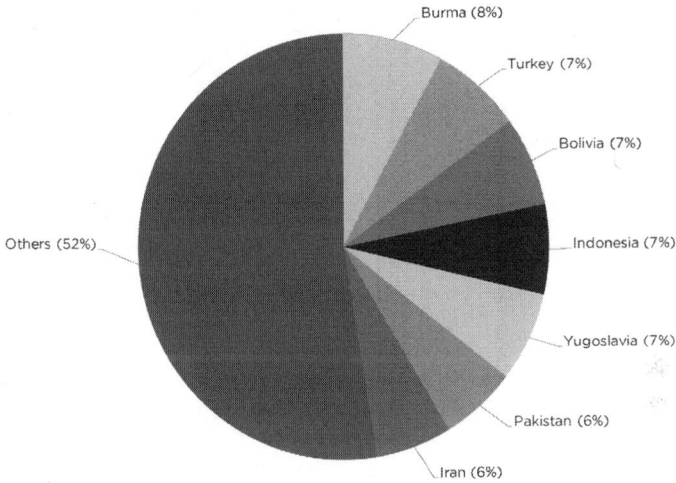

Pie chart: Burma (8%), Turkey (7%), Bolivia (7%), Indonesia (7%), Yugoslavia (7%), Pakistan (6%), Iran (6%), Others (52%)

in Figure 3.7 provides a typical picture of where technical advisors operated. Of the experts in the field, the largest group was in Burma, followed by Turkey, Bolivia, Indonesia, Yugoslavia, Iran, and Pakistan. The group included United States allies, but it was hardly a list of US priority countries. Instead, it favoured middle-sized non-aligned governments.

These technical advisors sought to build what might be called a "development world order."[58] The UN was seeking to build the world anew, and development gave it an ideal mission statement. The UN's major contribution to modernization theory was the idea of democratic planning, pioneered by postwar social-democratic governments in Britain, France, Saskatchewan, and elsewhere. Development planning, in Arturo Escobar's description, "involved the overcoming or eradication of 'traditions,' 'obstacles,' and 'irrationalities'; that is, the wholesale modification of existing human and social structures and their replacement with rational new ones."[59] The UN, without the apparent axe to grind of the United States, was a more welcomed and thus more effective channel to transmit the idea

Figure 3.8
An unidentified Egyptian worker operating a large radial drill at a machine shop in Port Fuad as part of a UN technical assistance project supporting the rehabilitation of the Suez Canal. (Source: UN Photo 146207)

of planning. Its model was not American liberalism; still less was it Soviet central planning. Through the TAA, it was helping to reconstitute a capitalist and Eurocentric world order, while at the same time trying to construct an interconnected "world in development" in which technical assistance would "change lives" and change the way the world was organized.[60] TAA officials could use the phrase "stages of development" well before it was popularized by American modernization theory's guru, Walt Rostow.[61]

The TAA acted from a position of power, as bearers of superior technical knowledge, but also from a position of relative weakness compared to wealthier US technical advisory services offering a different type of model. It did so in partnership with an emerging group of planners in less developed countries. Technical assistance also allowed the UN to build a world-girdling diplomatic service of its own. The array of Technical Assistance resident representatives established under UN auspices around the world formed a network that few governments could rival. By 1958, when the TAA folded into other UN departments, some 8,000 technical advisors had gone overseas and there were 39 Technical Assistance resident offices functioning as, in effect, UN development embassies to countries or regions. As a comparison, Canada by 1960 still had only four embassies in all of Africa.[62]

An example of development diplomacy is Keenleyside's successful effort to bring the Soviet Union into the UN technical assistance scheme. Moscow initially rejected technical assistance as a tool of American imperialism. But soon after dictator Josef Stalin's death in March 1953, it launched an economic offensive to penetrate less developed countries, especially non-aligned countries in Asia. As part of this effort, Moscow offered to contribute 4 million roubles, the equivalent of a million American dollars. In presenting this about-face, Soviet delegate Amasasp Aroutunian distinguished US "Point Four" aid sharply from the UN's technical assistance. The Soviet Union, he said, "had always held that technical assistance should be made available through the intermediary of the United Nations. By contrast, the United States 'Point Four' plan was entirely contrary to United Nations principles, and constituted a weapon of penetration and coercion."[63]

The Soviet offer came with strings. Most notably, the currency was to be entirely unconvertible. The TAA worked to find ways to draw the Soviet Union and its allies into the funding picture, despite an effort by Canada, Norway, and the United States to reject unconvertible Soviet and Czech contributions. For these Western powers, the danger was that the Soviets would use the UN channel to create bilateral links, with Soviet funds used to pay Soviet experts and provide Soviet equipment in Asian countries, and thereby create Soviet economic bridgeheads. This had to be resisted, but calls for all contributions to be fully convertible into other currencies foundered on the fact that British and French contributions, along with those of quite a few smaller donors, were not fully convertible either.

A further challenge came from Moscow's demand that Soviet contributions could go to the UN—meaning via the TAA—but not to any of its specialized agencies such as the World Health Organization or the Food and Agriculture Organization. The deal creating the UN Expanded Programme of Technical Assistance divvied up the funding pie between the TAA and specialized agencies. The Soviet offer threatened this carefully negotiated division of funds, for if one donor could alter the division of funds, then the entire package fell apart.

Consequently, the 1953 Soviet offer had to be rejected. At the same time, the TAA was desperately short of funds and relied for roughly half its income on the US grant, at constant risk of being cut or killed entirely by Congress. Keenleyside pushed Canada to raise its annual contribution as a means of pressuring other countries to do the same. But a large Soviet grant might provide a lifeline. With the Korean War ending in an armistice in 1953, a Soviet pledge to UN aid programs might also help encourage superpower cooperation, making a useful contribution to the UN mission of promoting global peace.

The UN and the TAA in particular looked for solutions. Keenleyside flew to Moscow to work out a deal after Soviet delegations to UN meetings proved unwilling to budge on their conditions. A series of "lurid" Soviet attacks on the UN's technical assistance contained some valid points, Keenleyside admitted. But he told his hosts that unless they removed their conditions, the UN could not accept their money. Keenleyside did not enjoy Moscow, complaining of its unattractive people bundled up against the cold and its "police state" atmosphere. However, he was impressed with Vice-Minister of Foreign Affairs Vasili Kuznetsov, who had once worked in a Detroit Ford Motors plant, and even with the "brilliant" Aroutunian, his chief tormentor in UN forums. In the end, Keenleyside got his way on the two key barriers by making concessions in other areas. The Soviet Union would allow the specialized agencies to use its funds, and consider partial convertibility if there was no way to use the full rouble amount on Soviet equipment and services. In exchange, the TAA and the agencies would look seriously at using more Soviet experts and try to spend more in the Soviet Union, including by allowing the WHO to buy Soviet medicines. "Our success was subsequently of real help to the Expanded Programme and all those participating in it," Keenleyside recalled. "It also added to T.A.A.'s popularity with the Specialized Agencies which had been both distressed and angered by the Russians' preference for us."[64]

In short, the Keenleyside mission was a triumph, reflecting both Keenleyside's individual leadership and the UN's broader desire to bridge cold war divides. Secretary-General Trygve Lie was soon suggesting to Pearson that if all aid funds flowed through the UN, aid would not become a cold war battlefield.[65] A Canadian working in the secretariat, Lloyd Herman, was seconded to TAA for a months-long study of how to use Soviet aid. Meanwhile, the US Congress embarked on another bout of considering cuts to the UN technical assistance grant. If a cut was the result, "we might expect that the Soviet offer of aid would come to play a significant part in the programme as a whole," Canada's UN mission reported.[66]

Moscow's entry into the world of technical assistance appeared as a threat in Washington, used to a dominant voice in much of Asia. To a lesser extent this was also true in London, which saw the Colombo Plan as an instrument to maintain its influence in South and Southeast Asia. But the technical assistance diplomats of the UN were playing a different game, using technical assistance as a way to reduce cold war tensions. To an extent, they had the backing of some smaller powers, including Canada, for a gentler approach to the Soviet Union. Hugh Keenleyside's 1954 Moscow trip was followed by a visit to the Soviet Union by Pearson in late 1955, the first by a NATO foreign minister after Stalin's death. Canada's role in technical assistance was significant, and Canada also had some sympathy for UN technical assistance diplomacy, led as it was by a former Canadian diplomat, Hugh Keenleyside.

Keenleyside formally retired from the UN in 1959 to become chairman of the British Columbia Power Commission, a recently nationalized public electricity utility. He continued as co-chairman of an enlarged British Columbia Hydro and Power Authority until 1969. In 1966, he published a well-received book on international aid.[67] Keenleyside rounded out his international experience as associate commissioner-general for the UN Conference on Human Settlements (Habitat) held in Vancouver in 1976.

Conclusion: Developing the World

Canada was slower off the mark than some to send aid to the Global South, but it soon came to be a major donor, especially important to the UN's technical assistance programs. Ottawa embraced multilateral channels for aid and became a leading supporter and advocate of the UN's aid work. It was not a solo "Samaritan state." Instead, it stressed what might be dubbed collective Samaritanism, working closely with others to deliver aid in ways that were seen as mutually beneficial to both donor and recipient. This theme of mutual benefit reached its pinnacle in 1969 with the release of *Partners in Development,* the report of the UN-sponsored Commission on International Development, chaired by Lester Pearson following his retirement as prime minister.[68] Canadian and UN thinking on development dovetailed in that report, the culmination of more than a decade of experience.

Multilateralism meant that Canada did not establish its own aid program in the 1950s as larger countries like the United States, Britain, and France were doing. It had an aid administration unit housed in the Department of Trade and Commerce, but the money flowed through multilateral mechanisms—capital assistance for infrastructure through the Colombo Plan, and most technical assistance through the UN and its specialized agencies. Keenleyside stood near the centre of early Canadian technical assistance thought, moving fluidly from UN official to shaper of Canadian public opinion to colleague and lobbyist of Canadian policy makers. His role helped to position Canadian aid in a multilateral, UN-centred position in the years to follow.

Canada's government gradually moved in the 1950s to becoming the leading booster, if not the top donor, to UN technical assistance. It could not effectively act alone, but its voice could be magnified in UN forums. The UN's relative success in the development aid field in turn reflected well on the world organization, which was as policy makers in Ottawa wished it. In technical assistance, Canada was a major player.

Technical assistance was mainly about economic development, but it was not solely a "Samaritan" program of giving. Its diplomatic aspects also helped the UN raise its global stature and try to cool superpower tensions. Aid was also diplomacy, a point recognized quite explicitly in Ottawa as well as in New York. Keenleyside's success in bringing the Soviet Union into UN technical assistance work was remarkable, given the close association in the public mind between technical assistance and US president Truman's foreign policy. Development diplomacy helped form a world order that promoted global integration at a time when decolonization and the Cold War raised fears of disintegration. In this sense, it also served Canadian foreign policy goals.

Notes

1   A. W. F. Plumptre to Escott Reid, 7 November 1950, RG 25, vol. 6574, file 11038-40, Library and Archives Canada (LAC).

2   Extract from cabinet conclusions, 1 November 1950, reprinted in Greg Donaghy, ed., *Documents on Canadian External Relations (DCER)*, vol. 16: *1950* (Ottawa: Supply and Services Canada, 1996), 1266–68.

3   See, for instance, Pearson to Doug Abbott, 17 January 1951, reprinted in Greg Donaghy, ed., *DCER*, vol. 17: *1951* (Ottawa: Public Works and Government Services Canada, 1996), 1042–45.

4   Extract from cabinet conclusions, 25 October 1950, reprinted in *DCER*, 16:1260–62.

5   Jonathan B. Bingham, *Shirt-Sleeve Diplomacy: Point 4 in Action* (New York: John Day, 1953), 21.

6   Truman's inaugural address, 20 January 1949, https://www.trumanlibrary.org/whistlestop/50yr_archive/inagural20jan1949.htm; Gilbert Rist, *The History of Development: From Western Origins to Global Faith*, 2nd ed. (London: Zed Books, 2002).

7   "Memorandum of points for consideration in the development of a twenty-year program for achieving peace through the United Nations," 6 June 1950, *Public Papers of the Secretaries-General of the United Nations*, vol. 1: *Trygve Lie, 1946–1953* (New York: Columbia University Press, 1969), 301.

8   John Meehan, *The Dominion and the Rising Sun: Canada Encounters Japan, 1929–41* (Vancouver: University of British Columbia Press, 2004), 16.

9   Hugh L. Keenleyside, *Memoirs of Hugh Keenleyside*, vol. 1: *Hammer the Golden Day* (Toronto: McClelland and Stewart, 1981), 457.

10 "Chinese Immigration," memorandum by Hugh L. Keenleyside, 30 December 1936, Keenleyside Papers, vol. 8, file: Canada and China; "The Oriental Problem in Canada," confidential report of the Board of Review, chaired by H. L. Keenleyside, LAC; Keenleyside Papers, vol. 11, file: Oriental Immigration, 1935–1939, LAC.

11 Diaries of William Lyon Mackenzie King, 17 March 1943, item 26243, http://www.bac-lac.gc.ca/eng/discover/politics-government/prime-ministers/william-lyon-mackenzie-king/Pages/item.aspx?IdNumber=26243&.

12 "Memorandum for the Prime Minister," Mackenzie King papers, MG 26 J4, vol. 284, LAC.

13 Shelagh Grant, "Hugh Llewellyn Keenleyside: Commissioner of the Northwest Territories, 1947–1950," *Arctic Profiles* 43, no. 1 (1990): 81.

14 David Quiring, *CCF Colonialism in Northern Saskatchewan: Battling Parish Priests, Bootleggers, and Fur Sharks* (Vancouver: University of British Columbia Press, 2004).

15 Diaries of William Lyon Mackenzie King, 16 November 1948, item 31923, http://www.bac-lac.gc.ca/eng/discover/politics-government/prime-ministers/william-lyon-mackenzie-king/Pages/item.aspx?IdNumber=31923&.

16 Robert Winters to J. W. Pickersgill, 3 February 1950, L. S. St. Laurent Papers, vol. 96, file D-54-D, LAC.

17 Keenleyside, *Memoirs*, vol. 2: *On the Bridge of Time* (Toronto: McClelland and Stewart, 1982), 326–27, 334; "Latin America: Expert Assistance Rendered to Date," S-0441-1417-01, United Nations Archives and Records Administration (UNARMS).

18 Glenn J. Dorn, "Pushing Tin: U.S.-Bolivian Relations and the Coming of the National Revolution," *Diplomatic History* 35, no. 2 (April 2011): 215–16.

19 Note on Secretariat inter-departmental meeting, 30 August 1949, S-0441-1417-04, UNARMS; Memo by Robenborg in history of Bolivia requests, 1 Oct. 1949, S-039-0022-09, UNARMS.

20 Report of the United Nations Preparatory Mission to Bolivia on Technical Assistance, 9 December 1949, S-0369-0022-09, UNARMS.

21 Report of the UN mission of technical assistance to Bolivia, 1951, Keenleyside Papers, vol. 8, file: Bolivia [1], LAC.

22 Keenleyside, *Memoirs*, 2:336.

23 Indonesian Ambassador to UK Subandrio, speech to Scottish Provisional Committee for War on Want, Glasgow, 21 November 1953; US Secretary of Agriculture Charles F. Brannan, cited in Charles Wolf Jr., *Foreign Aid: Theory and Practice in Southern Asia* (Princeton, NJ: Princeton University Press, 1960), 63.

24 Keenleyside Bolivia travel diary, Keenleyside Papers 30-12, LAC.

25 Ibid.

26 Robert J. Alexander, *The Bolivian National Revolution* (Westport CT: Greenwood Press, 1958), 245–47.

27 Working Paper 6: UN Technical Assistance in Bolivia, for Seminar on evaluation of UN Technical Assistance, McGill University, 11–12 March 1954, S-0441-1515-06, UNARMS.

28   Oral History Interview of Margaret Anstee, in *The Complete Oral History Transcripts from UN Voices*, CD-ROM (New York: United Nations Intellectual History Project, 2007), 47–48.

29   Ibid., 49.

30   St. Laurent to Keenleyside, 8 September 1950, St. Laurent Papers, vol. 96, file D-54-D, LAC.

31   Walter O'Hearn, "Keenleyside Favored For Major Post At United Nations," *Montreal Star*, 14 July 1950.

32   "Dr. Keenleyside," *Winnipeg Free Press* editorial, 16 September 1950.

33   Stursberg broadcast transcript, 9 September 1950, Keenleyside Papers, vol. 30, file: UNTAA appointment 1950, LAC.

34   Hugh Keenleyside, *International Aid: A Summary, with Special Reference to the Programmes of the United Nations* (Toronto: McClelland and Stewart, 1966), 230.

35   Keenleyside to Coldwell, 5 May 1952, Keenleyside Papers, vol. 12, file: Coldwell, M.J, LAC.

36   Keenleyside to Escott Reid, 8 October 1958, Escott Reid Papers, vol. 34, file: Keenleyside, Hugh L., LAC.

37   The case for Canadian participation in UN technical assistance was made successfully in External Affairs memorandum to cabinet, cabinet document 158-50, RG 25, vol. 3701, file 5475-DU-1-40[FP], LAC. Pledges rose from that point.

38   "Mr. Keenleyside's Trip to Canada," [1953], S-0441-1431-11, UNARMS.

39   Keenleyside speech on "Economic Development and Social Welfare as Roads to Peace," McGill University School of Social Work, 15 February 1955, Keenleyside Papers, 28-15, LAC.

40   Pearson speech to parliament, 21 February 1951, Canada, House of Commons, *Debates*, 21st Parliament, 4th Session, vol. 1, 537–38.

41   Almonte Ministerial Association to Louis St. Laurent, 12 May 1951, RG 25, vol. 6575, file 11038-40 [7.1], LAC; Memorandum from office of SSEA to Acting USSEA, 8 January 1954, RG 25, vol. 8389, file 11038-40 [15], LAC.

42   Minutes of Colombo plan group, 16 January 1953, RG 25, vol. 6576, file 11038-40 [11.1], LAC.

43   Australian Cabinet submission 339, 19 February 1953, A4940, C1050, National Archives of Australia (NAA); Cabinet submission 10, undated [June 1954], A4940, C1050, NAA.

44   Keenleyside personal letter to Pearson, 17 June 1953, in Donald Barry, ed., *DCER*, vol. 19: *1953*, 526–28.

45   Keenleyside to Pearson, 17 June 1953, Keenleyside Papers, vol. 25, file: Pearson, L.B., LAC.

46   Ibid., Keenleyside to Pearson, 10 August 1953.

47   Summary charts of pledges to EPTA, RG 25, vol. 6090, file 5475-DU-1-40[19.1], LAC; Keenleyside to Pearson, 15 November 1956, Keenleyside Papers, vol. 25, file: Pearson, L.B., LAC. Figures for charts drawn from Olav Stokke, *The UN and Development: From Aid to Cooperation* (Bloomington: Indiana University Press, 2009).

48   Figures and chart data from 1954 posts list, S-0441 series, UNARMS.

49   For instance, Cranford Pratt, ed., *Canadian International Development Assistance Policies* (Montreal: McGill-Queen's University Press, 1994).

50   TAA memorandum, John Fried to Keenleyside, 15 January 1952, S-0441-1416-01, UNARMS.

51   Recruitment letter, signed by David Judd, Technical Cooperation Service, Department of Trade and Commerce, 6 April 1956, RG 74/1980-81/36-7C-7-74, LAC.

52   Keenleyside 1952 welcome letter, S-0441-1483-03, UNARMS.

53   Keenleyside, *International Aid*, 220.

54   See, for instance, Karen Minden, *Canadian Development Assistance: The Medical Missionary Model in West China, 1910–1952* (Toronto: Joint Centre for Asia Pacific Studies, 1989); Richard R. Mallon, *The New Missionaries: Memoirs of a Foreign Advisor in Less-Developed Countries* (Cambridge, MA: Harvard Institute for International Development, 2000); Nick Cullather, "Modernization Theory," in *Explaining the History of American Foreign Relations*, 2nd ed., ed. Michael J. Hogan and Thomas G. Paterson (Cambridge: Cambridge University Press, 2004), 212–20; Gilbert Rist, *The History of Development: From Western Origins to Global Faith*, 2nd ed. (London: Zed Books, 2002); H. W. Arndt, *Economic Development: The History of an Idea* (Chicago: University of Chicago Press, 1987); M. P. Cowen and R. W. Shenton, *Doctrines of Development* (London: Routledge, 1996); Michael E. Latham, *Modernization as Ideology: American Social Science and "Nation-Building" in the Kennedy Era* (Chapel Hill: University of North Carolina Press, 2000); Ruth Compton Brouwer, *Modern Women Modernizing Men: The Changing Missions of Three Professional Women in Asia and Africa, 1902–69* (Vancouver: University of British Columbia Press, 2002); Sunil Amrith and Glenda Sluga, "New Histories of the United Nations," *Journal of World History* 19, no. 3 (2008): 251–74.

55   Carol Chin, "Beneficent Imperialists: American Women Missionaries in China at the Turn of the Century," *Diplomatic History* 27, no. 3 (2003): 327–52.

56   Ruth Compton Brouwer, "When Missions Became Development: Ironies of 'NGOization' in Mainstream Canadian Churches in the 1960s," *Canadian Historical Review* 91, no. 4 (2010): 661–93.

57   Mary M. Young and Susan J. Henders, "'Other Diplomacies' and World Order: Historical Insights from Canadian–Asian Relations," *Hague Journal of Diplomacy* 11 (2016): 351–82.

58   Ibid.

59   Arturo Escobar, "Planning," in Wolfgang Sachs, ed., *The Development Dictionary* (London: Zed Books, 2010), 149.

60 *I Saw Technical Assistance Change Lives* (New York: United Nations, 1952).

61 Speech by Arthur Goldschmidt, TAA, undated but from early 1950s, Eleanor M. Hinder papers, 770/7, State Library of New South Wales, Sydney, Australia; Walt W. Rostow, *The Stages of Economic Growth: A Non-Communist Manifesto* (Cambridge: Cambridge University Press, 1960).

62 David Owen, "The United Nations Expanded Program of Technical Assistance – A Multilateral Approach," *Annals of the American Academy of Political and Social Science* 323 (1959): 25–32; Robin Gendron, *Towards a Francophone Community: Canada's Relations with France and French Africa, 1945–1968* (Montreal: McGill-Queen's University Press, 2006).

63 Economic and Social Council debates, cited in Alvin Z. Rubinstein, *Soviets in International Organizations: Changing Policy toward Developing Countries, 1953–1963* (Princeton, NJ: Princeton University Press, 2015), 34–35.

64 Keenleyside USSR travel diary, Keenleyside papers, LAC.

65 R. A. MacKay to Jules Léger, 2 February 1956, RG 25, file 5475-DU-1-40 [15.2], LAC.

66 Canadian UN delegation to Under-Secretary of State for External Affairs, 4 April 1955, RG 25, file 5475-DU-1-40[13.1], LAC.

67 Keenleyside, *International Aid*.

68 *Partners in Development*, Report of the Commission on International Development chaired by Lester Pearson (New York: United Nations, 1969). On the report see Kevin Brushett, "Partners in Development? Robert McNamara, Lester Pearson, and the Commission on International Development, 1967–1973," *Diplomacy and Statecraft* 26, no. 1 (2015): 84–102.

PART 2

DEVELOPMENT, DIPLOMACY, AND TRADE, 1953–1991

During the 1960s foreign aid came of age. Its structures proliferated and professionalized, while the amount of aid money flowing rose steadily. The United Nations, previously handing out only technical assistance, moved into direct capital aid to development projects, by creating a Special Fund for development. The World Bank, soon after, created its own International Development Association. In 1965, the Special Fund and UN technical operations were amalgamated into the United Nations Development Programme (UNDP). American aid operations were consolidated under John F. Kennedy into a powerful new United States Agency for International Development. Other major donors followed suit with new agencies and new funding.

At the same time, governments in the Global South increasingly linked aid and trade. The first UN Conference on Trade and Development (UNCTAD) in March 1964 signalled the change. Donor nations and the Global South, recognizing that aid alone was insufficient to meet Southern demands for economic growth, met in Geneva to adjust the terms of North-South trade. Aid was increasingly rebranded as official development assistance (ODA, a term first used in 1969), a name change that reflected a more holistic approach to growth that bound together technical and capital aid, trade and financial policy, and multilateral coordination. As the UN noted in launching its first "development decade" in 1969, "development concerns not only man's material needs, but also the improvement of the social conditions of his life and his broad human aspirations. Development is not just economic growth, it is growth plus change."[1]

This global shift had a profound impact in Canada. The tentative structures and ad hoc programming of the 1950s gave away to elaborate structures and strategic planning. The small and flimsy aid organisation within the Department of Trade and Commerce was replaced in 1961 by the External Aid Office, a creaky fiefdom that staggered along under the hidebound direction of diplomat Herb Moran. Prime Minister Pierre Trudeau completed the transformation in 1968, when he established a free-standing office to handle aid operations, the Canadian International Development Agency (CIDA), with a broader mandate and more independent management. CIDA put more cash into the country's development mission and was more open to Canadian civil society input. Yet the new agency still reported to Canada's foreign minister through an interdepartmental committee that kept a wary eye on aid's potential contribution to meeting Canadian foreign policy and trade objectives.

So, then, what precisely did this transformation mean for Canadian aid? Was aid still servant to trade? Was it effective in advancing diplomatic and economic goals? Could civil society actors and individual policy makers really make a difference? And what of interactions between donor and recipient?

Aid, the four case studies in this section agree, was never purely humanitarian in motive, but was always an instrument of the Canadian state. However, their authors differ, sometimes quite dramatically, over aid's ability to meet objectives other than development and humanitarian goals, and over who influences aid policy. On the one hand, in his history of aid to Pakistan, Ryan Touhey found that Canadian largesse bought neither influence nor market access, only trouble. Pakistan was no helpless petitioner for Canadian help, but instead pursued its own political aims. The new CIDA structures did little to change this reality. On the other hand, for Stefano Tijerina, aid was a blunt but effective instrument of the promotional state, which successfully mobilized grants and gifts in pursuit of new markets in the Global South. Canada acted more as junior bully than Samaritan, bolstering a pro-Western regime in Colombia in ways that assisted US goals for the region.

Asa McKercher and Kevin Brushett also see aid as subservient to the Canadian state's economic and political objectives. Yet both offer a more sophisticated explanation for the dynamics of aid policy making. McKercher explores the heightened political debate around aid relations with Latin America that followed the Chilean coup in 1973, which ushered Canadian civil society actors into policy-making circles. They successfully challenged the autonomy of state actors, forcing them to revise their expectations and objectives. Using a similar archival approach, Brushett explores the career of aid administrator Lewis Perinbam, arguing that one individual can moderate and even subvert the state's capacity to use aid for its own ends. Both cases centre challenges to government aid policy from Canadian civil society, rather than from recipient governments. More professionalization in aid bureaucracies and more money for aid opened the doors for understanding aid as a function of triangular relationships between donor, recipient, and civil society.

Note

1   See http://research.un.org/en/docs/dev/1960-1970.

"A One Way Street": The Limits of Canada's Aid Relations with Pakistan, 1958–1972

Ryan Touhey

Canada's substantial Colombo Plan aid program in South Asia ran into increasingly serious trouble during the 1960s. This was especially true in Pakistan, the second largest recipient of Canadian aid, after India. Envious and scornful of Ottawa's complex and dynamic aid relationship with New Delhi, Pakistan became a fickle aid partner during this key decade.

Ottawa's Colombo Plan aid began with two broad objectives: to prevent communist influence in the region through economic development in South Asia; and to cultivate good will and influence for the West and Canada in India and Pakistan. For the most part, Canadian aid achieved its first aim, developing and retaining strong pro-Western constituencies in both countries. During the 1960s, however, Canadian aid to Pakistan became ever more entangled in Pakistan's animosity toward India. Pakistani governments critically assessed their share of Canadian aid against the volume and nature of aid sent to India, and found it wanting. Consequently, Canadian aid achieved only limited success in meeting Ottawa's second goal as its diverse and complex aid relationship with India consistently ran afoul Pakistani interests and expectations.

The early 1970s proved no different. Pakistan emerged from its disastrous civil war and subsequent clash with India in December 1971 truncated and weakened. Canada's aid program quickly reflected the new geopolitical balance on the subcontinent as Ottawa reduced the size and scale of its diplomatic mission in the former West Pakistan and channelled resources to East Pakistan, the newly independent and deeply impoverished state of Bangladesh. Despite its best intentions, the evolution of Canada's aid relationship with Pakistan reveals the difficulties Ottawa encountered in managing Pakistani geopolitical expectations while leveraging Canadian efforts to raise living standards in South Asia to cultivate political and commercial ties and influence in both India and Pakistan.[1]

Mutual distrust and antipathy characterized post-partition relations between India and Pakistan. Following the partition of British India into the independent states of India and Pakistan in August 1947, the two countries disputed control of the state of Kashmir, which soon joined India. Successive Canadian governments avoided taking positions on the dispute. Ottawa's policy was measured and not unusual. Other Western nations were equally wary of becoming embroiled in the subcontinent's Gordian knot. Pakistani authorities gradually bristled at Ottawa's approach and carefully monitored the form and value of Western aid to India. While Prime Minister Jawaharlal Nehru's India pursued a non-aligned foreign policy that often criticized Western positions, Pakistan emphasized its anti-communist outlook and close ties to the West. This calculated decision reflected a hope that the Western democracies would support Pakistani ambitions vis-à-vis Kashmir and isolate India internationally. Certainly, Pakistani officials hoped for more Western aid as a reward for their cold war geopolitical stance. At a minimum, they wanted Western leaders to question India's claim to any foreign aid given that its non-aligned policy tilted toward the communist Eastern Bloc.

Pakistani aspirations became increasingly noticeable during Prime Minister John Diefenbaker's tenure as Progressive Conservative prime minister from 1957 to 1963. The Diefenbaker government had inherited a robust aid connection with Pakistan from its Liberal predecessor in 1957. By the end of fiscal year 1958–59, Canada had contributed $96.3 million in total aid to Pakistan since 1951, making it the second largest donor state behind the United States.[2] Canadian aid projects in Pakistan focused

FIGURE 4.1
Canadian engineer Gilles Tenner with his unidentified Pakistani tribesman assistant at
the site of the country's signature Canadian project under the Colombo Plan, the Warsak
Hydroelectric and Irrigation Project. (Source: National Film Board, LAC e999920074-u)

primarily on energy infrastructure, most prominently the Warsak Dam
on the Kabul River in North-West Pakistan. Approved by the St. Laurent
government in 1953, the project was intended to provide badly needed
hydroelectric energy for West Pakistan and irrigate a major section of the
North-West Frontier Province. Diefenbaker toured the site during his November 1958 visit to Pakistan, affording him "a personal sense of identity
with Pakistani efforts to build the economic and industrial strength of the
country."[3] The Warsak Dam quickly emerged as a flagship Colombo Plan
project, with Ottawa contributing $36 million, its largest contribution to a
single project to date.[4]

Pakistani aid lobbying aimed above all to undermine Canadian aid
to India. In conversations and correspondence with their Canadian

colleagues, prominent Pakistani officials sought to isolate India and stop it from receiving increased Western aid. Minister of Commerce Zulfikar Ali Bhutto, for instance, emphasized Pakistan's ties with the West when he met Diefenbaker in 1959, explaining that "the unwillingness of Pakistan to accept aid from the Soviet Union" made it more dependent on the West for development assistance. Bhutto was not anticipating an increase in Canadian aid to Asia, Canadian diplomats concluded, so much as a larger share of the total allotment—presumably at India's expense. It might "be reasonable to increase Pakistan's share somewhat in the next few years if really effective projects are submitted," wrote Diefenbaker foreign policy advisor Basil Robinson.[5]

Pakistani leader General Mohammad Ayub Khan nourished divisions between India and the West in his correspondence with the Canadian prime minister, emphasizing his country's economic needs in contrast to India's. "Governments of this region," Khan wrote, "are confronted with the gigantic task of raising sub-human levels in order to meet the threat of the seductive promises of Communism." He reminded Diefenbaker that "India receives large assistance from the Communist world. These factors make our economic development more dependent on the assistance that we receive from friendly countries like Your Excellency's."[6] Two months later, following India's absorption of Portuguese-held Goa, Ayub Khan again criticized Indian foreign policy to Diefenbaker as inimical to Western interests, linking Western aid to Indian ambitions for regional dominance. Khan asserted that Nehru "will soft-pedal with the West to the extent that the Western aid is not put in complete jeopardy. In fact my view is that he firmly believes that the West will continue to pamper him, irrespective of what he does, so long as he can keep up some pretence of amiability."[7]

Diefenbaker detested non-alignment and developed a closer connection with the Pakistani leader General Mohammad Ayub Khan than with Nehru. Diefenbaker noted Pakistan's pro-Western tilt approvingly while casting a critical eye toward Nehruvian non-alignment. But while Diefenbaker confided to his friends of frustrations with Indian foreign policy, there was no significant shift in Canadian aid policy to India, to the growing chagrin of the Pakistanis.

Indeed, during the twilight of the Diefenbaker era, New Delhi and Ottawa seemed to draw even closer when border skirmishes between India and the communist People's Republic of China erupted into a full-scale Chinese invasion of northern India in the autumn of 1962. The unanticipated crisis shook India badly. While Pakistan watched with satisfaction, the Indian military suffered a series of defeats, forcing Nehru to compromise his policy of non-alignment and plead with Washington, London, Ottawa, and Canberra to send military support and equipment for his beleaguered forces. This Western group had no desire to see India falter, regarding it as the most important democratic nation in Asia, and responded in various degrees to the Indian request. Though Diefenbaker reacted cautiously, he still irritated Pakistan by offering limited amounts of financial and military help. But by the time most Canadian help arrived in 1963, Diefenbaker was gone, swept from office by Prime Minister Lester B. Pearson's new Liberal government, which inherited the tricky file.[8]

This new form of Canadian aid to India alarmed Pakistani authorities, who expressed concerns that military aid to India might be used against Pakistan. Pearson's government was sensitive to such fears, but affirmed Diefenbaker's commitments to India.[9] Zulfikar Ali Bhutto, now the Pakistani foreign minister, met with Paul Martin Sr., his Canadian counterpart, at the United Nations in September 1963. Bhutto repeated his objections to giving Western military aid to India, suggesting that some armaments were "already being turned against Pakistan." Martin replied that he was satisfied with India's "strong assurances" that Canadian military aid would not be used against Pakistan. As their discussion concluded, Bhutto retorted that "India's record had to be considered against that of Pakistan. While professing non-alignment India had fomented unfriendliness towards Western nations within India for many years." By contrast, Pakistan "had been firmly aligned with the West."[10]

If Martin hoped that his conversation with Bhutto had put paid to Pakistani concerns, he was wrong. Bhutto headed to Ottawa in October 1963 determined to raise the matter with Pearson. Former Canadian high commissioner to Pakistan Christopher Eberts attended the discussion and recorded the foreign minister's "lengthy and forceful presentation." Reverting to what had become an ever-present theme in the bilateral dialogue, Bhutto emphasized Pakistan's close ties with the West and its membership in Western military alliances SEATO and CENTO. India, he exclaimed, had no such ties! Pearson countered that Canadian military aid to India responded to a Chinese invasion across India's borders, insisting that Ottawa would not "do anything whatever to damage the interests of Pakistan." As the conversation reached its end, Bhutto commented favourably on the impact of Canadian Colombo Plan aid in Pakistan, particularly the Warsak hydroelectric and irrigation projects. The two also discussed a possible new bilateral project: Canadian help to construct a nuclear power plant.

As Bhutto and Pearson said their goodbyes, the prime minister reflected on his long-standing experience with South Asia, noting that "he had always enjoyed dealing with the Pakistanis, perhaps because of the directness of their approach; that he had a good deal of sympathy for Pakistan's position" on the problems Bhutto had expressed.[11] In appraising the visit, Deputy Foreign Minister Norman Robertson concluded that Bhutto had "only one substantive" interest: to see Western military aid to India scrapped.[12] The episode showed that even if Canadian aid to Pakistan was substantial and welcomed, it would not win Pakistani goodwill unless Ottawa was also ready to back Pakistan in its confrontation with India.

This lesson was driven home in September 1965 when border clashes between India and Pakistan over the Rann of Kutch erupted into open warfare. A confident Ayub Khan, believing that Nehru's successor, Lal Bahadur Shastri, was a weak and indecisive leader, decided to test India's mettle in Kashmir. Pakistan gradually infiltrated thousands of soldiers across the border to seize strategic points and encourage insurrection among Kashmir's majority Muslim population. India responded with an armoured invasion of Pakistan and made quick gains.

As the Pakistani army faced defeat, Ayub Khan's regime assailed Western diplomatic establishments and their staff. The Canadians were no exception. They endured numerous diplomatic slights, some bizarre, some serious, aimed at showing that the West, including Canada, had let Pakistan down. Communications between Ottawa and its posts in Pakistan were deliberately interrupted for extended periods. An anti-Western riot in Karachi led to Canada's flag being ripped down, and rioters smashed windows and caused "extensive damage" to the Canadian chancery. The Ministry of Foreign Affairs rebuffed Canadian requests for police protection for the mission. Pakistani annoyance also resulted in delayed approvals for RCAF aircraft evacuating Canadians and delays in granting landing permission for RCAF flights on behalf of the UN in September and December.[13] Canada's considerable bilateral aid presence did nothing to reduce Pakistani anger.

At first glance, Canada appeared to have been dragged into the Kashmir dispute as a result of its unwillingness to support Pakistan. However, a closer look suggests that Canadian aid to India, particularly Ottawa's substantial and ongoing nuclear assistance, had antagonized the Pakistanis. C. V. Cole, the only Canadian diplomat attached to the Rawalpindi office, reported that he had been "reminded a number of times not only by Ministry of foreign affairs officials but by other Pakistanis that Canada had given India the potential to make the bomb."[14] Paradoxically, Indian archival records reveal that India's foreign secretary believed that although Ottawa did not take sides on Indo-Pakistani disputes, Canada shared "excellent relations" with Pakistan. In his experiences with Canada's Department of External Affairs," he added, "there is some sympathy for Pakistan as the so-called weaker country, and this is particularly so on the Kashmir issue."[15]

The symbolic attacks on Canada in September 1965 marked a watershed in bilateral relations with Pakistan as Canadian officials began to ask themselves what aid had achieved for Ottawa. Indeed, Cole urged Ottawa to reprimand the Pakistanis sharply for their "poor behaviour" as in "the long run . . . this would have a more salutary effect on Canadian–Pakistan relations than any amount of economic assistance including the Karachi nuclear power plant" that Ottawa agreed to help construct and finance.[16] Marcel Cadieux, who took over as undersecretary in 1964, resolved to meet with the Pakistani high commissioner to express Ottawa's displeasure, confident that a polite but firm discussion might settle the matter.

John Weld, Canada's acting high commissioner in Pakistan, briefed Cadieux for the meeting. Weld described the lack of public knowledge in Pakistan about Canadian aid, and believed that the bilateral aid relationship deserved immediate attention. While Canada's public diplomacy efforts in Pakistan had failed to project Canada's aid efforts to the public, he clearly thought that most of the blame lay elsewhere. "We have been—like the weather," he argued, "taken for granted" in "our rather disinterested help to Pakistan," whereas Soviet and Chinese efforts received "front page treatment." Lack of "full cooperation" was another grievance. "In a number of areas relative to aid" Weld believed that "cooperation has been far from complete: e.g., Pakistani failure to provide satisfactory statistics regarding use of counter-part funds; failure of public bodies to obtain clearances to allow Canadian aid work to go forward; lack of proper housing and other amenities for Canadian-Colombo Plan technical assistance experts."[17]

Weld had reason to express frustration. By the end of 1965, Ottawa had provided approximately $230 million in grants and food aid to Pakistan, and remained its second largest aid donor. Most of the grants continued to be directed toward building Pakistan's energy needs. Major infrastructure projects such as the Warsak dam and a nuclear power plant were expected to make a considerable contribution to the Pakistani economy. Moreover, Ottawa had helped build several transmission lines and power houses, and welcomed over 500 students and bureaucrats to Canada for instruction and training.[18] Despite this record, Weld and his External Affairs colleagues were growing increasingly uncertain and skeptical about the benefits of Canadian aid for Canada and its larger strategic objectives in South Asia.

Pakistan had slowly but defiantly recalibrated its foreign policy in the aftermath of the Sino-India border war in 1962 to look for more reliable allies. Dissatisfied with the West, it sought to expand its ties with the People's Republic of China and the Soviet bloc. Concomitantly, Canadian officials warned Pearson, the "major casualty" of this "somewhat opportunistic" policy was Western influence. This much seemed clear from the September 1965 riots during which US Information Service offices "were destroyed" and the Canadian "chancery in Karachi sustained damage."[19] From the perspective of the Department of External Affairs, Canada was not to blame for "certain irritants" that had accumulated in the bilateral relationship. Rather, the tension reflected Pakistan's declining ties with the West and the perception that Ottawa had failed to support it in Kashmir while continuing to transfer Canadian nuclear technology and military assistance to India.[20]

The changing dynamic, and at times aggressive tone of bilateral interactions with Pakistani officialdom, prompted the Canadian high commission to monitor Pakistan's aid sensitivities more closely and apprise Ottawa of possible risks associated with aid to India. The assistant deputy minister of the Economic Affairs Ministry volunteered that "some Pakistani officials . . . resent what we are doing for the Indians" and expected Ottawa to make amends and "raise the ante." Canada's acting high commissioner advised Ottawa to treat Pakistan and India jointly rather than "plunging ahead with an Indian programme without regard to Pakistan." Doing otherwise "would land us in the soup in this country."[21]

During this period of growing bilateral political tension, Ottawa proceeded with its earlier agreement to permit General Electric Corporation Canada to sell a CANDU nuclear plant to Pakistan, further complicating aid relations. Deciding to proceed with the Karachi Nuclear Power Plant (KANUPP) reactor was fairly easy. Ottawa was determined to cultivate new markets beyond India for Canadian reactors and nuclear technology. And even if this second client was non-democratic Pakistan, the Canadian government could at least claim that Pakistan, like India, was a key member of the Commonwealth. Moreover, unlike India, Pakistan was an important regional western ally. Ottawa, therefore, appeared willing to look beyond the crucible of South Asian strategic tensions. Pakistan was also willing to purchase the necessary heavy water for the reactor from Canada, making a deal even more financially attractive.[22]

Negotiating nuclear safeguards proved much harder, and once again, Ottawa's aid plans became entangled in the tensions between New Delhi and Rawalpindi. India refused to accept safeguards on its nuclear reactors, which were supplied by Canada beginning in 1956, and eventually refused to sign the Nuclear Non-Proliferation Treaty (NPT) on the grounds that it did nothing to disarm countries that already had nuclear weapons. Pakistani officials bitterly commented that Canada was effectively giving India the ability to produce a nuclear bomb.[23] Yet Ottawa could hardly retreat from its Indian commitments. As McKercher, Tijerina, and Macdonald make clear in their respective chapters later in this volume, Canadian aid policy was irrevocably linked with Ottawa's "promotional" support for Canadian exports. Both the Canadian government and Atomic Energy Canada Limited were determined to keep India as a nuclear customer and were convinced that if Canada did not sell reactors to that country, other countries surely would. Worries about India's stance on non-proliferation were brushed aside in order to maintain Canada's most prominent nuclear customer.[24] Despite Anglo-American warnings that India might be developing nuclear weapons, Canadian policy makers clung blindly to their memories of India's non-violent struggle for independence under Nehru and Gandhi, which fostered hope that India would not choose that path.

Ottawa's unwillingness to tame Indian nuclear aspirations raised Pakistan's ire. The Pakistanis objected to stronger International Atomic Energy Agency–sanctioned safeguards on their own reactor deal with Ottawa, insisting that Pakistan receive the same limited safeguards that India had negotiated for the 1963 Rajasthan Atomic Power Project (RAPP I) CANDU reactor sale. That reactor had stricter safeguards than the original 1956 Canada-India Reactor (CIR) agreement, but it did not meet IAEA's revised standards for enhanced safeguards, which Ottawa supported strongly.

By August 1966, Weld worried that nuclear cooperation with India had become "a festering sore." Pakistani officials, believing that they faced discriminatory treatment, insisted that India was using the CIR reactor to produce weapons-grade plutonium. Weld also stressed that Pakistanis resented substantial Canadian wheat donations to India to help alleviate famine conditions. They regarded an offer of an extra one million dollars of food aid to Pakistan "as little more than a sop."[25] Ottawa appreciated the concerns raised, but barring a dramatic change in Indian actions, it refused to modify its nuclear policies to placate Pakistan. Nor were additional wheat allowances forthcoming for Pakistan.[26] Negotiations with India to conclude a third nuclear purchase, RAPP II, continued despite India's rejection of upgraded IAEA safeguards. Pakistan increased its lobbying efforts against the reactor sale, alleging that India was set to explode a nuclear device.

The allegations emerged just as Pearson's cabinet began to debate the proposed RAPP II sale. On 27 July, ministers agreed to finance the second phase of RAPP II if India accepted safeguards similar to those for RAPP I. Martin wanted more stringent safeguard requirements even though he suspected that the Pakistani charges were unfounded. The "best intelligence assessment," he informed Pearson, "is that the Indians have no present intention to explode a 'peaceful' nuclear device." Nonetheless, he and his diplomatic advisors believed it imperative to push India to accept IAEA safeguards. Given Ottawa's desire to see the IAEA succeed and to obtain as stringent safeguards as possible, it was critical that India agree. This was particularly so while Ottawa was simultaneously developing its nuclear relationship with Pakistan. The Pakistanis, perhaps hoping to drive a wedge between Ottawa and New Delhi, were now willing to adhere to IAEA safeguards.

As Weld prepared to return home to Ottawa, he prepared a valedictory despatch reflecting on his time in Pakistan. It focused on one of the few links between the two countries, bilateral aid. This was one of the first thorough assessments from the Canadian high commission to reflect on a relationship in decline against a backdrop of years of steady aid increases. Weld noted the contradiction between the fact that the two countries had "little common interest or outlook" and the ongoing "flow of our aid to this area."[27] He questioned whether Canadian aid was serving the benefit of Pakistanis or serving "a dictatorial government supported by an oligarchy of landowners, industrialists and generals." Previous high commissioners had avoided such a forceful description of the Khan government. On this issue, Weld underlined the extent to which Canadian aid policy turned a blind eye to undemocratic regimes provided they nominally aligned with Western interests. Pakistan, however, met that criterion less and less. Kashmir would remain a source of tension given that any neutral stance on the issue would meet with Pakistan's general disapproval. Essentially, aid had increased while political ties had ebbed, and trade remained negligible.

Suddenly cutting or reversing the aid flow, admitted Weld, would threaten relations. But what could be done? Weld advised that Canada continue to seek a "modest role" and "give aid which will bring ultimate benefits to the people rather than bolster a regime, but we should not become so directly involved as to be further drawn into the area."[28] Canada found itself in a unique but unwelcome position. India and Pakistan were its largest two aid recipients and nuclear export markets, but Canadian help had failed to translate into either political influence or solid ties. Despite Canadian pressure, India continued to pursue non-alignment and refused to sign the NPT, while Pakistan's favour waxed and waned depending on whether or not Canada regarded India in a negative light. Weld's report was read with appreciation and then promptly filed away. Uncomfortably aware that its substantial contributions to Pakistan no longer served its larger strategic interests, Ottawa did nothing. Meanwhile, Canadian aid continued to flow.

By the time Pearson left office in April 1968, relations with Pakistan were declining rapidly, with Islamabad largely to blame. That left Liberal prime minister Pierre Trudeau's new government with some difficult decisions regarding Canada's cumulative $296 million aid relationship with Pakistan. Canadian diplomats were increasingly skeptical of its value. In a letter to former Canadian diplomat John Holmes, Charles McGaughey, the Canadian high commissioner, wryly described his work in Pakistan as "never a dull moment, not with a $28 million a year aid programme and the Paks' management of their foreign policy." What other country, he asked rhetorically, could be friendly with the United States, the Soviet Union, and Communist China? "Non-alignment with a vengeance," McGaughey called it.[29] More officially, McGaughey described the underwhelming state of bilateral ties to External Affairs as "pretty much a one way street, us to them/us to them, and most of the traffic is our economic aid." And prospects ahead were even dimmer. The nuclear aid relationship was entering uncharted territory as Pakistan looked set to ignore an agreement "in principle" with Ottawa to transfer the nuclear safeguards on KANUPP to the IAEA.[30] This was a worrying sign given Bhutto's recent promise that "if India gets the bomb, we will eat grass but we will have one too."[31]

If McGaughey's time in Pakistan was far from dull, then one wonders how he would have described that of his successor—John Small, who replaced him in 1969. Though he had served in Pakistan between 1963 and 1965, Small was surprised at how much the destructive tensions since then had sapped Ottawa's political and aid ties with Pakistan. In an detailed assessment for headquarters, he emphasized that development assistance had "become the most important single factor in our relations with Pakistan." In order to renew relations, Small encouraged Ottawa to consider "a substantial increase in the activity and size" of Canada's aid program for humanitarian, political, strategic, and future economic reasons. Although he did not offer specific examples of what such an increase might entail, he argued that devaluing the aid relationship would affect Ottawa's ability to persuade Pakistan on bilateral and international matters of concern to Canada—especially nuclear safeguards. Small also advised External Affairs that it was high time to direct the "bulk of our aid" to East Pakistan at the expense of wealthier, politically dominant West Pakistan. By doing so, Small identified and sympathized with the long-standing East Pakistani grievance that it was consistently starved of Western development assistance.[32]

Domestic tensions in East Pakistan boiled over in the aftermath of the December 1970 national election, the first free election in the country's history, held in the wake of Ayub Khan's downfall. East Pakistan had long nurtured a grievance against West Pakistan for ignoring the country's eastern wing. For instance, during the 1965 war with India, East Pakistan claimed that the Pakistani government chose not to buttress its eastern defences. The eastern wing also received less foreign aid than the western wing. Culturally, Eastern Pakistanis believed that the central government looked down on the predominantly Bengali people and language of the eastern province. In December 1970, the Awami League, a party based entirely in East Pakistan, won the national election. West Pakistani leaders chafed at the idea of being governed by the Awami League, arresting the League's leader and placing East Pakistan under martial law. Civil war erupted. With Pakistani military forces ruthlessly quelling civil unrest and opposition, Bengali refugees poured into India.

The Canadian government recognized that there was little it could do to halt the conflict, though the war encouraged Ottawa to reassess its relationship with Pakistan. Small encouraged Ottawa to "salvage" and maintain a bilateral aid program and to act judiciously so as not to curtail whatever limited influence it could exercise.[33] Despite some opposition to Small's advice from Canadian diplomats in India, officials in External Affairs agreed with his analysis and argued against suspending development assistance.[34] The Trudeau government concurred. On 26 May 1971, Secretary of State for External Affairs Mitchell Sharp told the House of Commons that no new aid for Pakistan would be forthcoming, although Ottawa would continue with previously approved programs. Indeed, Canadian authorities proved rather considerate of Pakistani sensitivities, channelling Canadian aid to refugees in India through multilateral organizations rather than directly through CIDA.[35]

Regardless, Ottawa's willingness to send aid monies to Bengali refugees in India aggravated Pakistani authorities. For Islamabad, any form of aid going to India had a political purpose and a political message. Even aid earmarked for refugees helped India absorb the pressures created by the crisis. The military government, now headed by Agha Muhammad Yahya Khan, made its displeasure at Canadian (and Western) policy clear. Pakistani officials even pondered giving support to Quebec separatists and withdrawing from the Commonwealth.[36] Repeating its tactics of 1965, the Pakistani government disrupted diplomatic communications of foreign missions in Islamabad, violating the Vienna agreement on diplomatic relations that safeguarded freedom of diplomatic communications. Even social functions at the Canadian high commission could prove troublesome. In one incident, officials of the Pakistani Ministry of Foreign Affairs refused to attend a Canadian-hosted event because Indian officials were invited.[37]

Events on the subcontinent deteriorated further on 3 December 1971 when Pakistani troops attacked along the western frontier of India, frustrated beyond measure with India's support for the Awami League separatists. Indian forces easily rebuffed the attack and responded with a full invasion of East Pakistan. Within a matter of weeks Pakistani forces were defeated and the state of Bangladesh sprang into existence. India emerged clearly ascendant on the subcontinent as Pakistan, its military in tatters, lost over half of its population to the new state. A shrunken Pakistan soon turned to an urgent effort to develop nuclear weapons, leading Ottawa to end bilateral nuclear cooperation.

A truncated Pakistan meant that Islamabad dropped in terms of regional importance for Ottawa. The Canadian diplomatic and aid presence suffered as a result. As Small recalled, "when the dust had settled our [staff] complement was slimmer by four officers and several support staff."[38] One of those affected officers was responsible for aid matters. The high commissioner was philosophical about those changes, however, noting that new priorities, the creation of Bangladesh, and "the war-induced slowdown in trade, aid, and immigration justified the reduction in numbers." Looking back, Small believed that Canadian advice to Islamabad to restore democracy in East Pakistan and not to pursue conflict with India "had little effect."[39] In that regard, relations with East Pakistan followed the consistent pattern between Canada and Pakistan, confirming that Ottawa's foreign aid gave it little leverage.

Canadian aid to Pakistan started out with the brightest of hopes. A rich and established Commonwealth member extending a helping hand to its newly independent Asian partners amidst the early tensions of the Cold War and decolonization initially seemed a straightforward endeavour likely to earn Canada and the West easy credit. The transfer of aid presented an opportunity to promote the best of Canada's agricultural, educational, and technical abilities in South Asia, winning friends and markets, while relieving poverty. Ottawa's belief that it also had no imperial baggage, unlike other leading Western allies, produced a sense of exceptionalism in Ottawa and a view that Canada was unlike London or Washington. Ottawa's initial aid offerings, however meagre, would serve Western interests in stabilizing the region, fostering democracy, and promoting South Asian fraternity with the West. However, the partition of the subcontinent unleashed crippling sectarian and geopolitical tensions upon which Canadian aid hopes foundered in the decades to come.

Canadian aid to Pakistan during this tumultuous era was deeply entangled in Indo-Pakistani rivalry despite Ottawa's repeated attempts to avoid taking sides between the two quarrelsome neighbours. This approach was entirely sensible. Yet it also meant that Ottawa walked a tightrope over a widening chasm in the aftermath of the 1965 war, when a humiliated Pakistan shrilly denounced India's nuclear ambitions. Islamabad blamed Ottawa for enhancing India's chances of becoming a nuclear weapons state. Ottawa disagreed, viewing India and Pakistan simply as similarly lucrative markets for the Canadian nuclear industry. On this front, aid objectives and commercial hopes made for inauspicious policy outcomes. Canadian aid counted for little in the Pakistani calculus. What mattered was whether Canada gave Pakistan its fair share in relation to an unworthy India, and whether Canadian aid to India might harm Pakistan. Ottawa's desire to avoid taking sides meant that it struggled to respond to Pakistani concerns.

The fraught history of Canadian aid to Pakistan matters today because it illustrates, as Keith Spicer's *A Samaritan State?* did in 1966 and Stephen Brown does in this collection, how little political leverage aid provides. Gratitude is an unsteady foundation for any bilateral relationship. Moreover, this disappointing bilateral history also reminds us of how reluctant policy makers sometimes are to reassess and re-evaluate their course of action despite clear indications of trouble. The slow collapse of Canada's aid program in Pakistan froze Ottawa diplomats and officials, who failed to grasp how little their efforts meant in Islamabad, and who were then unable to redefine what Canada wanted from its sizeable aid ties with Pakistan. Thus, as the 1970s dawned, aid relations with Pakistan came to mirror Canada's problematic relationship with India.[40] Only the brutal South Asian war in 1971 and its consequences managed to jolt Canadian thinking. As the geopolitical environment on the subcontinent descended into crisis, Canadian policy makers in Ottawa and at the high commission in Islamabad became increasingly conscious of their limited influence.

Pakistan's political goodwill, they concluded, would continue diminishing as long as Canada remained unwilling to curtail its ties to India. The optimistic hopes of Canada's aid architects to Pakistan in the 1950s were now a faded dream.

Notes

1   Little has been written on Canada's relations with Pakistan, and what has been written is dominated by the writings of former Canadian officials. Former high commissioner to Pakistan John Small wrote a useful vignette of his time in Islamabad: see Small, "From Pakistan to Bangladesh 1969–1972: Perspective of a Canadian Envoy," in David Reece, ed., *Special Trust and Confidence: Envoy Essays in Canadian Diplomacy* (Ottawa: Carleton University Press, 1996), 209–38. Diplomat Earl Drake has an interesting chapter of his experience as a young foreign service officer in Pakistan from 1956 to 1958 in his memoir *A Stubble-Jumper in Striped Pants* (Toronto: University of Toronto Press, 1999). H. Basil Robinson provides details of John Diefenbaker's visit to Pakistan in *Diefenbaker's World: A Populist in Foreign Affairs* (Toronto: University of Toronto Press, 1989). Former Canadian diplomat and head of the Commonwealth secretariat, Arnold Smith, provides useful nuggets on the Canadian reaction to the Pakistani civil war in *Stitches in Time: The Commonwealth in World Politics* (Don Mills, ON: General Publishing, 1981). Historians have slowly begun to write on Canada's relationship with Pakistan: see Ryan Touhey, "Dealing in Black and White: The Diefenbaker Government and the Cold War in South Asia 1957–1963," *Canadian Historical Review* 92, no. 3 (Sept. 2011): 429–54; see also Touhey, "Commonwealth Conundrums: Canada and South Asia During the Pearson Era," in *Mike: Lester Pearson, Pearsonianism, and Canadian Foreign Policy,* ed. Asa McKercher and Galen Perras (Vancouver: University of British Columbia Press, 2017), 251–74.

2   Notes on Pakistan and its relations with Canada, 20 March 1959, RG 25, vol. 7210, file 9678-40, Library and Archives Canada (LAC).

3   Cited in Denis Smith, *Rogue Tory: The Life and Legend of John G. Diefenbaker* (Toronto: Macfarlane Walter and Ross, 1995), 304.

4   Trevor Lloyd, *Canada in World Affairs 1957–1959* (Toronto: Oxford University Press, 1968), 199–200.

5   Memorandum from Basil Robinson to John Diefenbaker, 22 October 1959, RG 25, vol. 7210, file 9678-40, LAC.

6   Ayub Khan to John Diefenbaker, 14 October 1961, John G. Diefenbaker (JGD) Papers, file MG 01/XII/A/270, Diefenbaker Canada Centre Archives, Saskatoon (DCA).

7   Ibid., Khan to Diefenbaker, 23 December 1961.

8   See RG 25 vol. 10417, file 27-20-5-India, Subject: Military Assistance – Training Assistance – India, LAC. Canada provided $6.6 million worth of aid on a grant

basis, including: 8 Dakota Aircraft, 5 Otter aircraft, 36 Harvard aircraft, 500 Tons of electrolytic nickel, 16 Caribou aircraft on concessional financing, and military clothing.

9   Norman Robertson to Paul Martin, 28 June 1963, RG 25 vol. 5449, file 11384-G-40, LAC.

10 Canadian Delegation, New York to External Affairs, 30 September 1963, RG 25 vol. 10555, file 20-1-2-PAK, LAC.

11 Ibid., Memorandum of conversation between Pearson and Bhutto, 1 October 1963.

12 Ibid., External Affairs to Karachi, 8 October 1963.

13 C. V. Cole, Legal Division to Commonwealth Division, 12 January 1966, RG 25, vol. 10055, file 20-1-2-PAK, LAC.

14 Ibid.

15 Prime Minister's Visit to Canada by C. S. Jha, 1 June 1965, Indian Ministry of External Affairs records, File 873.Div(AMS)/65, National Archives of India.

16 Ibid.

17 Weld to Under-Secretary of State for External Affairs (USSEA), 31 January 1966, RG 25, vol. 10055, file 20-1-2-PAK, LAC.

18 Pakistan and Canada, briefing note, 18 February 1966, RG 25, vol. 10055, file 20-1-2-PAK, LAC.

19 Pakistan and Canada, briefing note, 22 April 1966, L. B. Pearson Papers, vol. 247, file 840/P 152 Conf, LAC.

20 Ibid.

21 Rawalpindi to USSEA, 21 April 1966, RG 25, vol. 10055, file 20-1-2-PAK, LAC.

22 See Duane Bratt, *The Politics of Candu Exports* (Toronto: University of Toronto Press, 2006), 121–22.

23 Cole, Legal Division to Commonwealth Division, 12 January 1966, RG 25, vol. 10555, file 20-1-2-Pak, LAC.

24 See Ryan Touhey, *Conflicting Visions: Canada and India in the Cold War World* (Vancouver: University of British Columbia Press, 2015), chaps. 1–2, 5–8, 10.

25 Weld to External Affairs, Dispatch 448, 12 August 1966, vol. 10055, file 20-1-2-Pak, LAC.

26 External Affairs to Rawalpindi, Dispatch K-397, 19 September 1966, vol. 10055, file 20-1-2-Pak, LAC.

27 Rawalpindi to Ottawa, 11 July 1967, RG 25, vol. 10836, file 20-1-2-Pak, LAC.

28 Ibid.

29 McGaughey to John Holmes, 15 May 1968, John W. Holmes Papers, F2260 54-1 pt. 2., Trinity College Archives, Toronto.

30 Islamabad to Ottawa, 22 August 1968, RG 25, vol. 10836, file 20-1-2-Pak, LAC.

31 Rawalpindi to Ottawa, 11 July 1967, RG 25, vol. 10836, file 20-1-2-Pak, LAC.

32 John Small to USSEA, 31 March 1970, RG 25, vol. 10836, file 20-1-2-PAK, LAC.

33 John Small, "From Pakistan to Bangladesh 1969–1972: Perspective of a Canadian Envoy," in Reece, *Special Trust and Confidence*, 227.

34 Bureau of Asian and Pacific Affairs to SSEA, 12 June 1971, RG 25, vol. 8914, file 20-India-1-3-Pak, LAC. See also Small, "From Pakistan to Bangladesh," 228.

35 Ralph Collins to James George, 13 May 1971, RG 25, vol. 8914, file 20-India-1-3-Pak, LAC.

36 Cited in Smith, *Stitches in Time*, 139.

37 The author is grateful to Greg Donaghy for sharing an extract on the "War in South Asia" from a draft of the history of the Department of External Affairs. See John Hilliker, Mary Halloran, and Greg Donaghy, *Canada's Department of External Affairs*, vol. 3: *Innovation and Adaptation, 1968–1984* (Toronto: University of Toronto Press, 2017), 116–20.

38 Small, "From Pakistan to Bangladesh," 231.

39 Ibid.

40 See Touhey, *Conflicting Visions*.

5

One Size Fits All? Canadian Development Assistance to Colombia, 1953–1972

Stefano Tijerina

With the exception of Haiti and the Commonwealth Caribbean, the nations of the Western Hemisphere remained largely excluded from Canada's bilateral aid agenda until 1968. As earlier chapters in this collection make clear, Canadian aid programs in the 1950s and early 1960s were geared toward South and Southeast Asia as part of the Commonwealth's Colombo Plan. Extending official development assistance (ODA), however, was not considered a viable foreign policy strategy for building relations in Central and South America, and portions of the Caribbean.[1] Instead, Ottawa policy makers largely responded to Canadian private sector interest in establishing an official bridgehead in the Western Hemisphere. Government was intended to play, as US historian Emily Rosenberg expresses it, a "promotional" role helping Canadian business compete against other Western private interests.[2] "Government support of private business activities," argued Canadian historians K. J. Rea and Nelson Wiseman, "has been a dominant theme in Canadian economic history."[3]

Canadian governments shared Washington's operating "assumption that the growing influence of private groups abroad would enhance the nation's [external] strategic and economic position."[4] It also believed that "private impulses, more than government policies," would facilitate capitalist expansion across the Americas. Fearful that Canada's smaller private sector would fare poorly against American and European competition, Ottawa recognized the need for a more aggressive promotional state.[5] Consequently, the Canadian government implemented a series of government-business strategies in order to expand their trade relationships in the region, including the establishment of official diplomatic relations, the advancement of trade missions, and eventually the implementation of ODA policies in the 1970s.

Official diplomatic relations were established in the region during the 1940s and early 1950s, a process spearheaded by a 1941 trade mission to Latin America headed by Liberal trade minister J. A. MacKinnon.[6] The close government-business partnership in the region was reaffirmed in 1953, when another Liberal trade minister, C. D. Howe, led a second "goodwill" trade mission to Latin America, leaving little space for ODA initiatives. Commonwealth and Francophone ties in the Caribbean, promoted by anglophone and francophone interest groups in Canada, eventually resulted in ODA hemispheric initiatives, finally reaching other selective portions of the hemisphere in 1963 through the Inter-American Development Bank (IDB).[7] Bilateral aid allocations for Latin America came five years later, as part of Prime Minister Pierre Trudeau's trade diversification strategy, which targeted ODA to "places and projects" where Canada's "bilingualism . . . expertise . . . experience . . . resources and facilities" could "make possible an effective and distinctively Canadian contribution."[8]

In the search for instruments to enhance the Canadian promotional state, ODA surfaced as a crucial tool to advance private interests in the region. A market-driven aid agenda, tailored for parts of the Latin American region throughout the 1970s, reaffirmed the dominant class theory of the promotional state advanced by such Canadian scholars as Cranford Pratt, who argued that business elites played an influential role in the design of Canadian foreign policy.[9] The 1953 "goodwill" trade mission, the 1956 sale of Canadian jet fighters to the Colombian air force, and Trudeau's market-driven ODA initiatives illustrate the promotional state in action. In these three instances the Canadian government served as a facilitator for business interests, helping them secure an advantageous position within the Colombian market through the experience of a seasoned bureaucracy.

Colombia was one of the nations targeted by the Canadian government-business partnership because its resources and economic potential remained untapped as civil war in the 1950s blocked foreign interests from fully capitalizing on the nation's modernization.[10] The country was among the first recipients of Canadian multilateral development aid after 1963, through the IDB, which provided US$50 million for Canadian procurement over a five-year period, giving Canadian business market access.[11] The country subsequently became one of the key ODA recipients under Trudeau's expanded program. These aid ventures allowed Canada to enter the multilateral game in the region and enhance its bilateral trade relations.[12] The Colombian case study illustrates the exploitative and opportunistic nature of Canadian ODA, answering the titular question of Keith Spicer's book, *A Samaritan State?*, with a resounding negative.

For Spicer, Canadian aid was motivated by a combination of three broad "humanitarian, political and economic considerations."[13] Colombia's experience suggests that the motive was almost purely economic. Specifically, the case study in this chapter illustrates the tensions that Stephen Brown highlights between self-interest and altruism at the institutional level, revealing how the government-business partnership used ODA policies to advance business interest in Colombia through such signature projects as the Alto Anchicaya hydroelectric project. It juxtaposes the cold war political strategies discussed by Asa McKercher with the market-driven approach that was dominant in Colombia. Ultimately, it focuses on the international relations that unfolded between the two countries prior to and during the implementation of Trudeau's diversification policies, complementing the macro-strategic views outlined by Laura Macdonald in chapter 11 of this volume.

Howe's "Goodwill" Trade Mission

Canadian-Latin American relations grew steadily during the Second World War. Venezuela, for example, emerged as a key supplier of oil for the Canadian economy, replacing Colombia by the mid-1940s.[14] By the early 1950s, Canada had established diplomatic relations with the majority of nations across the Western Hemisphere, intensifying trade with the region.[15] Canada, indicated the Department of Trade and Commerce, had achieved an advantageous position in the region as a result of the war, which it would continue to occupy as the region turned toward new trade partnerships to replace industrial and technological imports that had traditionally come from war-torn Europe.[16] This trend incentivized Canada's private sector to focus on the expansion of the Latin American and Caribbean markets.

Liberal prime minister Louis St. Laurent's government embraced this policy, sending its minister of trade and commerce and defense production, C. D. Howe, on a trade mission to the region. Howe's mission was to market the "Canada" brand and seek opportunities for Canadian business. The mission had as objectives the strengthening of Canadian ties to the region and the promotion of Canadian "goodwill" to establish a "broad basis of trust and mutual interest" as the first step in the construction of a long-term trade relationship with key local actors.[17] It was an effort to secure markets across Latin America at a time when American, European, and other Western countries were also prospecting for trade in the region.

Howe, who was fighting accusations from the Progressive Conservative opposition that the government was "losing its markets abroad," celebrated Latin America's trade potential. He reminded his critics that under successive Liberal governments trade with Latin American had grown from $33 million in 1938 to $560 million.[18] The embattled minister emphasized the importance of trade in the region of the world "with the fastest growing population" and an accelerated "industrial progress."[19] He recognized that Colombia and many of its neighbours were going through social, structural, legal, economic, and institutional transformations, but insisted that Canada, like other advanced industrial nations, should take "advantage" of these changes.[20] The area's adoption of a market-driven economic development model, increasing modernization, economic expansion and "high production, rising living standards and increasing import requirements" clearly justified the mission.[21]

In January 1953, Howe embarked on a five-week tour to nine countries, including Brazil, Argentina, Uruguay, Venezuela, Colombia, Dominican Republic, Haiti, Cuba, and Mexico.[22] The mission included a small group of government officials and seven Canadian businessmen "drawn from widely representative branches of the Canadian economy."[23] Howe and several of the business representatives were familiar with parts of Latin America, and some of them were fluent in Spanish.[24] Representatives included D. W.

FIGURE 5.1
In the aftermath of the Second World War, Canadian business tapped the promotional state for help prospecting new markets. Canadian trade minister C. D. Howe, who led a delegation to several South American countries in January 1953, is shown here at a wreath-laying ceremony in Venezuela. (Source: Industry, Trade and Commerce/LAC, PA-181128)

Ambridge, president and general manager, Abitibi Power and Paper Company, of Toronto, representing the Canadian Chamber of Commerce; J. M. Bonin, managing director of La Cooperative Agricole de Granby, representing the Chamber of Commerce of the Province of Quebec; J. S. Duncan, chairman and president of Massey-Harris Company, representing the Canadian Manufacturers' Association; Alex Gray, president of Gray-Bonney Tool Company of Toronto, representing the Canadian Exporters' Association; F. L. Marshall, vice-president of export for the House of Seagram, representing the Canadian Inter-American Association; K. F. Wadsworth, president and general manager of Maple Leaf Milling Company; and Clive B. Davidson, secretary of the Canadian Wheat Board.[25]

The mission spent just four days in Colombia, dividing its time between Bogotá and Barranquilla. In Bogotá, the Canadian delegates met

with "staunch anticommunist" Roberto Urdaneta Arbeláez, who was acting president on behalf of conservative leader Laureano Gómez, who had
stepped down from power for health reasons.[26] They arrived right in the
middle of *La Violencia*, a bitter civil conflict pitting left-leaning guerrillas
against the government and producing more than 13,000 citizen deaths in
1952 alone.[27] Nonetheless, the Canadians felt that they had encountered
a favourable business climate backed by a government willing to increase
trade with Canada and the rest of the world.

Mission delegates also met with the directors of Colombia's central
bank, Banco de la República, the president and officials from the merchant
fleet Flota Mercante Grancolombiana, executives from the Colombian
Coffee-Producers Federation, and representatives from various business
conglomerates.[28] The main objective of these meetings was to develop and
enhance direct trade between the two countries in order to avoid "indirect
trade through third countries," and more particularly through the United
States.[29] The meeting with executives from the Flota Mercante Grancolombiana, for example, provided the Canadians with an opportunity to discuss
the expansion of direct trading routes and the continuation of shipbuilding
contracts held by Canadian Vickers in Montreal, which had built the fleet's
first-generation cargo ships in 1949.[30]

Representatives from the Canadian Wheat Board also met with government officials in order to discuss Colombia's wheat import policy, since
Canadian wheat producers were eager to sell their excess production to
countries across Latin America.[31] The Canadian wheat lobby capitalized on
recent changes sparked by economist Lauchlin Currie's influential World
Bank report from 1950. Even though Colombia was a self-sufficient food
producer, the report recommended that it shift its production to export
crops and import those that were produced inefficiently; wheat, argued
the World Bank, was one of these inefficient crops.[32] By 1953 the Laureano
Gómez administration had implemented policies to decrease the production of domestic wheat, thus increasing imports. This justified the presence
of Clive B. Davidson from the Canadian Wheat Board, who was interested in securing most of these imports for Canadian producers.[33] The new
arrangement stipulated that "Colombian importers" would have "a greater opportunity to plan ahead . . . and be in a position to buy more wheat
from Canada in those periods when local production" was insufficient.[34]

Stefano Tijerina

Although no sales contracts were finalized, the Canadian government-business partnership provided the Wheat Board with an opportunity to serve as a bridge for exporters anxious to secure access to the Colombian market.

Besides meeting with government officials, key industrialists, and leading businessmen, Howe and his colleagues met with Canadian-owned companies already operating in Colombia.[35] These included the pharmaceutical laboratories of Frost and Company and the local branch of the Royal Bank of Canada.[36] It was clear to the Canadian government-business partnership that what was needed in markets like Colombia's was a larger role for the promotional state in further advancing Canadian business interests. Canadians were already present in banking, oil, pharmaceuticals, aluminum, wheat, and shipbuilding, but Colombia had a "highly diversified economy" and a "strong financial position," which meant that there were still many untapped business sectors.[37] Howe's report indicated that trade with countries like Colombia could "be expanded to still much greater levels."[38] Canada, he told the House of Commons, needed to increase its position in one of the "world's major trading areas," adding that this effort would be left "primarily" in the hands of "Canadian businessmen."[39]

There was no need for Canadian ODA in the Americas of the 1950s. According to the St. Laurent government, the region needed more Canadian private investment, stronger trade ties, direct bilateral trade relations to eliminate the US middleman, and an increase in direct contact between customers and suppliers.[40] The mission showed that there were federal institutions such as the Department of Trade and Commerce that were willing to cooperate with the private sector in order to achieve these goals. This level of institutional commitment was seen firsthand three years later with the sale of Canadian jet fighters to the Colombian Air Force, revealing the effectiveness of the Canadian promotional state.

Sale of F-86 Jet Fighters to Colombia

Colombians were engulfed in General Rojas Pinilla's military coup four months after Howe's mission. Pinilla's overthrow of the Laureano Gómez administration set a new tone for Colombia's foreign relations. His efforts to bring the Colombian civil conflict to a peaceful resolution and to eradicate the roots of communism across the country were undermined by his brutal use of force and growing unpopularity. Yet this did not inhibit Western nations from praising his valiant struggle against the communist guerrillas. Under these circumstances Canadair, a subsidiary of US giant General Dynamics, was able to close a deal with the Colombian government for the sale of F-86 jet fighters. Canadair's experience in Colombia showed that military aid could help bridge Canadian business and political interests in the region.[41]

Through a letter of intent issued in February 1956, the Colombian government agreed to purchase six F-86 jet fighters from Canadair.[42] There was a need to modernize and strengthen the Air Force in order to combat communist guerrillas from the air, and Canadair, according to the Pinilla administration, had the right solution.[43] The negotiations that unfolded revealed how Canadair effectively lobbied through Canada's departments of Trade and Commerce, Defence Production, and External Affairs in order to close the deal. It was a challenging transnational negotiation because the government-business partnership had to convince the US and North Atlantic Treaty Organization allies that Canada's military aid would help contain communism in Colombia, and that, contrary to NATO policy, it made good sense to provide aid to an undemocratic, military regime. The transaction marked the first sale of Canadian jet aircraft to Latin America and the first time a deal of this kind occurred outside NATO and the Commonwealth.[44]

Canadair eagerly responded to the Colombian letter of intent, immediately requesting a formal export permit from St. Laurent's government. In addition to quickly drafting a joint submission to cabinet on the company's behalf, the Department of Trade and Commerce established a clear division of labour between itself, External Affairs, and Defence Production. The Canadian government, it was agreed, should provide Canadair with political, production, and commercial support to push the deal forward.[45]

There was especially strong support for the sale from Howe and his senior-most advisors in the departments of trade and commerce and defence production. The transaction would open doors to more Canadian businesses in Colombia and "stimulate" sales of military equipment across the world. Moreover, expanded sales of military equipment beyond NATO and the Commonwealth would help Canada penetrate the international arms sales market. It also promised to reduce Canadair's overall F-86

Stefano Tijerina

FIGURE 5.2
The sale of Canadair F-86 jet fighters to Colombia in 1956 helped stimulate the company's global military sales and consolidate the business-government partnership that lay at the heart of the promotional state. (Source: Department of National Defence/LAC, PA-067557)

production costs, representing a considerable savings on similar aircraft for the Royal Canadian Air Force."[46]

There were post-sales benefits to be taken into account too. In addition to the sale of the jet fighters, Canadair had negotiated a contract to establish overhaul and service facilities. This potentially represented a hundred jobs for Canadian technicians together with further sales of Canadian equipment, parts, and technology. New business opportunities might also be generated from the sale, including contracts for management and maintenance of radio and telecommunications.[47] It was evident that the government was working on behalf of Canadair's corporate interests, convinced that this international trade was good for the Canadian economy.

Howe pushed this initiative forward knowing that there was opposition within cabinet. Some ministers worried that the sale might irritate the

United States and the United Kingdom, both traditional suppliers in this market. They also feared the impact that the sale might have on Canada's global reputation. Moreover, Canadian support for one of the region's many military dictatorships might alienate the "liberal and progressive forces" that Canada supported and turn the South American left against Canada.[48] Other cabinet members were nervous that the deal might endanger other Canadian capital and business interests in Colombia, undermining bilateral trade relations. For good measure, Secretary of State for External Affairs Lester B. Pearson warned that the sale of jet fighters to Pinilla's military regime contradicted Canada's Colombo Plan aid policies in Asia, where the Commonwealth opposed arm sales to undemocratic regimes.

A week later, Pearson withdrew his opposition, telling cabinet "that it would be difficult to refuse to sell to a country which wished to develop its legitimate defense and which was in an area of the world where there was no tension at the moment." Furthermore, he added, it was important to consider the negative implications that this would have on the "maintenance of the Canadian aircraft industry."[49] On 20 March 1956, Pearson sent a memorandum to his cabinet colleagues making a strong case for the sale. He reiterated the justifications offered by Sharp, explaining that there was no doubt that Colombia would obtain the planes from another supplier if Canada did not release them. Colombia, he added, "was the best friend that Canada had in South America and it would be difficult to explain why the export of the aircraft could not be permitted."[50] The foreign minister recommended approving the export permit. On 22 March 1956, cabinet agreed.[51]

In the summer of 1956, six F-86 aircraft were finally delivered to the Colombian Air Force, marking Canada's emergence "as a supplier of jet aircraft in Latin America."[52] Canada's private sector interests had prevailed over its political interests. Canadian military aid to Colombia showed that the government-business partnership was effective in advancing Canadian interests in the region. Canadian business would continue to set its eyes on the Colombian market throughout the late 1950s and 1960s, but the increasing presence of American and other Western corporate competition made it harder for Canadian companies to succeed. In the search for new business strategies to overcome this emerging challenge, the Canadian government-business partnership set its eyes on ODA as a means of gaining ground over their regional competition.

ODA and the "Third Option"

The 1953 "Goodwill Mission" and the jet fighter sale revealed the effectiveness of Canada's government-business partnership as a policy instrument for expanding Canadian business interests across the Western Hemisphere. They helped reinforce the idea in Canadian political circles that the direction of Canadian-Colombian bilateral relations should be determined by market forces and that any aid initiatives should be directed toward this end. Increased American bilateral aid encouraged Canada to seek similar options to provide its private sector with even greater market opportunities. In 1963, Lester B. Pearson, elected prime minister in April of that year, decided to channel multilateral technical assistance to Colombia through the IDB, reaffirming the commitment to a business agenda. The US$50 million secured by Colombia for the procurement of Canadian services and technology over a five-year period provided Canadian business considerable access to this emerging market.[53] By the time the first cycle of multilateral loans had lapsed, Pierre Trudeau, elected prime minister in April 1968, was prepared to adopt trade diversification policies to strengthen Canada's position in Latin America.

From its start in 1968, and especially after it adopted its "third option" trade diversification strategy in 1972, Trudeau's government embraced Latin American markets as important to Canada's future economic development. Inevitably, this meant stepping up Canada's regional presence to help its private sector compete in these lively markets, which were actively investing in infrastructure and imported technology for their economic development projects.

Socialist and Communist nation-building models, on display in Cuba, Chile, and Argentina, were competing against capitalism, prompting US presidents John F. Kennedy and Lyndon B. Johnson to respond with Alliance for Progress aid initiatives. It was under these circumstances that the Trudeau government opted to implement a third option for Latin America that included bilateral ODA as a key component of the nation's foreign policy strategy. And Colombia, where an increasingly better-educated and consumer-friendly society was flourishing, was a prime target. ODA and technical assistance, hoped Ottawa, would increase Canadian investment, strengthen commercial relations, promote direct trade, and consolidate that direct connection between Canadian and Colombian consumers and producers.

The Trudeau government's 1968 ministerial mission to Latin America, headed by Foreign Minister Mitchell Sharp, represented the first step toward a more aggressive and strategic hemispheric policy that would allow Canada to compete against other foreign interests.[54] One of the mission's conclusions was that bilateral tied aid policies needed to be part of any successful regional strategy because the United States, Japan, Britain, and other Western competitors were pursuing similar approaches in Colombia and across the region to secure markets and other economic benefits. After a searching external policy review, in 1970 Trudeau's government issued the white paper *Foreign Policy for Canadians*, which reflected this self-interested doctrine.[55]

Trudeau's white paper acknowledged that there was a need to promote Canada's "goodwill" through humanitarian aid across the developing world but that there was also a need to utilize ODA to satisfy Canadian domestic interests. External aid, it argued, could provide initial sources of financing for the purchase of Canadian goods and services, and help Canadian business acquire the on-the-spot experience vital for growing commercial interests overseas.[56] Canadian aid, the government argued, would help prepare Canada to respond to market demands across Latin America. Sectors of the government lobbied on behalf of the private sector, making market-driven aid a priority. For example, the deputy minister of industry, trade and commerce, J. F. Grandy, argued that bilateral and multilateral ODA for Latin America should "contribute as far as possible to Canadian participation in capital projects and to the development of commercial markets," parallel to basic aid objectives.[57] Priority, added Grandy, should be given to "programmes designed to put Canadian firms in a favorable position to compete."[58] Trade was a realistic way in which Canada could develop a clear-cut policy that would bring it close to the region.[59]

The implementation of Trudeau's new policy coincided with an aggressive Colombian effort to seek foreign investment and external aid funds to finance national modernization and large-scale economic development projects. The nation was transitioning from an Import Substitution Industrialization (ISI) economic development model, which used high tariffs to promote local production, toward a market-driven model increasingly dependent on foreign technical assistance and investment. Colombia had established an economic planning department (Departamento Nacional de Planeación) in 1958, was engaged in training a technocratic class, and was implementing the economic development recommendations issued by the 1950 World Bank mission and the Alliance for Progress Initiative under the 1960–1970 Decennial Plan.[60] Through the 1960s, it was aggressively seeking development aid and foreign investment across the international system, strategically forcing donor nations to compete against each other for economic development opportunities in Colombia.

Canada's decision to enter this market was almost inevitable, given that other similar middle powers had responded to Colombia's demands for ODA. The 1970 World Bank *Report on Economic Growth of Colombia*, the first country economic report to be published by the bank, justified Canada's decision to focus on the Colombian market.[61] The report indicated that Colombia had achieved rates of growth in real income considerably above the historical average, with gross domestic product growing 6.1 per cent in 1968, 6.5 per cent in 1969, and approximately 7.0 per cent in 1970, compared to growth of less than 5 per cent throughout the 1950s and early 1960s.[62]

Canadian ODA policy parameters stipulated that aid could be offered to developing nations based on "the degree of poverty" of the recipient nation, the level of "self-sustaining growth," the availability of "good projects and programmes," the degree of "determination they are bringing to the mobilization of their own resources," or according to sectors in which Canada had particular expertise.[63] Ottawa's decision to direct multilateral and bilateral aid funds to Colombia in the early 1970s suggested that the South American nation met the criteria set by the policy review.

After the 1968 ministerial mission, the Canadian government approved a series of ODA initiatives, including a loan of US$12 million to the Colombian government for the construction of the Barranquilla thermoelectric project, and provided Bogotá with an insured line of credit for the import of firefighting equipment via the Export Credits Insurance Corporation.[64] Ottawa also agreed to provide Colombia's newly created economic development entity, Fondo Financiero de Proyectos de Desarrollo (FONADE), with a US$1 million loan to explore foreign investment feasibility projects that would bring the two nations closer together.[65]

One of the most significant outcomes of Canada's external policy review was a decision to select Colombia as one of the four strategic Latin American areas of focus.[66] In fiscal year 1971–72, the government shifted its allocation of external aid funds, reducing funds for Africa, and for the first time, allocating monies to Latin America.[67] The Canadian International Development Agency (CIDA), responsible for steering this reallocation, set a clear course for hemispheric policy. The shift that took place in 1970 increased the allocation of development assistance to Latin America, channelled most of it to Colombia, Brazil, Peru, and Central America, and geared that aid toward technical assistance.[68]

In addition to choosing Colombia as a strategic partner, the Canadian government and the directors of the new Crown corporation, the International Development Research Centre (IDRC), chose Bogotá as IDRC's Latin American headquarters.[69] This placed Colombia, which soon became the target of Canadian technical assistance programs and IDRC projects, at the centre of Canada's regional ODA efforts. There was a clear policy intention to balance tied-aid technical assistance projects with more grassroots-based economic development research projects.

The IDRC's direct involvement in Colombia would be in the area of agricultural research, particularly cassava research. Together with the Ford, Kellogg, and Rockefeller foundations, the United States, and the Netherlands, the IDRC began to cooperate with the Centro Internacional de Agricultura Tropical (CIAT), which had been created by the Consultative Group on International Agricultural Research in 1967. This agricultural research centre would become one of the greatest promoters of agro-industry in Colombia and a voice for UN policies to increase global food security. In the 1970s, IDRC's CIAT funding would come to represent the core of Canada's multilateral development aid to Colombia.

Through multilateral policy-recommending bodies such as the Consultative Group on International Agricultural Research, industrialized nations and their non-profit organizations interested in promoting the agro-industrial model came together to push their agendas in countries like Colombia. CIAT's initiatives were a clear example of the cooperative effort between local and foreign interests whose objective was to promote a model of agriculture that, from the technical point of view, would benefit developing nations struggling to move away from small crop agriculture.[70]

Stefano Tijerina

The CIAT initiatives, in part supported by Canada's ODA policy, hastened Colombia's transition away from food self-sufficiency and toward the international commercialization of food production and consumption. This also signalled the arrival of a political and bureaucratic culture that relied on foreign advice and depended on top-down approaches to external aid in order to make policy decisions.in the area of food production. Research centres like CIAT became an influential voice in the economic development decision-making processes, handing power to foreign governments, private actors, scientists, and academics, who were committed not to local well-being but to the science and effectiveness of agricultural production as a solution to global food scarcity.[71]

In the 1970s there was little space for a humanitarian agenda when it came to ODA initiatives for Latin America, and Colombia's experience was a testament to this. External aid for the region was designed to help recipient nations "judiciously apply technology for the purpose of tapping their underutilized natural resources" through capital-intensive technical assistance projects and tied-aid projects.[72] CIDA allocated a total of US$2 million to Colombia from the total of US$9.5 million allocated to Latin America for 1971–72.[73] This aid went toward education, forestry, fisheries, and community development programs, while multilateral funding went to IDRC and capital-intensive projects paid through the IDB.[74] This included funding for feasibility and pre-investment projects, telecommunication facilities, port facilities, airport facilities, technical universities, and the financing and construction of energy projects.[75] This complemented and reinforced the Canadian business presence in the Colombian market, where Canadian companies already dominated several sectors. They controlled a large portion of the commercial paper and pulp and paper industry through Canadian paper manufacturer Kruger's Colombian subsidiary, Papeles Nacionales S.A. Canadians also controlled 54 per cent of the aluminum market through Montreal-based Alcan's subsidiary Aluminio de Colombia, and 41 per cent of copper imports to Colombia.[76]

Through IDB funding, Canada became an important investor in the development of Colombia's energy grid. Canadian "know how" and experience in hydro and thermal power enjoyed a comparative advantage in Colombia since the country depended so heavily on those two powers. Power boiling equipment, non-aircraft gas turbines, electric power machinery, and technical "know how" was imported through tied-aid programs.[77] Canada's private sector would become heavily involved with the construction of the Corporación Autónoma Regional del Cauca's (CVC), Alto Anchicayá hydroelectric project, and the Termonorte de Barranquilla project on Colombia's Atlantic coast, spearheading in the early 1970s the nation's energy policy.[78]

Between 1970 and 1975, CIDA allocated a total of US$7.8 million to Colombia, placing Colombia among the top ten recipients of Canadian ODA.[79] Fifty-five per cent of the bilateral funding was directed to social policy programs, while another 30 per cent went to CIAT.[80] Behind these policy initiatives lay the idea that bilateral and multilateral ODA initiatives would allow recipient nations to secure their natural resources for future industrial use, generating income and economic prosperity for the nation, facilitating conditions for greater income equality, and thus resulting in peace, security, and political stability.[81] Technical assistance would help reduce the gap between rich and poor, and potentially increase the demand for Canadian foodstuffs, industrial raw materials, capital equipment, and technology. "Inevitably," observed External Affairs, "to the extent that the standard of living of the mass of the people rises, there will be . . . opportunities for the sale of a wider variety of Canadian consumer goods."[82] This theoretical justification for ODA, questioned by Spicer in his book, *A Samaritan State?*, became clear in the 1970s under the implementation of the policy for Latin America, as illustrated by the history of Canadian ODA to Colombia.

Canadian ODA, as both Ted Cogan and Asa McKercher underline elsewhere in this volume, came under increased scrutiny in the 1970s. The debate over aid for Latin America pitted supporters of a market-driven ODA agenda against those favouring a humanitarian and social justice aid agenda.[83] This bitter debate persisted throughout the Cold War and into the early 1990s, usually favouring the market-driven agenda as neo-liberal policies were adopted by Colombia and other Latin American nations. By the mid-2000s, however, this policy debate was finally put to rest. Under Conservative prime minister Stephen Harper's government, aid began to lose its relevancy as it was replaced by Canadian foreign direct investment, an increasingly important element in the government-business partnership. Foreign direct investment reduced the accountability often tied to

ODA, making it a more favourable option to advance Canadian business in the region. Understanding the historical dynamics of the Canadian "promotional state" in Colombia helps clarify present bilateral realities and the implications for the broader Canadian-Latin American relationship.

Notes

1   For more on the initial stages of Canadian ODA, see Keith Spicer, *A Samaritan State? External Aid in Canada's Foreign Policy* (Toronto: University of Toronto Press, 1966).

2   For more information on the dynamics of the promotional state see, for example, Emily S. Rosenberg, *Spreading the American Dream: American Economic and Cultural Expansionism 1890-1945* (New York: Hill and Wang, 1982). For more on the Canadian government acting as a promotional state see, for example, Dominique Brégent-Heald, "Vacationland: Film, Tourism, and Selling Canada, 1934–1948," *Canadian Journal of Film Studies* 21, no. 2 (2012): 27–48, and for more on the Canadian government's role in the advancement of Third Option policies through promotional state strategies see Gordon Mace and Gérard Hervouet, "Canada's Third Option: A Complete Failure?" *Canadian Public Policy* 15, no. 4 (Dec. 1989): 387–404.

3   K. J. Rea and Nelson Wiseman, eds., *Government and Enterprise in Canada* (Agincourt, ON: Methuen, 1985).

4   Rosenberg, *Spreading the American Dream*, 38.

5   Ibid.

6   For more on the opening of Canadian diplomatic missions in Latin America see D. R. Murray, "Canada's First Diplomatic Missions in Latin America," *Journal of Interamerican Studies* 16, no. 2 (May 1974): 153–72.

7   Keith Spicer, "Clubmanship Upstaged: Canada's Twenty Years in the Colombo Plan," *International Journal* 25, no. 1 (Winter 1969–70): 27. For more on the francophone lobby in the Caribbean see Maurice Demers, "Promoting a Different Type of North-South Interactions: Québécois Cultural and Religious Paradiplomacy with Latin America," *American Review of Canadian Studies* 46, no. 2 (2016): 196–216. For more on the Commonwealth policy see, for example, Ralph R. Paragg, "Canadian Aid in the Commonwealth Caribbean: Neo-Colonialism or Development?." *Canadian Public Policy* 6, no. 4 (Autumn 1980): 628–41.

8   Spicer, "Clubmanship Upstaged," 27.

9   For more on the dominant class theory and its impact on Canadian foreign policy see, for example, Cranford Pratt, "Dominant Class Theory and Canadian Foreign Policy: The Case of the Counter-Consensus," *International Journal* 39, no. 1 (Winter 1983–84): 99–135; and Leo Panitch, ed., *The Canadian State: Political Economy and Political Power* (Toronto: University of Toronto Press, 1977). On the nature of the Canadian government-business partnership see, for example, Geoffrey Hale, *Uneasy Partnership:*

The Politics of Business and Government in Canada, 2nd ed. (Toronto: University of Toronto Press, 2018); and Don Nerbas, *Dominion of Capital: The Politics of Big Business and the Crisis of the Canadian Bourgeoisie, 1914–1947* (Toronto: University of Toronto Press, 2013).

10   On Colombia's early economic development process see Charles Berquist, *Café y Conflicto en Colombia (1886–1910); La Guerra de los Mil Días, sus Antecedentes y Consecuencias* (Bogotá: Ancora Editores, 1981); Vernon Lee Fluharty, *Dance of the Millions: Military Rule and the Social Revolution in Colombia* (Pittsburgh: University of Pittsburgh Press, 1957); and James Henderson, *Modernization in Colombia: The Laureano Gómez Years, 1889–1965* (Gainesville: University Press of Florida, 2001). For more on Canada's involvement in the modernization of Colombia see Stefano Tijerina, "A 'Clearcut Line': Canada and Colombia, 1892–1979" (PhD diss., University of Maine, 2011).

11   David R. Morrison, *Aid and Ebb Tide: A History of CIDA and Canadian Development Assistance* (Waterloo, ON: Wilfrid Laurier University Press, 1998), 55.

12   Tijerina, "'A 'Clearcut Line.'"

13   Spicer, *A Samaritan State?*, 4.

14   For detail see Robert C. Fisher, "'We'll Get our Own': Canada and the Oil Shipping Crisis of 1942," *The Northern Mariner* 3, no. 2 (April 1993): 33–39.

15   See Murray, "Canada's First Diplomatic Missions in Latin America."

16   Department of Trade and Commerce, *Postwar Trade Reviews: Colombia and Venezuela* (Ottawa: King's Printer, 1946), 1–2.

17   Canadian Goodwill Trade Mission to Latin America: Statement by the Minister of Trade and Commerce, Mr. C. D. Howe, made in the House of Commons, 26 February 1953, Canada, Department of External Affairs Information Division, *Statements and Speeches* (Ottawa, 1953), 3.

18   N. R. D., "The facts about prosperity: Mr. Howe on trade," *Winnipeg Free Press*, 4 August 1953, 1.

19   Canadian Press, "Trade with Latin America well founded," *Winnipeg Free Press*, 9 January 1953, 32.

20   Ibid.

21   Canadian Goodwill Trade Mission to Latin America, 2. On the mission's justifications see Canadian Press, "Trade with Latin America well founded," *Winnipeg Free Press*, 9 January 1953, 32.

22   Canadian Goodwill Trade Mission to Latin America, 2.

23   Ibid.

24   Howe was particularly familiar with Argentina since he had worked as a commercial engineer, selling grain elevators in the region during the 1930s. See "Howe Plans Seek Trade South America," *Lethbridge Herald*, 8 November 1952, 2.

25   Canadian Goodwill Trade Mission to Latin America, 3.

26 President Laureano Gómez's administration had been instrumental in pushing for diplomatic relations with Canada, finally closing the deal in March 1953. See also Canada, Department of External Affairs (DEA), *Report of the Department of External Affairs 1953* (Ottawa: Queen's Printer and Controller of Stationery, 1954), 15.

27 Henderson, *Modernization in Colombia*, 355.

28 Canadian Goodwill Trade Mission to Latin America, 8.

29 Ibid., 4.

30 Tim Colton, "General Cargo Ships Built in Canada Since WWII," http://shipbuildinghistory.com/canadaships/freighters.htm.

31 Canadian Goodwill Trade Mission to Latin America, 8.

32 See Lauchlin Bernard Currie, ed., *The Basis of a Development Program for Colombia* (Washington: World Bank, 1950), 8–16.

33 Canadian Goodwill Trade Mission to Latin America, 8.

34 Ibid.

35 Ibid.

36 United Press, "Mission quits Colombia: Canadian group heads for Ciudad Trujillo of Dominican Republic," *New York Times*, 2 February 1953, 34.

37 Canadian Goodwill Trade Mission to Latin America, 8.

38 Ibid., 11.

39 Ibid.

40 Ibid., 8.

41 Although Canadair was a subsidiary of General Dynamics at the time, the planes were built in Canada and generated profits for Canadian secondary sectors as well as revenues for Canadian investors.

42 L. B. Pearson, Memorandum to Cabinet: Proposed Export of F-86 Aircraft to Colombia, 20 March 1956, reprinted in Greg Donaghy, ed., *Documents on Canadian External Relations (DCER)*, vol. 23: *1956–57, pt. 2* (Ottawa: Canadian Government Publishing, 2002), 1408–9.

43 Ibid.

44 Memorandum by Head of American Division, 19 October 1956, in *DCER*, 23, pt. 2:1411–12.

45 Informal Note by the Department of Trade and Commerce, 27 February 1956, reprinted in *DCER*, 23, pt. 2:1403–4.

46 Jules Léger, Memorandum for the Secretary of State for External Affairs, reprinted in *DCER*, 23, pt. 2:1402–3.

47 Ibid.

48 Ibid.

49 Cabinet Conclusions, 15 March 1956, reprinted in *DCER*, 23, pt. 2:1407.

50 L. B. Pearson, Memorandum to Cabinet, 20 March 1956, reprinted in *DCER*, 23, pt. 2:1408–9.

51 Cabinet Conclusions, 22 March 1956, reprinted in *DCER*, 23, pt. 2:1410–11.

52 Memorandum by Head, Latin American Division, 19 October 1956, reprinted in *DCER*, 23, pt. 2:1411–14.

53 Morrison, *Aid and Ebb Tide*, 55.

54 For more information on the 1968 mission, see Stefano Tijerina, "Ahora o Nunca: La Misión Ministerial Canadiense a América Latina de 1968 y su Impacto en las Relaciones Bilaterales con Colombia," *Perspectivas Colombo-Canadienses* 2 (2009): 10–29.

55 DEA, *Foreign Policy for Canadians* (Ottawa: Queen's Printer, 1970).

56 Ibid., 10.

57 J. F. Grady to Paul Gérin-Lajoie, 22 November 1972, RG 25, vol. 11784, file 38-1-CIDA, Library and Archives Canada (LAC).

58 J. F. Grady to Paul Gérin-Lajoie, 12 December 1972, RG 25, vol. 11784, file 38-1-CIDA, LAC.

59 Department of Industry, Trade and Commerce (ITC), Draft for Ministerial Meeting of October 23, 1968 held at the East Block: The Ministerial Mission to Latin America – Policy Guidelines, RG 20, vol. 2586, file 20-204-2-1, LAC.

60 Ontario, Department of Economics and Development, Applied Economic Branch, Office of the Chief Economist, *Colombia: A Market for Canadian Products* (Toronto, 2 December 1968), 4.

61 Dragoslav Avromovic, ed., *Economic Growth of Colombia: Problems and Prospects; Report of a Mission Sent to Colombia in 1970 by the World Bank* (Baltimore, MD: Johns Hopkins University Press, 1970), v.

62 Avromovic, *Economic Growth of Colombia*, 1.

63 DEA, *Foreign Policy for Canadians: International Development* (Ottawa: Queen's Printer, 1970), 18.

64 "Financiación de Proyectos Ofrece la Misión Canadiense," *El Tiempo*, 1 November 1968, 5A.

65 Ibid.

66 Canadian International Development Agency (CIDA), "Memorandum to the Cabinet: The Allocation of Canadian Development Assistance Funds for the Fiscal Year 1971–1972," RG 25, vol. 11784, file 38-1-CIDA, LAC.

67 For external aid allocations see ibid., Appendix 1.

68 CIDA, "Memorandum to Cabinet," 15.

69 International Development Research Centre (IDRC), *IDRC at 40: A Brief History* (Ottawa: IDRC, 2010), 6.

70 Consultative Group on International Agricultural Research, "Summary of Proceedings: Third meeting of the Consultative Group on International Agricultural Research," Ottawa: Department of External Affairs, 1 and 2 November 1972, RG 25, vol. 11784, file 38-1-CIDA, LAC, 1.

71 For detail on early IDRC contributions to CIAT see Consultative Group on International Agricultural Research, "Summary of Proceedings," especially Appendix 2.

72 IDRC, *IDRC at 40*, 13.

73 CIDA, "Memorandum to the Cabinet," 22.

74 IDRC, *IDRC at 40*, 15.

75 DEA, *Foreign Policy for Canadians: Latin America* (Ottawa: Queen's Printer, 1970), 13.

76 Applied Economic Branch, Office of the Chief Economist, *Colombia*, 50.

77 Ibid.

78 República de Colombia, Departamento Nacional de Planeación, *Las Cuatro Estrategias*, ed. Departamento Nacional de Planeación (Bogotá, 1972), 303, 311.

79 Morrison, *Aid and Ebb Tide*, 457.

80 IDRC, *International Development Research Centre Projects 1970–1981* (Ottawa: IDRC, 1982), 53–359.

81 DEA, *Foreign Policy for Canadians: Latin America*, 11–19.

82 Ibid., 16.

83 For more on the debate over Canadian ODA policy in Latin America during the 1970s see Stefano Tijerina, "Canadian Official Development Aid to Latin America: The Struggle Over the Humanitarian Agenda, 1963–1977," *Journal of Canadian Studies* 51, no. 1 (Winter 2017): 217–44.

Samaritanos canadienses?: Canadian Development Assistance in Latin America during the Trudeau Years

Asa McKercher

In *A Samaritan State? External Aid in Canada's Foreign Policy*, Keith Spicer offered a dim view of Canadian aid programming in Latin America. Stressing that closer ties with countries in the region could be promoted through normal diplomatic and economic channels, he worried that aid expenditures in Latin America would create endless demands for ever larger sums, diverting money and attention away from more important priorities in the Commonwealth and French-speaking Africa. For Canada, the Western Hemisphere was of "limited concern."[1]

Spicer's outlook approximated that of successive Canadian governments, which have generally confined their interest in Latin America and the Caribbean to trade and investment while focusing their attention elsewhere. "Geographically, the United States screens Canada from Latin America," admitted Prime Minister Pierre Trudeau's government in 1970. "This is a constant factor which will always condition Canada's relations with the area south of the Rio Grande."[2] However, under Trudeau Canada expanded its involvement in Latin America through the government's first official development assistance programs for the region. Initiated in 1970, these bilateral programs were a significant sign that Canadian interest in development, which had traditionally focused on Asia, Africa, and the Commonwealth Caribbean, had now extended to Latin America.

This chapter explores the establishment and implementation of Canadian ODA for Latin America during the Trudeau years. Development assistance was an important manifestation of Canada's belated interest in the region and a sign that Ottawa's horizons seemed to extend beyond trade and investment. However, this ODA was bounded by several factors that underscore wider issues surrounding not just Canada-Latin America relations but development assistance in general in the rapidly changing decade of the 1970s: the connection between ODA and economic and security interests; the relationship between human rights performance and aid disbursements; and the domestic political controversies created by spending tax dollars abroad. To explore these interconnected issues and the ways in which they conditioned Canada's ODA in Latin America, this chapter looks specifically at programs in Cuba and Chile, two countries enmeshed in the hemisphere's cold war struggles. Overall, Canadian ODA during the Trudeau era underlines the extent to which, the symbolism of development programs aside, economic self-interest, especially trade promotion and protecting investment, has continued to define much of Canada's official dealings with Latin America. But this, as Laura Macdonald notes in her chapter, is a focus that civil society groups have challenged vigorously.

Canada's early aid program ignored Latin America, long seen in Ottawa as Washington's responsibility. Stirred by the quickening pace of the region's revolutionary politics after 1959, Lester B. Pearson's Liberal government set aside $10 million annually for the Inter-American Development Bank (IDB) in 1964, but refused to become a formal member of the bank.[3] For the government's foreign policy critics, including incoming Liberal prime minister Pierre Trudeau, elected in April 1968, this limited multilateral engagement was insufficient in a region that was virtually in Canada's backyard. In his first major foreign policy speech as prime minister, Trudeau affirmed the need for Canada "to take greater account of the ties which bind us to other nations in this hemisphere." Significantly, he urged Canadians to acknowledge the "economic needs" of their Caribbean and Latin American neighbours.[4] Five months later, as a token of interest, five Trudeau cabinet ministers, together with the heads of ten government agencies, embarked on a month-long trek to Argentina, Brazil, Chile,

Colombia, Costa Rica, Guatemala, Mexico, Peru, and Venezuela. Their report made clear that there was a need for Canadian assistance. "Economic and social development is the principal task facing all the countries the mission visited," it noted, adding that development was "given high priority" in discussions with each government visited. Overall, the ministers recommended increasing export credits and insurance, joining the IDB, and introducing bilateral ODA programs.[5]

If the ministerial visit fired imaginations, then it was a slow burn, for Latin America was excluded from the mandate of the newly formed Canadian International Development Agency (CIDA). Still, the Trudeau government's 1970 white paper on foreign policy, *Foreign Policy for Canadians*, gave official blessing to the idea of bilateral ODA for the region. Portraying Canada as a "distinctive North American country firmly rooted in the western hemisphere," the document observed that the countries of the Americas needed Western-style development, supported by developed countries such as Canada. In an analysis steeped in modernization theory, the study affirmed that it was likely that the "judicious application of technology may well bring all the countries of that region to the point of economic 'take-off.'" Until they reached that stage, however, governments required outside support, and the document recommended continuing IDB contributions, initiating bilateral technical assistance, increasing support for NGOs, and "encouraging the private sector to participate in Latin American development" through investment. The benefit for Canada would be an expansion of trade prospects that "would enhance Canadian sovereignty and independence," a major concern for the Trudeau government, which worried about economic reliance on the United States. This approach suggests that, prior to the publication of the Third Option paper, in 1973—a strategy to diversify Canada's economy away from the United States—Latin America already figured in Ottawa's trade diversification schemes.[6] This mix of economic self-interest and enthusiasm for development typified the Canadian approach to Latin America.

Foreign Policy for Canadians heralded a relative increase in official Canadian involvement in Latin America. Between 1970 and 1976, Ottawa sent four ministerial trade missions and the prime minister to the region, and joined both the Pan American Health Organization (1971) and the Inter-American Institute of Agricultural Sciences (1972), new channels for

Canadian technical assistance. More important, in 1972 Canada became a permanent observer at the Organization of American States (OAS), stopping short of formal membership. Meanwhile, in 1970 CIDA initiated a bilateral ODA program for Latin America, the first one launched since 1961–62, when aid to francophone Africa was instituted.[7] CIDA funding for projects in Latin America was limited to $10 million, though spending soon grew. While Canadian IDB money backed the construction of large-scale infrastructure projects, CIDA's initial programs were focused on small-scale technical assistance. The aim, a CIDA report explained, was "to transfer skills and knowledge rather than capital, allowing Latin Americans to use their own resources, both physical and human, more effectively for economic and social development."[8]

In addition to a growing suite of bilateral projects, Canada increased its activities in the IDB. In May 1972 Canada officially joined the IDB, committing $100 million over the next three years, plus $202 million to the bank's fund for special operations. All loans made with Canadian money had to be approved jointly by Canada's government and the IDB. "Together with bilateral assistance," CIDA boasted, IDB funding "will raise Canada's over-all Latin American program to about four times its former level."[9] In an indication that development in itself was not the sole justification for development spending, CIDA touted Latin America as "a very important potential market for Canadian exports and a source of valuable imports that will improve the Canadian standard of living." IDB membership, the agency hoped, "should open up" new markets.[10] By 1978, Canada had $400 million committed to the bank, with most of it spent on large signature projects.

After four years of programming, CIDA funding for Latin America received a major boost. In 1974, following a visit to several countries in the region, CIDA President Paul Gérin-Lajoie launched what the agency called "sweeping changes" to programming, including a raft of new bilateral technical assistance agreements and a concomitant increase in funding, nearly doubling spending in Latin America. Moreover, the number of personnel in CIDA's Latin American division was doubled.[11] These changes reflected Gérin-Lajoie's personal interest in the region, including his sense of *Latinité*, the notion that French Canadians shared an innate bond with Latin Americans. He would embark on several tours of countries in the Western Hemisphere, including Cuba, which, as noted below, became an

Asa McKercher

aid recipient under his watch and largely at his initiative.[12] Gérin-Lajoie's tenure at CIDA (1970–77) represented a period of intense Canadian interest in Latin American development.

Canadian multinational firms had long played a major role in Latin American economic development, and since the 1968 ministerial mission, promoting Canada's economic interests had been critical to how Canadian ODA in the region was conceived. The connection between development and Canadian business was signified by CIDA's close ties with the Canadian Association for Latin America (CALA), a business organization formed in 1969 to promote Canadian investment in Latin America and supported with CIDA funds. Close cooperation with CALA, explained CIDA in 1976, was bringing a "new view" to Canadian development efforts in Latin America, which included "alternative proposals" for bilateral ODA by "establishing contact between businesses and industries in Latin America and Canada."[13] The interplay between private economic interests and public development efforts typified the Canadian government's prioritization of economic interests in Latin America, already a source of criticism for activists concerned by CIDA's efforts in the region.[14]

Criticism of Canada's government over close links between development and business mounted as the context for delivering foreign aid became more complicated in the mid-1970s. Throughout the decade, both globally and in Canada, human rights advocates, progressive development specialists, and political economists devoted increasing attention to the interconnected issues of global poverty, international human rights, and the overseas actions of Western multinational corporations.[15] Motivated by these issues, some observers, most notably the Latin American Working Group, became deeply critical of Canadian financial involvement in and foreign policy toward Latin American countries with strongly authoritarian governments, including Brazil, Argentina, Uruguay, and, especially, Chile.

In September 1970, Chileans had elected a Marxist government under Salvador Allende. For CIDA, which began planning its Latin American programming that year, Chile was not eligible for bilateral programming because its per capita income was too high, an issue, Laura Macdonald notes in her chapter, that has generally limited Canadian aid disbursement in Latin America. However, observing the Allende government's "commitment" to development and surmising, correctly, that US assistance would decline (given Washington's opposition to Allende), Canadian officials made a slight change in policy in early 1971, approving a limited aid program aimed at "supporting the new regime in its development efforts" in education, agriculture, and community development.[16] Although most of the $10.4 million allocated for Latin America in fiscal year 1971–72 would be spent in Colombia, Brazil, and Ecuador, Chile was eligible to receive up to $100,000 and to draw on a $1 million regional projects fund, designed to bankroll a single long-term project.[17]

Given the fraught political situation within Chile itself—Allende's coalition government faced considerable opposition not only from the Chilean middle class and conservatives but also from the radical left, which sought a wholesale revolution—CIDA officials were careful in allocating ODA. One official surveying the domestic political situation warned that efforts by "hard-line Marxists" within the government to "indoctrinate the masses against the existing institutions of the country" necessitated caution. Chile's ruling coalition comprised both responsible social democrats and irresponsible radicals, who "may run off with the ball" and embarrass Canada "with a project likely to be . . . contentious in the context of contemporary Chilean politics."[18] In the end, the Chileans submitted a modest request for $87,000 in technical assistance for the mining industry, a major element of the national economy.[19] CIDA also began planning for a $1 million forestry project, and, through the IDB, Canada offered Chile a $4.32 million development loan for the State Technical University and a $4.3 million loan for the country's telephone and telegraph systems.[20] Additionally, Ottawa agreed in 1972 to reschedule Chilean debt.[21] Collectively, Canadian efforts alleviated some of the economic and financial pressure faced by the Allende government as a result of US President Richard Nixon's secret directive to make Chile's economy "scream."[22]

In Chile, economic pressures produced political chaos, which led to the September 1973 overthrow of Allende's government by the military under General Augusto Pinochet. That December, with the military junta's campaign of repression against Chilean leftists ongoing, and with public criticism directed toward the Trudeau government for its recognition of the regime and its initial refusal to accept refugees, Ottawa halted its bilateral ODA program in Chile.[23] In effect, this meant an end to the forestry project and the suspension of future assistance. However, Canada continued to pay out the balance of the $87,000 mining project as well as the two IDB projects.

Reviewing economic policy toward Chile in light of the coup and ongoing criticism of Canada's response to the resulting humanitarian crisis, officials from External Affairs (DEA), Industry, Trade and Commerce, and Finance agreed that further disbursements would be limited by "Canadian public opinion," which was "highly sensitive" to the junta's human rights violations. In effect, this decision represented a partial victory for Canadian human rights activists. However, officials noted that with the new regime encouraging foreign investment, "Canadian companies have re-entered the market and are actively looking for business opportunities," especially in mining, a blow to activists anxious to hamstring the junta.[24] A subsequent interdepartmental meeting in March 1974 approved the policy of avoiding new development assistance for Chile "until next autumn or until the termination of the state of emergency in Chile, whichever came first." This committee did not envisage a formal termination of aid as a means of showing disapproval of the junta, a move already taken by the British, French, and other western European governments. Rather, officials judged that "conditions in Chile are not propitious to the resumption of technical assistance."[25] Clearly, human rights concerns were factored into the decision to allow the petering out of Canadian aid to Chile, but Ottawa's position was not to make this point explicit. In a pattern that played out with assistance to Cuba as well as in Guatemala and El Salvador, Canadian policy downplayed the use of ODA as a lever to control the actions of other governments, a sign that respect for state sovereignty was paramount. Concerns for domestic politics and human rights were understated.

While Ottawa ruled out using the suspension of development assistance to send a message regarding human rights violations in Chile, other Canadian economic links with the country were expanded, generating intense criticism from Canadians concerned with human rights violations. They especially objected to increased export credits and insurance coverage through the Export Development Corporation (EDC), and continued support for Chilean debt relief through multilateral financial channels. Such measures were viewed as evidence that the Trudeau government was aiding the junta—and through export credits, was doing so with taxpayers' dollars. Though CIDA had nothing to do with these financial decisions, critics judged it complicit as there seemed to be little difference between its loans and those advanced to Chile by multilateral banks. The *Comité de Solidarité Québec-Chili*, the leading solidarity group in Québec, denounced Gérin-Lajoie for his "vote with the US bourgeoisie for loans made in Chile by the World Bank and the Inter-American Development Bank."[26] In addition to urging an end to Canadian investment in Chile, activists exhorted the government to suspend CIDA aid and EDC support until Pinochet promised "the respect and protection of human rights."[27] Representing the Catholic Church and mainline Protestant denominations, the Canadian Council of Churches implored government ministers to prioritize "the struggles of the Latin American peoples toward justice and liberty, rather than the interests of the Canadian business community."[28]

Ottawa responded by maintaining a distinction between economic and development questions and human rights issues, a position adopted not just on Chile, but in general. In a 1976 summary defending support for World Bank loans to Chile, diplomat Eric Bergbusch wrote that Canada did "not condone curtailment of human rights in Chile or elsewhere." Decisions, he continued, were based "on development related criteria and that such loans should not be used to exert political leverage." Rather, foreign capital would promote economic development, which would "be more effective in changing undesirable characteristics of regimes with which we may disagree than overt political pressure."[29] This viewpoint aligned with Canadian economic interests but not with the promotion of human rights. Yet Ottawa was at least consistent across the ideological spectrum, for in addition to supporting Chile's reactionary junta, it also provided ODA to communist Cuba.

Canadian aid for Cuba, a country sanctioned and embargoed by the US, crossed a significant cold war boundary. Though Canada had maintained diplomatic and economic ties with Fidel Castro's government since the Cuban revolution in 1959, it had carefully restricted the types of goods traded, and minimized the importance of the relationship. Under Trudeau's strategy of expanding relations with Latin America, Canada embraced Cuba more openly and warmly, transforming the country into a leading Canadian export market in the region.[30] As part of this embrace, in early 1971, officials in the Department of External Affairs debated establishing an ODA program for Cuba in response to Cuban signals that it desired to tap into the new Canadian funding available for the hemisphere.

While Ken Brown, Canada's ambassador in Havana, pressed for aid to strengthen a growing relationship, Marcel Cadieux, the Canadian ambassador in Washington, warned against any move that would anger the Americans and "have the rather curious result of placing us with the Soviet Union," which backed Cuban development. Weighing these two divergent views, Klaus Goldschlag, director general of the department's Bureau of Western Hemisphere Affairs, decided that the benefits of a limited assistance program outweighed any drawbacks. Even though Cuba was a communist state with a mismanaged economy, he insisted that the country was "one of our best commercial customers in Latin America" and that aid might lead to further exports. Although a backlash from the United States and regional right-wing governments was possible, he concluded that there "is no innate reason why foreign policy should not from time to time break new ground."[31] Canadian ODA for Cuba would be ground breaking, indeed.

Goldschlag's conclusion, along with a Cuban funding request for two small technical assistance projects on language training and audiovisual instruction, filtered their way into a memorandum that Foreign Minister Mitchell Sharp put to cabinet in July 1971. These projects, Sharp admitted, were innocuous, but their symbolic and political importance was large. Not only would Cuba be the first communist country to receive Canadian aid but it remained "a willing and cooperative member of the Soviet camp which actively lends itself to the furtherance of Soviet designs in the Western Hemisphere." While such considerations might normally disqualify it from receiving aid, Sharp worried that the island's exclusion from CIDA aid would send a negative message to Havana just as Canada sought more cooperative relations. Moreover, there was "no doubt" that Castro's government was committed to development policies redressing "social inequality," an effort that should be encouraged. Given these competing factors, cabinet agreed to a development funding program for Cuba, but one limited in scope.[32]

Cabinet's decision opened the door to Canadian ODA to Cuba, a remarkable development given the political and international climate of the Cold War. To meet the two Cuban technical assistance requests, funding was directed through the Canadian University Service Overseas (CUSO), which placed Canadian students on development projects abroad. In early 1973 CIDA offered a $1.1 million grant for a three-year program that sent engineering faculty from Canadian universities to Cuba and brought Cuban students to study in Canada; provided veterinary assistance in tackling an African swine fever outbreak; and paid for more CUSO language training.[33] These modest technical assistance projects were a first step to a larger Canadian development effort in Cuba. Certainly, CIDA officials, including Gérin-Lajoie, were soon planning to triple Cuban program funding annually. As the resulting sum would rival Canadian efforts in Colombia, Peru, and Brazil, major regional recipients of Canadian ODA, undersecretary (or deputy minister) A. E. Ritchie reminded Gérin-Lajoie of cabinet's support for a limited program, noting that "total aid should not be out of proportion to our interest in Cuba or Latin America."[34]

For advocates of a closer Canada-Cuba relationship, this development spending, however limited, was welcomed. In January 1974, Malcolm Bow, Brown's successor in Havana, had an hour-long private meeting with Castro. The loquacious Cuban leader expressed how "enthusiastic" he was about Canadian aid programs.[35] The following month, a CIDA team led by Gérin-Lajoie visited the island for a five-day tour of Cuban agricultural and educational facilities. Speaking to accompanying reporters, Cuban president Osvaldo Dorticós Torrado praised the way that "relations are developing between our two countries," while Gérin-Lajoie characterized the visit as a "springboard" to deeper relations.[36] Indeed, the CIDA trip resulted in technical agreements for loans and grants with spending commitments well above cabinet's "limited" directive.[37]

Back in Ottawa, officials in External Affairs were concerned by Gérin-Lajoie's enthusiasm. Prior to the CIDA president's departure, Sharp had urged him to keep ODA to Cuba in balance with overall assistance to the rest of Latin America, reminding him that under the 1971 cabinet decision funding for Cuba would be approved only on a project-by-project basis. Instead Gérin-Lajoie promised an ODA package of $6–7 million in soft loans and $3–4 million in grants over three years to fund public health, pharmaceutical, and animal health initiatives. He also encouraged Cuba to submit additional projects for consideration and agreed to a joint study of long-term CIDA-Cuba cooperation. "All of the above points represent a considerable departure from the policy which was agreed," complained External Affairs staff, who worried that Cuban expectations were being raised to unrealistic heights.[38]

Indeed, CIDA wanted even more. It soon emerged that it was planning, without consulting the diplomats in External Affairs, to offer Cuba soft loans and grants worth $23.5 million over four years, making Cuba the largest recipient of Canadian ODA in Latin America. Ritchie pushed back, convincing the enthusiastic CIDA president to withdraw this grandiose proposal.[39] In the end, Cuba received a $10 million program loan over three years beginning in 1976–77, on top of the almost $5 million in technical assistance and loans extended between 1972–73 and 1975–76. In all, between 1972 and 1978, Cuba received $14.88 million in Canadian aid. In addition, as part of Ottawa's efforts to expand trade and investment with Cuba, the EDC made available a $100 million line of credit.[40]

From the start, assistance to Cuba provoked criticism within Canada. Amid media stories of cabinet infighting and reports that CIDA was trying to conceal the extent of its assistance package from public scrutiny, former Liberal cabinet minister Paul Hellyer publicly denounced the aid program, and members of the Progressive Conservative opposition wondered why taxpayers' money was being sent to a "totalitarian state."[41] The situation worsened in late 1975, when Cuba's armed forces intervened in Africa in support of anti-colonial fighters in Angola, sparking opposition demands that the government withhold its aid "until such time as the government in Cuba withdraws."[42] Between January 1976 and 1978, opposition members of Parliament introduced over a dozen motions calling for a halt to CIDA spending and EDC credits. When a Cuban spy ring was later discovered in Montreal, Douglas Roche, a Progressive Conservative MP and human rights activist, angrily declared that "whatever good CIDA's agricultural projects are doing in Cuba, it is not possible to support them when Cuba finds the resources to send troops" abroad or spy on Canada.[43]

In defending his government's position, Trudeau insisted that it was "not Canadian policy to base our aid on all aspects of the foreign policy of a country receiving it." Canada's aid program, he explained, "is not linked to the ideology of a particular country."[44] This stance—on display with both right-wing Chile and communist Cuba—reflected traditional Canadian policy, but it failed to appease critics who had begun to link aid, foreign

Figure 6.1

The decision to extend Canadian aid to communist Cuba as cold war tensions remained high exposed CIDA to sharp criticism from critics inside and outside the government. In this cartoon, Canadian aid to Cuba is depicted as simply reinforcing the Soviet Union's military might. (Source: Andy Donato/*Toronto Sun*/LAC e999920085-u) policy, and human rights. Given such criticism of the already controversial Cuban aid program, it was not surprising when CIDA officials announced in February 1977 that existing programs would expire once funding ran out at the end of fiscal year 1977–78 and that no new projects were planned. Aid to Cuba had become too controversial. In May, when asked by Roche if the government would cut aid to exert pressure on Cuba, Foreign Minister Don Jamieson assured him that the government was "phasing down, or at least winding up" its Cuba programs. He gave no public indication that this was being done to exert pressure on Havana.[45]

By February 1978 program spending had completely dried up, encouraging ministers to terminate Cuba's eligibility for further CIDA aid in July. Canadian officials stressed that the decision not to pursue the CIDA program in Cuba was not aimed at forcing change in Havana.[46] Rather, Cuban diplomats were informed that Cuba's intervention in Africa and its nefarious intelligence operations, including an attempt by Cuban spies to recruit a Canadian tour guide, made it impossible to defend development spending in Canada.[47] The last CUSO program was ended in 1980, when a new foreign minister, Mark MacGuigan, secured cabinet agreement to terminate it. More assertive than Jamieson, MacGuigan explained publicly that Canada had been willing to assist the Cubans "up until the point when Cuba decided that it could afford the luxury of despatching expeditionary forces to Africa. Clearly it then had no more need for Canadian aid, given its new priorities."[48]

Aid to Chile and Cuba was indisputable evidence of the Trudeau government's interest in Latin America and in development in the region. Yet there were clearly limits to this policy of engagement, limits reflected in the low level of aid funding relative to other regions of the globe, and in Ottawa's continuing focus on using aid to secure Canadian economic interests. More significantly, the domestic debate over assistance to Chile and Cuba in the 1970s underlined foreign aid's increasingly controversial nature and its indissoluble links to human rights and the political behaviour of recipient states. Over the course of this pivotal decade, Canadian observers of government development programs grew more vocal in linking aid and human rights performance. Indeed, there was a change in the understanding of sovereignty and the legitimacy of interfering in another state's domestic affairs that made aid to Chile and Cuba especially difficult for the Trudeau government. "The Government of Canada should reduce to a minimum its material assistance to, and symbolic approval of, governments that commit gross violations of human rights," stated Progressive Conservative MP Douglas Roche, summimg up the new consensus in 1979.[49]

In response to such criticisms, government leaders were keen to emphasize, as Trudeau did, that Canada had "not made it a condition of our assistance to starving people in the third world that their government be above reproach."[50] He insisted that development assistance should be spent regardless of a government's internal, domestic actions. This thinking fit with the Trudeau government's stance on promoting international human rights at the bilateral level, where policy was motivated by a very traditional and scrupulous respect for state sovereignty and the notion that a government was uniquely responsible for its own domestic sphere. It was consistent too with Trudeau's fear of external meddling within Quebec, whose separatist forces were reaching their apogee at the end of the decade. When limits were drawn, as was the case with Chile and Cuba, they reflected strong domestic pressures, which made continuing development programming too politically costly for the government.

Notes

1 Keith Spicer, *A Samaritan State? External Aid in Canada's Foreign Policy* (Toronto: University of Toronto Press, 1966), 62.

2 Canada, Department of External Affairs (DEA), *Foreign Policy for Canadians: Latin America* (Ottawa: Information Canada, 1970), 5. On the Trudeau government and Latin America, see Brian Stevenson, *Canada, Latin America, and the New Internationalism: A Foreign Policy Analysis, 1968–1999* (Montreal: McGill-Queen's University Press, 2000); James Rochlin, *Discovering the Americas: The Evolution of Canadian Foreign Policy Towards Latin America* (Vancouver: University of British Columbia Press, 1994).

3 Cabinet Conclusions, 3 December 1964, RG 2, vol. 6265, Library and Archives Canada (LAC).

4 DEA, *Statements and Speeches* 68/17, 29 May 1968.

5 Canada, *Preliminary Report of the Ministerial Mission to Latin America, October 27–November 27, 1968* (Ottawa: DEA, 1969).

6 DEA, *Foreign Policy for Canadians: Latin America*, 5, 6, 12, 28.

7   CIDA, *Canada and the Developing World: CIDA Annual Review 1970–1971* (Ottawa: Information Canada, 1971), 4.

8   CIDA, *Annual Review 1972–1973* (Ottawa: Information Canada, 1973), 32.

9   "Canada in IDB," *CIDA Contact*, June 1972.

10 "Stronger ties with Latin America: Canada joins regional bank," *Cooperation Canada*, July/August 1972.

11 CIDA, *Annual Review 1973–1974* (Ottawa: Information Canada, 1974), 40.

12 "Latin American Visit," *CIDA Contact*, April 1976; David Morrison, *Aid and Ebb Tide: A History of CIDA and Canadian Development Assistance* (Waterloo, ON: Wilfrid Laurier University Press), 123.

13 "New View of Latin America," *CIDA Contact*, September 1976; "CIDA Knows What's Good for Business," *Last Post*, January 1975; And see RG 25, vol. 9045, file 20-4-CALA, LAC.

14 Latin American Working Group, *Canadian Aid: Whose Priorities? A Study of the Relationship between Non-Governmental Organizations, Business, and the Needs of Latin America* (Toronto: Latin American Working Group, 1973).

15 See, for example, Stephanie Bangarth, "'Vocal but not particularly strong?': Air Canada's Ill-fated Vacation Package to Rhodesia and South Africa and the Anti-Apartheid Movement in Canada," *International Journal* 71, no. 3 (2016): 488–97.

16 Tansley to Gérin-Lajoie, 16 March 1971, RG 25, vol. 8636, file 20-1-2-CUBA, LAC.

17 CIDA to Santiago, "Status Report – Bilateral Technical Assistance Programme," 25 May 1971, RG 25, vol. 12049, file 38-9-1-Chile, LAC.

18 Santiago to DEA, D-242, 27 September 1971, RG 25, vol. 12049, file 38-9-1-Chile, LAC.

19 Smith, "Technical Assistance: Chile," 5 May 1971, RG 25, vol. 12049, file 38-9-1-Chile, LAC.

20 CIDA to Santiago, tel. 2249, 28 September 1972, and Notes for GWP Liaison Visit, November 1972 – Santiago, RG 25, vol. 12049, file 38-9-1-Chile, LAC.

21 Aid and Development Division, "Chilean Debt," 5 July 1973, RG 25, vol. 11919, file 38-6-1-Chile, LAC.

22 Quoted in Jonathan Haslam, *The Nixon Administration and the Death of Allende's Chile: A Case of Assisted Suicide* (London: Verso, 2005), 98.

23 DEA to Santiago, tel. 517, 21 December 1973, RG 25, vol. 11919, file 38-7-1-Chile, LAC. On public reaction and pressure on the government, see John Hilliker, Mary Halloran, and Greg Donaghy, *Canada's Department of External Affairs*, vol. 3: *Innovation and Adaptation, 1968–1984* (Toronto: University of Toronto Press, 2017), 160–63.

24 Nutt, "Minutes of Interdepartmental Meeting on Economic Policy toward Chile," 5 February 1974, RG 25, vol. 11919, file 38-7-1-Chile, LAC.

25 Ritchie to Minister, 28 March 1974, RG 25, vol. 11919, file 38-7-1-Chile, LAC.

26 "Noranda et l'état Canadien s'entendent à merveille avec la dictature chilienne," *Chili-Québec Informations*, Avril 1976. Translation mine.

27 Coalition on Canadian Policy Towards Chile, "Canada and the Rights of the Chilean People," March 1976, MG 32 C26, vol. 79, file 7, LAC.

28 Canadian Council of Churches, "Canadian Policy Toward Chile," 9 October 1974, MG 28 I103, vol. 495, file 18, LAC.

29 DEA to Washington, EDC-74, 19 January 1976, RG 25, vol. 11919, file 38-7-1-Chile, LAC.

30 Robert Wright offers a warmer view of Trudeau's dealings with Cuba than do Greg Donaghy and Mary Halloran. See Robert Wright, *Three Nights in Havana: Pierre Trudeau, Fidel Castro and the Cold War World* (Toronto: HarperCollins, 2007); and Greg Donaghy and Mary Halloran, "*Viva el pueblo Cubano*: Pierre Trudeau's Distant Cuba, 1968–78," in *Our Place in the Sun: Canada and Cuba in the Castro Era*, ed. Robert Wright and Lana Wylie (Toronto: University of Toronto Press, 2009), 143–62.

31 Havana to DEA, tel. 16, 8 January 1971, Washington to DEA, tel. 30, 5 January 1971, and Goldschlag, "Technical Assistance to Cuba," 4 March 1971, RG 25 vol. 8636, file 20-1-2-CUBA, LAC.

32 Memorandum to Cabinet, No. 757-71, 29 June 1971, RG 55, box 6, file 5075-4/C962, LAC; Cabinet Conclusions, 22 July 1971, RG 2, vol. 6381, LAC.

33 "Assistance to Cuba," *CIDA Contact*, March 1973; "$1 Million to Send Professors to Havana, Ottawa's Plan," *Globe and Mail*, 23 January 1973.

34 Ritchie to Gérin-Lajoie, 19 September 1973, RG 25, vol. 11922, file 38-1-7-CUBA, LAC.

35 Havana to DEA, tel. 36, 9 January 1974, RG 25, vol. 16074, file 20-1-2-CUBA, LAC.

36 Lionel Martin, "Canada, Cuba Forming Ties through CIDA," *Globe and Mail*, 12 February 1974.

37 "Visit to Cuba and Haiti," *CIDA Contact*, March 1974.

38 Aid and Development Division to PDM, 4 March 1974, RG 25, vol. 12050, file 38-9-1-CUBA, LAC.

39 Aid and Development Division to PDE, 9 August 1974, RG 25, vol. 12050, file 38-9-1-CUBA, LAC.

40 Gotlieb to Minister, 17 May 1978, RG 25, vol. 16074, file 20-1-2-CUBA, LAC.

41 "Secret Sugarplum to Cuba Splits Cabinet," *Globe and Mail*, 21 December 1974; "CIDA Conceals Full Amount of Huge Aid Package to Cuba," *Ottawa Journal*, 7 May 1975; Paul Hellyer, "CIDA's Proposed Agreement with Cuba Shows Need for Review of Aid Programs," *Ottawa Citizen*, 6 June 1975; Canada, House of Commons, *Debates*, 24 April 1975, 5196.

42 Canada, House of Commons, *Debates*, 20 November 1975, 9272; "End Aid to Cuba House Urged," *Globe and Mail*, 27 January 1976.

43 Canada, House of Commons, *Debates*, 1 February 1977, 2628.

44 Canada, House of Commons, *Debates*, 3 February 1976, 10572, and 6 February 1976, 10703; "PM rejects aid cut," *Globe and Mail*, 10 February 1977.

45 "Canadian Aid to Cuba Slowly Winding Down," *Montreal Gazette*, 11 February 1977; Canada, House of Commons, *Debates*, 8 May 1977, 5229.

46 Brief for Minister Regan, 18 April 1980, RG 25, vol. 15285, file 55-26-1-CUBA, LAC.

47 Korth to file, 13 December 1978, RG 25, vol. 16074, file 20-1-2-CUBA, LAC.

48 DEA, *Statements and Speeches* 82/12, 31 March 1982; P. Whitney Lackenbauer, ed., *An Inside Look at External Affairs during the Trudeau Years: The Memoirs of Mark MacGuigan* (Calgary: University of Calgary Press, 2002), 128–29.

49 Douglas Roche, "Toward a Foreign Policy for Canada in the 1980s," *International Perspectives* (May/June, July/August 1979), 6.

50 Canada, House of Commons, *Debates*, 2 March 1977, 3574.

"Trotsky in Pinstripes": Lewis Perinbam, CIDA, and the Non-Governmental Organizations Program, 1968–1991

Kevin Brushett

On a warm fall night in October 1991, hundreds of people arrived at La Maison du Citoyen in Hull, Quebec to say farewell to their cherished colleague Lewis Perinbam, who was leaving CIDA after more than twenty-two years of public service in the cause of international cooperation. At the "roast" celebrating his achievements Perinbam modestly reminisced on the "small part" he had played in shaping Canada's international development assistance policy over the course of four decades. "Contrary to widely-held misconceptions," he continued, the federal government "can be an exciting and creative place to work in if you just remember two rules. . . . Never ask any questions to which the answer may be no; and forgiveness is usually easier to obtain than permission."[1]

That night, in an "Ode to Lewis," colleagues feted his long career in the "North-South" business. They ribbed him about his vast range of contacts: "for sure it is exaggeration that Lewis knows half of every nation." They marvelled at his ability to work the bureaucracy and the politics of development assistance: "his approach to issues was varied and deft, he bowed to the right and kept peace with the left." And they knowingly winked at his innovative means of administration: "On working methods, there was purity of intent and much obscurity of content. Of budgetary rationale controllers saw new maps of hell."[2] But former CIDA President Marcel Massé struck a more sober note. His remarks emphasized Perinbam's special influence on the development of Canadian aid programs by confirming his status as what Ottawa journalist Sandra Gwyn once called a "Guerilla Bureaucrat."[3] Perinbam, at least outwardly, did not look the part of a guerilla bureaucrat. He was clean-shaven, well-dressed, and did not stand on his head in the hallways of CIDA's offices. Rather, Massé remembered him as a "Leon Trotsky in pin-stripes" whom he claimed "work[ed] by stealth altering the substance of programs and initiatives without necessarily changing their appearance." "He got away with [so much]," Massé continued, "because he was so quiet—no one noticed his underground activities until they were fait accomplis." Above all, Perinbam adhered to American activist Abbie Hoffman's dictum that "the first duty of a revolutionary is to get away with it."[4] And get away with it, he did. Between 1969, when he arrived in Ottawa to head up the fledgling NGO Division at CIDA, and 1991, when he retired as vice-president of CIDA's Special Programs Branch, he took full advantage of support inside and outside Ottawa to revolutionize Canadian aid policy on many different fronts. What began as an innovative but relatively modest $5 million commitment to helping voluntary organizations carry out development projects in the Global South became by the time Perinbam retired a $330 million program funding hundreds of NGOs and thousands of projects. Equally important, he had turned the NGO Division into a much larger Special Programs Branch, which launched innovative programs including the Industrial Cooperation Program, Management for Change, Africa 2000, and the Youth Initiatives program.[5]

Since the publication of Keith Spicer's *A Samaritan State?* a half-century ago, the word "revolutionary" has generally not been used alongside Canadian development assistance policy. More often than not, CIDA has been variously critiqued for its ineffectiveness, its mixed and often conflicting objectives, and its role in maintaining Canada's economic and political hegemony vis-à-vis the peoples and nations of the Global South.[6] While many of these critiques have merit, there is one field where Canada once stood out as both innovative and effective: its engagement with the voluntary sector through various NGO programs.[7] As head of CIDA's NGO Division and later the Special Programs Branch, Perinbam was directly responsible for many of these innovative programs. Aid consultant David

Protheroe has referred to CIDA's expansionary and innovative period between 1968 and 1978 as a "near golden age" when Canadian development assistance policies so "thoroughly and ubiquitously" lived up to "middle power ideal[s]."[8] Though some of that shine has since worn off, Canadians' continued commitment to humanitarian and development-focused assistance policies has been due in no small part to Perinbam's deft management of his portfolio in these early years.

Lewis Perinbam was born in the town of Johore Bahru, in what is now Malaysia, in May 1925 to Indian immigrant parents Mary and Dr. Joseph Perinbam. Lewis left Malaysia at age nine to live with his uncle in Glasgow, Scotland, so that he could pursue his education. That education was cut short at eighteen when he received the tragic news of the brutal death of his father at the hands of Japanese occupation forces. Accused of hiding British and Chinese nationals as mental hospital patients, he was tortured by Japanese soldiers and then forced to dig his own grave before his execution. Perinbam eventually returned to Scotland to finish his studies at the University of Glasgow School of Engineering, from which he graduated in 1947. Worried that his Indian heritage would hinder his job prospects, he went to London to work for the Indian High Commission, where he eventually became involved with World University Service (WUS), a non-governmental organization established in the aftermath of the First World War to aid foreign students in need, including those fleeing Nazism in Europe during the 1930s and 1940s. By the early 1950s, WUS had gained "a solid reputation for its study tours, seminars, workshops and conferences."[9] In 1953, Lewis learned of an opportunity to put the Canadian branch of WUS on a more stable footing. He jumped at the opportunity. "I had become fascinated with Canada's history," he recalled, "as a country rooted in different cultures and whose citizens embraced values and principles, which did not prompt them to dominate others. I was excited therefore when WUSC invited me to Canada."[10]

For the rest of the 1950s, Perinbam criss-crossed the country helping to knit the various World University Service Canada (WUSC) branches into a cohesive and ambitious national organization. Though Canada's commitment to diversity attracted him to the country, he thought that Canadians could be parochial and that they had much to learn from working in conjunction with people whose lives and circumstances were very different from their own.[11] Paul Davidson, former WUSC executive director, remembered that even "at functions filled with movers and shakers," Perinbam "could usually be found talking in a corner to an 18-year-old," encouraging them to learn and serve abroad.[12] Even so, he rarely missed an opportunity to "network," which his wife Nancy Garrett later claimed he had invented before it was even a term. For example, it was on a 1957 WUSC trip to Ghana that Perinbam first met Pierre Trudeau; it was a relationship he assiduously cultivated, becoming one of the future prime minister's advisors on development issues.[13] Over the next half-century, Perinbam courted other world leaders, from Swedish prime minister Olof Palme to the Aga Khan and Prince Charles, as well as development experts from the World Bank to the Indian government, to build both an official and unofficial network to support a more egalitarian approach to what David Engerman calls "Development Politics."[14]

Perinbam's work at WUSC earned him enough plaudits to win him a job in 1959 as secretary general of the Canadian National Commission for UNESCO, where he continued to promote international cooperation among young people. Even in this early period, he was already writing to Prime Minister John Diefenbaker about organizing student work exchanges in the Global South. That idea eventually came to fruition in 1961 with the foundation of Canada's "Peace Corps," the Canadian University Service Overseas (CUSO). Though CUSO had many founding fathers, it was Perinbam who turned the idea into reality by personally borrowing $10,000 from the Carnegie Foundation and another $3,000 from Ontario Teachers' Federation to send the first volunteers to Ghana.[15] Perinbam remained active in CUSO even though his work with UNESCO and later with the World Bank kept him largely in New York. All of his work with WUSC, UNESCO, CUSO, and the World Bank equipped him to head up CIDA's new non-governmental organization program. In fact, Perinbam had lobbied the Diefenbaker government to support an NGO program as early as 1963. When CIDA's first president, Maurice Strong, came calling, Lewis essentially wrote his own job description.[16]

Perinbam's arrival in Ottawa in 1969 coincided with a momentous change in the Ottawa bureaucratic environment. The late 1960s represented what Sandra Gwyn has called "The Twilight of the Mandarins," when the old guard of . . . generalists were replaced by "trendy operators"

FIGURE 7.1
The youthful Lewis Perinbam brought a cosmopolitan sensibility to CIDA, which he joined in 1969. (Source: Unknown photographer/LAC e999919838-u)

and "altruistic technocrats." These were what Trudeau would call "new guys with new ideas." This renewed civil service followed the self-confident and assertive tone of its new leader and, as a result, Ottawa "crackled with energy," resembling "neither Camelot nor Athens so much as a cross between the Harvard Business School, Berkeley in the free speech era, and a utopian commune."[17]

CIDA, which grew out of the External Aid Office (EAO), was one of the epicentres of this dramatic growth and change in the Ottawa bureaucracy.[18] To fulfill his commitment to increase the size and scope of Canada's international development portfolio, outgoing Prime Minister Lester B. Pearson handed the reins of Canadian aid policy development over to the young and ambitious Maurice Strong.[19] Strong and his successor Paul Gérin-Lajoie leveraged increased public and political attention to development issues to staff CIDA with a degree of expertise that would allow it to speak as "the voice" on Canadian international development policy, much to the consternation to those in the Department of External Affairs who insisted that aid policy should remain subservient to Canada's larger political and economic interests. Until Strong arrived, the EAO was considered a "career backwater" and was "seriously hampered by the fact [it did] not have personnel overseas who are thoroughly familiar with ... field conditions overseas."[20] CIDA benefited from this expansionary period in Ottawa to recruit ten of the top fifteen graduates accepted into the government's administrative trainee program in 1969.[21]

As one of Strong's first-class recruits, Perinbam did not take long to build a small but substantial empire within CIDA. Initially, the NGO Division began with a modest budget of $5 million and a similarly modest set of objectives. As the work of Ted Cogan and Tamara Myers has outlined, the division grew out of the Centennial International Development Program and its hugely popular Miles for Millions walkathons.[22] Hoping to capture this outpouring of concern for development, the NGO Division was established with four broad objectives:

1. To broadly serve Canadian interests;

2. To enable CIDA to tap non-governmental expertise;

3. To stimulate NGO developmental activities to create a multiplier effect on Canada's overall development assistance effort; and

4. To encourage Canadians to become more involved in and aware of Canada's international development program.[23]

While more than two-thirds of the original NGO budget of $5 million went to supporting CUSO and Canadian Executive Service Overseas (CESO) volunteers, by the time Perinbam became vice-president of the Special Programs Branch in 1974, their share of the NGO budget had fallen to less than half. More important, during the same time, the number of NGOs working with CIDA rose from 20 to 200, with 617 projects receiving funding. The growth of the NGO program to $31 million by 1975 faithfully represented CIDA's philosophical approach to development by promoting social justice and stimulating self-sustaining development. By the end of the 1980s, the budget of Perinbam's Special Programs Branch (SPB) had tripled in size. Over its two decades of existence, the SPB invested more than $2 billion in funds while attracting another $6 billion in cash, goods, and services. When Perinbam retired, Canada was dispensing more than 10 per cent of its development assistance through NGOs, twice as much as the next largest donor.[24] Though most of the programs Perinbam oversaw in the SPB constituted less than 10 per cent of Canadian aid disbursements, these projects did much to help developing nations achieve important social objectives while simultaneously stimulating public support at home for international development.[25] As one of his early NGO Division recruits remembered, under Perinbam it was "harder to turn down proposals than to fund them."[26] Despite this permissive approach, Margaret Catley-Carlson, CIDA president in the 1980s, noted on one of Perinbam's annual performance reviews that the SPB operated "without any [of the] major problems of accountability [and] mismanagement . . . that have plagued other parts of the Agency."[27]

Not surprisingly, Perinbam's NGO Division quickly became known among the civil society sector as "our" department. Perinbam's cultivation of NGO support was crucial in building what David Black's chapter in this volume calls CIDA's "organizational essence" as a "development organization" committed first and foremost to poverty alleviation and a more just international social, economic, and political order.[28] The NGO umbrella organization, the Canadian Council for International Co-operation (CICC), noted that its members thought "well of their relations with CIDA and that the relationship had been 'positive, valuable, and beneficial.'"[29] A decade later, Ian Smillie, head of CUSO, wrote Perinbam to laud their relationship as "perhaps one of the most progressive and least selfish in the world." Writing in 1983, during a difficult period in CUSO's history, when internal divisions between radicals and pragmatists, French and English, were tearing it apart, Smillie insisted that its survival was due in large part to the "confidence that [Perinbam] . . . had placed in . . . CUSO."[30] Though at times Canadian NGOs worried that the division was steering them "down [the] garden path strewn with government goodies and lo and behold to 'priorities' and 'directives'" that were not their own, for the most part their relationship with the division was constructive and non-coercive.[31]

Yet, Perinbam's relationship with his former NGO colleagues was not without its strains. From the beginning, some in the NGO community, such as CUSO returned volunteer Grant Wanzell, worried about what their "blood relationship with CIDA" might do to their independence. Would NGOs become nothing more a "junior CIDA corps" and their role diminished to mere "governmental employment and placement agenc[ies?]"[32] By the mid-1970s, those concerns had worked their way up to CUSO executive director Murray Thomson, who worried that Perinbam and CIDA had become "servants of the very *status quo* [they were] working to change." "Perinbam" he continued, "saw things in terms of the 1960s . . . [and although] he was always talking about innovations and new ideas . . . when we came up with . . . new and innovative ideas . . . he was more interested in his own." Others commented that the NGO Division had begun to meddle in the projects submitted for approval, too often "behav[ing] as if they wished they were their own clients."[33] During this period, CIDA often seconded staff to various NGOs, including CUSO, while NGO volunteers and staff moved freely between their organizations, CIDA, and the CCIC, thus blurring the line between government and civil society.[34] For his part, Perinbam thought that NGO leaders had become "wooly naïf[s]," and dismissed the increasingly conspiratorial nature of their criticisms.[35] "There's an assumption that the government must be against them," he lamented. "They don't realize that we don't get up in the morning and say: 'What are we going to do to the NGOs today?'"[36] On more than one occasion, Perinbam warned his former NGO colleagues that "when CIDA gets knocked so does the NGO program" and the strength of "their Division" depended on the strength of CIDA itself.[37]

Despite these periodic tensions, Perinbam and the NGOs operated on the same wavelength when it came to the nature and purpose of development policy. Their general confidence in Perinbam's leadership was due to a number of factors, not least of which was the fact that Perinbam embodied what political scientist Cranford Pratt called "humane internationalism," an ethos that championed aid policy that was ethical, cooperative, and non-coercive.[38] Throughout his career, Perinbam emphasized that aid must avoid becoming a new form of colonialism. As earlier chapters in this volume by David Webster and Jill Campbell-Miller note, although Canadian aid officials entered aid relationships in privileged and powerful positions vis-à-vis their counterparts in the Global South, many (but not all) of them understood that success depended on a dialogue between equals.[39] For this reason, Perinbam insisted that it must be founded on the idea of "partners not patrons" engaged in a common enterprise to lift all peoples to prosperity and dignity.[40] Canadians, he reminded one audience, could not become leaders in development if they allowed their relationships with the developing world to be "a vehicle for domination or exploitation under the guise of 'partnerships,' whether by governments, NGOs, or the private sector."[41] This notion of partnership not only influenced the NGO program but was also central to other SPB programs such as the Business and Industry Program (1978) and the Management for Change (1981) initiative, which were established to share Canadian entrepreneurial and administrative acumen with nascent enterprises in the Global South.[42] Although these two programs created some anger in the NGO community because of their emphasis on the "profit motive," Perinbam later remembered them as among the initiatives of which he was most proud.[43]

While Perinbam firmly believed that NGOs were the perfect means to build international partnership in development, he could be critical of the gaps in their theory and practice. Addressing the annual meeting of CARE in May 1971, Perinbam pointedly asked whether the NGO challenged their fundraisers to examine "the real causes of hunger, sickness and illiteracy," or compared "the expenditures on war and armaments with those for . . . the war against poverty."[44] For him, NGOs that did not sufficiently reflect on their practices were "in danger of being like the rich man who tossed a penny to the beggar to relieve his own conscience . . . while avoiding the question of why there is a beggar at all."[45] Similarly, he often criticized NGOs for spending resources on their public image rather than on building links with the peoples of the Global South. The developing world, he argued on another occasion, was right to be "apprehensive and fearful [of] the waves of developmentalists . . . and so-called partners" who arrived to "rescue them from their poverty [but] who appear to have taken the place of missionaries of old."[46] In this vein, he saw the value of indigenous NGOs that could pinpoint the incompatibility between Northern theories and Southern realities.[47] Looking back from the perspective of recent critiques of NGOs' effectiveness in fighting global inequalities, Perinbam's analyses were remarkably prescient. Nonetheless, his unwavering devotion to their overarching cause at times reflected more liberal rather than revolutionary tendencies in his own strategies and approaches to IDA and global poverty.[48]

The way that Perinbam and his NGO Division tapped into the expertise and zeal of returned volunteers was another factor in building trust with the NGO community. It doubtless helped that many of these new CIDA recruits came from Perinbam's old stomping grounds at CUSO. Some were part of the initial hiring flurry in late 1969, while others, such as Dale Posgate, one of the original fifteen CUSO volunteers to serve in India, found their way to CIDA later. Historian Ruth Compton Brouwer puts the number of CIDA employees who were former CUSO volunteers at nearly 40 per cent, leading one of Perinbam's recruits, Elizabeth McAllister, to claim that "it seemed liked *everyone* had worked for CUSO." Indeed, by the early 1970s, this group had become known, both for good and for bad, as the "CUSO Mafia."[49] Sheila Batchelor, one of Perinbam's initial recruits, remembers that "before all the i's were dotted and t's crossed for the establishment of the NGO Division [Perinbam] gather[ed] around him . . . a talented enthusiastic group of mainly young people whom he handpicked to be the core of the NGO Division." Most of us, she continued, "had grassroots overseas experience or had been involved with NGOs in some capacity. We were gung ho, full of energy, and convinced that it was our generation who would finally change the world. Above all, we were highly individualist and strong willed. There was not one shrinking violet in our midst."[50] Other notable CUSO recruits to the NGO Division included Ronald Leger, who later became involved in Inter Pares, as well as Nigel Martin, who became head of OXFAM Quebec and a director of the CCIC. Martin in particular remembered coming to Ottawa as a "young angry product of the 1960s," skeptical of how much he would accomplish inside the "big monster . . . aka 'The Government.'"[51]

Perinbam's managerial style attracted returned volunteers and encouraged them to carve out long careers in government. His colleagues remembered him as an "anti-bureaucrat" engaged in "disruptive innovation" who manoeuvred his way through official Ottawa.[52] Under Perinbam's guidance the NGO Division and the SPB became the emotional heart and soul of CIDA because he "ma[de] things happen, and [did] not simply administ[er] the status quo." Other colleagues remembered him not as an ideologue but as someone who sought out people with different dreams and ideas, never simply "yes people."[53] This was particularly true when it came to choosing his replacement at the NGO Division, Romeo Maione, a long-time social activist in the Catholic Church and Quebec labour movement, and the first executive director of the Canadian Catholic Organization for Development and Peace (CCODP). Maione inherited Perinbam's "drive and passion to enable others to do wonderful things."[54]

Perinbam's commitment to broadening the horizons at CIDA also applied to recruiting and supporting women. Sheila Batchelor remembered Perinbam as a "lifelong champion of women in the workplace . . . [who] provided us with an atmosphere of professional acceptance and instilled in us the confidence in our abilities which later allowed us to make our way in other much less positive work milieus."[55] Perinbam's performance reviews consistently commented highly on his support for "affirmative action." Indeed, under his leadership CIDA became among the first to institute a Women in Development (WID) approach to minimize the gendered implications of traditional development programming.[56] It was no coincidence that MATCH International, the world's first international development NGO run by and for women, was established with the support of the NGO Division in 1976.

The NGO program also won accolades as an efficient and effective means of delivering development assistance while simultaneously engaging Canadians' support for CIDA's larger program. Officials in the departments of External Affairs and Industry, Trade and Commerce (ITC), the "senior members" of the interdepartmental consultation body known as the Canadian International Development Board (CIDB), judged the NGO program to be a cost-effective means of delivering aid. They also liked that it could be more "flexible, adventurous and experimental" than official bilateral programs, which were constrained by government-to-government negotiations.[57] As one diplomat noted, "All too often bilateral and multilateral aid was held hostage to the interests of governments not those of their citizens."[58] Officials praised the NGO program as "a magnificent contribution to real development at the lowest level . . . organizations receiving assistance staffed by 'dedicated, industrious people who assist[ed] . . . their . . . friends . . . to a better life through better habits . . . skills . . . and greater self-respect."[59] Others noted that the program was an excellent means of providing development assistance in countries where Canada could not or did not want to mount bilateral programs, particularly nations whose human rights records were poor. For example, most Canadian aid to Haiti during the 1970s was carried out through the NGO program, because as one Canadian embassy official observed, "we don't want the government to become involved or even to set priorities."[60] The NGO program was also important in re-establishing Canadian ties with Uganda in the aftermath of the 1973 coup.[61]

Nonetheless, as the NGO program grew during the 1970s, some government officials, particularly in External Affairs, became increasingly uneasy about its direction and purpose. Though most agreed that the program should be kept free from "bureaucratic red tape and excessive control," others contended that there were "inherent dangers of maintaining this concept . . . in the face of the expected future growth"[62] Some of these anxieties stemmed from "Doubting Thomases," Perinbam claimed, who conjured up all kinds of "lurid pictures of what might happen if public funds were misused."[63] Canadian diplomats also worried that the NGO Division too often departed from "established policy" and insufficiently reviewed project proposals, leading to too many "risky ventures."[64] According to them, the idea behind the NGO program was for CIDA to keep a "low profile while at the same time helping an organization, usually Canadian, make a worthwhile contribution to development."[65] However, the expansion of the program meant that CIDA's role was becoming "much more [blatantly] interventionist."[66] External Affairs also worried about the lack of experience among CIDA officials and the absence of project oversight by embassy and mission officials. It did not help that even within CIDA the NGO branch jealously guarded its programs and rarely consulted with their colleagues.[67] Officials also disliked Perinbam's frequent trips abroad to monitor Canadian NGO projects, which often shaded into "inappropriate" consultation with foreign leaders, development experts, and indigenous NGOs. How much he shared about official Canadian policy is unclear, but External Affairs more than once complained about documents leaked by the NGO Division.[68]

A perfect example of External Affairs' growing concerns with the NGO program was the Christian Action for Development in the Caribbean (CADEC) project. In the early 1970s, the United Church of Canada, in association with the Caribbean Council of Churches, applied to CIDA for help funding community development projects in the region. By 1975, the Canadian high commissioner in the Barbados, Larry Smith, was complaining to Perinbam about CADEC projects and the overall direction of the NGO program in the region. In his sharply worded dispatch, Smith produced a litany of administrative complaints about his experiences with NGO Division–sponsored projects. But the crux of his complaint was political. Too many NGO projects were creating difficulties for Canadian missions abroad, because they were unconcerned with "the impact the[ir] work . . . ha[s] on our broader inter-governmental or inter-country relationships." He reminded Perinbam that despite the arms-length relationship between CIDA and the NGOs, "people tend not to make the distinction between Canadian government activity and Canadian private activities." Foremost in Smith's mind was CADEC's monthly newsletter, which carried articles highly critical of regional governments as well as Canadian multinational corporations operating in the region. Smith ended his missive by admonishing Perinbam's lack of attention to program administration. "You keep assuring us," he wrote, "that procedures were being tightened up . . . but as yet there has been little evidence of this."[69]

Perinbam's response reflected both his concern and his ability to defend the NGO program from internal pressures that would make it little more than a "door opener" to advance short-term Canadian political and economic interests in the developing world.[70] First, he deflected criticism of the administrative issues to the United Church and officials in External Affairs who had not passed the requisite information up the chain of command. More importantly, he went straight to the issue that underlay External Affairs' growing resistance to the NGO program, that organizations such as CADEC were critical of governments and established interests in the Global South. "On the one hand," Perinbam wrote, "you state that [CADEC] is 'doing good work, operates at the grass-roots level, encourages economic and social development, and promotes regional cooperation.'" "On the other hand," he continued "you say that it 'comments frequently and publicly on political matters often critically of governments.'" "The same," he reminded Smith, "can be said of many highly respectable Canadian NGOs such as the churches, universities and unions." Indeed, Perinbam chastised Smith for questioning the sincerity and integrity of CADEC "when its directors include people like [renowned development economist] Sir Arthur Lewis, the Archbishop of Jamaica, the Anglican Bishop of Barbados and the President of the Caribbean Development Bank." Perinbam finished his letter to Smith claiming that he was "not here to plead for CADEC. . . . All I ask is for some clear guidance as to *what you wish us to do*."[71]

Fears that the NGO Division was transferring control over Canadian development policy to its beneficiaries became more pointed when Perinbam put forward the proposition of directly funding indigenous organizations such as CADEC through an International NGO program rather than through Canadian-based organizations. CIDA President Paul Gérin-Lajoie and Perinbam believed that too many development projects were conceived by Canadians rather than by peoples in the developing world.[72] From the start, Perinbam had always sought more "constructive evaluation[s] of Canada's development assistance program in [both] a national and international perspective."[73] To sell the program to the naysayers on the CIDB, CIDA argued that an INGO program would "improve the effectiveness of the program by enlarging its scope and thrust."[74] Improved efficiency and transparency notwithstanding, External Affairs repeatedly asked that it be removed from CIDA's 1975 Strategic Plan. According to External Affairs, the original rationale for the NGO program was to purchase a domestic constituency to support Canada's existing aid programs and policies, not for foreigners to design their own. To them the INGO program represented the naïve and wooly-headed thinking so characteristic of CIDA's early years. To cite Larry Smith again, such an approach to development was a "very crude method of subversion" based on the assumption at CIDA that "governments do not represent the people . . . [and] must therefore be circumvented." "Even if we subscribe to such an untenable international philosophy," he continued, "we might ask ourselves whether [Canada] would welcome a workshop on general preferences or . . . on the merits of Marxist central planning sponsored by Chile or Cuba."[75] Another commentary noted that "there's a difference between a domestic [Local Initiatives Project] and one operated internationally by a foreign government, and as such External Affairs should be deeply opposed to CIDA sponsoring the activities of indigenous NGOs."[76] In the end, Perinbam's persistence won the day.

The final area where Perinbam sought to foster a narrative of humane internationalism was through extensive consultation with NGOs both at home and abroad. Like many in the NGO community, he believed that their "primary *raison d'être* was not the collection and transfer of money from private citizens, but the representation of the Third World voice in

Kevin Brushett

FIGURE 7.2
Lewis Perinbam, 1987.
(Source: Unknown
photographer/LAC
e999919839-u)

the structures that perpetuate their continuing underdevelopment."[77] For those in CIDA this was the rationale behind what would eventually become the Public Participation Program (PPP), which funded such development education programs as the annual Ten Days for World Development. To officials in External Affairs the program was supposed to provide "a dependable base of public support for the continued expansion" of the Canadian aid program by "providing a more informed but constructive tone" to political debates over the magnitude and complexity of the issues involved.[78] It was not long before they believed that CIDA had created a monster. With significant CIDA funding many NGOs mounted "education" programs that strongly criticized not only Canadian aid policy but also Canada's role in global economic relations. These criticisms reached a fever peak during the World Food Conference in Rome in 1974, when Canadian

NGOs criticized the government's approach to combating the global food crisis. Hoping to avoid another embarrassment during the 1976 UNCTAD IV meetings, Eric Bergbusch, head of the aid and development division in External Affairs, made it clear that CIDA's support to NGOs "should be of such proportions that they can [act] in their proper function as observers" and not "mount a counter-delegation."[79] By the early 1980s, External Affairs had also come to worry about the increased human rights emphasis of groups such as the Latin American Working Group, the Toronto Committee for the Liberation of Southern Africa, the Taskforce on the Churches and Corporate Responsibility and GATT-Fly, which critiqued Canada's economic policies toward economies in the Global South. Although few of these organizations received direct monies through the PPP program, they were all part of the development education network established by CUSO, Oxfam, and the Inter-Church Fund for International Development, with significant political and financial support from Perinbam's NGO and Special Branch programs. Though Perinbam at times criticized his NGO colleagues for biting the hand that fed them, their activism more often than not strengthened CIDA's hand vis-à-vis the more conservative stakeholders on the CIDB. As David Morrison argues in the conclusion to his history of CIDA, Perinbam's original investment in a strong and vibrant voluntary sector had helped it resist pressures from other aid "stakeholders," namely DEA and ITC, to make IDA serve non-development objectives.[80]

Conclusion

In his seminal study of Canadian development assistance, *A Samaritan State?*, written a half-century ago, Keith Spicer adopted a thoroughly realist approach. Humanitarian motives for development assistance, he wrote, were "a fickle and confused policy stimulant derived from personal conscience. [They are] not an objective of government." "To talk of humanitarian 'aims' in Canadian foreign policy," he continued, "is in fact to confuse policy with the ethics of individuals molding it, to mix government objectives with personal motives."[81] With this in mind, what then do we make of someone like Lewis Perinbam, who for more than two decades not only embodied the humanitarian impulse in Canadian international development assistance policy but also translated it into practice at some of the highest levels of the Canadian state and beyond? For one, as the work of both Stephen Brown and Rebecca Tiessen reminds us, institutions, including impersonal government bureaucracies, are not monolithic entities. They are composed of individuals imbued not only with motives and values but also, in Perinbam's case, with the skill, acumen, and charisma to steer innovative policies through the forbidding channels of the state apparatus and also to shape those very processes and institutions in fundamental ways.[82] Equally important, it echoes David Engerman's call to historians of international development to "investigate rather than assume the paramountcy of the state in intergovernmental relations such as economic development" by examining the "tensions and politics *within* national governments" to better map and explain the "world development made."[83]

Recent critiques of Canada's development assistance policy note that its current ineffectiveness stems in part from the fact that it has long lacked a champion with sufficient power to institute strategic direction.[84] Certainly that was not true of Perinbam. Indeed, as his original boss Maurice Strong wrote on his retirement, "the fact that Lewis managed to develop such a vast work within the bosom of a bureaucratic process that seldom understood and rarely welcomed the ungovernable ways of non-governmental organizations is a small miracle of immense proportions."[85] To be sure, larger state structures constrained those activities by pushing particular ideas in directions that required significant compromise. For all the praise that Perinbam received as an "anti-bureaucrat," he also assiduously pursued alliances with the powerful in Ottawa, and elsewhere, that could advance CIDA's agenda. For some in the NGO community, Perinbam's management of his insider/outsider position too often leaned toward the "liberal urge within CIDA," a term not always meant as a compliment.[86] Ever the pragmatist, he was often ready to accept "half a loaf"—to echo another title from the history of Canadian development assistance—despite censure from the jealous guardians of the humane internationalist counter-consensus. But as Massé reminded his audience at Perinbam's farewell, "the first duty of a revolutionary is to get away with it."[87]

Notes

1   Notes for Remarks by Lewis Perinbam at a "Roast" organized in his honour by his colleagues and friends, 9 October 1991, Lewis Perinbam Papers, vol. 6, file 24, Library and Archives Canada (LAC).

2   "An ode of farewell to Lewis Perinbam, Ottawa, 9 October 1991," Perinbam Papers, vol. 6, file 24, LAC.

3   Sandra Gwyn, "The Twilight of the Ottawa Man," *Saturday Night*, January 1971.

4   Talking Points for Marcel Masse to roast Lewis Perinbam, Hull, Quebec, 1991, Perinbam Papers, vol. 6, file 24, LAC.

5   "Biography and Administrative History," Perinbam Papers, LAC, http://collectionscanada.gc.ca/pam_archives/index.php?fuseaction=genitem.displayItem&rec_nbr=3930960&lang=eng&rec_nbr_list=3930960,3714081,200799,100 026.

6   For example, see the following classic statements: Kim Richard Nossal, "Mixed Motives Revisited: Canada's Interest in Development Assistance," *Canadian Journal of Political Science* 21, no. 1 (1988): 35–56; Jamie Swift and Brian Tomlinson, eds., *Conflicts of Interest: Canada and the Third World* (Toronto: Between the Lines, 1991); Robert Carty, Virginia Smith, and Latin American Working Group, *Perpetuating Poverty: The Political Economy of Canadian Foreign Aid* (Toronto: Between the Lines, 1991); Stephen Brown, ed., *Struggling for Effectiveness: CIDA and Canadian Foreign Aid* (Montreal: McGill-Queen's University Press, 2012); Cranford Pratt, ed., *Canadian International Development Assistance Policies: An Appraisal* (Montreal: McGill-Queen's University Press, 1994); David R. Morrison, *Aid and Ebb Tide: A History of CIDA and Canadian Development Assistance* (Waterloo, ON: Waterloo University Press, 1998).

7   Tim Brodhead and Cranford Pratt, "Paying the Piper: CIDA and Canadian NGOs," in Pratt, *Canadian International Development Assistance Policies*, 87–119; and Tim Brodhead, Brent Herbert-Copley, and Anne-Marie Lambert, *Bridges of Hope?: Canadian Voluntary Agencies and the Third World* (Ottawa: North-South Institute, 1988). For a critique of the NGO program see Nikolas Barry-Shaw and Dru Oja-Jay, *Paved With Good Intentions: Canada's Development NGOs From Idealism to Imperialism* (Halifax: Fernwood, 2012).

8   David Protheroe, "Canada's Multilateral Aid and Diplomacy," in Pratt, *Canadian International Development Assistance Policies*, 29–30.

9   WUSC-EUMC, "History," accessed 8 December 2016 from http://wusc.ca/en/about-us/about-us-page-1.

10 Masse Notes for Remarks, Perinbam Papers, vol. 6, file 24, LAC.

11 CUSO International West, "Nancy [Garrett] tells me about Lewis Perinbam – Podcast # 72," http://cuso-vso.mypodcastworld.com/738/nancy-tells-me-about-lewis-perinbam-podcast-72.

12   Philip Fine, "OBITUARY: Lewis Perinbam: International education pioneer," *University World News*, Issue 11, 13 January 2008, http://www.universityworldnews.com/article.php?story=20080110161218471.

13   Lewis occasionally accompanied Trudeau on foreign visits concerning aid issues, including the 1975 Commonwealth Heads of Government meeting in Jamaica. He was also on the Trudeau family's annual Christmas card list.

14   "An Ode of Farewell to Lewis Perinbam," 9 October 1991, Perinbam Papers, vol. 6, file 24, LAC. For the way in which international development often took place through informal networks see David Engerman, "Development Politics and the Cold War," *Diplomatic History* 41, no. 1 (Jan. 2017): 14–19.

15   Jack Cahill, "Lewis Perinbam, Quiet Civil Servant is a man of imagination and daring," *Toronto Star*, 19 February 1984, F5.

16   Richard Harmston, email correspondence, 1 February 2017.

17   Richard Gwyn, *Northern Magus: Pierre Trudeau and Canadians* (Toronto: McClelland & Stewart, 1980), 95. Although the nature of the civil service changed during these years by attracting significant numbers of francophones and women, the culture of the "new mandarinate" remained thoroughly white male and anglophone into the 1980s. Perinbam would later chair the *Task Force on the Participation of Visible Minorities in the Federal Public Service*. See Lewis Perinbam, *Embracing Change in the Federal Public Service* (Ottawa: Treasury Board, 2000).

18   The EAO began with approximately 40 employees in the early 1960s, grew to 492 in 1970 as CIDA, and then to 1020 by 1976. Public Service Commission of Canada, *Annual Reports*, 1962–1977.

19   According to David Morrison, Strong accepted Pearson's offer of leading a revamped EAO only if it had significant input on policy development. Morrison, *Aid and Ebb Tide*, 59–61.

20   Minutes of Informal Discussions concerning the External Aid Board, 12 October 1966, RG 25, vol. 11784, file 38-1-CIDA, LAC; Martin Desmules, « Histoire du volontariat international au Québec : Le cas du service universitaire canadien outre-mer – SUCO » (Maitrise en histoire, Université du Québec à Montréal, 2009), 18.

21   Ruth Compton Brouwer, *Canada's Global Villagers: CUSO in Development, 1961–86* (Vancouver: University of British Columbia Press, 2013), 188; Morrison, *Aid and Ebb Tide*, 64.

22   Ted Cogan, "Selling Foreign Aid in the 1960s: Public Opinion, Civil Society and the Demise of SHARE CANADA," Canadian Historical Association Annual Meeting, Brock University, 2014; Tamara Myers, "Local Action and Global Imagining: Youth, International Development, and the Walkathon Phenomenon in Sixties' and Seventies' Canada," *Diplomatic History* 38 (2014): 282–93.

23   Original Mandate of the NGO Division, CCIC Papers, vol. 11, file: CCIC-CIDA Consultation, 22–28 November 1976, LAC.

24   Brodhead and Pratt, "Paying the Piper," 95.

25   Though CIDA was sometimes criticized for its wasteful and ineffective programs, particularly on the bilateral side, Canadian popular support for international development as a whole remained fairly positive between the late 1960s and the early 1990s. See Alain Noel, Jean-Philippe Therrien, and Sebastien Dallaire, "Divided over Internationalism: The Canadian Public and Development Assistance," *Canadian Public Policy* 30, no. 1 (2004): 29–46; and Ian Smillie, "Canada," in Ian Smillie and Henny Helmich (in collaboration with Tony German and Judith Randel), eds., *Public Attitudes and International Development Co-operation* (Paris: OECD, 1998).

26   Anne Sutherland in The Lewis Perinbam Memory Book, Perinbam Papers, vol. 20, file 21, LAC.

27   Performance Review and Appraisal, March 1988, Perinbam Papers, vol. 4, file 16, LAC.

28   See David Black, chapter 12 of this volume. On organizational essences see Marie-Eve Desrosiers and Philippe Lagassé, "Canada and the Bureaucratic Politics of State Fragility," *Diplomacy and Statecraft* 20, no. 4 (2009): 659–78

29   CCIC Brief to the Standing Committee on External Affairs & National Defence, 29 April 1975, Oxfam Canada Papers, vol. 85, file 37, LAC, 2; Richard Harmston, email correspondence, 1 February 2017.

30   Ian Smillie to Perinbam, 29 July 1983, Perinbam Papers, vol. 3, file 36, LAC.

31   CCIC-CIDA Consultation October 1976, Part II, Kenrie Marshall to Romeo Maione, 17 August 1976, CCIC Papers, vol. 10, file: NGO-CIDA Consultation 5–7 October 1976, LAC; Brodhead and Pratt, "Paying the Piper"; Brodhead, Herbert-Copley, and Lambert, *Bridges of Hope?*.

32   Grant Wanzel, Annual Report of the Interim Chairman of the CUSO/SUCO Returned Volunteers Network, Part Two – A Critical Analysis of CUSO/SUCO 1968/69, CUSO Papers, vol. 43, file 11, LAC.

33   Ian Smillie, The *Land of Lost Content : A History of CUSO* (Toronto: Deneau, 1985), 272.

34   Richard Harmston, email correspondence, 1 February 2017.

35   Smillie, *Land of Lost Content*, 103.

36   Ibid., 266.

37   Notes for Remarks by Lewis Perinbam, CIDA/NGO Consultation, 5 October 1976, CCIC Papers, vol. 10, LAC; MG 28 I367, vol. 10, file: NGO-CIDA Consultation, 5–7 October 1976, LAC.

38   See, in particular, Cranford Pratt, "Humane Internationalism and Canadian Development Assistance Policies," in Pratt, *Canadian International Development Assistance Policies*, 334–70.

39   See chapters 1 and 2 in this volume by Jill Campbell-Miller and David Webster.

40   "Partnership in Development: The Role of Non-Governmental Organizations," Address to WUSC, 3 September 1969, Perinbam Papers, vol. 9, file 3, LAC.

41   Lewis Perinbam, "Developing countries need real partners, not crippling patronage," *Canadian Speeches* 11, no. 7 (November 1997): 26–37.

Kevin Brushett

42 Notes on an Address "Quest for Justice" to the CUSO Annual General Meeting, 2 December 1972, Carleton University, Perinbam Papers, vol. 9, file 4, LAC; Notes for an Address on "The Third World: Threat or Promise" to the First Global Conference on the Future, 22 July 1980, Harbour Castle Hilton Hotel, Toronto; Perinbam, "Developing countries need real partners."

43 CUSO International West, "Nancy [Garrett] tells me about Lewis Perinbam – Podcast # 72"; and Morrison, *Aid and Ebb Tide*, 128–29, 171–72.

44 "The Role of the Voluntary Agency in International Development," to the World Conference of CARE on the occasion of its 25th Anniversary, 13 May 1971, Mayflower Hotel, Washington, D.C., Perinbam Papers, vol. 9, file 4, LAC.

45 "The Role of the Voluntary Agency in International Development," Perinbam Papers, vol. 9, file 4, LAC.

46 Notes for the Consultation with Non-Governmental Agencies and Groups, 19 April 1972, Perinbam Papers, vol. 9, file 4, LAC; Perinbam, "NGOs Lead the Way to International Equality," *Canadian Speeches* 16, no. 1 (March/April 2002).

47 Address on "Changing Times and Changing Challenges for NGOs" to the Caribbean and Latin America Regional Conference, Kingston, Jamaica, 1 November 1990, Perinbam Papers, vol. 10, file 6, LAC.

48 For a recent critique of limits of NGO and CSO action that echoes Perinbam's concerns see Nicola Banks and David Hulme, "The Role of NGOs and Civil Society in Development and Poverty Reduction," Brooks World Poverty Institute, University of Manchester Working Paper, 2012, http://hummedia.manchester.ac.uk/institutes/gdi/publications/workingpapers/bwpi/bwpi-wp-17112.pdf. See also Michael Barnett, *Empire of Humanity: A History of Humanitarianism* (Ithaca, NY: Cornell University Press, 2011), 195–219; and Barry-Shaw and Oja-Jay, *Paved With Good Intentions.*

49 Brouwer, *Canada's Global Villagers*, 187–88.

50 Lewis Perinbam Memory Book, Perinbam Papers, vol. 20, file 21, LAC.

51 Ibid.

52 Richard Beattie in Lewis Perinbam Memory Book, Perinbam Papers, vol. 20, file 21, LAC. The phrase "disruptive innovation" comes from Nigel Martin, cited in Richard Harmston, email correspondence, 1 February 2017.

53 Ronald Leger in Lewis Perinbam Memory Book, Perinbam Papers, vol. 20, file 21, LAC.

54 Richard Harmston, email correspondence, 1 February 2017.

55 Sheila Batchelor in Lewis Perinbam Memory Book, Perinbam Papers, vol. 20, file 21, LAC.

56 Rebecca Tiessen, "Gender Equality and the 'Two CIDAs': Successes and Setbacks, 1976–2013," in Stephen Brown, Molly den Heyer, and David Black, eds., *Rethinking Canadian Aid* (Ottawa: University of Ottawa Press, 2014), 195–210.

57 Meeting of the CIDB, 7 March and 19 March 1973, RG 25, vol. 11788, file 38-1-CIDA-ALLOC, LAC.

58 Peter Hoffman to Romeo Maione re Trip to South America, 1 November 1978, RG 25, vol. 11796, file 38-1-CIDA-NGO, LAC.

59 W. J. Burnett to W. J. Jenkins, 14 March 1974, RG 25, vol. 11785, file 38-1-CIDA, LAC; Memorandum to the Interdepartmental Committee on Development Assistance, 24 March 1972, RG 25, vol. 11788, file 38-1-CIDA-ALLOC, LAC.

60 L. A. H. Smith to Barry Steers, 20 October 1971, RG 25, vol. 11794, file 38-1-CIDA-NGO, LAC.

61 Canadian High Commission in Nairobi to CIDA, 2 November 1973, RG 25, vol. 11794, file 38-1-CIDA-NGO, LAC.

62 Interdepartmental Committee on Development Assistance, Summary of Discussion, 5 September 1973, RG 25, vol. 11794, file 38-1-CIDA-NGO, LAC.

63 Notes for Remarks by Lewis Perinbam, 5 October 1976, CCIC Papers, vol. 10, file: NGO-CIDA Consultation 5–7 October 1976, LAC.

64 Interdepartmental Committee on Development Assistance, Summary of Discussion, 5 September 1973, RG 25, vol. 11794, file 38-1-CIDA-NGO, LAC.

65 Memorandum to ECD, 7 February 1973, RG 25, vol. 11794, file 38-1-CIDA-NGO, LAC.

66 Aubrey Morantz, Checklist of Issues in Our Relationship with CIDA, 13 August 1973, RG 25, vol. 11791, file 38-1-CIDA-EA, LAC.

67 Memorandum to ECD, 7 February 1973, RG 25, vol. 11794, file 38-1-CIDA-NGO, LAC.

68 Jacques Roy to Perinbam, 19 February 1980, RG 25, vol. 11791, file 38-1-CIDA-EA, LAC.

69 L. A. H. Smith to Perinbam, 4 February 1975, RG 25, vol. 11795, file 38-1-CIDA-NGO, LAC.

70 Robert Carty, "Giving For Gain: Foreign Aid and CIDA," in *Ties that Bind: Canada and the Third World*, ed. Richard Swift and Robert Clarke (Toronto: Between the Lines, 1982), 162.

71 Perinbam to L. A. H. Smith, 11 March 1975, RG 25, vol. 11795, file 38-1-CIDA-NGO, LAC.

72 Paul Gérin-Lajoie, "Rediscovering a Sense of Adventure," Address to the Annual Meeting of the CCIC, 9 June 1972, UCCA Papers, vol. 83.018, file 4-4, LAC.

73 Memorandum to the Minister, 20 October 1971, RG 25, vol. 11784, file 38-1-CIDA, LAC.

74 Paul Gérin-Lajoie, Memorandum for the Minister, 2 November 1973, RG 25, vol. 11794, file 38-1-CIDA-NGO, LAC.

75 L. A. H. Smith, Memorandum on CIDA Initiative in Non-Governmental Organizations Programme, 16 June 1972, RG 25, vol. 11794, file 38-1-CIDA-NGO, LAC.

76 Klaus Goldschlag, Memorandum on the CIDA Initiative in Non-Governmental Organizations Programme, 26 June 1972, RG 25, vol. 11794, file 38-1-CIDA-NGO, LAC. The Local Initiatives Program was a 1970s federal program run by Manpower and Immigration ostensibly to address seasonal unemployment through programs that

might also provide "community betterment." Many of these projects, however, became centres of opposition to federal government programs such as urban renewal. See J. M. Keck, "Making Work: Federal Job Creation Policy In The 1970s" (PhD diss., University of Toronto, 1995).

77 B. Ward to M. Lapointe, 17 February 1976, CCIC Papers, vol. 11, file: NGO-CIDA Relations, LAC.

78 Draft Report, n.d., Andrew Brewin Papers, vol. 81, file 4: Development Parliamentary Sub-Committee on International Development 1969–70, LAC.

79 E. J. Bergbusch to Roger Wilson, 16 March 1976, RG 25, vol. 11795, file 38-1-CIDA-NGO, LAC.

80 Morrison, *Aid and Ebb Tide,* 451.

81 Keith Spicer, *A Samaritan State? External Aid in Canadian Foreign Policy* (Toronto: University of Toronto Press, 1966), 11.

82 Stephen Brown, "Canada's Foreign Aid before and after CIDA: Not a Samaritan state," *International Journal* 68, no. 3 (2013): 501–12; and Tiessen, "Gender Equality and the Two CIDAs."

83 Engerman, "Development Politics and the Cold War," 18. Emphasis mine.

84 Adam Chapnick, "Canada's Aid Program: Still Struggling After Sixty Years," *Behind the Headlines* 65, no. 3 (May 2008): 11.

85 Maurice Strong, "Message for the Lewis Perinbam Dinner," 9 October 1991, Perinbam Papers, vol. 6, file 24, LAC.

86 Some Hypotheses on CIDA Bilateral Funding of NGOs, September 1977, CCIC Papers, vol. 11, file: CIDA-NGO Relations, 1976-82, LAC. See also Barry-Shaw and Oja-Jay, *Paved With Good Intentions.*

87 See Clive Sanger, *Half a Loaf: Canada's Semi Role Among Developing Countries* (Toronto: Ryerson Press, 1969). Talking Points for Marcel Masse, Perinbam Papers, vol. 6, file 24, LAC.

PART 3

IMAGERY AND SYMBOLISM

The flowering of UN and Colombo Plan aid was a godsend for Canadians in search of a new self-image. English Canada's national identity tottered insecurely after the Second World War as imperial Britain retreated, leaving Canadians uncomfortably alone in North America with the US colossus and reliant on a US-led military alliance, the North Atlantic Treaty Organization (NATO), to retain a link with Europe. By the 1960s and 1970s, the national identity crisis was acute. A surging American cultural and economic presence north of the border and the growth of nationalist sentiment in Quebec raised deep questions about what it meant to be Canadian.

The answer, at least in part, lay in foreign affairs. Aid, alongside peacekeeping and CanLit (as Canadian literature was nicknamed), gave Canadians a renewed sense of self and an international identity as good Samaritans. Postwar aid and national identity were intrinsically linked. It was hardly coincidental that the early aid administrator, the former English colonial Nik Cavell, deliberately changed his name to don a distinctly Canadian identity. Aid official Lewis Perinbam did not need to change his name, but he too cast off his former nationality as he entered and transformed Canadian aid operations. And there were others.

The three chapters in this section explore elements of this relationship between foreign aid and national identity in Canada, teasing apart image and reality. Aid, a novel venture in unfamiliar parts of the world, was always going to be a hard sell, as Ted Cogan's chapter explains. Aware of the ongoing need for public support, successive Canadian governments portrayed aid as quintessentially "Canadian," a simple extension of Canada's natural role as global peacemaker. This made aid bipartisan, a project of all political parties, helping to build a sense of national unity and consensus. If the Canadian state was promotional, its audience was internal as much as international—perhaps more so.

Sonya de Laat's study of CIDA's extensive photography collection also holds up a mirror to Canadian identity. CIDA's imagery helped define (and constantly redefine) Canada as a steadfast and immutable "caring" and "helpful nation." Striking pictures of poverty and Canadian efforts to help convinced Canadians that their country was working for good causes in other lands.

Indeed, this very self-identity as a "Samaritan State" would spur Canadian citizens into one of the greatest mass giving campaigns in the country's history, Nassisse Solomon argues in her chapter. Images of starving children encouraged Canadians to mount a national mass relief effort for the victims of the Ethiopian famine in the mid-1980s. The country's most prominent singers gathered as "Northern Lights" to make a video telling Canadians that "tears are not enough"—donations were needed more. The fundraising campaign allowed thousands to feel a direct connection to helping starving Ethiopians and to feel proud of their country for coming to the rescue.

But identity hides as much as it reveals. Federal politicians justify aid as inherently Canadian, but jostle behind the scenes for geopolitical and economic advantage. CIDA's imagery projects an unperturbable air of national caring and concern, while its agendas shift, obscuring aspects of Canada's ODA worthy of debate and criticism. Solomon's chapter ends by peeking at the brutal underside of African famine relief in the 1980s, including the manipulation of famine imagery, the politics of food distribution on the ground, and the persistent negative framing of Africa. Examining Canadian aid through its imagery suggests that it has been more effective in shaping Canadian self-images than in ending poverty.

8

Building a Base: The Growth of Public Engagement with Canadian Foreign Aid Policy, 1950–1980

Ted Cogan

Canadian foreign aid came of age in the three decades after 1950 in a climate that was often less than hospitable. Most Canadians, including politicians and civil servants, had little direct experience with, or knowledge of, the underdeveloped world. This reality made it challenging, both practically and politically, to build a stable base of support for foreign aid in Canada. These challenges were soon compounded by significant economic and reputational concerns. The needs of the developing world were constantly expanding at a time when domestic claims on the public purse were growing and Canada's economic outlook was becoming increasingly unstable. Furthermore, as foreign aid funding grew, so too did scrutiny by the press and various civil society groups engaged in development assistance work. To address all these challenges, successive federal governments came to the conclusion that effective foreign aid programming was, in part, contingent on managing public support.

The efforts of politicians and civil servants to build public support for foreign aid were focused on two audiences. The first audience was the electorate at large. In approaching this audience, successive governments sought to increase awareness about international development and build broad support. The second key audience were stakeholder groups, like churches, universities, NGOs, and businesses, which had established interests in foreign aid. The government saw members of these groups as key allies, as they had the knowledge and experience necessary to form a core domestic constituency for foreign aid.

Gaining the support of these two audiences required different approaches. The government had a built-in advantage among stakeholder groups in that these groups were well aware of the complex and growing needs of the underdeveloped world and understood that a large-scale intervention was needed to address them. Efforts to build support among stakeholder groups were, therefore, focused primarily on policy and funding.

The electorate was also increasingly aware of the needs of the underdeveloped world. However, the electorate's understanding of these needs generally lacked the depth necessary to appreciate immediately why a problem that had always primarily been addressed through private charity now required government intervention. Furthermore, foreign aid had to compete for funding and public support with other new policy initiatives, like medicare, that had more direct impact on the everyday lives of Canadians.

Accordingly, it became clear that a compelling narrative would be essential to build broad-based public support for foreign aid. In order to define the national interest in aid, and thereby justify government involvement, successive Canadian ministries made clear appeals to established notions of national identity, often portraying foreign aid as quintessentially "Canadian" and a clear extension of the role Canada ought to be playing in the world. These same governments also took steps to enable their stakeholder partners to amplify and legitimate these narratives of support for foreign aid.

However, the presence of a compelling narrative for government-sponsored foreign aid did not, in itself, ensure that a stable base of political support for foreign aid would emerge. Indeed, public support for foreign aid was often placed on unstable footing as a result of economic challenges, negative press coverage, and divisions within the foreign aid community.

Until recently these efforts to build public support for foreign aid and the challenges they faced have remained underexplored in the scholarly literature. Indeed, it has often been assumed by commentators that aid has no real domestic constituency, and historians like Adam Chapnick have described public support for foreign aid as "fickle and shallow."[1] The lack of domestic interest in aid is certainly reflected in the literature on the motivations underlying foreign aid policy, which has traditionally been outward looking.[2] However, aid practitioners, as well as scholars David Morrison, Tim Brodhead, Cranford Pratt, and Carol Lancaster have long claimed that complex networks of public support for aid do exist and can exert influence over policy under the right circumstances.[3] As Sean Mills has recently pointed out, the histories of these networks of public support are complex and only just beginning to be written.[4] Most of these recent histories explore how civil society has shaped Canadian aid policy, often apart from or in opposition to government. This chapter complements this literature by offering a preliminary overview of how governments framed foreign aid policy for their publics and attempted to build support for it through civil society networks.

The Colombo Plan and the Search for Narrative, 1950–1957

The federal government initially struggled to come up with a narrative to explain why it was launching its first foreign aid program, the Colombo Plan. The initial delay in framing foreign aid for the Canadian public can be explained in part by the small size of the program, which represented only one-tenth of one per cent of the federal budget in 1951.[5] However, the relatively small size of the program did not mean that it escaped public or media attention. During Prime Minister Louis St. Laurent's final six years in power, the foreign aid program was largely responsible for the near tripling of the budget of the Department of External Affairs.[6] The novelty of the foreign aid program and the fact that it was undertaking work that had traditionally been financed by private charity naturally piqued public interest. This increased interest forced a reluctant government to come to terms with how it was going to present foreign aid to Canadians.[7]

The St. Laurent government faced three practical challenges in framing foreign aid for the Canadian public. First, it could not rely on appeals to necessity or precedent to create a narrative for its aid policy. It would have not been immediately apparent to the lay Canadian why intervention by their government was necessary to shore up the underdeveloped world, as opposed to some combination of private charity and increased contributions from current and former colonial powers. As Jill Campbell-Miller explains elsewhere in this volume, there was some precedent for the Colombo Plan, but it was weak at best. Canada's reconstruction efforts in Europe after the Second World War provided a model of sorts, but unlike those efforts the Colombo Plan was focused on Commonwealth Asia, a distant corner of the world where few Canadians had any deep connections. Furthermore, Canada's most recent attempt at aid in Asia, a $C90 million reconstruction and export credit program offered to the Chinese Kuomintang government, had fared poorly. Indeed, it was so mired in controversy that critics dubbed it "Operation Sinkhole."[8]

Second, the difficulties presented by the lack of an obvious foreign aid narrative were compounded by the fact that the St. Laurent government's interests in the Colombo Plan were complex and difficult to present succinctly to the public. Traditionally, the Colombo Plan has been seen as driven by a desire to shore up the support and economic security of Commonwealth Asia during the Cold War.[9] However, ensuring "stability in backward countries" was only one of a number of Canadian interests listed in Colombo Plan briefing material.[10]

The crushing $13.5 billion war debt Britain owed to its current and former colonies was of equal concern to Canada at the Colombo Conference in January 1950. Canada had recently loaned the British $1.25 billion, and the fact that British were struggling to repay the $13.5 billion that they owed to their colonies did not bode well for Canada getting its money back.[11] As the British proposed to address their financial struggles by seeking economic concessions that would have harmed Canada, Ottawa's interest in Britain's finances becomes clear. How Canada's concerns about British finances related to the Colombo Plan and more broadly to regional security in Asia was, however, a bit more difficult to explain.

In essence, the Colombo Plan was designed to simultaneously address concerns about regional security in Asia and British finances by providing a source of funds to underwrite the kind of economic development that would shore up Britain's current and former Asian colonies against communist influence and do so in a way that would take pressure off the British to finance this economic development work directly through quickly repaying its war loans. To explain why it was participating in this scheme, the federal government essentially had to explain to Canadians that Britain's colonies had loaned it $13.5 billion during the Second World War which they now desperately needed back in order to fund the kind of economic development that would stave off communist advances. Canadians would then need to know that Britain could not afford to pay back these loans as a result of a complex financial crisis. Furthermore, Canadians would need to understand that this state of affairs threatened Canada, as it was against its long-term interests for communism to gain a stronger foothold in Asia because Canada also had an outstanding loan it needed the British to repay, and because the British were proposing to deal with their economic problems, in part, by seeking economic concessions that would have been harmful Canada. Add to this complexity the fact that the British financial crisis did not turn out to be as bad as economists originally thought it would be, and that communist-fuelled conflict on the Korean peninsula erupted much sooner than experts expected, and it becomes clear why it was difficult to define a narrative to sell the Colombo Plan to the Canadian public in the 1950s.

Third, the government faced a challenge in framing the Colombo Plan for the public because St. Laurent's cabinet was strongly divided as to whether and to what extent Canada should support it. Though Secretary of State for External Affairs Lester B. Pearson returned from the Colombo conference with a cautious enthusiasm for foreign aid, most ministers were either firmly against the scheme or, like St. Laurent, skeptical. By early 1951, Pearson was able to win over the Colombo Plan's most influential critic, Finance Minister Douglas Abbott, and a $25 million contribution was approved by the government, but the question of public approval remained open.[12]

With the Korean War now fully under way, the Colombo Plan's usefulness in the fight against communism offered a clear and convenient narrative and one that the government initially embraced. However, in the long term, this was a problematic narrative for the St. Laurent government because it did not reflect their apprehensions about the effectiveness of the Colombo Plan as a weapon in the fight against communism. Pearson admitted privately that at best the plan might provide partial immunity against "the attractions of Communism." At worst, however, the plan had the potential to divert funds that could more effectively be used to fight communism through rearmament.[13]

The government's inability to settle on a narrative was reflected in its initial reluctance to discuss the plan or even foreign aid more broadly. This reticence did not go unnoticed on the opposition benches. In June 1951, Progressive Conservative opposition spokesperson John Diefenbaker rose in the House of Commons to observe that as "far as the Colombo Plan is concerned, I doubt whether it has been sold to our own people. When I spoke about it on one occasion in this house I received three letters condemning me for supporting a proposition to give assistance to South America."[14] Diefenbaker's speech came at the tail end of a strong public outcry for Canada to do more to address an ongoing famine in India and was representative of broader frustration with the government's unwillingness to adequately engage with the Canadian public on the foreign aid file.

Indeed, St. Laurent's government was largely caught off guard by the public's demand for action during the 1951 Indian famine. A memorandum for Pearson, written at the height of the famine, notes that in light of the situation in India, the Colombo Plan has "manifested not only a surprising volume of editorial comment but a remarkable degree of enthusiasm for a Canadian contribution."[15] Though the famine subsided before the government was able to pull together a Canadian response, it took careful note of public interest in the file, as well as the criticisms levelled. The result was a clear sense that the government would need to do a better job articulating its foreign aid policy.[16] As Greg Donaghy discusses elsewhere in this volume, the hiring of master storyteller Nik Cavell was particularly profitable in this regard.

A 1951 Department of External Affairs media survey indicated that the anti-communist narrative that the press attached to foreign aid in the early days of the Colombo Plan was gradually giving way to a more "humanitarian" narrative during the Indian famine.[17] In response, Pearson, who had always been uncomfortable with the idea of playing to communist fears when framing foreign aid for the Canadian public, began to abandon this narrative for a more humanitarian one. By the mid-1950s, the St. Laurent government as a whole began to mirror this shift toward a more moralisitic and internationalist tone. Speeches emerging from ministers' offices began to emphasize Canada's obligations to the developing world and how increasing interdependence in the global community placed "upon the favoured peoples of the world the obligation to remember what they

Ted Cogan

owe to other nations and peoples of the world less fortunate than themselves."[18] This moral internationalist framework was designed to appeal to Canadians' increasing sense of themselves as a "middle power" that could make meaningful contributions to the improvement of the postwar world.

Diefenbaker and the Commonwealth Turn, 1957–1963

Diefenbaker faced few of the challenges that St. Laurent confronted when trying to garner support for foreign aid from the Canadian public. By the time Diefenbaker was elected in June 1957, foreign aid had overcome its growing pains. Diefenbaker even presided over a popular expansion and reorganization of Canada's foreign aid program. Initially, his government seemed to understand the interest of certain segments of the Canadian public in the program. His first secretary of state for external affairs, Sidney Smith, said there was no policy area that "should receive greater approval and endorsation [sic] from Canadians," and Diefenbaker's personal interest is well established in his memoirs, which contain a strong defence of his foreign aid record.[19]

The Diefenbaker government also benefited, at least early on, from the fact that it had a clear vision of where foreign aid fit in its broader international policy goals and how it planned to appeal to Canadians' shared identities to win support for its aid policy. Diefenbaker's foreign policy was ultimately rooted in a desire to preserve Canadian autonomy in global affairs. He was neither the rabid anti-American that some have accused him of being, nor did he make a habit of letting his personal affinity for Crown and Commonwealth get in the way of acting in Canada's best interest.[20] Rather, Diefenbaker saw the Commonwealth as a force strong enough to balance an ever-increasing American influence that he felt threatened Canada's independence.

In the Colombo Plan, Diefenbaker saw an opportunity to build a stronger Commonwealth and for Canada to play a leadership role in a global arena that was not quite so dominated by the Americans. This had strong appeal, and in the months immediately following the 1958 election, a 34-page policy memorandum was written that outlined an aid strategy that vigorously promoted Commonwealth identity.[21] Diefenbaker was clear that "the first consideration in external aid programs should be to raise

FIGURE 8.1
Successive Liberal and Conservative governments promoted the Colombo Plan as
quintessentially Canadian. Canada Post issued a stamp in June 1961 to mark the plan's tenth
anniversary, highlighting Canada's signature contribution in Pakistan, the Warsak Dam.
(Source: Canada Post/LAC)

the standard of living within the Commonwealth, for I consider the Commonwealth the greatest instrument for freedom the world has ever seen."[22] This strategy was reflected in speeches and other public engagements that emphasized the Colombo Plan's Commonwealth origins and how it could instill shared values, promote cooperation, and ultimately create a more peaceful world.[23]

In the early years of his mandate, Diefenbaker backed this rhetoric with significant investments in foreign aid funding. Most of these investments were rolled out as part of the 1958 Commonwealth Economic and Trade Conference in Montreal after other Commonwealth economic programs failed to come to fruition. This turned the Montreal Conference into a launching pad of sorts for new Commonwealth aid initiatives. The most significant announcement was a $15 million increase in the Colombo Plan budget to $50 million a year for three years, fully double its original budget.[24]

The Diefenbaker government underscored the notion that foreign aid was compatible with Canadian ideals by emphasizing how foreign aid was a modern interpretation of long-held Canadian values of generosity and mutual assistance. The paper outlining the government's public relations strategy for aid suggested that it be portrayed as the modern equivalent of a working bee, as a gathering of Commonwealth neighbours from which Canada had benefited in the past during its "pioneering days" and to which it now owed a debt of service.[25]

This narrative was moderately successful in reaching Canadians in the early years of Diefenbaker's government, whose efforts received a broadly positive, if subdued, reception from the public and the press.[26] However, public opinion of Diefenbaker's aid policy began to change in 1960 as a result of a series of factors both within and outside his control. Most important, the prime minister was unable to adapt his messaging on Commonwealth solidarity to suit the decade's significant transformations in national identity.

Debates over the role nuclear weapons would play in Canadian defence policy in the early 1960s sparked a wave of peace activism that spanned the country. Calls for the defence budget to be slashed in favour of increased foreign aid became increasingly commonplace.[27] Well publicized humanitarian crises and the proliferation of "starving baby appeals" in an increasingly visual media landscape also led to frequent calls for more aid.[28] Canadians wrote to Diefenbaker complaining of lost sleep, telling stories of the images of "hungry faces" that were burned into their minds, and pleading emotionally for guidance on what to do.[29] At the same time, Diefenbaker's capacity to respond to these calls was shrinking as the postwar economic boom that had underwritten much of the aid growth in the first half of his mandate weakened, plunging Canada into a recession in 1960.[30]

Diefenbaker's own attitude toward aid also deteriorated sharply following US president John F. Kennedy's visit to Ottawa in May 1961. During the visit, Kennedy asked the prime minister to increase Canada's foreign aid commitment. Diefenbaker, facing economic problems at home, rejected the request, telling one advisor bluntly, "I'm going to think of Canada for the next 14, 15, 16, or 18 months."[31] He conveyed this to Kennedy, who nevertheless used a parliamentary address to press Canada to "do more," blindsiding his host.[32] Kennedy's appeal was enthusiastically endorsed by the press but firmly rebuffed by an angry Diefenbaker as "something we cannot accept."[33]

Under pressure at home and abroad, Diefenbaker instinctively defended his foreign aid record through a Commonwealth lens. He assured Canadians that the country was doing its part for its most important Commonwealth allies. However, this defence too often came across as an appeal to Empire and was increasingly ineffective in a nation that was turning away from thinking of itself in British terms and looking for opportunities to define its own place in global affairs. Diefenbaker's decision to cut Commonwealth aid by $8.5 million in 1962–63 largely destroyed the credibility of this already ineffective defence. The cuts were widely decried as "a posture of gross national callousness."[34]

The challenges Diefenbaker faced in building public support for foreign aid were highlighted again when aid re-emerged as an issue in the 1963 election campaign. Two weeks before Canadians were set to vote, retired US general Lucius Clay, whom Kennedy appointed to lead an inquiry into American foreign aid, released comments critical of Canada's aid record. The Canadian press jumped on the comments, siding with the general.[35] Diefenbaker's instinct was, once again, to invoke the Commonwealth and disparage the American "interlopers." With typical bluster he exclaimed: "When some other nations start pointing out to us what we should do let me tell you this, that Canada was in both wars a long time before some other nations came in. . . . Let it be clear that in the last war for a period of 15 or 18 months, freedom was in the custody of the British Commonwealth of Nations. . . . We don't need any lessons as to what Canada should do after the record of service in two world wars."[36] Diefenbaker's argument was that Canada needed to assert its independence from American dominance in the aid field and that the Commonwealth was the obvious vehicle through which it could do this, as it had always been. His problem was that Canadian support for the United States was on the rise, in no small part due to Kennedy's charismatic appeal.[37] Moreover, those Canadians concerned about American dominance were increasingly drawn to the views of politicians like Walter Gordon, who offered a vision of an independent Canada that required no Commonwealth counterbalance.[38] Diefenbaker's rhetoric, wrapped in the language of Empire, appeared hopelessly out of date.

Pearson and Internationalist Aid, 1963–1968

This sense that Diefenbaker was stuck in the past, when combined with indecision about nuclear questions and continuing economic problems, saddled him with a reputation as an ineffective and indecisive leader who did not understand the role Canadians wanted their nation to play in a rapidly changing world. This created an opening for Prime Minister Lester B. Pearson's Liberals, who won the 1963 election. As part of his foreign policy platform, Pearson campaigned against the Progressive Conservative cuts to foreign aid, and his victory gave him room to increase Canadian foreign aid substantially, pushing funding to new levels and tapping new sources of public support.

In terms of foreign aid leadership, especially on the political level, the Pearson years were unmatched. Pearson's history with the file combined with the personal commitment to aid that both he and Secretary of State for External Affairs Paul Martin exhibited created unrivalled opportunities for growth. It was also a key time in the transition between identities in Canada.

Though an Anglophile, Pearson found the trappings of Empire "tiring" and largely abandoned Diefenbaker's Commonwealth aid rhetoric. This was part of a broader shift away from the idea of balancing American and British influence and toward embracing an identity that was homegrown, or at least presented as such.[39] To this end, Pearson moved to create a Canadian flag, establish a Canadian national anthem, and reconcile Canada's historic linguistic and cultural duality. On the aid front, Pearson offered a reinvigorated version of the internationalist message he had employed during the St. Laurent years. He also took significant steps to build public support beyond the usual speeches and media liaison.

The Pearson government's messaging on foreign aid reflected the internationalism of its leader, often emphasizing that "the great purpose of international statesmanship today must be to improve the living standards of all the world's peoples and to make possible a better life for all."[40] Pearson often insisted that aid ought to be more than charity, that it was best understood as an obligation and a moral imperative. While in opposition Pearson clearly articulated this point in a speech at McGill University, saying that Canadians must "root out of our minds the idea, and reject the attitudes that flow from it, that this kind of assistance is a form of charity; 'baksheesh' for the poor neighbour. It is no more charity than the obligation of a more fortunate province in our own federation to assist the less wealthy by equalisation payments imposed on the taxpayer through federal legislation."[41]

It was no mistake that Pearson mentioned foreign aid and equalization payments in the same breath. For Pearson, "nationalism and internationalism were two sides of the same coin."[42] His vision of a more equal and united Canada was inextricably linked to his vision of a more equal and united world. Consequently, when his government presented foreign aid to the Canadian public, it played heavily on themes of international involvement, peace, and unity, themes that were important to Canadians, emphasizing their independence and national pride.

Of course, the moral imperatives present in Pearson's foreign aid policy were accompanied by strategic calculations. Internationalism is predicated on the assumption that the fate of any one state is highly dependent on the well-being of other states. Accordingly, the Pearson government adopted a foreign aid policy that focused on expanding the geographic reach of Canadian aid and, in particular, encouraging multilateral cooperation. The end goal was to increase the breadth and impact of Canadian aid, thereby increasing international unity and decreasing the potential for economically motivated conflict.[43]

Much of the actual work of fulfilling this vision was left to Martin, whose support of foreign aid eclipsed his leader's in many ways.[44] Martin announced a substantial renewal of the aid program in November 1963 that expanded its financial and geographic scope. He secured cabinet approval for a policy that aimed to spend $400 million, or 0.7 per cent of GNP, on aid by 1969–1970 as well as another $150 million for a concessional loan program.[45] Martin also doubled the amount of money that Canada spent on multilateral aid, eventually reaching five times the Organisation for Economic Co-operation and Development average on multilateral aid.[46] Furthermore, he secured approval for a substantial geographic expansion of the aid program, which soon came to embrace the Caribbean, French Africa, and Latin America. The growth of the French African aid program was especially important in securing increased support for foreign aid in

Quebec, where there was increasing agitation for a foreign policy that better reflected the country's cultural duality.

The Pearson government also took a significant interest in expanding and formalizing relationships with two other key stakeholder groups, NGOs and business, in an effort to grow domestic support for foreign aid. The Canadian University Service Overseas (CUSO) received the External Aid Office's (EAO) first NGO grant, over Martin's initial objections, in part because there was a strong hope that returned CUSO volunteers would play a key role in building support for foreign aid in Canada.[47] To build on public interest in Canada's 1967 Centennial celebrations the Pearson government also worked with NGOs to present the Centennial International Development Programme (CIDP). This program leveraged the idea of Canada providing a "birthday gift" to the developing world during the centennial year as a means to educate Canadians about foreign aid through community teach-ins and Miles for Millions walkathons.[48]

Similarly, the government tried to build greater support for foreign aid in the business community by hiring a director general for the External Aid Office (EAO) with private sector roots. Herbert Moran, the incumbent, was a talented administrator but limited in his capacity to innovate or build bridges with the private sector. Roby Kidd, director of the Overseas Institute of Canada, pressed the need for change in a letter to Martin. Kidd was adamant that now was "not the time for a routine appointment giving reward to an able and faithful civil servant." Ottawa needed "a Director General who will not only keep costs down . . . and get along well with your department but will stimulate business, university and other organizations to pull their weight."[49] The advice of Kidd and others was heeded, and the Pearson government chose Maurice Strong, the dynamic young president of Power Corporation, as the EAO's next director general.[50] Strong was given a clear mandate to "encourage greater participation in international development on the part of the private sector in Canada."[51]

Enthusiasm for new partnerships, public participation, and for foreign aid in general reached its zenith around this time. Former diplomat and Glendon College president Escott Reid delivered an address that echoed across the country, calling for a second golden age of Canadian foreign policy rooted in a "Canadian crusade . . . against world poverty."[52] Media coverage of foreign aid was extensive and broad ranging.[53] Canadians who wrote on the subject to Pearson and Martin were frequently supportive, often effusively so, and encouraged them to do more. "My wife and I want to express to you our joy in hearing that your government has decided to increase foreign aid by 50%," wrote Flemming Holm, a typical correspondent. "We hope that . . . further increases will soon be made in these very constructive efforts to build world peace, welfare, and good will."[54]

However, like the Diefenbaker government, Pearson's government faced increasing challenges on the aid file that made it difficult to keep pace with public opinion and demands for aid growth. Higher inflation meant that more of the new revenue the government realized from economic growth had to be used to cover the its own rising costs. This meant that, short of raising taxes, there was less "new money" to be spent on aid and that the money that was being spent was less effective. It also put pressure on Canadian pocketbooks and led to demands that aid spending be restrained in favour of domestic economic assistance.

Moreover, Pearson faced a changing media landscape that was becoming more adversarial toward political leaders and focusing more on investigative journalism.[55] This shift resulted in the first widely published foreign aid scandals, including coverage of unspent foreign aid funds, allegations that a large shipment of powdered milk was wasted as a result of substandard packaging, and a two-month-long saga involving substandard medical aid for Vietnam that resulted in parliamentary hearings. This increase in coverage, and the fact that it was far less deferential to the government, prompted more and more Canadians to question the wisdom of Pearson's approach to foreign aid.[56] These economic and reputational challenges led to an increasingly volatile mixture of Canadians who were disappointed with the government's aid record on the one hand, and of Canadians who felt that aid should be slashed in favour of aiding economically distressed Canadians on the other. Typical of the former group was Iain Macdonald, who wrote to tell Pearson that many Canadians "remain quite discontent with current governmental attitudes towards foreign aid in general. That Canada should remain tenth among nations in such a vital matter is to me, in considering your own experience and record, not quite comprehensible."[57] Macdonald's views toward aid contrast sharply with those of Roy Keitges, who wrote to tell Pearson "that any political leader who announced that he was going to eliminate all foreign aid and spend the money in Canada for Canadians would receive the largest majority of votes ever recorded in a Canadian election."[58] Pearson never tested this theory and left office having substantially expanded the foreign aid program in both financial and geographic terms and having engaged with the public and stakeholder groups in new and meaningful ways. This did not mean, however, that all those who were newly, or more deeply, engaged with aid supported the government's approach to the file.

Trudeau's Troubling Times, 1968–1980

While public support for foreign aid remained strong into the early Trudeau years, it was clear that significant tensions between aid advocates and the government were brewing just below the surface. The environment in which these tensions began to surface was strongly influenced by Trudeau's own complex engagement with aid policy and foreign policy in general. He had no intention of "owning" the file, in the manner Pearson had, but was strongly committed to pursuing a new bureaucratic and policy posture at External Affairs.[59]

In a philosophical sense, Trudeau's geopolitical outlook on aid did not differ significantly from Pearson's. Trudeau shared the internationalist perspective that aid, properly conceived, could help promote international unity and decrease the potential for economically motivated conflict. However, he eschewed the moralism that defined Pearson's mandate and was privately critical of the idea that the underdeveloped world could ever achieve living standards comparable to Canada.[60] Accordingly, the Trudeau government's practical approach to foreign aid, as outlined in its comprehensive foreign policy review, focused on promoting foreign aid that was more directly tied to Canada's domestic interests and produced demonstrable and "lasting improvement[s]" in the underdeveloped world.[61]

Trudeau also had a keen personal interest in the developing world, one that reflected his views on Canadian identity. He felt that aid was one of the areas in which Canada could make a difference, and saw it as an area of foreign affairs through which Canada could express its cultural duality. As a result, in its initial years the Trudeau government was enthusiastic about foreign aid and made significant efforts to grow public support. However, as political and economic challenges arose in the later years of its first mandate, enthusiasm waned and the spotlight the Trudeau government had once shone on foreign aid dimmed.

Trudeau was not above playing to the crowd when discussing foreign aid, even declaring in 1968 that "the world must be our constituency."[62] However, he made it clear that Canada could not "afford to cling to the conceptions and role-casting which served us in our international endeavours of three decades or more."[63] He went on to insist that his government would "be exploring all means of increasing the impact of our aid programmes by concentrating on places and projects in which our bilingualism, our own expertise and experience, our resources and facilities, make possible an effective and distinctively Canadian contribution."[64]

This exploration took the form of a formal aid policy review published in 1970 as part of his broader review of Canadian diplomacy. The review reflected Trudeau's sense of Canada's global identity, skillfully merging his internationalism with a commitment to the developing world and an insistence that foreign policy better reflect domestic interests. In defining a new public narrative for foreign aid the report contended that a "society able to ignore poverty abroad will find it much easier to ignore it at home; a society concerned about poverty and development abroad will be concerned about poverty and development at home. We could not create a truly just society within Canada if we were not prepared to play our part in the creation of a more just world society. Thus our foreign policy in this field becomes a continuation of our domestic policy."[65]

This subtle turn away from Pearson's overt moralism toward a narrative that more explicitly included domestic aims was accompanied by plans to further increase engagement with key stakeholder groups and to further broaden the franchise of foreign aid in Canada through communication and education programs.

Significant progress was made when the External Aid Office was transformed into the Canadian International Development Agency in 1968. The increased resources put at CIDA's disposal permitted signifcant growth in communications work. Most notably, CIDA's Information Division was upgraded to become the Communications Branch in 1971 and began to produce more innovative public relations material. In an attempt to better inform and educate the public, by the mid-1970s, CIDA had developed three major new publications. *Contact*, a monthly newsletter, and *Cooperation*

Canada, a bimonthly magazine, combined CIDA news with general international development content in order to broaden their appeal, especially as educational resources. CIDA also published *Action*, a tabloid featuring the work of Canadian NGOs, four times a year.[66] In addition, CIDA began to devote significantly more effort to the production of educational resources, including classroom kits and films.

However, the principal means by which CIDA sought to grow public support was through partnerships with stakeholder groups, especially NGOs, churches, universities, and businesses.[67] Among these groups, NGOs were the most important allies and were seen as having the greatest potential to condition public opinion. In building bridges with the organizations, CIDA benefited substantially from its decision to hire individuals like Lewis Perinbam. As Kevin Brushett discusses in Chapter 7, Perinbam played a pivotal role in growing CIDA's first formal NGO program. Under his watch, support for NGOs increased from an original budget of only $5 million to over $78 million a decade later.[68] Even more important for the agency's public engagement activities was the founding of CIDA's Development Education Program in 1971. This program provided funding for groups like the Canadian Council for International Co-operation and CUSO to provide formal development education programs to the Canadian public.

Informal lectures by returned missionaries and volunteers had long been a staple of Canada's church basements and community halls, but there was a sense within government and the broader aid community by the early 1970s that this sort of ad hoc educational programming was ineffective at driving public support. A report written for the CCIC in 1973 argued that "what Canadians understand about the Third World is generally primitive: starving children, 'primitive' living conditions, lack of technology, 'inferior' cultures. Consequently, their desire to relate to the Third World is not matched by the knowledge to do so in an informed and effective way."[69] To tackle this problem, the CCIC created the Development Education Animateur Programme (DEAP), one of the earliest and most influential public education programs funded by CIDA. DEAP helped precipitate a shift in public education about development away from "saying that conditions of underdevelopment exist" toward explorations of "why they exist."[70] As a result, many NGOs began devoting more of their resources to small

FIGURE 8.2

As public support for CIDA declined in the mid-1970s, CIDA stepped up its information programming. This CIDA poster from the 1980s trumpets the agency's efforts to deliver food aid. (Source: Lucie Chantal/LAC e-999920124-u)

grassroots educational efforts that allowed them to make stronger connections to their communities and better educate Canadians about the need for aid.

This shift by no means marked the end of larger consciousness-raising efforts. While NGOs like the CCIC and CUSO were developing grassroots programming, Canada's major Christian churches (Anglican, Catholic, Lutheran, Presbyterian, and United) launched a new large-scale development education campaign, Ten Days for World Development, that was strongly supported by the federal government. Ten Days was launched in 1971 to leverage the long-standing involvement of Canada's churches in development work and their unrivalled weekly attendance of 8.3 million people to bring the message of development to Canadians who were not attracted to programs like DEAP.[71] Ten Days focused on local events that would appeal to a broad array of Canadians, including sermons, hunger suppers, poster exhibitions, essay contests, and panel discussions. The organization also sponsored a high-impact national program that used church leaders and prominent speakers from the developing world to garner significant media attention.[72]

At the same time, the federal government pursued a stronger relationship with the university community. Universities represented a unique nexus of individuals responsible for shaping the next generation of Canadians and individuals with the technical expertise to help shape development policy and support increasingly sophisticated development projects. As early as 1951, St. Laurent recognized the important role universities could play in "increasing understanding and co-operation amongst peoples of the world."[73] It is not unsurprising then that the federal government began funding university-based development research, field work, and programming on an ad hoc basis in the 1950s. What followed was a substantial push for the "internationalisation" of Canadian universities. In 1961 the state of the so-called "international curriculum" focused on the Global South in Canadian universities was described as "inexcusable" and "a sad disservice to the present generation of university students."[74] Reports were commissioned, and curriculums gradually improved through the 1960s. In 1970, "research into the problems of the developing world" was given a significant boost when the federal government authorized the creation of the International Development Research Centre, though universities remained concerned that its focus would be too narrow to support all the projects they wished to undertake.[75] Consequently, CIDA commissioned two more reports on partnerships between the university community and the government. Eight years of committee hearings and further studies followed until CIDA finally created an Educational Institutions Program within the NGO Division to liaise with universities. This program was upgraded to division status in 1980 in further recognition of the importance of partnerships with the university sector.[76]

Simultaneously, the government was rapidly expanding its partnerships with the business community. During the Trudeau government's foreign policy review the Department of Trade and Commerce had argued forcefully that Canada's foreign aid should better reflect its commercial interests. While aid never became as commercially oriented as Trade and Commerce would have liked, significant shifts in that direction did occur in the Trudeau years. A formal Business and Industry program was created in 1969 and was substantially expanded with the creation of the Industrial Cooperation Program in 1978. In a concerted effort to expand the base of foreign aid, this program shifted the focus of CIDA's dealings with the business community from large resource, engineering, and consulting firms to small and medium-size businesses. Efforts were also made to help Canadian businesses win more multilateral aid contracts and to encourage them to import more goods from the developing world. These programs were popular within the business community, and a substantial increase in CIDA's financial commitments to business partnerships followed as a result, with funding increasing from $250,000 in 1977–78 to $7.2 million in 1980–81.[77] The programs were equally popular within government for creating, as one official put it, a lot of "small winners" in the business community who were now more meaningfully engaged with aid policy.[78]

Despite Trudeau's efforts to expand the foreign aid franchise and grow public support for its aid activities, his government, like its predecessors, faced several challenges in managing public engagement. First, and most important, there was a split in the base of public support between Canadians who supported foreign aid on traditional charitable terms and Canadians who supported newer and more radical development philosophies. The former group continued to support foreign aid, much as they had since the 1950s, by urging through letters, petitions, editorials, and other means

Ted Cogan

that the government "accelerate the assistance it is giving to developing countries."[79] However, emboldened in part by their success in securing the reluctant Trudeau government's support for relief efforts in Biafra, many NGOs and their supporters began to take a more combative stance toward official foreign aid policy.[80] Funding increases were quickly replaced by systemic change as the primary goal of many of Canada's most influential international development advocates. This shift was part of a global movement of advocacy inspired by the rise of dependency theory, a call for a systemic redistribution of global wealth in favour of the developing world that grew in popularity in the late 1960s and 1970s.[81]

During this time Canada's major Christian churches attempted to build a formal "Coalition for Development" made up of a broad range of civil society groups that recognized that "the North American economic system from which we benefit so liberally is an exploitive system that takes more from the developing world than it gives"[82] The coalition folded after only a few years, largely because it lacked stable funding, but many of its former members continued to work together to press the government for systemic change. The churches developed project GATT Fly to research and advocate for fairer international trade practices, DEAP began to focus its education efforts on the role of social change in achieving economic development, and CUSO moved away from its "do-gooder" past toward a highly political, "more active, more public identification with the unrepresented of the world."[83] This shift toward advocacy of systemic change in the global economy put many of these groups on a collision course with the federal government, still wedded to the existing liberal international order. The vast majority of development NGOs, including church development organizations, received a large proportion of their funding through CIDA, and most of these grants required that the funds not be used in support of domestic political advocacy. Yet many NGOs believed that true development could only be achieved by levelling the economic playing field at home as well as globally. Consequently, they could hardly avoid expressing opinions on domestic economic and social issues, inviting conflict with their Ottawa funders. In the late 1970s, the government clamped down on the use of CIDA funds by NGOs for domestic purposes, destroying any hope of meaningful cooperation between NGOs and the government to build support for foreign aid.

Meanwhile, outside the NGO community, the prospect of encouraging more Canadians to support aid was hindered by mounting spending scandals, a spate of negative media reports, and another economic downturn. In the mid-1970s Canadian newspapers, especially the new *Toronto Sun*, began to report heavily on CIDA mismanagement and waste with blazing tabloid headlines like "CIDA: Is it a Sick Joke?" "The Trouble with Foreign Aid," "CIDA Shenanigans in Haiti," and "What's Going on at CIDA?"[84] Though the level of coverage was, at times, unjustified, there was certainly no shortage of problems in Canada's foreign aid regime, a fact borne out by reports from the Auditor General in 1976 and 1979. These reports identified a worrying lack of financial controls alongside a host of policy blunders. Canadians erupted angrily at the loss of improperly packaged seed potatoes worth $60,000, and sighed with despair at the $1.4 million spent to refit the *MV Gulf Guard*, a fishing boat repeatedly refused by the Columbian government as "unsuitable."[85] These blunders were amplified by the media and, after 1976, by the white supremacist–led Citizens for Foreign Aid Reform (C-FAR), which injected unprecedented vitriol into the debate. Letters to the prime minister became more pointed. It is "bad enough that we allow a horde of employables [sic] at home to collect unemployment money," wrote H. L. Blatchford, "but why are we giving $633.8 millions of our citizens' hard-earned cash to indigent strangers."[86]

Blatchford's letter also hints at the other major obstacle to growing support for foreign aid during the Trudeau years—the economy. Trudeau and his chief foreign policy advisor Ivan Head were, in fact, supportive of some of the systemic changes to the global economic order advocated by Canadian NGOs and their supporters.[87] In 1975, against the advice of the Department of External Affairs, Trudeau had even called for the advent of a global economic system that was "truly universal and not confined to or favouring groups defined along geographic or linguistic or ideological or religious or any other lines."[88] Privately, however, he recognized that there was little political support at home for changes in economic policy that would devastate the low-tech manufacturing sector in Canada by permitting the widespread entry of cheaper goods from the developing world. This was especially true in the aftermath of the 1973 oil crisis, which helped generate a prolonged period of economic malaise in Canada.

Ted Cogan

The effect of this economic downturn and CIDA's flagging reputation is clearly reflected in Gallup polls from the era. Support for foreign aid expansion among Canadians surveyed fell from 60 per cent in 1974 to 51 per cent in 1978.[89] This shift in public support, combined with more limited economic resources and widespread reports of mismanagement within CIDA, resulted in the first cuts to foreign aid since 1962. Between 1978 and 1980 the foreign aid budget was cut by over $33 million. More significant "cuts" came at the end of the fiscal year as CIDA lost its special authority to roll over unspent funds from year to year in 1978. By 1980, CIDA had lapsed or left unspent over $300 million.[90]

Conclusion

It is impossible to say if these cuts would have been smaller or less money would have been left on the table if relations among foreign aid stakeholders had been better in the late 1970s. A great many externalities influence foreign aid policy, and given the formidable challenges inherent in international development work it can be easy to forget the role played by domestic electorates. However, it is clear that after initially struggling to define a public narrative for foreign aid, successive federal governments have paid a great deal of attention to how aid is presented to the Canadian public. These portrayals most often reflected the incumbent government's view of Canadian identity and of Canada's place in the world, from the more internationalist view of the St. Laurent and Pearson years to the Commonwealth-focused narrative of the Diefenbaker years to the hybrid approach taken during the Trudeau years. These portrayals also influenced the direct appeals and stakeholder partnerships that Canadian governments nurtured to expand and solidify a political base for aid. Expansion proved easier than consolidation. In good times, Canadians were eager to support foreign aid and the opportunities for international involvement it presented. In the face scandal or economic malaise, however, support for foreign aid was often more tepid. Despite significant efforts and ever more sophisticated techniques, between 1950 and 1980 federal governments only managed to build and maintain an unstable base of support for foreign aid in Canada. Given the natural ebb and flow of the economic cycle and the propensity for challenges to arise when executing complex development projects in distant countries, this was, perhaps, all that could realistically expected.

Notes

1   Carol Lancaster, *Transforming Foreign Aid: United States Assistance in the 21st Century* (Washington, DC: Peterson Institute, 2000), 50. Adam Chapnick, "The Politics of Reforming Canada's Foreign Aid Policy," in *Struggling for Effectiveness: CIDA and Canadian Foreign Aid*, ed. Stephen Brown (Montreal: McGill-Queen's University Press, 2012), 312.

2   See, for example: Kim Richard Nossal, "Mixed Motives Revisited: Canada's Interest in Development Assistance," *Canadian Journal of Political Science* 21, no. 1 (1988): 35–56; Réal Lavergne, "Determinants of Canadian Aid Policy," in *Western Middle Powers and Global Poverty: The Determinants of the Aid Policies of Canada, Denmark, the Netherlands, Norway and Sweden*, ed. Olav Stokke (Uppsala, Sweden: Scandinavian Institute of African Studies, 1989), 33–89; Roger Young, "Canadian Foreign Aid: Facing a Crisis of its Own?," *Journal of Canadian Studies* 19, no. 4 (1985): 28–41; Phillip Rawkins, "An Institutional Analysis of CIDA," in *Canadian International Development Assistance Polices: An Appraisal*, ed. Cranford Pratt (Montreal: McGill-Queen's University Press, 1994), 156–85. Robert Carty, Virginia Smith, and Latin American Working Group, *Perpetuating Poverty: The Political Economy of Canadian Foreign Aid* (Toronto: Between the Lines, 1981); Richard Swift and Robert Clarke, eds., *Ties that Bind: Canada and the Third World* (Toronto: Between the Lines, 1982); Jamie Swift and Brian Tomlinson, eds., *Conflicts of Interest: Canada and the Third World* (Toronto: Between the Lines, 1991); Grant L. Reuber, "The Trade-Offs among the Objectives of Canadian Foreign Aid," *International Journal* 25, no.1 (1969): 131; Peyton V. Lyon, R. B. Byers, and D. Leyton-Brown, "How Official Ottawa Views the Third World," *International Perspectives* (Jan.–Feb. 1979): 12; Cranford Pratt, "Ethics and Foreign Policy: The Case of Canada's Development Assistance," *International Journal* 43, no. 2 (1988): 264–301; Douglas Roche, *Justice not Charity: A New Global Ethic for Canada* (Toronto: McClelland and Stewart, 1976); Peter Wyse, *Canadian Foreign Aid in the 1970s: An Organizational Audit* (Montreal: Centre for Developing Area Studies, McGill University, 1983); Keith Spicer, *A Samaritan State? External Aid in Canada's Foreign Policy* (Toronto: University of Toronto Press, 1966), 11; Michael Tucker, *Canadian Foreign Policy: Contemporary Issues and Themes* (Toronto: McGraw-Hill Ryerson, 1980), 234–36.

3   David R. Morrison, *Aid and Ebb Tide: A History of CIDA and Canadian Development Assistance* (Waterloo, ON: Wilfrid Laurier University Press, 1998), 442, 451; Tim Brodhead and Cranford Pratt, "Paying the Piper: CIDA and Canadian NGOs," in *Canadian International Development Assistance Policies: An Appraisal*, ed. Cranford Pratt (Montreal: McGill-Queen's University Press, 1994), 96; Cranford Pratt, "Humane Internationalism and Canadian Development Assistance Policies," in *Canadian*

International Development Assistance Policies: An Appraisal, ed. Cranford Pratt (Montreal: McGill-Queen's University Press, 1994), 334; Lancaster, *Transforming Foreign Aid*, 50; Carol Lancaster, *Foreign Aid: Diplomacy, Development, Domestic Politics* (Chicago: University of Chicago Press, 2007), 21–22.

4   Sean Mills, "Popular Internationalism: Grassroots Exchange and Social Movements," in *Canada and the Third World: Overlapping Histories*, ed. Karen Dubinsky, Sean Mills, and Scott Rutherford (Toronto: University of Toronto Press, 2016), 246.

5   Canada, Department of Finance, *Public Accounts of Canada for the Fiscal Year Ended March 31, 1951 and Report of the Auditor General* (Ottawa: King's Printer, 1951).

6   Canada, Department of Finance, *Public Accounts of Canada for the Fiscal Year Ended March 31, 1957* (Ottawa: Queen's Printer, 1957).

7   See Andrew Brewin, "We Can't Sidetrack Economic Aid," *People's Weekly*, 30 September 1950; "We Can't Dodge This," *Saturday Night*, 7 November 1950; "What Is Canada Doing?" *Globe and Mail*, 23 January 1951.

8   Andrew Brewin, "Canadian Economic Assistance to Under-Developed Areas," *International Journal* 5, no. 4 (1950): 306; Robert B. Bryce, *Canada and the Cost of World War II: The International Operations of Canada's Department of Finance, 1939–1947*, ed. Matthew J. Bellamy (Montreal: McGill-Queen's University Press, 2005), 158, 163.

9   Morrison, *Aid and Ebb Tide*, 1.

10   Section 38 Technical Assistance for Economic Development of Under-Developed Countries, Undated, Lester B. Pearson Papers (LBP), vol. 22, file: Commonwealth Foreign Ministers Conference – 1950, Library and Archives Canada (LAC).

11   Curt Cardwell, *NSC 68 and the Political Economy of the Early Cold War* (New York: Cambridge University Press, 2011), 133.

12   Abbott to Pearson, 30 January 1951, Douglas LePan Papers (DVL), vol. 7, file 73 – Colombo Plan, LAC; Cabinet Conclusions, 7 February 1951, Privy Council Office Records (PCO), vol. 2647, LAC.

13   Pearson to Abbott, 17 January 1951, DVL Papers, vol. 2, file 13, SSEA – Memoranda, telegrams, etc., LAC.

14   Canada, House of Commons, *Debates*, 15 June 1951, 4168.

15   Memorandum for the Minister: Proposal for New Offer of Wheat to India, 4 May 1951, DVL Papers, vol. 7, file 74 – Colombo Plan, LAC.

16   On the challenges the St. Laurent government faced in getting its foreign policy message out through the media, see Patrick H. Brennan, *Reporting the Nation's Business: Press-Government Relations During the Liberal Years, 1935–1957* (Toronto: University of Toronto Press, 1994).

17   Ibid.

18   Lester B. Pearson, "The World We Live In" (statement to the Seventh International Conference of Social Work, Toronto, 27 June 1954), Department of External Affairs (DEA), *Statements and Speeches* 54/34.

19   Sidney Smith, "Aspects of Canadian Foreign Policy" (statement in the House of Commons, Ottawa, 26 November 1957), DEA, *Statements and Speeches* 57/44; John G. Diefenbaker, *One Canada: Memoirs of the Right Hon. John G. Diefenbaker*, vol. 2 (Toronto: Macmillan, 1976), 74, 108, 110, 114–18, 126–28, 137, 140–47, 163, 183–84, 192–94, 199, 200–201, 203.

20   On Diefenbaker's supposed extreme anti-Americanism, see Jamie Glazov, *Canadian Policy Toward Khrushchev's Soviet Union* (Montreal: McGill-Queen's University Press, 2002). For discussion of Diefenbaker's personal feelings toward the Crown and Commonwealth, see H. Basil Robinson, *Diefenbaker's World: A Populist in Foreign Affairs* (Toronto: University of Toronto Press, 1989), 4. For a discussion of Diefenbaker's practical approach to relations with Britain and the Commonwealth, see Bruce Muirhead, "From Dreams to Reality: The Evolution of Anglo-Canadian Trade During the Diefenbaker Era," *Journal of the Canadian Historical Association* 9, no. 1 (1998): 243–66.

21   This memorandum was most likely written by O. J. Firestone, a prominent economist in the Department of Trade and Commerce, though its authorship cannot be definitively attributed. Canada's Attitude Towards Less Developed Countries, 27 October 1958, John Diefenbaker Papers (JD), file F231 Foreign Aid 1958, Reel M-9425, LAC.

22   Diefenbaker, *One Canada*, 2:110–11.

23   See, for example, Diefenbaker, "The Living Commonwealth of Today" (address to the Commonwealth Trade Conference, Montreal, 18 September 1958), DEA, *Statements and Speeches* 58/36.

24   "Commonwealth Trade and Economic Conference," *External Affairs* 10, no. 10 (1958): 235–38.

25   Canada's Attitude Towards Less Developed Countries, 27 October 1958, JD Papers, file F231 Foreign Aid 1958, Reel M-9425, LAC.

26   For letters in support of Diefenbaker's foreign aid policy, see JD Papers, file 802 – Economic Assistance Abroad, Reel M-8900, LAC. This file also contains letters of opposition, though they were far fewer in number. For representative coverage in the media, see: "Canada Outdoes U.S. Assistance to Pakistanis," *Globe and Mail*, 15 July 1957; "Canada Planning More Foreign Aid Despite Few Mutterings," *Quebec Chronicle Telegraph*, 29 June 1958; "Canada Takes Part: Aid for Development Is Pledged to India," *Globe and Mail*, 29 August 1958; "Canada to Boost Economic Aid," *Globe and Mail*, 19 September 1958; "Foreign Aid Derby: Canada Has a Winner in Pakistan Dam," *Ottawa Journal*, 14 March 1959.

27   See, for example, Mrs. A. G. Blair to Diefenbaker, 26 May 1960, JD Papers, file 802 – Economic Assistance, Reel M-8900, LAC.

28   The most prominent humanitarian crisis at the time was the Congo Crisis, a period of upheaval that followed the Republic of the Congo's independence from Belgium. For detail, see Kevin Spooner, *Canada, the Congo Crisis, and UN Peacekeeping, 1960–64* (Vancouver: University of British Columbia Press, 2009).

29 See, for example, Dorothy Janas to Diefenbaker, 13 February 1961, JD Papers, file 802. C749 – Economic Assistance Abroad – Congo, Reel M-8900, LAC.

30 Philip Cross and Philippe Bergevin, *Turning Points: Business Cycles in Canada since 1926* (Toronto: C.D. Howe Institute, 2012).

31 Robinson, *Diefenbaker's World*, 196.

32 Canada, House of Commons, *Debates*, 17 May 1961, 4964.

33 "U.S. Takes Canada for Granted," *Toronto Star*, 21 May 1961.

34 C. C. Thomson to Diefenbaker, 29 October 1962, JD Papers, file 805 – Economic Assistance Abroad, Reel M8901, LAC.

35 "Seek to Cut Washington Program: Report Charges Canada Lagging on Foreign Aid Clay Group Also Critical of Recipients," *Globe and Mail*, 25 March 1963.

36 "U.S. Late Joining World Wars," *Globe and Mail*, 25 March 1963.

37 Gallup Canada Inc., "Canadian Gallup Poll # 300," *ODESI*, January 1963, http://odesi2.scholarsportal.info; Gallup Canada Inc., "Canadian Gallup Poll # 302," *ODESI*, April 1963, http://odesi2.scholarsportal.info.

38 See Stephen Azzi, *Walter Gordon and the Rise of Canadian Nationalism* (Montreal: McGill-Queen's University Press, 1999).

39 There is debate in the literature on Canadian identity in this period about when and to what extent British influence over Canadian identity waned. See, for example, Phillip A. Buckner, ed., *Canada and the End of Empire* (Vancouver: University of British Columbia Press, 2005); José Eduardo Igartua, *The Other Quiet Revolution: National Identities in English Canada, 1945–71* (Vancouver: University of British Columbia Press, 2006); and C. P. Champion, *The Strange Demise of British Canada: The Liberals and Canadian Nationalism, 1964–68* (Montreal: McGill-Queen's University Press, 2010).

40 Lester B. Pearson, "Eighteenth Session: An Assembly of Opportunity" (address before the Eighteenth Session of the United Nations General Assembly, New York, 19 September 1963), DEA, *Statements and Speeches* 63/19.

41 Pearson to the McGill Conference on World Affairs, 17 November 1959, Paul Joseph James Martin Papers (PJJM), vol. 195, file 5, LAC.

42 Lester B. Pearson, *Mike: The Memoirs of the Right Honourable Lester B. Pearson*, vol. 2: *1948–1957*, ed. John A. Munro and Alex I. Inglis (Toronto: University of Toronto Press, 1973), 32.

43 Kim Richard Nossal, Stéphane Roussel, and Stéphane Paquin, *The Politics of Canadian Foreign Policy*, 4th ed. (Montreal: McGill-Queen's University Press, 2015), 150–55.

44 Greg Donaghy, *Grit: The Life and Politics of Paul Martin Sr.* (Vancouver: University of British Columbia Press, 2015), 204.

45 Cabinet Conclusions, 14 November 1963, LAC.

46   Multilateral aid allocations increased from $C12.19 million in 1963–64 to $C28.11 million in 1966–67. Canada, Department of External Affairs, External Aid Office, *Annual Review: 1966–1967* (Ottawa: Queen's Printer and Controller of Stationery, 1967). In 1965–66 Canada spent 27.8 per cent of its ODA on multilateral aid compared to an OECD average of 5.6 per cent; Morrison, *Aid and Ebb Tide*, 54.

47   Lester B. Pearson, "Canadian Youth Serves the Developing Countries" (address to CUSO, Ottawa, 1 October 1965), DEA, *Statements and Speeches* 65/25.

48   Tamara Myers, "Blistered and Bleeding, Tired and Determined: Visual Representations of Children and Youth in the Miles for Millions Walkathon," *Journal of the Canadian Historical Association* 22, no. 1 (2011): 245–75; Tamara Myers, "Local Action and Global Imagining: Youth, International Development, and the Walkathon Phenomenon in Sixties' and Seventies' Canada," *Diplomatic History* 38, no. 2 (2014): 282–93.

49   J. R. Kidd to Pearson, 5 April 1966, LBP Papers, vol. 144, file 352 E98.1 Pers. & Conf. – Gov. Admin., LAC.

50   Martin himself was also a close ally and personal friend of Strong. See, for context, Donaghy, *Grit*, 259–60.

51   Memorandum to all Employees of the External Aid Office, 28 September 1967, PJJM Papers, vol. 225, file 7, LAC.

52   Escott Reid, "Canada in World Affairs: Opportunities of the Next Decade," Address, Annual Dinner of the Canadian Centenary Council, Ottawa, 1 February 1967. See also Escott Reid, Canada and Foreign Economic Aid, 13 October 1967, PJJM Papers, vol. 234, file 89-2, LAC; "A Crusade Against World Poverty," *Ottawa Journal*, 13 October 1967; and Escott Reid, "Canadian Foreign Policy, 1967–1977: A Second Golden Decade?," *International Journal* 22, no. 2 (1967): 171–81.

53   See, for example, "Foreign Aid Hike Planned," *Winnipeg Free Press*, 29 August 1963; "Le Canada est prêt à aider la nouvelle université du Ruanda," *Le Droit*, 29 August 1963; Bruce Macdonald, "A Sense of Shame on Foreign Aid," *Globe and Mail Magazine*, 5 October 1963; Pat Whelan, "Heads Can be Held Higher: Canada Aid Stands Out," *Windsor Star*, 29 November 1963; "Beef Up Foreign Aid . . . but Spend It Wisely," *Vancouver Sun*, 21 November 1963; "Foreign Aid Gets U.S. Praise," *Toronto Star*, 31 December 1963; "Le Canada enverra plus de professeurs à l'étranger," *Le Devoir*, 29 January 1964; "Indies Group Pledged Aid by Canada," *Globe and Mail*, 4 November 1964; "Tanzania wants aid by Canada," *Vancouver Province*, 22 March 1965; "Canada to give India $10M Worth of Food," *Quebec Chronicle Telegraph*, 17 February 1966; "Martin demandera $45,000,000 pour l'Inde," *L'action Catholique*, 24 March 1966; "Pearson tacks warning on aid to Middle East" and "Canada Doubles Food Aid," *Halifax Chronicle Herald*, 27 June 1967; "Le Canada consacrera $5 millions au transport aérien dans les Antilles," *La Presse*, 17 January 1968.

54   Flemming Holm to Pearson, 5 December 1963, LBP Papers, vol. 264, file 802 World Relations – Economic Assistance Abroad, LAC.

55   Patrick H. Brennan, "'A Good Man for the Middle Innings': Lester Pearson and the Media, 1963–1968," in *Pearson: The Unlikely Gladiator*, ed. Norman Hillmer (Montreal:

McGill-Queen's University Press, 1999), 117–30; Paul Rutherford, *When Television Was Young: Primetime Canada 1952–1967* (Toronto: University of Toronto Press, 1990).

56 See, for example, "A mystery in Canada's aid," *Globe and Mail*, 25 July 1966; "Inquiry ordered in milk," *Windsor Star*, 3 November 1967; "Calls Canada's Aid to Vietnam a Mess, *Winnipeg Free Press*, 3 November 1967; "Foreign aid director disputes criticism of Vietnam program," *London Free Press*, 4 November 1967; "Canada was thanked for moving doctor, Martin's aide says," *Globe and Mail*, 4 November 1967; "Ottawa Promises More Aid to Injured Vietnamese," *Montreal Gazette*, 9 December 1967.

57 Iain T. M. Macdonald to Pearson, 4 October 1964, LBP Papers, vol. 264, file 802 World Relations – Economic Assistance Abroad, LAC.

58 Roy Keitges to Pearson, 2 January 1964, LBP Papers, vol. 264, file 802 World Relations – Economic Assistance Abroad, LAC.

59 John Hilliker, Mary Halloran, and Greg Donaghy, *Canada's Department of External Affairs*, vol. 3: *Innovation and Adaptation, 1968–1984* (University of Toronto Press, 2017), 9–11.

60 J. L. Granatstein and Robert Bothwell, *Pirouette: Pierre Trudeau and Canadian Foreign Policy* (Toronto: University of Toronto Press, 1990), 265.

61 Quoted in Granatstein and Bothwell, *Pirouette*, 265; Trudeau, "Canada and the World" (A Policy Statement by Prime Minister Pierre Elliott Trudeau issued on 29 May 1968), DEA, *Statements and Speeches* 68/17.

62 Ibid.

63 Ibid.

64 Ibid.

65 DEA, *Foreign Policy for Canadians: International Development* (Ottawa: Queen's Printer, 1970), 9.

66 Morrison, *Aid and Ebb Tide*, 496.

67 DEA, *Foreign Policy for Canadians: International Development*. Canada, House of Commons, "Minutes and Proceedings of Evidence of the Sub-Committee on International Development Assistance of the Standing Committee on External Affairs and National Defence," 1971; CIDA, *Strategy for International Development Cooperation, 1975–1980* (Ottawa: Information Canada, 1975); Canada, House of Commons, "Minutes and Proceedings of Evidence of the Sub-Committee on International Development Assistance of the Standing Committee on External Affairs and National Defence," 1976.

68 CIDA, *Annual Review 1979–1980* (Ottawa: Minister of Supply and Services, 1980).

69 Description of the CIDA Development Participation Program (1971–1973), May 1973, Canadian Council for International Co-operation Records (CCIC), vol. 12, file: NGO-CIDA PPP Correspondence and Submissions 1977–1981, LAC.

70   Yvon Madore, Animation and International Development Education, CCIC Records, vol. 56, file: DEAP Background Information and Exposition of Aims and Purposes of Programme; Report 1974–1975, LAC.

71   This figure is an estimate. Church attendance statistics for Canada are less reliable prior to 1980. Lance W. Roberts, *Recent Social Trends in Canada, 1960–2000* (Montreal: McGill-Queen's University Press, 2005), 365–66.

72   Minutes 19–20 September 1972, Canadian Council of Churches Records (CCC), vol. 42, file 42-11 Interchurch Consultative Committee on Development and Relief Minutes 1972–1973, LAC.

73   Louis St. Laurent, "The Universities and International Understanding in the Free World" (address at special Convocation at the University of Western Ontario, London, 7 March 1951), DEA, *Statements and Speeches* 51/10.

74   Francis Leddy, quoted in Norma Walmsley, *Canadian Universities and International Development* (Ottawa: Association of Universities and Colleges of Canada, 1970), 7.

75   International Development Research Centre Act, RSC 1985, c. I-19.

76   Morrison, *Aid and Ebb Tide*, 171.

77   Ibid., 172.

78   Ibid., 210.

79   Roy E. Webster to Trudeau, 18 June 1969, Pierre Elliott Trudeau Papers (PET), vol. 460, file 802 World Relations Economic Assistance Abroad Jan.–Sept. 1969, LAC.

80   See Stephanie Bangarth, "The Politics of African Intervention: Canada and Biafra, 1967–1970," in *From Kinshasa to Kandahar: Canada and Fragile States in Historical Perspective*, ed. Michael K. Carroll and Greg Donaghy (Calgary: University of Calgary Press, 2016), 53–72.

81   For an example of the use of dependency theory during this period, see Walter Rodney, *How Europe Underdeveloped Africa* (London: Bogle-L'Ouverture Publications, 1972).

82   First Triennial Assembly, 24–28 November 1969, CCC Papers, vol. 2, file 1 Triennial Meetings – Minutes, LAC.

83   "CUSO, Trends," *Forum* (CUSO Newsletter), January 1974.

84   Richard Gwyn, "CIDA: Is it a 'Sick Joke'?" *Ottawa Journal*, 11 January 1975; "The Trouble with Foreign Aid," *Time*, 2 June 1975; Morton Shulman, "CIDA Shenanigans in Haiti," *Toronto Sun*, 11 January 1977; "What's Going on at CIDA?" *Globe and Mail*, 16 February 1977.

85   Canada, Office of the Auditor General, *Report of the Auditor General to the House of Commons (Fiscal Year Ended 31 March 1976)* (Ottawa: Minister of Supply and Services, 1976); Canada, Office of the Auditor General, *Report of the Auditor General to the House of Commons (Fiscal Year Ended 31 March 1979)* (Ottawa: Minister of Supply and Services, 1979).

86   H. L. Blatchford to Trudeau, 16 July 1974, PET Papers, vol. 318, file 352/I61 –
      Government – Federal Government Administration, LAC.

87   For details, see Greg Donaghy, "A Wasted Opportunity Canada and the New
      International Economic Order, 1974–82," in *Canada and the United Nations: Legacies,
      Limits, Prospects*, ed. Robert Teigrob and Colin McCullough (Montreal: McGill-
      Queen's University Press, 2017), 183–207.

88   Pierre Trudeau, "The Contractual Link – A Canadian Contribution to the Vocabulary
      of Co-operation" (remarks at the Mansion House, London, 13 March 1975); Ivan L.
      Head and Pierre Elliott Trudeau, *The Canadian Way: Shaping Canada's Foreign Policy,
      1968–1984* (Toronto: McClelland and Stewart, 1995), 147.

89   Gallup Canada Inc., "Canadian Gallup Poll # 413," *ODESI*, June 1978, http://odesi2.
      scholarsportal.info; Gallup Canada Inc., "Canadian Gallup Poll # 371," *ODESI*,
      December 1974, http://odesi2.scholarsportal.info.

90   Canada, Department of Finance, *Public Accounts of Canada, 1978* (Ottawa: Minister
      of Supply and Services, 1978); *Public Accounts of Canada, 1979* (Ottawa: Minister of
      Supply and Services, 1979); and *Public Accounts of Canada, 1980* (Ottawa: Minister of
      Supply and Services, 1980).

9

Pictures in Development: The Canadian International Development Agency's Photo Library

Sonya de Laat

> Images captured by the photographer's eye give us insight, can communicate some of the poetry and drama of others' lives, can make the people of the Third World become real in our imaginations. Because it is so important to our future, the Canadian International Development Agency (CIDA) has built up a valuable resource [the International Development Photo Library] to help Canadians see our world better.
>
> —Monique Landry, Minister of External Relations, 1987[1]

With these words, Monique Landry invited Canadians to become spectators of lives that were lived at a geographical, cultural, economic, and political distance. They were invited to do so through the rich visual resources of the Canadian International Development Agency's International Development Photo Library (IDPL), more colloquially known as the CIDA Photothèque. Since its public launch in 1987, and with photographs that have spanned

CIDA's 45-year existence, the IDPL has been indispensable in building the agency's legitimacy and public support. Described in 2000 as "one of the world's leading holdings of images of southern-hemisphere countries and people," the IDPL features diverse social documentary photography.[2] For over a generation, CIDA mobilized photography from its collection in publications, travelling exhibitions, and educational material to try to shape Canadians' conscience, imagination, and perceptions of life in the developing world, while also building Canada's international reputation as a caring and helpful nation.[3] For scholars, the pictures are invaluable for accessing official views and for tracing shifting conceptions and practices of development.

The Photothèque images reflect changes in public sentiments and global aid trends, including who is worthy of attention, how aid recipients are imagined, and what practices were used for foreign assistance. In approaching photography as a cultural phenomenon that is much more than a technology for making pictures, this chapter explores the history and content of the IDPL and its role in mediating social relations within a national and global aid system. As the aid sector undergoes a renewed period of external critique and self-reflection, this chapter is an invitation to consider this collection, and historical photography more generally, as being simultaneously of the past and a site of contemporary civil engagement.

Recent studies of aid agency visual media and strategies have expanded the definition of humanitarians and what constitutes humanitarian actions, while adding historical depth to critiques of humanitarian photography.[4] This chapter explores the Photothèque collection and considers its relevance for further academic study through a brief history of the IDPL, a broad thematic overview of its content, and an exploration of the significance of this collection for aid historians and practitioners. Along the way, opportunities for future research are identified. While photography is of historical and rhetorical significance, the chapter concludes with an invitation to consider photography as opening a civic space in which modes and powers of signifying and mediating global and local relations can be questioned and negotiated.

Sonya de Laat

Developing a Photo Library of International Development

The history of the IDPL reaches further back in time than the year of its official launch. Even before CIDA's inception in 1968, staff members of the External Aid Office, which preceded CIDA, were making photographic records of their job experiences overseas. In its first decade, CIDA's use of photography was mainly for internal accountability and training purposes, as there was little in the way of general, let alone expert, knowledge about conditions in developing countries.[5] The photographs were commissioned and used by the Briefing Centre, whose role it was to train development officers before they headed into the field and to debrief them on their return.[6] Photographs from this period were dominated by images of development officers and local staff pictured in front of project signage or equipment, or their involvement in infrastructure project activities (Figure 9.1). These first photographs were rarely shared beyond the agency; they were not intended for public consumption.

During this first decade, however, the Canadian public's exposure to life in the "Third World," to use the terminology of the day, was expanding. Expo '67 created a momentum that propelled and heightened Canadian public interest in all things global. Other events held in the agency's first decade, including the United Nations Conference on Human Settlements (Habitat) hosted by Vancouver in 1976, further bolstered interest in and knowledge of the world beyond Canada's borders.[7] By this time, CIDA was attracting employees with theoretical and practical knowledge of developing countries. CIDA benefited from those who found international development appealing "not only to idealism but also to a sense of adventure and/or the exotic."[8] As Canadians were demonstrating an interest in global cultures, CIDA expanded its educational mandate, turning its attention to informing the broader Canadian public about life in the developing world.

By CIDA's tenth anniversary, the Briefing Centre began contracting "highly skilled reporters" and photographers in order to improve the "depth and diversity" of the collection.[9] One internal document asked photographers "to record: CIDA projects in all sectors; all aspects of daily life, both rural and urban; landscape, geography, flora and fauna, and urban environments. People are to be included as often as possible."[10] The operating philosophy considered informing Canadians about daily life in developing countries—particularly through images that represented local people as active participants in development—as the more ideal and democratic way of generating support for CIDA and its official development assistance projects without having to be prescriptive or didactic.[11]

The relationships CIDA developed with its photographers further encouraged a democratic approach. Contracted photographers worked relatively independently, at times piggybacking CIDA assignments onto those from other aid organizations for which they also worked.[12] The result was a field of view that extended beyond CIDA projects. The pictures that came back represented a new aesthetic for CIDA that differed greatly from the images originally made for the Briefing Centre. Replacing the more didactic training photographs were evocative and formal portraits of people and life in the developing world. Less visible in the photographs were CIDA development officers facilitating overseas projects. The focus became the people who were (or were meant to become) recipients of Canada's official development assistance. In 1983, the Briefing Centre collection was transferred to CIDA's Public Affairs Branch, and in 1985, with growth in the wealth and breadth of the collection, the decision was made to create a publicly accessible International Development Photo Library.[13]

The library was officially launched in 1987 with the travelling exhibition *Development* (Figure 9.2). The intention of the Photothèque was that it would be a "professional photo-library available to the public as an educational resource."[14] The IDPL's main clients were CIDA's Public Affairs Branch and government departments, but other non-government agencies and media also made use of the photographs.[15] The library, with its twenty-year-old collection, had already become a rich repository of culture, life, and conditions in parts of the world that many Canadians would only ever come to know through photography. Over the course of the following decades, IDPL photography would be centrally featured in CIDA's publications, including magazines such as *Development*, *Action Plans*, and *Global Citizenship in Action*, as well as numerous policy briefs, newsletters, handbooks, and reports. These publications represented some of the more formal public engagement documents.

Building on the success of the inaugural *Development* exhibit, CIDA recognized the affective asset of the photographs themselves: their capacity to mediate emotional ties between Canadians and foreign assistance. CIDA

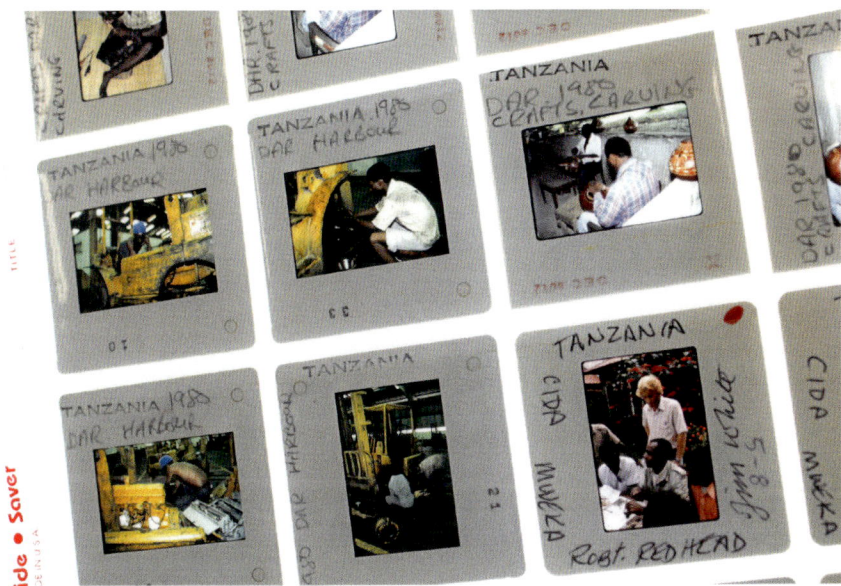

FIGURE 9.1
Photographs by CIDA staff for the Briefing Centre.
(Source: LAC/Global Affairs Canada TCS00196-
1988-056 2000816725)

FIGURE 9.2
Catalogue cover for the Development exhibit, 1987.
(Source: Global Affairs Canada)

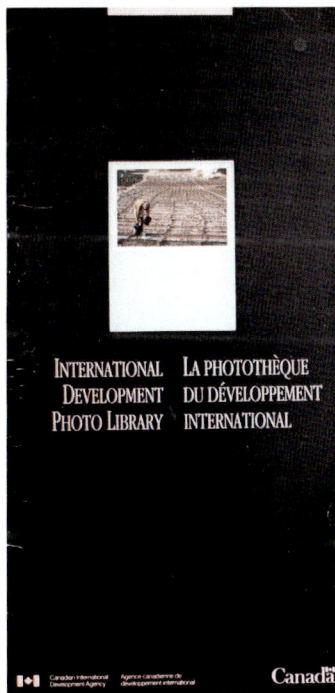

INTERNATIONAL   LA PHOTOTHÈQUE
DEVELOPMENT   DU DÉVELOPPEMENT
PHOTO LIBRARY   INTERNATIONAL

Canadian International   Agence canadienne de
Development Agency   développement international

Canada

FIGURE 9.3
Twenty-fifth anniversary exhibition promotion, 2010. (Source: Global Affairs Canada)

FIGURE 9.4
Photographer David Barbour's winning picture for the World Press Photo Award, Egypt, 1985. (Source: Global Affairs Canada/David Barbour)

Sonya de Laat

FIGURE 9.5
Example of a positive representation of development assistance, Philippines, 1988.
(Source: Global Affairs Canada/ David Barbour)

FIGURE 9.6
Example of a negative development picture, Bangladesh. Part of Development Exhibition, 1987. (Source: Global Affairs Canada/David Barbour)

FIGURE 9.7
Example of an "everyday" picture, representative of a smaller subset of the IDPL collection, Botswana, 1982. (Source: Global Affairs Canada/Crombie McNeill)

joined forces with the Canadian Museum of Contemporary Photography (CMCP) to produce travelling photography exhibits that were more accessible for a larger swath of Canadians.[16] Joint CIDA-CMCP exhibitions included *Other Children* (1989) and *Rights and Realities* (1995), first exhibited at the World Conference on Women in Beijing. Finally, but in no way less significant, in the 1990s, CIDA created a nationwide school education program on international development. The educational material created for the Development Information Program leaned exclusively on Photothèque images.

In 2010, the library celebrated its twenty-fifth anniversary, and marked it with another travelling exhibition (Figure 9.3). By this point, the collection included the work of many award-winning Canadian photographers, including four who received the internationally renowned World Press Photo Award: Dilip Mehta (1984), David Barbour (1985), Roger LeMoyne (1999), and Lana Šlezić (2007). David Barbour's winning photograph was made while on assignment for CIDA in Egypt the same year the IDPL was started, setting a standard of excellence for the collection (Figure 9.4).

By the time CIDA was dissolved in 2013, with much of its programming either disappearing or merging into the Department of Foreign Affairs, Trade and Development, now Global Affairs Canada (GAC), the IDPL had already become the victim of changing political, economic, and technological times. Despite the quality of the photography and the high profile of the photographers, already in 2010 the IDPL stopped acquiring photographs.[17] Today, the IDPL collection consists of some 150,000 photographs composed of the original Briefing Centre photographs, the pictures made by commissioned photographers, and the corporate collection.[18]

At its height, from the mid-1980s to mid-2000s, the IDPL would go on to serve many functions for CIDA, from raising its profile in a time when it encountered its first intense external critiques to bolstering its legitimacy when it faced its first budgetary cuts after decades of growth.[19] The IDPL would also have unforeseen impact that resonates still today. In the context of the history of humanitarianism, the IDPL emerged at a time of global intensification and expansion of aid activity that brought with it intense media scrutiny. Marked by events such as the catastrophe of the Ethiopian famine followed by the horrors of genocide in the Balkans and Rwanda, humanitarianism in the mid-1980s to mid-1990s underwent a period of disillusionment. The following sections situate the IDPL in the larger visual humanitarian context, and consider the significance of the IDPL for humanitarian and development action going forward.

Situating the IDPL and Its Themes

In the recent survey of the International Committee of the Red Cross (ICRC) photographic library, Valérie Gorin called the collection "encyclopedic" because of its broad coverage of humanitarian themes and historic crises.[20] Like the CIDA Library, the ICRC collection started with photographs made by delegates on the job. The collection grew when the ICRC commissioned professional photographers in similar ways and for similar public relations reasons as CIDA did. The ICRC also included donated and purchased photographs to round out the collection, transforming it into a visual memory project of humanitarianism, albeit from one institution's perspective. Rather than a repository of historical memory, the CIDA Photothèque was an active and contemporary source of information on life in the developing world—a resource for Canadians to learn about the people, daily activities, labour practices, and work conditions in distant and unfamiliar lands for current and future ODA activities. The IDPL is nowhere near as encyclopedic as the ICRC library, which stretches back to the mid-nineteenth century and covers a range of humanitarian concerns from conflicts to natural disasters to development. CIDA's 45-year project is much more modest, yet it is a robust example of a particular moment in the history of humanitarian photography, a subset known as *development photography* that ballooned after the end of the Second World War.[21]

Humanitarian photography is defined as "mobilization of photography in the service of humanitarian initiatives across state boundaries."[22] It is as old as the medium itself and encompasses pictures made by missionaries, reformers, professional and amateur photographers, and professional humanitarians. Beginning in the mid-nineteenth century, its two dominant forms included "atrocity photographs" and the visual form of the "humanitarian narrative."[23] Atrocity photographs, such as piles of corpses resulting from conflict or epidemic, or photographs of "living skeleton" famine victims, were meant to raise awareness of suffering, all the while shocking spectators into action. People campaigning for emergency relief or political

reform often wrestled with their consciences over using this type of imagery, knowing the risks of feeding people's morbid curiosities and possibly
titillating some spectators. Such shocking photographs also risked utterly
shutting down spectators' ability to generate any action other than looking
away out of disgust or fatigue.[24]

Meanwhile, the visual form of the humanitarian narrative emulated
what had, until the popularization of photography, been the dominant
mode of expression and persuasion of reform writers.[25] Conventionally, the
humanitarian narrative centred on the progressive story revolving around
a victim (idealized as innocent and passive) who was suffering at the hands
of a perpetrator (a disease or condition if not a person), only to be rescued
by the hero (predominantly presented as active, white, and superior
in some way).[26] The visual humanitarian narrative may have included
elements of atrocity for added "truth" effect, but its main concern was on
building a visual narrative of salvation and supremacy that emulated the
written narratives. Both atrocity and humanitarian narrative photography
coexisted through the period of the two world wars. New technologies and
approaches then emerged enabling photographers to represent visually and
share human experiences and emotions by focusing on individual portraits,
bringing a human face to wartime and postwar suffering.[27]

The end of the Second World War and the onset of the cold war conflict
between Soviet totalitarianism and Western democracy ushered in an era
of decolonization within the former European colonies in Asia and Africa.
Aid agencies, many of which had materialized during and after the war,
turned their attention from relief and reconstruction to development.

With the shift in geopolitical trends, development photography also
changed, becoming a distinctive style of humanitarian photography.
Representing local aid recipients as participants in their own social, political, and economic uplift proved to be visually challenging since there
were no immediate affective or shocking focal points such as those that
came with natural disasters or conflict. To create more visually stimulating
imagery, and to bring a human face to development projects, development
iconography turned to the personal portrait style generated and honed by
war photographers.[28] The aim of this photographic approach was a focus on
the active role of recipients rather than Western aid providers. To this end,
there emerged a "'deliberate positivism' in imagery "showing self-reliant

and active people of the South," smiling and actively participating in determining their own destiny.[29]

As optimistic and innovative as such imagery might have appeared, development agencies recognized, and were swayed by, the financial benefits that came from negative imagery. Thus, pictures of severely malnourished children with bloated bellies (a symptom of kwashiorkor), with flies on their eyes, or with runny noses represented the flip side of development aid appeals.[30] These types of negative imagery became the focus of a passionate critique within the aid sector in the last decades of the twentieth century. Ultimately, that critique pointed out a paradox in the iconography of suffering: the attempt at doing good contributed to demoralizing and dehumanizing the very subjects that humanitarians and their organizations pledged to help.[31] Accused of having become "merchants of misery" by exploiting and perpetuating stereotypes that objectified, essentialized, and infantalized victims and their communities in an effort to further organizational ends, aid actors adopted codes of conduct and ethics guidelines that have been adhered to with varying degrees of success.[32]

The IDPL emerged within this context, and its photographers and staff were sensitive to the critiques.[33] As an entity of a development agency, the IDPL also followed some of the same visual practices that circulated through the international aid sector. The Photothèque collection includes pictures with positive and negative content, but there is little in the collection that can be considered atrocity photography.[34]

By and large, the photographs CIDA distributed in its official publications, educational material, and public relations posters and calendars were of the optimistic development photography sort characterized by smiling faces of children and adults, often in close-cropped portraits filling the pages and covers (Figure 9.5). Many take on the form of the humanitarian narrative, even if Canada-as-hero is only gestured at through farming, transportation, education and health equipment, or the CIDA logo (see Figure 9.3).

A large proportion of CIDA exhibition photographs consist of harsher depictions of the lived realities of people in poorer parts of the world (Figure 9.6). In these pictures, sober-looking individuals stand in ankle-deep mud between makeshift houses, or children of all ages crowd into one-room schools, and long lines of women wait under the hot sun for food or water. While less uplifting, they are not of a sort that would make spectators cringe, and turn away in disgust. The IDPL's acquisitions program was about counteracting, and presenting an alternative narrative to, the "pornographies of suffering" swirling around at the time.[35] By and large, the Photo Library successfully avoided succumbing to the temptation to exploit extreme misery. That being said, media scholars have recently put forth critiques of this positive development photography. While originally lauded as a corrective to the numbing aspect of atrocity pictures or the superiority inherent in humanitarian narratives, this critique sees positive pictures as concealing difference and perpetuating deep-seeded biases that see people in different geographic or social locations as perpetually dependent and ignorant beings.[36]

That a mixture of positive and negative themed photographs constitutes the IDPL is not surprising given the history of humanitarian photography and the emergence of development as an ideological and practical form of aid. There is, however, a unique set of photographs also interspersed throughout the Photothèque that insist on being reconciled with the broader collection. This other set of photographs had their origins in the Briefing Centre's training program and were never intended for public consumption or mass circulation. These photographs depict rather mundane, everyday content such as civil institutions and infrastructure in Rwanda, shop windows in Botswana, and domestic scenes of CIDA families enjoying rest and relaxation while employed overseas (Figure 9.7). They are neither obviously positive nor negative, as they fall outside the typical development photography genre. Their presence in the collection opens new lines of questioning about the representation of development and the mediation of social relations associated with it.

Situating the IDPL in broader histories and themes of humanitarian photography anchors the CIDA collection within the larger history of humanitarianism: a time when national governments were finding economic and political benefits in foreign aid assistance. Consideration of the role of photography in shaping the meaning, interpretation, and understanding of CIDA and Canadian ODA requires exploring the ways in which photography can be analyzed.

Signification in and Significance of the IDPL Collection

Until recently, dominant approaches in photography studies and criticism focused on the politics of representation and semiotics, or, put simply: the pictures' content and symbolic meaning. Historians have long treated photography as a more or less static artifact. It has been used predominantly illustratively, depicting who was present at what event, and the details of their physical appearance or that of the places in which they appear. Historical photographs have been considered as pictures *of* the past: of what has already been socially and politically achieved.[37] Photographs have also long been recognized for their rhetorical force, and as such have been sources for accessing dominant ideological and emotional trends that structure images of people as worthy of receiving or providing care. Photography is widely acknowledged as shaped by ideologies, politics, economics, and socio-cultural constraints that form along changing hegemonic lines.[38] CIDA's photography can certainly be seen in this light considering that the pictures were commissioned, curated, and captioned by agents of the state. Recent trends in visual theories propose shifting attention to the actors and arena of activity beyond the content and frame of the picture to locate photography's greater cultural and political forces. Here, briefly, is a consideration of the CIDA Photothèque collection with these long-standing and more recent visual theories in mind.

As Ted Cogan demonstrates in the preceding chapter, discourse and popular conceptions of development assistance altered throughout Canada's development assistance history. Through a combination of changes in political leadership and public interests, impressions of international aid would shift already before CIDA's inception. By the time of the IDPL's official launch in the mid-1980s, its content had significantly moved away from pictures of large-scale infrastructure and capital projects to a focus on individuals and lives in developing countries.

While part of a global trend for visual representations of development and humanitarian action, this focus on the people and places where CIDA operated presented several significant opportunities for the agency. Paying particular attention to recipients or potential recipient communities reflected dominant public perceptions and discourse of Canadian aid in the 1970s and 1980s. The focus on people in developing countries, whether

Sonya de Laat

living in difficult conditions of poverty and deprivation or working in situations made possible by CIDA, would be the central subject matter of the IDPL for the coming decades.

According to the 1987 *Development* exhibition catalogue, the photographs on display "provide us with clues that enable us to be aware of our differences." With that in mind, Figure 9.6, which was part of that exhibition, presumably equates those differences with global structures of inequality that need correcting. Such a message certainly suited the moral internationalist and global justice perspectives that originated from the L. B. Pearson and Pierre Trudeau governments and upon which the IDPL's operational imperatives were founded.[39] When juxtaposed alongside other images from the IDPL collection, such as those in Figures 9.4 and 9.5, a narrative structure emerges that legitimated the existence and presence of CIDA. The combination of pictures of people in developing countries in apparently negative and positive situations built a narrative that could foster a particular emotional (and subsequently political) stance toward aid and toward those on its receiving end. The negative photographs symbolized life without, or before, CIDA support. Meanwhile, the positive pictures symbolize a progressive outcome following Canadian development assistance. In concert, they work to evoke a set of emotions that shape an impression of and legitimate the agency's actions.

The result is a CIDA iconography that bolsters uncritical support for CIDA's work, for who could deny the importance of Canadian ODA in the presence of those sorrowful and smiling faces? The combined positive-negative portrait photographs adapted with ease to changes in political leadership while continuing to build support at the risk (or benefit) of distracting attention from CIDA's actual actions (or inactions). With a focus on this visual narrative, CIDA's public image could remain consistent despite regular changes in political leadership and agendas.[40] This consistent representation concealed behind a veil of altruism potentially contentious projects or decisions that could go virtually unnoticed by the public eye. While further research might detect subtleties within the collection associated with ideological differences of political leadership, on the whole the dominant messaging remained relatively unchanging.

More recent visual theories reconsider photography as an event rather than a technology for making pictures. According to the visual culture scholar, Ariella Azoulay, the "invention of photography was the creation of a new situation in which different people, in different places, can simultaneously use a black box to manufacture an image of their encounters: not an image of *them*, but of the encounter itself."[41] As such, all the people involved in that encounter, including all subsequent spectators of the picture, are necessary to realizing the photographic event. The photographer and the distributor of the pictures may have (professional, political, economic) intentions with the images, but when photography is considered an event it is no longer the photographer's vantage point, their intended meaning, that is the only—or even the dominant—one. As an event and an encounter, photography "can no longer be seen as a personal property, but [as] a complex set of relations" in which "everyone gain[s] the opportunity to see through the gaze of another."[42] In this sense, the invention of the camera is not just a new mechanical technology to make pictures, but one that creates a new "civil space" within which bonds and responsibilities are forged between those implicated in or articulated to the photographic situation. With this approach, photography inherently invites the possibility of "restoring and re-establishing as many links as possible between the photograph and the situation in which it was taken."[43]

These recent theories open new lines of inquiry, inviting analysis of the entire IDPL collection, questioning the events and actors associated with it rather than just the content or frame of individual pictures. Doing so expands the field of vision in development photography and explores its role in mediating social relations within development assistance. Indeed, a look at Phototèque content even invites critical reflection about global structures of inequality and mechanisms of exclusion.[44]

Some of the "everyday" photographs that appear in the IDPL and that originate from the Briefing Centre are instructive here. Figure 9.7, for instance, may well have been made disinterestedly, with the intention of showing what types of shops Canadians might expect to find for their own convenience upon their arrival in Botswana. Other photographs made for the benefit of development officers exhibit more self-conscious irony. For instance, Dilip Mehta made exposures of typical Canadian civil servants enjoying a moment of repose in their expat housing compound in Bangladesh. Behind them a local dark-skinned Bangladeshi labourer waters the garden. The scene, as Mehta composed it, reflects traditional, hierarchical colonial relationships. Mehta is an Indo-Canadian photographer and visual artist, which may have contributed to a more critical stance.

The photographs of shops, banks, and domestic activities present an "everyday" that is distinct from the "daily life in the developing world" depicted in CIDA publications and exhibitions. These are much more ambiguous and introduce the possibility of questioning CIDA's actions and presence: Why here? For what purpose? What is the relationship between CIDA and the developing nation on the receiving end of Canadian ODA? What is being concealed behind the expressions of the evocatively portrayed aid recipients? In what way do cultural or social positions (e.g., gender, class) from CIDA photographers shape their field of vision? Given that CIDA photographers were not always picturing specific CIDA projects, but rather the life in countries in which they operated, what details were Canadians learning about Canadian development assistance activities? Considering the consistency of CIDA's image despite changes in political agendas and ideologies, were Canadians being presented an equally homogenous view of the Third World or of development assistance? To what extent were there distinctions being made, in educational material or exhibitions, between actions taken in different countries? To what extent were Canadians enabled to distinguish between life in Botswana and Rwanda, or Nicaragua and Nigeria?

As aid agencies globally, and Global Affairs Canada itself, undergo ongoing renewal processes, resources such as photographic libraries and picture archives are invaluable entry points for self-reflection. They are also indispensable and yet underutilized wells for exploring the relationships built, fostered, neglected, and rebuilt between those on the giving, receiving, and spectating sides of aid.[45]

Conclusion

> ... one thing I am always looking for in my photographs is a kind of cross-current. I never want the photograph to be just one thing, one mood, one idea. Rather, it should be a place where multiple, often contradictory, impressions overlap.
>
> —Roger LeMoyne, photographer[46]

Roger LeMoyne's comment is built on an approach to interpreting photography that remains bound by the frame of the image. If nothing else, recent innovations in photographic theory expand the field of vision beyond the picture's borders. LeMoyne's instincts are correct, even though not explicit; photography is not "just one thing," it is always open to different signification, in spite of anyone's intentions. Considering the event of photography rather than the product of the photograph reveals that the medium is inherently a point of convergence, a place where different points of view intersect and have an opportunity to interact. In the event of photography, spectators come to the photographs at different historical moments or with different political and social positions in relation to the image. Considering photography in this way renders all of the Photo Library pictures, not just the outlier "everyday" pictures, civic spaces that invite reflection and debate about the relations mediated and represented in them.

Images from the Canadian International Development Agency's Photothèque helped shape Canada's identity at home and abroad as a caring, helpful nation. Sharing portraits of apparently positive and negative examples of daily life in developing countries enabled CIDA to appear unchanging despite regular changes in political leadership and agendas. The development iconography the IDPL acquired and mobilized, while building broad and relatively constant support for CIDA, could also conceal aspects of Canada's ODA that might be points of debate or critique.

Until recently, photographic theories would conclude that the IDPL photographs could only illustrate past CIDA activities or be resources for accessing dominant political and social ideologies. Photographic theories that explore the arena of activity beyond the border of the pictures and seek out the disruptive force of contingency inherent in photography offer opportunities to use the Photothèque pictures to think about social relations in development work. Mediations and representations from the past can inform considerations of those today, something that is especially relevant in the present era of reflection and renewal in development. As the line between subjects and creators blurs with the growth and accessibility of social media, the knowledge of histories of representations is enriching and valuable to future development relations.

Notes

I am grateful to Mary Bramley and Blaine Marchand for their insights and recollections about the origins and functions of the IDPL. I would also like to thank Bramley and her colleague Paul Richer of the IDPL for their assistance in scouring the library collection on my behalf, as well as Library and Archives staff and members of the Canadian Network of Humanitarian History for their additional supports. I would also like to thank Stephanie Colvey for sharing her insights as a photographer who began her photographic career with CIDA.

1   Canadian International Development Agency (CIDA), *Development: CIDA's Photographic Library* (Ottawa: Government of Canada, 1987), 2.

2   Blaine Marchand, "Lives Lived," *Globe and Mail*, 4 November 2000, A24-5.

3   It is worth noting that a rich scholarly debate exists around the concept of development. I use the term here not to signal allegiance to any one point of debate but because it is the language (and ideology) of Canada's official aid program.

4   Heide Fehrenbach and Davide Rodogno, eds., *Humanitarian Photography: A History* (Cambridge: Cambridge University Press, 2015); Kevin Grant, "Christian Critics of Empire: Missionaries, Lantern Lectures, and the Congo Reform Campaign in Britain," *Journal of Imperial and Commonwealth History* 29, no. 2 (2001): 27–58. Sharon Sliwinski, *Human Rights in Camera* (Chicago: University of Chicago Press, 2011).

5   Personal communication with Mary Bramley, 14 December 2016.

6   According to Morrison, the Briefing Centre was created in 1969 to take "a more professional approach to preparing Canadians for placements abroad." David R. Morrison, *Aid and Ebb Tide: A History of CIDA and Canadian Development Assistance* (Waterloo, ON: Wilfrid Laurier University Press, 1998), 66.

7   Personal communication with Blaine Marchand, 17 February 2017.

8   Morrison, *Aid and Ebb Tide*, 64–74.

9   The Briefing Centre and the Public Relations Branch were both under the auspices of CIDA's Communications Department. CIDA, *Development*, 1–27.

10 CIDA, n.d., internal IDPL document, provided by Bramley.

11 Personal communication with Blaine Marchand, 17 February 2017.

12 While ownership remained with CIDA, photographers were allowed to use the pictures they made for the agency for non-profit, self-promotional purposes. Stephanie Colvey, photographer, personal communication, 27 July 2017. Also see personal communication with Mary Bramley, 14 December 2016.

13 According to Marchand, one of the key figures in creating the CIDA Photothèque was Roberta Borg (1943–2000), who, coincidentally, had previously worked with the National Film Board to create the "highly acclaimed Habitat film series, which premiered at the United Nations Habitat Conference in Nairobi." Blaine Marchand, "Lives Lived," *Globe and Mail*, 4 November 2000, A24-5.

14 CIDA, *Development*, 1–27.

15 During the 1980s and 1990s, more than 50 per cent of the IDPLs clients were civil society organizations who required professional photography for their promotional material.

16 The CMCP is now part of the National Gallery of Canada. Their archives include documents and material related to the joint CIDA-CMCP photography exhibits.

17 As a result, CIDA began to "beg, borrow, and steal" from other departments or purchase photographs on an as-needed basis. A project to put some 90,000 digitized photographs onto a publicly accessible online portal was quietly scuttled at the time of the agency's merger. Despite the completion of hours of vetting, culling, editing, and making Web-ready, the project did not go ahead due to platform incompatibility between the different departments' operating systems; see personal communication with Mary Bramley, 14 December 2016.

18 The IDPL is a public collection; however, access to it is limited. Another 8,291 original Briefing Centre photographs from 1972 to 1985 are housed, and accessible upon request, at Library and Archives Canada; these are among the first pictures made by professional photographers for the agency. The corporate collection consists of photographs of ministers and CIDA personnel performing official duties. For the sake of brevity, I do not include these photographs in this paper, as they were not explicitly a part of CIDA's education and information practices. It bears noting that this by no means diminishes the space for civil engagement opened up by their existence.

19 Morrison, *Aid and Ebb Tide*, 313.

20 Valérie Gorin, "Looking Back over 150 Years of Humanitarian Action: The Photographic Archives of the ICRC," *International Review of the Red Cross* 94, no. 888 (2012): 1349–79, http://doi.org/10.1017/S1816383113000568.

21 The genre has earned its own social media hashtag: #DevPix.

22 Fehrenbach and Rodogno, *Humanitarian Photography*, 1.

23 Valérie Gorin, "'Millions of Children in Deadly Peril': Utilisation des d'enfants affamés par Save the Children pendant l'entre-deux guerres," *Revue Suisse D'histoire* 37: Special Issue on Media And Famines (2014): 95–112; Thomas W. Laqueur, "Bodies, Details, and the Humanitarian Narrative," in *The New Cultural History*, ed. L. A. Hunt (Ann Arbour: MPublishing, University of Michigan Library, 1989), 176–204.

24 Heather D. Curtis, "Picturing Pain: Evangelicals and the Politics of Pictorial Humanitarianism in an Imperial Age," in Fehrenbach and Rodogno, *Humanitarian Photography*, 22–46; Karen Halttunen, "Humanitarianism and the Pornography of Pain in Anglo-American Culture," *American Historical Review* 100, no. 2 (1995): 303–34; Kevin Rozario, "'Delicious Horrors': Mass Culture, The Red Cross, and the Appeal of Modem American Humanitarianism," *American Quarterly* 55 no. 3 (2003): 417–55.

25 Laqueur, "Bodies, Details, and the Humanitarian Narrative," 176–204.

26 Gorin, "Millions of Children in Deadly Peril," 95–112; Laqueur, "Bodies, Details, and the Humanitarian Narrative," 176–204.

27   Davide Rodogno and Thomas David, "All the World Loves a Picture: The World Health Organization's Visual Politics, 1948–1973," in Fehrenbach and Rodogno, *Humanitarian Photography*, 223–48.

28   Jorgen Lissner, *The Politics of Altruism: A Study of the Political Behaviour of Voluntary Development Agencies* (Geneva: Lutheran World Foundation, 1977).

29   Nandita Dogra, "'Reading NGOs Visually'—Implications of Visual Images for NGO Management," *Journal of International Development* 19, no. 2 (2007): 163; Henrietta Lidchi, "Finding the Right Image: British Development NGOs and the Regulation of Imagery," in *Culture and Global Change*, ed. T. Skelton and T. Allen (London: Routledge, 1999), 275–96; Ian Smillie, *The Alms Bazaar: Altruism Under Fire – Non-Profit Organisations And International Development* (London: Intermediate Technology, 1995).

30   Jeremy Benthall, *Disasters, Relief and the Media* (London: I.B. Tauris, 1993).

31   Suzanne Franks, *Reporting Disasters: Famine, Aid, Politics and the Media* (Oxford: Oxford University Press, 2014); Dennis Kennedy, "Selling the Distant Other: Humanitarianism and Imagery – Ethical Dilemmas of Humanitarian Action," *Journal of Humanitarian Assistance* 28 (Feb. 2009): 1–25; Arthur Kleinman and Joan Kleinman, "The Appeal Of Experience: The Dismay of Images: Cultural Appropriations of Suffering in our Times," *Daedalus* 125, no. 1 (1996): 1–23.

32   Jorgen Lissner, "Merchants of Misery," *New Internationalist* 6, no. 1 (1981): 1–11; General Assembly of the Liaison Committee of Development NGOs to the European Communities, *Code of Conduct Images and Messages Relating to the Third World* (1989): International Federation of the Red Cross, *Code of Conduct in Disaster Relief* (1994), http://www.ifrc.org/en/publications-and-reports/code-of-conduct/.

33   See personal communication with Mary Bramley, 14 December 2016.

34   Sensitive images include photographs such as childbirths. These types of photographs have not been published but may have been used for internal organizational purposes.

35   See personal communication with Mary Bramley, 14 December 2016.

36   Nandita Dogra, *Representations of Global Poverty: Aid, Development and International NGOs* (New York: I.B. Tauris, 2014).

37   Pierre Bourdieu, *Photography: A Middle-Brow Art*, trans. Shaun Whiteside (Stanford, CA: Stanford University Press, 1990).

38   Allan Sekula, *Photography Against the Grain: Essays and Photo-Works 1973–1983* (Halifax: Press of the Nova Scotia College of Art and Design, 1984); Judith Butler, "Torture and the Ethics of Photography: Thinking with Sontag," in *Frames of War: When Is Life Grievable?*, ed. Judith Butler (London: Verso, 2009), 63–100; Susan Sontag, *Regarding the Pain of Others* (New York: Picador, 2003); John Tagg, *The Disciplinary Frame: Photographic Truths and the Capture of Meaning* (Minneapolis: University of Minnesota Press, 2009).

39   Ted Cogan's chapter in this volume.

40 While underlying Canadian financial interests in ODA has been a criticism, it need not be. An attempt to conceal or deny such interests when they do exist is much worse.

41 Ariella Azoulay, *Civil Imagination: A Political Ontology of Photography* (London: Verso, 2012), 92–93.

42 Ibid., 113.

43 Ibid., 86.

44 See also Butler, "Torture and the Ethics of Photography," 63–100.

45 Recent photo-based oral history projects that focus on the experiences and perceptions of the people (or their community members) in the photographs have emerged in collaboration with the opening up of visual archives. Not all of them are humanitarian or development specific. *Project Naming* is supported by Library and Archives Canada and aims to identify individual Inuit people contained in that photographic archive collection; see Carol Payne, "'You Hear It in Their Voice': Photographs and Cultural Consolidation among Inuit Youths and Elders," in *Image and Memory: Oral History and Photography*, ed. Alexander Freund and Alistair Thomson (London: Palgrave, 2011), 97–114. For a recent project on refugees in UNHCR photographs, see Caroline Lenette, "Writing with Light: An Iconographic-Iconologic Approach to Refugee Photography," *Forum Qualitative Sozialforschung*, 17, no. 2 (2016), http://dx.doi.org/10.17169/fqs-17.2.2436. For a project learning from people in contemporary aid photographs, see S. Warrington and J. Crombie, *The People in the Pictures: Vital Perspectives on Save the Children's Image Making* (London: Save the Children UK, 2017), https://resourcecentre.savethechildren.net/node/12425/pdf/the_people_in_the_pictures.pdf.

46 From LeMoyne's online biography: http://rogerlemoyne.com/bio.

Sonya de Laat

"Tears Are Not Enough": Canadian Political and Social Mobilization for Famine Relief in Ethiopia, 1984–1988

Nassisse Solomon

On 1 November 1984, the Canadian Broadcasting Corporation's flagship evening news program, *The National*, aired a four-minute editorial on the devastating famine in Ethiopia by reporter Brian Stewart. This short clip scaled the depths of human suffering with its vivid depictions of apocalyptic famine, and has since been credited as the impetus driving the Canadian government and thousands of ordinary Canadians to respond to the humanitarian crisis on the African continent. Canadians, Progressive Conservative MP Reg Stackhouse told his colleagues, were "shocked by television reports of mass starvation in Ethiopia."[1] These morbid and haunting images enabled Progressive Conservative prime minister Brian Mulroney and his secretary of state for external affairs, Joe Clark, to galvanize non-partisan support for a broad humanitarian rescue mission. Consequently, between 1984 and 1988, the Ethiopian famine became a unifying national cause and "clarion call" to international action for Canadians from coast to coast.[2]

The global response to what was widely referred to as the "African crisis" was immediate and largely unprecedented in its scope and level of citizen engagement.[3] Canada was no different. Canadian engagement with the Ethiopian famine crisis was multifaceted and extended across the political and social spectrum. Inspired by the federal government's determination to assume an unusually high-profile leadership role in fostering various forms of participatory and citizen-engaged politics, Canada and Canadians embodied, and even aspired to exceed, the tenets of "good Samaritanism" that Stephen Brown explores in his chapter. Notions of altruism and humanitarianism articulated by politicians and citizens alike reflected Brown's premise that true altruism required that "a state, like a person, should be generous to complete strangers without any self-interested motive." By 1985, nearly a million Canadians had donated "an average of $60 each to help save 30 million Africans from starvation."[4] During the four years of sustained public support for Ethiopian relief, a wide variety of Canadians in and outside of government joined together in a socio-political phenomenon that was later dubbed the "Mulroney model."[5]

Canada provided more aid to Africa than to any other region of the Global South between 1980 and 2011.[6] Yet there has been little scholarly examination of the socio-political implications of Canadian involvement in Ethiopian/African famine relief efforts. Most discussions of the famine relief campaign in Canada are subsumed as mere footnotes in discussions of Canadian foreign policy under Mulroney, diminishing the fervour and determination of Canadians and their government to collaborate in tackling famine eradication in Africa. This chapter examines the ways in which Canadian involvement with the Ethiopian famine was distinct and unparalleled in its range of state and non-state actors, and in its level of public support for, and engagement with, famine relief efforts. It explores too how exposure to the difficult challenges of humanitarian relief sowed the seeds for popular disenchantment and the resurgence of domestic partisan divisions. The "Samaritan State" was clearly an ephemeral phenomenon.

The Samaritan State Rallied

Ubiquitous publicity about the Ethiopian famine through multiple media forums fostered close government and public cooperation in Canada aimed at eradicating famine in Africa. The African famine encouraged several facets of Canadian society, many with no prior exposure to foreign aid questions, to merge into a truly "Samaritan State." New Democratic Party

MP Pauline Jewett attributed "steadfast public support to the cause" as an outcome of the "global village" created by television.[7] Without doubt, as anthropologist Sonya de Laat discusses in chapter 9, the *"aestheticization"* and "the packaging of famine as a shocking and dramatic crisis" was integral to the discursive construction and the rallying of both political and public support for famine relief in the Horn of Africa. The plight of the millions of people in the afflicted regions was undeniably desperate, and much of the photographic coverage of the famine featured close-ups of the most emaciated individuals. The images of famine victims and the endless cover stories devoted to the Ethiopian crisis permeated Canadian and Western consciousness, then and later.[8]

The Ethiopian famine was one of the first foreign policy crises encountered by Mulroney's Progressive Conservative government, elected in early September 1984.[9] Responding to Stewart's CBC newscast, Foreign Minister Joe Clark told his party's caucus on 7 November that it "is our duty as a people to respond." He continued: "We will treat Ethiopia as an all-party matter. . . . We want support from all Canadians. . . . MPs should contact service clubs and local mayors and ask them to lend their efforts to provide aid. . . . One of the faults in past Canadian foreign policy was that the Canadian people were shut out."[10] Clark and his compatriots were doubtless influenced by lessons learned from Canada's mishandling of the Biafran crisis in Nigeria nearly two decades earlier. While Biafra quickly faded from popular memory in the aftermath of the Nigerian civil war, historian Stephanie Bangarth argues that "the lessons learned, the tactics employed by mainstream churches, NGOs, and individuals, and the pressure brought to bear on the federal government would serve both as a foundation on which to build future humanitarian relief operations in Africa and as an example of the importance of public mobilization."[11]

The prime minister too was moved by the "tragedy of vast starvation and death," and a desire not to repeat errors of governments past, when he promised the House of Commons to "provide leadership and assistance in this grave crisis" despite a towering national deficit, the prospect of a tough budget, and campaign promises to create more jobs.[12] Opposition members echoed the prime minister's sentiments because, as Liberal MP Jean Chrétien explained, "no one wants to be partisan about this issue."[13] The national consensus in November 1984 held that "although Canada has

FIGURE 10.1
Canadians of all kinds, including an ad hoc celebrity pop group, the Northern Lights, rallied to the Ethiopian cause. The band's Christmas-themed song, "Tears Are Not Enough," topped the charts in 1985. (Source: Bruce Allen Agency, LAC e999920081)

its problems, we are fat compared with those countries."[14] Ever the canny populist, Chrétien was right in noting that all Canadians wanted the government to do more and that this was "not the time to cut foreign aid."

From the outset of concerted relief efforts, Progressive Conservative leaders were convinced that the crisis was a concern not only for the government but also "for the people of Canada."[15] Hence, Clark asked "the help of Members of Parliament throughout the House of Commons, and of citizens across the country to ensure that the Government acts and that the people act to do what we can to stop the starving in Ethiopia." The foreign minister's call to action was met with resounding chants of *"Hear, Hear!"*

Official enthusiasm was echoed by the Canadian public. An ad hoc group of Canadian musical stars and celebrities, Northern Lights, repeated the government's call to action in an iconic charity pop song, "Tears Are Not Enough," that topped the charts for 1985.[16] Featuring news stories like

"Artisans donate work to aid famine victims"[17] and "Canucks pledge $1.5 M,"[18] press headlines illustrated the public's engagement with the issue. The entire country was moved by the televised images of refugee camps and mass starvation, resulting in an outpouring of support typically characterized as "magnificent," with more than 500,000 Canadians donating about $35 million to Africa by May 1986.[19]

The optimism and determination that marked popular humanitarianism in Canada was infectious and far reaching. Over the course of four years, acts of relief were carried out by a variety of state and non-state actors, including churches, community groups, and schools as well as individual professionals from a range of fields with different levels of expertise.[20] Heightened public awareness and engagement with the issue of famine in Africa, particularly in Ethiopia, widened the space in Canada for a proliferation of discourses on the global duties and obligations of the state and its citizens, culminating in acts of "humanitarian internationalism."[21] University of Toronto political scientist Cranford Pratt defined "humane internationalism" as "an acceptance that citizens and governments of the industrialized world have ethical responsibilities towards those beyond their borders who are suffering severely and who live in abject poverty."[22]

In their collective response to the famine, Canadians demonstrated their commitment to this philosophy in spades. As early as 13 November 1984, Progressive Conservative MP Jim Edwards captured the national mood when he recounted how the Kiwanis Club of Edmonton was "recommending to its board of directors an expenditure of $10,000 for Ethiopian and African relief."[23] Edwards described how he had received a call from an Edmonton doctor, who volunteered to spend his six-week vacation in Ethiopia at his own expense. That, Edwards insisted, was "the true spirit of Canadian internationalism."[24]

The national feeling persisted. Early in the second year of the relief effort, a survey conducted by the government's chief pollster, Allan Gregg, found that the majority of Canadians surveyed "were more concerned about global problems of hunger and starvation than [domestic] economic problems."[25] Gregg characterized this finding as the prevalent attitude among Canadians and not just "a passing fad."[26] In March 1986, Gregg's final report, entitled *Canadians and Africa: What Was Said*, highlighted the fact that in alignment with previous surveys, one in five Canadians continued "to cite world hunger and poverty as their second major issue of concern."[27]

During the peak famine relief effort, the Canadian government was truly in tune with the national mood. Indeed, political scientist Kim Nossal later asserted that if populism in politics is measured by a willingness to involve as many "ordinary people in the policy process as possible or practicable," then the "Mulroney government had an evident populist streak."[28] In recent years, foreign affairs critics have cited this period as exemplary, contrasting it with the apathetic attitude of successive governments in their responses to other subsequent African crises.[29]

Impassioned by a visit to the drought and famine–ravaged East African nation in December 1984, Clark several times underscored the Mulroney government's commitment to taking leadership in this cause. Instead of relying on established mechanisms in the Department of External Affairs or CIDA, the Mulroney government appointed David MacDonald as its Emergency Coordinator for African Famine, effectively creating "a new *ad hoc* layer of political administration."[30] MacDonald was given the resources to develop a separate office to oversee all the relief activities of the government, NGOs, and private citizens, enabling Canadians to respond to the ensuing "human crisis in the most effective way possible."[31] MacDonald was effectively granted an implicit form of "super ministerial role and access," allowing him to overcome bureaucratic barriers and to request immediate action directly from departments, powers that he credits as key to the successes of his team and its mission.[32]

MacDonald was clearly the right man for the job. Over the course of his term as relief coordinator, MacDonald won the hearts and trust of the Canadian public, often using quiet diplomacy to "defuse criticism of Canadian food aid operations during a critical period."[33] First elected to Parliament from Prince Edward Island in 1965, he was a skilled political operative, who served as a cabinet minister in Joe Clark's short-lived Progressive Conservative government in 1979 before losing his seat in 1984. An ordained United Church minister, MacDonald enjoyed a sterling reputation in Ottawa as a man of conscience. He championed aid to the breakaway Nigerian province of Biafra in 1968–69 and opposed the imposition of the War Measures Act to crush the radical Front de libération du Québec in October 1970.[34] Happy to rise above partisan differences, as an opposition MP MacDonald joined Liberal prime minister Pierre Trudeau's "Futures Secretariat," a group of national opinion leaders promoting "public interest in Third World issues."[35] MacDonald's appointment reflected the Mulroney government's bipartisan approach to famine relief. MacDonald surmises that he was asked by the government because they needed someone who could tackle bureaucratic impediments, as well as "somebody they knew really well and trusted."[36] "There was a lot of spontaneous combustion" he recalled, "of people who wanted to do something meaningful."[37] In his report *Africa's Famine and Canada's Response,* MacDonald outlines in great detail the ways in which Canadians from coast to coast responded in what he characterizes as both traditional and "new and imaginative ways."[38]

Relief Across The Spectrum

One of the earliest public initiatives that MacDonald highlights was a Halifax-based "adopt-a-village" airlift on Christmas Eve organized by Haligonians working with John Godfrey, president of Kings College University, and the Ottawa-based World University Service of Canada (WUSC). "I see it as an alliance of people in the community of all ages," commented Godfrey. "What makes this thing great is that we've got 19 year olds with 69 and 42 year olds who are working together on it, each bringing his own skills and patience. It's been a real trip for students in the Maritimes who have been talking to air force Colonels and helping to order planes around."[39] The effort, MacDonald emphasized, quickly led to the "twinning" of Canadian communities in the Maritime provinces with a number of Ethiopian villages. Through twinning, Canadians from coast-to-coast became invested in helping individual Ethiopian communities. Canadians were seeking long term change, and the practice of twinning came to be seen as a sustainable strategy to ensure that a humanitarian crisis of this magnitude would not reoccur.[40]

The experience with Gode, one of six Ethiopian villages in WUSC's four-month-old Ogaden-wide emergency program that was matched up with a Canadian city, was not unusual. Inspired by Godfrey's effort, a small group of students at the University of Toronto secured their school's backing, obtained space in the International Student Centre, and began fundraising. Students, staff, and faculty were challenged to support a community with a $12 donation, or a dollar per month, the price of a cup of coffee.[41] Barbara Treviranus, one of the Toronto villagers, recalls her involvement in the start of this initiative as empowering to a fourth-year undergraduate interested in international development.[42]

When twinning was "adopted" as an International Youth Year activity by local broadcaster City TV, plenty of media coverage followed.[43] Dubbed the *village twinners*, the organizers ensured widespread participation in their effort by publicizing it across the city's subway system and by engaging Mayor Art Eggleton, who attached an appeal on Gode's behalf to the city's July tax bill.[44] Rallying the city of Toronto proved to be a cinch, with almost twenty Toronto "Villagers" schools cooperating "to aid Gode with awareness weeks, all night dances and popcorn sales."[45] By the time activist Dawn Mac-Donald visited Gode in February 1986, this Toronto group had raised over "$60,000 with an estimated further $40,000 coming from various school and church campaigns in progress."[46] Canadian youth were once again emblems of the nation's commitment to a worthy international cause.[47]

Citizens in more rural settings were also engaged in agitating for long-term change through cooperative action. In the summer of 1986, for instance, Susan James of the Guelph African Relief Network (GAFRN) wrote Ontario premier David Peterson, petitioning the provincial government to focus on "community-to-community" action between the province and Africa.[48] GAFRN, characterized as "an informal grouping of . . . agencies and organizations working either in development assistance or in education in international development," was a typical small-scale Canadian initiative. It aimed to bolster "sustained individual personal involvement by both Canadians and Africans" and wanted more done by Canadian governments to rally their public into greater displays of international humanitarianism. "We believe," said James, urging the premier to action, "that the response we have observed here to the challenge of the African drought and famine, has opened a door to much higher levels of engagements of Ontario people and their communities with Africans and development actions in Africa."[49]

GAFRN members believed that deeper ties between Guelph and Africa would have a long-lasting impact, and were consequently seeking the support of their provincial government in bringing their efforts at local city council to fruition. The group hoped that the province would support an exchange of health care providers, broaden the existing activities of colleges and universities in sharing both students and teachers, create more opportunities for African students to come to Ontario schools and universities through a revised fee structure, and initiate the sharing of provincial and municipal methods of planning natural resource and agricultural resource assessment and development. All of these suggestions were indicative of the fact that Canadian relief efforts would inevitably veer into activities that might be considered as foreign policy initiatives embedded in conceptualizations of development emerging from the Mulroney government's willingness to engage its citizens in participatory forms of politics.

GAFRN, like other relief organizations, participated in the national "Forum Africa" consultation meetings, which invited Canadians to "evaluate the African crisis, learn from it and to reflect on the role they could play in the recovery of those African countries suffering from famine."[50] Forum Africa was initiated by the federal government on 4 September 1985 in the city halls of Ottawa and Hull; by February 1986, more than fifty communities across six regions of the country had held symposium sessions.[51] Though the impetus for these meetings came from the Office of the Canadian Emergency Coordinator, it was intended that community-based organizations, including humanitarian groups, churches, education, business, unions, municipalities, and the media would assume responsibility for the program. Ultimately, "Forum Africa" underlined the federal government's capacity and willingness to leverage existing networks and resources to spearhead Canada-wide engagement on a foreign aid issue.

Overall, the level of public and political engagement with the famine in Ethiopia was impressive, cross-sectional, and yet, also cause for reflection. Based on reports produced by MacDonald and his team, ideas of personal sacrifice to help Ethiopians were palatable to many Canadians, so long as the sacrifice was for the greater good. Perhaps the most poignant and hard-hitting examples of devotion to the cause were the demonstrations of support from Canadians who themselves were faced with economic hardship. John Amagoalik, co-chairman of the Inuit Committee on National Issues, told a news conference that most Inuit of his "generation have all been affected, directly or indirectly, by famine."[52] Inuit representatives were soon scheduled to tour Ethiopia, and they placed an emphasis on the fact that they identified "with others who live in harsh conditions and suffer from famine."[53]

In another example, Nancy Leavitt from Edmonton wrote to Clark offering $125. Leavitt, a full-time student and mother of three teenagers, clearly felt the sacrifice at home was worth the price of helping the "starving children of Ethiopia."[54] "I trust this money will go for food and not arms," she wrote, explaining that she had told her own children that their Christmas will not be an elaborate one, but that they will "all have a clear conscience" knowing that they did their utmost to contribute. Irrefutably, the African famine of this period elicited mass compassion from Canadians from all walks of life.

Channelling Relief

Mass awareness of the African famine ultimately served a twofold purpose as it enabled mass mobilization and ultimately mass consumption of the issues as presented by the media. In addition to the shock value of the footage rendered, representations of the famine were also arguably packaged to elicit moral imperatives to act. Over the course of the four years of sustained famine relief efforts by the Canadian government and its citizens, Ethiopia would receive the most attention of the twenty-one African nations afflicted by famine or in receipt of "abnormally high" international food aid in this period.[55]

Most of Canada's Official Development Assistance (ODA) program was administered by CIDA, and assistance reached Ethiopia in this period through four principal channels: bilateral arrangements, multilateral channels, special Canadian programs, and Canadian businesses supported by CIDA.[56] By the early 1980s, food experts had already deemed that "Africa's population was rapidly outstripping food production."[57] Hence, the main CIDA objective in Ethiopia was food security, and it focused its efforts on providing food aid and investing in bilateral projects through NGOs, the Africa 2000 program, a Business Cooperation Branch's Industrial cooperation program, and a joint CIDA–International Development Research Centre project.[58] It is through assistance from CIDA's Special Programs Branch that the direct participation of Canadians was elicited, in support of the Canadian government's "efforts to promote self-reliance and meet basic human needs in developing countries."[59]

From the outset of the government's relief effort, it was widely recognized that Canada had on "a per capita basis and in terms of absolute figures, contributed the most towards food aid in Ethiopia."[60] In total, through regular CIDA programs and the Special Fund for Africa, set up in response to the 1984–85 drought, Canada supplied Ethiopia with well over 100,000 tons of food in 1984–85, with a value of more than $39 million. This represented almost one-quarter of Canada's total food aid to Africa.[61] In addition to increased food aid and assistance from the bilateral and Special Programs Branch, Ethiopia was the principal recipient of funds from the $65 million Special Fund for Africa and the $20 million African Recovery Fund in 1984–85.[62]

The Politics of Aid

By the early 1980s, as Ted Cogan points out in his chapter in this volume, foreign aid had already become a politically charged subject in Canada. This was no less true when it came to dealing with the famine-stricken regions in Africa. The efforts of Liberal prime minister Pierre Trudeau to increase aid to Ethiopia in 1983–84 in anticipation of its looming famine had drawn sharp criticism from the Progressive Conservative opposition.[63] In January 1984, for instance, Progressive Conservative MP Ron Stewart had called into question both the nature, and the implications of, Canadian aid to Ethiopia. Stewart was especially concerned by reports from the European Parliament that Western aid to Ethiopia was being sent onward to the Soviet Union, Canada's cold war adversary. Moreover, citing reports that the Ethiopian government was "spending 40% of its budget on its army—instead of feeding its starving citizens," he questioned CIDA's prudence in allocating $10 million in food aid to Ethiopia. While members of his conservative party supported aid when and where it was needed, Stewart insisted that accountability and transparency on the part of the recipient nation should be weighted heavily. The MP further contended that Liberal economic policies had put Canada "in the same league as Mexico, another bankrupt nation." "The taxpayers' hard earned dollars," Stewart concluded, should not be spent "propping up inefficiently run, one-party dictatorships that are politically unfriendly both to us and to the entire notion of democracy and human rights."[64]

Given pre-existing patterns of partisan conflict over aid, it is noteworthy that the overwhelming public and political response to the Ethiopian crisis after November 1984 swept away concerns regarding the Ethiopian government and the efficacy of the CIDA's aid delivery system. Yet, as political scientist Mark W. Charlton argues in *The Making of Canadian Food Aid Policy*, the Ethiopian famine remained a contentious affair. In his book, Charlton outlines the heated debates over the morality of providing aid to a government with a clear track record of human rights abuses. In particular, Charlton underscores how the resettlement programs of the Ethiopian government were perceived to be "genocidal and coercive" policies by many aid agencies and government critics, some of whom wanted to withhold aid as an appropriate response.[65]

At least initially, Foreign Minister Clark easily quelled fears that either the brutal civil war or a corrupt Ethiopian government might disrupt aid. "The Government and authorities of Ethiopia," he confidently asserted, "are doing everything that is possible in very difficult circumstances to ensure that aid that comes from the rest of the world to help starving people in Ethiopia, will get to those people."[66] MacDonald insisted that the "quiet diplomacy approach" adopted by him and his team was effective at getting aid to where it was needed the most.[67] While publicly reassuring Canadians that the Ethiopian government was allocating Canadian aid responsibly, MacDonald channelled some aid through NGOs, which were able to funnel it to the severely afflicted provinces of Eritrea and Tigray, rebel strongholds.[68] Anxious to help, most Canadians trusted Clark and MacDonald to bring their hopes for Ethiopia to fruition.

However, by early 1988, it was increasingly difficult to deny the evidence of gross misconduct. Eyewitness accounts and official reports documented villages being burned and food being stored until rotten or sold to the highest bidders. Instead of sending cheques to their MPs, Canadians were soon sending petitions demanding an "end to the hostilities in Ethiopia."[69] With the easing of the drought in 1986, many donors were also increasingly aware of the need to include long-term rehabilitation with relief assistance.

Consequently, by April 1988, the focus of discourse within both the Canadian government and the public sphere shifted from celebratory support for relief assistance to more pointed expressions of concern and criticism over the political and moral implications of providing aid to Ethiopia.

Nassisse Solomon

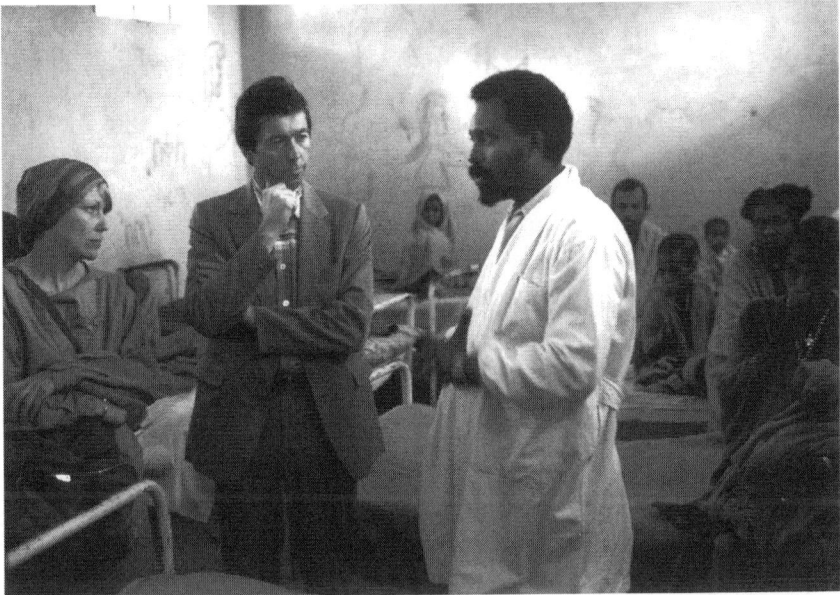

FIGURE 10.2
Advisor Marie-Andrée Lalonde-Morisset and Emergency Coordinator for African Famine David MacDonald meet with an unidentified Ethiopian doctor on a visit to a hospital in Mekele, Ethiopia, in 1985. (Source: David MacDonald Collection/LAC e999919818)

A typical petition delivered by Liberal opposition leader John Turner, with "1,200 signatures from Vancouver and across the country," called on the government to lead "an international development and peace initiative for the immediate cessation of hostilities and internal violence in Ethiopia."[70] Four years into the nationwide famine relief campaign, Canadians were arguably seeking more systemic change to deal with the circumstances in East Africa.

Winnipeg MP Bill Blaikie, the NDP's foreign policy spokesperson, became an especially trenchant critic of the government's relationship with the Ethiopian state. When inquiring about Ottawa's ability to get food through to the Ethiopian provinces of Tigray and Eritrea, often described by parliamentarians as "rebel territories," Blaikie insisted that Clark assure the House of Commons "and through this house to the Government of Ethiopia and to others that are concerned, that there is a place where Canada will draw the line." Blaikie demanded to know when Canada would "say that the humanitarian need for food to get to starving people, regardless of the political circumstances is paramount in Canadian policy."[71] Blaikie's criticisms would signal the end of the popular campaign, as Ethiopian famine relief became too complicated for the general public and the government to remain as fervently engaged as they were in November 1984.

Implications: The Legacy of a Period of Fanfare

During this intersecting period in Canadian and Ethiopian history, the impetus to act was provided on 1 November 1984, and widespread social action was mobilized by conceptualizations of what it meant to be a Canadian citizen. Consequently, the Ethiopian famine served as a clarion call for global citizenship and altruism for Canadians from coast to coast.

The implications of these relief efforts would be far reaching, with important consequences for Canadian aid policy and foreign relations. In their assessment of this era, political scientists Nelson Michaud and Kim Nossal argue that the Progressive Conservatives did not come into power in 1984 with a clearly articulated foreign policy agenda.[72] Yet, forced to reckon with an international catastrophe within days of its election, this government demonstrated leadership in their handling of this international crisis.

More important, the Progressive Conservative response to the Ethiopian crisis, alongside the coordinating efforts of MacDonald and his team, set a benchmark for increased involvement of NGOs in the policy-making and policy-implementation process.[73] During the course of MacDonald's mandate as emergency coordinator, public concern for the African situation remained constant. According to the Decima poll commissioned in February 1986, Canadians continued to believe that "Canada should continue in its role as one of the more generous nations in assisting African recovery and development."[74] Thus fortified, in March 1986 MacDonald's final report confidently offered a series of recommendations for further Canadian involvement in Africa.

One direct outcome of the ongoing public interest and opposition pressure for the Mulroney government to act was the Africa 2000 operation. Conceived as a long-term policy and program commitment, Africa 2000 would encompass all Canadian ODA involvement in Africa.[75] Described as more than "a financial kitty," Operation Africa 2000 was essentially a

Canadian policy commitment made for fifteen years, allocating an initial $150 million from existing CIDA funds over the course of five fiscal years for special initiatives in Africa. The central focus of the operation was policy, with a particular emphasis on agriculture, reforestation, food security, and women. In the aftermath of the Ethiopian famine, Canada provided more official development assistance to Africa than to any other region every year from 1980 until 2011.[76]

Ultimately, as Charlton points out, the famine also contributed to the reassessment of Canada's handling of aid in conflict-ridden regions. "In circumstances where CIDA lacks confidence in the overall priorities of the recipient government," he explains, CIDA resorted to "alternative [NGO] channels to ensure that the food is reaching the specific populations in need."[77] Critics like Charlton have argued that in spite of the "public relations" successes of the Mulroney government's approach of "quiet diplomacy" during the Ethiopian famine relief efforts, there is lingering uncertainty over the ethics of providing aid to governments with ongoing internal conflicts and poor human rights records, especially when food aid is being utilized as a weapon.

Within the collective Western psyche and memory, the famine year of 1984–85 remains the international benchmark for Ethiopian, and by implicit extension, "African suffering." The horrifying images of emaciated children and adults, as well as deaths en masse, mobilized Canadians to collective acts of humanitarian internationalism in a distant corner of the world afflicted by drought, famine, and brutal civil war.[78] Starving children, argues University of Maryland media scholar Susan D. Moeller, were, and still are, "the famine icon," signifying "a moral clarity to the complex story of famine."[79] Typically, images from Ethiopia rarely "situate[d] the child as a victim or survivor of a particular historic event nor belonging to a family, community, or nation."[80] Consequently, the Ethiopian famine soon became symbolic of and synonymous with all "African suffering."

Cultural historians and economists have characterized the 1980s in both the United States and the United Kingdom as a decade of greed and an era of "conspicuous consumption."[81] The Western culture of excess was stoked by a raging cold war, the conservative politics of American president Ronald Reagan and British prime minister Margaret Thatcher, the boom and bust of housing markets, high interest rates, and strong inflation. Yet "kids" of the 1980s across the West contended that there was "no excuse for political apathy."[82] The politics of the decade, British journalist and film-maker Sarfraz Manzoor has asserted, "felt like a blood sport and it bled into popular culture."[83] This was the Western political and cultural climate in which the British-led international movement "Band Aid" was born, accelerating into an international singularity/success. Economist Richard B. McKenzie cautions against mischaracterizing the 1980s as simply a decade of greed. Political and social engagement, he argues, also mean that it was a decade of social activism too, when "total private charitable contributions by living individuals, bequests, corporations and foundations, reached record highs."[84] It is within this paradigm of both excess and polarities that Bob Gedolf's "Band Aid" phenomenon took off; embraced by American and Canadian celebrities alike, it fuelled a moment of mass compassion in Canada. "Band Aid" was a larger than life socio-cultural/socio-political phenomenon across the entire Western hemisphere.

The 1984–85 famine relief campaign remains within living memory for many Canadians a lingering beacon of hope for the permanent eradication of famine on the African continent. Deemed a watershed moment in contemporary history, the famine and relief effort continue to be referenced frequently in the nomenclature of African famine news.[85] In early April 2016, for instance, when news of another apocalyptic-scale famine surfaced in international headlines, CBC reporter Margaret Evans reminisced that "Band Aid" was the first concerted response of its kind, raising over $150 million for relief.[86] Discourses surrounding yet another endemic bout of drought and famine had much historical symbolism and resonance. However, in response to criticisms that "history was simply repeating itself," Canadian diplomat Philip Baker stressed that the real story of African famine relief thirty years on ought to focus on the preparedness of the Ethiopian government in averting the kind of human catastrophe that occurred in 1984–86. In addition to providing an opportunity for self-aggrandizing reverence about a period of unparalleled mass compassion displayed by the West, memories of the famine also sealed the fate of Ethiopia, linking it "in the minds of many as forever associated with hunger and death."[87]

The pervasive blending of politics and culture made relief efforts during the 1984–86 period unique both internationally and domestically. Some critics have argued that the Band Aid phenomenon was part and parcel of the Reagan administration's efforts to wage cold war battles through humanitarian assistance."[88] Canada, others have argued, had no obvious political agenda for aiding Ethiopia, aside from improving its own international status by remaining a high-profile donor.[89] As a result, Canadian engagement with the famine crisis of 1984–85 was irrefutably multifaceted and pervasive across the political and social spectrum. Canada's UN Ambassador Stephen Lewis insisted that Canadians effectively demonstrated that they were members of "a generous, caring society."[90] Lewis further argued that the commitment of Canadians to multilateralism was real because, as he explained at one Forum Africa session, "the internationalism which we adhere to is rooted deeply in the psyche of Canadians."[91]

The construction of famine relief as a moral imperative, one widely embraced in the mid-1980s, perhaps gave rise to its own demise. One of the unintended outcomes of the very scale and intensity of the relief fanfare of 1984–86 may be contemporary donor fatigue, also characterized as "compassion fatigue" by Moeller.[92] In 2011, Conservative minister of international development Bev Oda announced that Canadians had given roughly $70 million to registered charities for African drought relief between July 6 and September 16.[93] Yet UN Secretary General Ban Ki-Moon estimated that at least $700 million in aid would still be required for that year alone. In the 1984–85 period, there was a total of $59.9 million dollars provided to Ethiopia in ODA.[94] In spite of the larger amounts raised and contributed by the government in subsequent years, African famines no longer attract the public attention that they once did.

Donor fatigue also reflects the deeply entrenched challenges of dealing with famine. The ideal of famine eradication, often promoted in mid-1980s, was a far more complex goal than the immediate emotional satisfactions sought by the general donor population. The politics of famine (famine reporting and famine relief efforts), both in 1984–86 and arguably now, illustrate that famine is often embroiled in much more nuanced political, economic, and environmental ecologies than depicted by the reductive media. African famine and its solutions cannot simply be framed as neat binary narratives of nature versus man, or good versus evil, or altruism versus capitalism. Thus, while images of starving women and children continued to elicit the empathy of Canadian and international publics, the rhetoric surrounding the complexities of the political conundrums within the region were, and still are, off putting.

Enshrouded in the memory of the unprecedented international response to the crisis of the mid-1980s is a peripheral discourse on environmental degradation and future catastrophe prevention. In the immediate aftermath of the 1984–86 famine, frontline aid workers were already predicting that relief efforts would not be enough to abate future catastrophes. Canadian aid agencies warned that even the most immediate and basic challenges faced by Africa's drought-stricken zones were not going to be overcome by 31 March 1986, when Mulroney's government told MacDonald to wind down his office.[95] Indeed, less than a year later, in December 1987, the World Food Program reported that Ethiopia, Mozambique, Malawi, Angola, Somalia, and the Sudan needed 2.3 million tons of food, almost twice as much as pledged by donor countries.[96] Not surprisingly, faith in the value of relief wavered.

Yet the relief efforts of 1984–86 still matter and demand attention. The headlines trumpeting the mass engagement of a Canadian public and its government in efforts to abate the unfolding tragedy in Ethiopia have made the campaign a modern parable for African famine. For many Canadians engaged with relief efforts during this period, 1984 continues to serve as a harbinger of hope—a hope that was the impetus to mobilize citizens around the world into action for positive change, changes that were once thought permanent.

Notes

1   Reg Stackhouse, Canada, House of Commons, *Debates*, 7 November 1984, 20.

2   Jack Hinde from Owen Sound, Ontario, wrote to Clark to let him know that he had "made an excellent start as Minister of External Affairs. Encouraging relief for Ethiopia was a clarion call that most Canadians will respond to." Cited in David MacDonald, Canadian Emergency Coordinator, *The African Famine and Canada's Response: For the Period from November 1984–March 1985* (Ottawa: Secretary of State, 1985), 52.

3   Tanja R. Muller makes the assertion that the Ethiopian Famine was a watershed event for humanitarian action in "'The Ethiopian Famine' Revisited: Band Aid and The Antipolitics of Celebrity Humanitarian Action," *Disasters* 37, no. 1 (2013): 61. Intimately involved in rallying Canadian public support and the delivery of aid to Ethiopia and other afflicted African nations, David MacDonald characterizes this

period as a "unique" fundraising effort for Africa. Author interview with David MacDonald, 28 March 2017.

4   *Forum Africa: Canadians Working Together*, Report by the Honourable David MacDonald, Canadian Emergency Coordinator/African Famine, on a series of Community Meetings from September 1985–February 1986, published March 1986, 5.

5   Editorial, "Follow The Mulroney Model to Alleviate Africa's Famine," *Globe and Mail*, 4 August 2011, http://www.theglobeandmail.com/opinion/editorials/follow-the-mulroney-model-to-alleviate-africas-famine/article589484/.

6   Stephen Brown, "Canadian Aid To Africa," in *Canada-Africa Relations: Looking Back, Looking Ahead*, ed. Rohinton Medhora and Yigadeesen Samy (Waterloo, ON: Centre for International Governance Innovation and Carleton University, 2013), 181–82.

7   Pauline Jewett, Canada, House of Commons, *Debates*, 16 November 1984, 307.

8   John Sorensen, "Mass Media and Discourse on Famine in the Horn of Africa," *Discourse and Society* 2, no. 2 (April 1991): 225.

9· Nelson Michaud and Kim Richard Nossal, "The Conservative Era in Canadian Foreign Policy, 1984–93," in their edited collection *Diplomatic Departures: The Conservative Era in Canadian Foreign Policy, 1984–93* (Vancouver: University of British Columbia Press, 2001),15.

10 Cited in Brian Mulroney, *Memoirs, 1939–93* (Toronto: McClelland and Stewart, 2007), 331–32.

11 On lessons learned from the Biafran Tragedy, see Stephanie Bangarth, "The Politics of African Intervention: Canada and Biafra, 1967–70," in *From Kinshasa to Kandahar: Canada and Fragile States in Historical Perspective, ed.* Greg Donaghy and Michael Carroll (Calgary: University of Calgary Press, 2016), 55.

12 Brian Mulroney, Canada, House of Commons, *Debates*, 7 November 1984, 39.

13 Jean Chrétien, Canada, House of Commons, *Debates*, 16 November 1984, 306.

14 Ibid.

15 Joe Clark, Canada, House of Commons, *Debates*, 7 November 1984, 28.

16 "Tears are Not Enough." *Historica Canada*, http://www.thecanadianencyclopedia.ca/en/article/tears-are-not-enough-emc/.

17 "Artisans donate work to aid famine victims," *Globe and Mail*, 23 March 1985, E7.

18 "Canucks pledge $1.5 M," *Toronto Sun*, 15 July 1985.

19 Bruce Ward, "Conscience, Faith in Man Propel MacDonald," *Ottawa Citizen*, 24 June 1986.

20 MacDonald's Canadian Emergency Coordinator's Report on *The African Famine and Canada's Response* highlights the fact that the Kinsmen Club of Kingston, Ontario, helped to raise enough funds to send a voluntary medical team to Ethiopia in February 1985, at p. 24.

21 Cranford Pratt, "Middle Power Internationalism and Global Poverty," in his edited collection *Middle Power Internationalism: The North-South Dimension* (Montreal: McGill-Queen's University Press, 1990), 5.

22 Ibid.

23 James Stewart Edwards, Canada, House of Commons, *Debates*, 13 November 1984, 200.

24 Ibid.

25 The survey by Toronto-based Decima Research found that Canadians surveyed in early February wanted foreign aid to be exempt from government cuts. "Foreign Aid Workers Determine Strong Relief Effort to Continue," *Evening Telegram* (St. John's), 18 February 1986.

26 Ibid.

27 *Canadians and Africa: What Was Said*, A Report for the Honourable David MacDonald, Canadian Emergency Coordinator/African Famine of a Nationwide Survey by Decima Research Ltd. Conducted in February 1986, 7.

28 Kim Richard Nossal, "Opening Up the Policy Preference: Does Party Make A Difference?," in Michaud and Nossal, *Diplomatic Departures*, 283.

29 In particular see Tony Burman, "Ebola: Canada Forgets Its Leadership in Ethiopian Famine," *Toronto Star*, 1 November 2014, https://www.thestar.com/news/world/2014/11/01/ebola_canada_forgets_its_leadership_in_ethiopian_famine.html; and Brian Stewart's "When Brian Mulroney was Great," CBC News, 14 May 2009, https://www.cbc.ca/news/canada/when-brian-mulroney-was-great-1.859343.

30 Nossal, "Opening Up the Policy Preference," 283.

31 Joe Clark, Canada, House of Commons, *Debates*, 7 November 1984, 28.

32 Author interview with David MacDonald, 28 March 2017.

33 Mark Charlton, *The Making of Canadian Food Aid Policy* (Montreal: McGill-Queen's University Press, 1992), 170.

34 Bangarth, "The Politics of African Intervention," 53–72. See also Ward, "Conscience, Faith in Man Propel MacDonald."

35 Ken MacQueen, "David MacDonald Excited By Challenge in Ethiopia," *Ottawa Citizen*, 11 December 1984.

36 Ibid.

37 Author interview with David MacDonald, 28 March 2017.

38 *African Famine and Canada's Response*, 24.

39 Cited in *The Varsity*, 6 June 1985, https://archive.org/stream/thevarsity106/thevarsity106_djvu.txt.

40 *Forum Africa*, 9.

41 Author Interview with Barbara Treviranus, one of the original Toronto villagers, 5 December 2017.

Nassisse Solomon

42   Ibid.

43   Email exchange with Barbara Treviranus, 10 November 2017.

44   Dawn MacDonald, "Ethiopia," *Toronto Star*, 8 February 1986. WUSC was funded from CIDA through the Special Programs Branch. See "Canadian International Development Agency Program Definition Mission 362/4311 Ethiopia, May 4–24, 1987: Team Notes," David MacDonald Papers, vol. 225, file 1, Library and Archives Canada (LAC).

45   Ibid.

46   Ibid.

47   Historian Tamara Myers makes this argument about the powerful symbolism of juxtapositions of the able-bodied and committed Canadian youth in contrast to the "needy third world child" in "Blistered and Bleeding, Tired and Determined: Visual Representations of Children and Youth in the Miles for Millions Walkathon," *Journal of the Canadian Historical Association* 22, no. 1 (2011): 267.

48   Susan James to David Peterson, 14 July 1986, David MacDonald Papers, vol. R12287, file 229-9, LAC.

49   Ibid.

50   David MacDonald to Monique Vezina, in *Forum Africa*, 2.

51   *Forum Africa*, 7.

52   Canadian Press, "Inuit Group off to Ethiopia For Tour of Famine Hit Areas," David MacDonald Papers, vol. R12287, file227, clippings file, December 1984–May 1986, LAC.

53   Ibid.

54   *African Famine and Canada's Response*, 22.

55   Angola, Burkina Faso, Burundi, Botswana, Cape Verde, Chad, Kenya, Lesotho, Mali, Mauritania, Morocco, Mozambique, Niger, Rwanda, Senegal, Somalia, Sudan, Tanzania, Zambia, and Zimbabwe are the other African nations listed in *African Famine and Canada's Response*, 36.

56   Ibid.

57   Brian Jeffries, "Dateline Nairobi: African Tragedy," *Maclean's*, 4 August 1980, 8.

58   CIDA, "Country Profile: Ethiopia," in file folder "Media Kit 1988," David MacDonald Papers, vol. R12287, file 219, LAC, 3.

59   Ibid., 7.

60   Jean Chrétien, Canada, House of Commons, *Debates*, 7 November 1984, 22.

61   CIDA, "Country Profile: Ethiopia" in file folder "Media Kit 1988," David MacDonald Papers, vol. R12287, file 219, LAC, 3.

62   Ibid.

63   The Trudeau Government had promised to achieve an ODA/GNP ratio of 0.7 per cent by 1990. See David R. Morrison, *Aid and Ebb Tide: A History of CIDA and Canadian Development Assistance* (Waterloo, ON: Wilfrid Laurier University Press, 1998), xv.

64 Ron Stewart, Canada, House of Commons, *Debates*, 26 January 1984, 704.

65 Charlton, *The Making of Canadian Food Aid Policy*, 170.

66 Joe Clark, Canada, House of Commons, *Debates*, 7 November 1984, 22.

67 Author interview with David MacDonald, 28 March 2017, and also in Charlton, *The Making of Canadian Food Aid Policy*, 170. For press coverage of a Canadian delegation's visit to the Ethiopian Highlands, in particular, see "Canadians, UN reject Ethiopian Abuse Charges," *Ottawa Citizen*, 19 March 1986.

68 Charlton, *The Making of Canadian Food Aid Policy*, 170.

69 John Turner, Canada, House of Commons, *Debates*, 13 April 1988, 14424–25.

70 Ibid. Other examples include one presented by Howard McCurdy (Windsor Walkersville) with 1,200 signatures, and another from Carole Jacques (Montreal-Mercier) with more than 1,300 names.

71 Bill Blaikie, Canada, House of Commons, *Debates,* 3 May 1988, 15083.

72 Michaud and Nossal, "The Conservative Era in Canadian Foreign Policy," 22.

73 Nossal, "Opening Up the Policy Preference," 281.

74 Africa 2000 Briefing Book, David MacDonald Papers, LAC.

75 Ibid.

76 Brown. "Canadian Aid To Africa," 181. Brown asserts that in 2010–2011, 38 per cent of Canadian international assistance went to Africa and six of the top ten recipients were in sub-Saharan Africa, namely Ethiopia, Tanzania, Mozambique, Ghana, Mali, Sudan, and Senegal.

77 Charlton, *The Making of Canadian Food Aid Policy*, 87.

78 Drought and famines were a recurring issue on the African continent during the late 1960s and 1970s (e.g., Biafra). In Ethiopia, the famine of 1977 was within living memory for many of its people during the catastrophe of 1984. See Brian Jeffries, "Dateline Nairobi: African Tragedy," *Maclean's*, 4 August 1980, 8.

79 Susan Moeller, *Compassion Fatigue: How the Media Sell Disease, Famine, War and Death* (New York: Routledge, 1999).

80 Myers, "Blistered and Bleeding," 253.

81 David Oliver Relin, "When Greed Was Good: The 1980s Will Go Down in History as a Decade of Excess," *Scholastic Update* 123, no. 12 (1991): 14, http://link.galegroup.com/apps/doc/A10561158/AONE?u=lond95336&sid=AONE&xid=bef1257f.

82 Sarfraz Manzoor, "The Diamond Decades: The 1980s," *Telegraph* (London), 31 May 2012, https://www.telegraph.co.uk/culture/culturenews/9289961/The-Diamond-Decades-The-1980s.html.

83 Ibid.

84 Richard B. McKenzie, "Was It a Decade of Greed?," *The Public Interest* 106 (Winter 1992): 92.

85   CBC reporter Margaret Evans references the legacy of this period in Canada and beyond in the 20 April 2016 feature news report entitled "Ethiopia on the Edge" for CBC's program *The National*, http://www.cbc.ca/player/play/670401603927; for international comparatives and references see James Jeffrey. "Ethiopia Drought: How Can We Let This Happen Again? This Time Around Ethiopia is Competing With War-Torn Syria and Yemen for International Funds," *Aljazeera*, 25 January 2016. http://www.aljazeera.com/indepth/opinion/2016/01/ethiopia-drought-happen-160121084103587.html.

86   Evans, "Ethiopia on the Edge." For more information in this regard see Nassisse Solomon, "1984: The Parable of Ethiopian Famine and Foreign Aid," http://activehistory.ca/2016/05/1984-the-parable-of-ethiopian-famine-and-foreign-aid/.

87   Evans, "Ethiopia on the Edge."

88   Alexander Poster, "The Gentle War: Famine Relief, Politics, and Privatization in Ethiopia, 1983–1986," *Diplomatic History* 36, no. 2 (April 2012): 399, 400.

89   Stephen Lewis, as quoted in Brian Stewart's "When Brian Mulroney Was Great," CBC News, 14 May 2009, https://www.cbc.ca/news/canada/when-brian-mulroney-was-great-1.859343.

90   *Forum Africa*, 36.

91   Ibid.

92   Moeller, *Compassion Fatigue*, 98.

93   Gloria Galloway, "What's Next for the $70-million Canadians Donated to East Africa," *Globe and Mail*, 5 October 2011, https://www.theglobeandmail.com/news/politics/whats-next-for-the-70-million-canadians-donated-to-east-africa/article559407/.

94   CIDA, *Food Crisis in Africa*, 1985, 7.

95   "Famine Report Key: Keep up the good work," *Ottawa Citizen*, 31 March 1986, David MacDonald Papers, LAC.

96   Canadian Press, "Act before thousands starve, Geldolf Says of Ethiopia Tour," *Vancouver Sun*, 21 December 1987, C5.

PART 4

THE POLITICAL ECONOMY OF CANADIAN AID, 1980–2018

Canada's development project stumbled in the mid-1980s and never recovered. After the pinnacle of Canadian public participation and self-perception as a humanitarian nation, evident in Nassisse Solomon's chapter on Ethiopian famine relief, compassion fatigue set in. A struggling economy and a looming national debt crisis exposed CIDA to closer scrutiny and recurring budget reductions, beginning in 1989. Aid funding fell precipitately after the election of Jean Chrétien's Liberals in 1993, as total government spending contracted and aid was slashed more than most sectors—declining from 3 per cent of federal government tax revenues to less than 1.5 per cent.[1] Among the first programs to go were CIDA's public engagement efforts, depriving the agency of its popular support at this vulnerable juncture.

At the same time, the political economy of global aid shifted to the right. Conservative governments in London and Washington and their allies at the World Bank and the International Monetary Fund championed a hardline capitalist neo-liberal agenda that imposed untested structural adjustment programs (SAP) across the Global South, reducing public spending and introducing free market liberalism.

Under president Marcel Massé and his successors, the Canadian International Development Agency embraced these reforms, aligned its aid with Ottawa's trade priorities, and beefed up its efforts in middle-income countries. At the same time, structural adjustment overturned earlier aid exchanges like those described by Jill Campbell-Miller in her chapter, which gave India a strong influence over Canadian aid policy. The change in focus obscured the once-clear rationale for an independent aid agency, and CIDA eventually succumbed to mounting pressures to merge with the Department of Foreign Affairs and International Trade, a shotgun marriage consummated in 2013.

Part 4 is an exercise in contemporary history that contextualizes the challenges of the last three decades. All three chapters take a critical perspective, ranging from Laura Macdonald's emphasis on Canadian business and civil society influences, to David Black's institutional focus on CIDA's final years, to Stephen Brown's revisiting of themes struck half a century ago in Keith Spicer's pioneering work on Canadian aid, *A Samaritan State?* Through very different analytical lenses, they come to strikingly similar conclusions that indicate a decline in Canada's aid capacity and relevance on the global stage.

For Macdonald, Canadian aid in Latin America has always followed the contours of the northern country's foreign politics, especially its foreign commercial policies. This has long encouraged high levels of Canadian investment in Central and South America, especially in such key sectors as mining, where Canadian investment leads the way. Ottawa's stress on promoting trade, outlined in Stefano Tijerina's case study of Colombia, continued in later years and throughout the region. But so too did the increasing role of civil society. As MacDonald writes, strong civil society actors have emerged both in Canada and in the region with a robust political stake in Canadian ODA. Regional aid policy, she argues, was, and is, shaped by the historic tensions between commercial stakeholders and civil society.

CIDA may have been harmed by its increased stress on business and reduced focus on civil society, an emphasis going back to the days of Hugh Keenleyside and Lewis Perinbam, and a former CIDA priority as described in chapters by Ted Cogan and Sonya de Laat. David Black's chapter on CIDA's institutional culture and the agency's 2013 merger with Canada's foreign ministry is just as historically determined. CIDA's demise, he argues, is rooted in the 1990s, when it embraced neo-liberal policy prescriptions to win favour with the World Bank, the IMF, and key Ottawa decision makers. The shift strained CIDA's identify as "an organization committed to poverty alleviation." Whereas CIDA had once provided space for policy experimentation, it had abandoned that role and was no longer able to advance the case for its own preservation. It was a far cry from the pioneering days of Nik Cavell!

Stephen Brown's closing reflections on the contemporary relevance of *A Samaritan State?* reprises the section's historical motif. Spicer erred in his pious hope that aid might return gratitude and political dividends. That was neither true in Pakistan in the 1950s nor Afghanistan in the 2000s. Yet Spicer's insistence on clarity of purpose and long-term enlightened self-interest are helpful remainders to policy makers to avoid short-term political or economic distractions. Though Canada does not emerge from this examination as a Samaritan state, many of Spicer's thoughts still hold up well, even in a time of decline for Canada's role in global development.

Note

1   See http://www.progressive-economics.ca/2017/05/03/a-tale-book-ended-by-2-trudeaus-canadas-foreign-aid-since-1970/.

Canadian Development Assistance to Latin America

Laura Macdonald

Canadian development assistance policies toward Latin America mirror the evolution of Canada's broader foreign policy relations with the region, and thus provide important insight into Canada's changing identity and role in the world. Canada's early ties with Latin America were weak and intermittent, and even as more recent governments have shown greater interest in the region, they have failed to develop deep and sustained ties with hemispheric partners and institutions.[1] Similarly, levels of development assistance were minimal in the early years of the Canadian aid program, and while Canadian assistance to Latin America increased substantially over the last several decades, it never rivalled levels provided to Africa (see David Black's chapter in this volume). Latin America is the world region with the highest levels of inequality, where high levels of poverty exist alongside extreme wealth. However, most Latin American states are classified as middle-income developing countries and the region is not viewed as the highest priority for aid aimed primarily at reducing poverty (Haiti is the main exception to this generalization and has been the principal recipient of Canadian aid in the region in recent years). Therefore, motivations for delivering development assistance based on pity, compassion, or "humane internationalism"[2] are not predominant in Canadian aid to Latin

America, where other motivations tend to prevail (the chapter in this volume by Tijerina displays some of these non-humanitarian motivations for development assistance in the case of Colombia).

This chapter reviews the history of Canadian development assistance to Latin America and examines how aid policy has interacted with broader foreign policy objectives over time. At least since the 1980s Canadian policies can be read as a form of dialogue between state and societies (both Canadian and Latin American). Societal determinants of aid policy tend to predominate in this relationship, as opposed to institutionalist factors, which, as David Black discusses in his chapter in this volume, played an important role in the Africa program. These determinants include geopolitical and security interests, commercial considerations, and political and ideological factors. Compared to support for other regions, Canadian aid to Latin America is shaped by the tension between relatively strong Canadian commercial interests in the region and pressures from highly mobilized civil society. Under Prime Minister Stephen Harper's Conservative government, aid was increasingly instrumentalized[3] and commercial objectives became more prominent, although they never entirely pushed out other motivations.

The chapter begins with a brief discussion of the early history of Canadian development assistance to Latin America, and then explores the politicization of Canadian aid beginning in the 1970s, and the increase in Canadian interest in the region between the 1980s and early 2000s, as reflected in aid policy. The third section considers the policies of the Harper government, which adopted an explicit Americas Strategy. In some ways similar to the efforts of Pierre Trudeau's Liberal government in the 1970s, it identified the region as a key foreign policy priority as part of the broader objective of expanding and diversifying Canadian economic interests in the world. Aid policies played an important role in this strategy, and development assistance was increasingly instrumentalized in response. The chapter concludes with some reflections on the initial changes under the Justin Trudeau government, which has rhetorically shifted away from an emphasis on commercial objectives, toward a greater emphasis on human rights, gender, and a revalorization of the contribution of civil society partnerships in the aid enterprise. It seems likely that while we will see greater balance between diverse objectives and greater input from civil society in establishing policies under the Trudeau government, the policies of the Harper era have established a certain pathway that may be difficult to escape.

Early History

Latin America was overlooked in the early years of Canada's official aid program, as a result of the country's traditional cultural and foreign policy ties. The Colombo Plan, as Jill Campbell-Miller explains in this volume, initially concentrated on supporting newly decolonized countries of the British Commonwealth, first in Asia and eventually in the English-speaking Caribbean and Africa. Canada thus expressed its willingness to contribute to the cold war endeavour of supporting and stabilizing former British colonies.[4] In contrast, Canada stayed out of Latin America, which was viewed as part of the US sphere of influence and not necessarily a congenial location for Canadian engagement. Canada's early relationship with the region was symbolized by its failure to join the principle hemispheric multilateral organization, the Organization of American States (OAS). Canadian officials and politicians felt they had little to gain from membership in a body that became increasingly subject to US whims, and there was little social support for greater involvement in hemispheric affairs in this early period.[5]

Mirroring this foreign policy position, Canada's development assistance commitments in the region remained limited. However, in 1964 Canada pledged $10 million in assistance for the Inter-American Development Bank (IDB). According to Keith Spicer, the rationale for the decision to begin providing aid to Latin America was largely based on foreign policy motivations. Among these were the idea that engagement would give Canada enhanced influence on US policy and a deeper understanding of Latin American "revolutionary forces" (which were an increasing concern after the 1959 Cuban revolution). Moreover, aid would help enhance "people-to-people" relations. Spicer expressed concern, however, that such a commitment might also spread Canadian skills too thin and lead to ever-increasing demands for aid to the region. He dismissed the decision to support the IDB as a token of "Canada's necessarily limited concern for Latin America," and hoped that it would not lead to increased commitments that might "undermine more valuable older relationships."[6] While Spicer valued aid as a way to expand Canadian ties with the world, he was modest in terms of the world regions he thought Canada should engage with, perhaps reflecting public opinion in English-speaking Canada.

The only exception to the general lack of civil society interest in the Americas beyond the United States came from Quebec, where there existed cultural and religious affinities with the region, in contrast with Anglo-Canada, where commercial interests in the region predominated. The idea of "*Latinité*" was adopted by the Catholic Church and secular Quebec intellectuals like Pierre Trudeau, who occasionally wrote about Latin America's social and economic issues in *Cité Libre,* the influential journal he co-founded.[7] Maurice Demers has documented extensive connections between Catholics in Quebec and in Mexico. Citizens in these two locations saw their cultural identities as interconnected, he argues, and used these ties to expand their political capital. Mexican Catholics, for example, used the support of co-religionists in Canada and the United States in their struggles with the post-revolutionary Mexican state.[8] Spicer, for his part, refers to the concept of *Latinité* dismissively as "recalling mystical ties of Latin civilization."[9]

According to David Morrison, emerging support for the establishment of a Latin American regional bilateral assistance program was the only one influenced to any significant extent by non-governmental pressures, referring to the government's desire to appeal to the francophone population in Quebec by projecting a bilingual and bicultural Canadian identity.[10] Support for assistance to Latin America would thus represent a counterweight to the emphasis within the aid program on the British Commonwealth. Overall levels of assistance remained extremely low, however, perhaps reflecting the weakness of civil society pressures as well as official disinterest in this period. By 1968, development assistance to Latin America represented only 3 per cent of the total aid budget.[11]

Latin America took on increased foreign policy relevance after Trudeau's election in April 1968 when his government sought to diversify Canada's foreign political and economic relations beyond its traditional partnership with the United States. As the chapters in this volume by Asa McKercher and Stefano Tijerina detail, Trudeau embraced Latin America to find new partners in the Americas and in recognition of the region's growing importance in the context of a move away from the cold war

FIGURE 11.1
Prime Minister Pierre Trudeau pursued deeper Canadian involvement in Latin America, which he embraced as a counterweight to US influence. He is shown here with Cuban leader Fidel Castro during his controversial visit to the island nation in January 1976. (Source: Duncan Cameron/LAC e999920086)

bipolar system. Trudeau's shift toward Latin America also reflected his commitment to greater cultural and geographic diversity. The appointment of Paul Gérin-Lajoie, an ally from Quebec, as CIDA president in 1970 signalled this intention. According to Morrison, Gérin-Lajoie drew upon a network of former Catholic missionaries and lay activists to "spearhead programming," which grew rapidly during his tenure, focusing on agriculture, forestry, fisheries, and community development.[12] During the period 1970 to 1976, bilateral aid to Latin America almost quadrupled to $34.5 million. At the same time, the presence of Canadian NGOs in the region expanded rapidly. By 1975, there were fifty-four Canadian NGOs operating there, receiving 28 per cent of their budget from CIDA.[13]

While multilateral cooperation was considered a longer-term priority, in 1972 Canada took on special observer status in the OAS and fully joined the IDB. The 1973 Chilean coup, in which General Augusto Pinochet's brutal military thugs overthrew elected President Salvador Allende, signalled a shift in the nature of the state-society relationship as a determinant of Canadian decision making on development assistance. After this point, the state-led nature of Canadian involvement declined as a result of the increased mobilization and activism of Canadian civil society actors with direct ties to the region and local civil society counterparts. New domestic actors emerged in this period, most notably the Inter-Church Committee on Human Rights in Latin America (ICCHRLA) and the Latin American Working Group (LAWG). Throughout the coming years, these civil society actors would become effective in pushing for an aid program that would respond to their demands for greater attention to human rights and social justice.

As a result of increased recognition on the part of state, business, and civil society of the importance of Latin America to Canadian interests and values, the Canadian aid commitment to the region grew steadily in this period. In fiscal year 1960–61 only Belize figured in the list of the top twenty recipients of bilateral ODA; over the period 1965–66 to 1975–76, no Latin American country appeared on this list except Chile in fiscal year 1970–71. By the five-year period 1975–76 to 1979–80, assistance to the Americas represented 11.9 per cent of total bilateral ODA, but dropped to 8.2 per cent in the next five-year period (1980–85).[14]

Overall, before the 1980s Latin American remained a secondary concern in Canadian aid policy, reflecting the common perception that Canadian interests there were minimal, and worries that involvement in the region, then clearly under US hegemony, could lead to undesirable conflict with US interests. While commercial and non-governmental interests were growing, they were not yet sufficiently powerful to overcome this fundamental reluctance.[15]

1980s—Politicization of Canadian Aid Program in Latin America

The politicization of Canada's relationship with Latin America, a process started in the early 1970s, accelerated steadily through the 1980s. There was a substantial increase in this decade in the level and intensity of Canadian involvement in the region, largely driven by the outbreak of a major crisis in Central America. The emergence of a series of guerrilla movements in response to long-standing oppressive dictatorships led to a number of civil wars in Central America. The victory of the leftist *Frente Sandinista de Liberación Nacional* (FSLN) in Nicaragua led to a militaristic response by American President Ronald Reagan, as well as the use of US Agency for International Development (USAID) funding in support of the remaining repressive regimes in El Salvador, Honduras, and Guatemala. While contacts between civil societies in different parts of the hemisphere were previously limited and largely occurred through religious channels, the Central American crisis brought Latin American concerns closer to Canadians and secular NGOs, building on contacts established by missionaries and laypeople decades earlier. It soon led to strong pressure on the Canadian state from civil society for a more independent approach to Latin America, different from that of the United States.

The politicization of Latin American civil society meant that decisions about aid (by both state and civil society) took on ever more political connotations.[16] Moreover, Latin American NGOs assumed greater protagonism in the aid dynamic as increasingly political Latin American NGOs pressured Canadian NGOs to redefine their joint relationships, moving away from more paternalistic forms of aid.

In response to these political dynamics, Canadian NGOs pushed for: increased aid for Nicaragua; elimination of official assistance to El Salvador and Guatemala; increased assistance to regional institutions; admission of Central American refugees to Canada; and support for the regional peace process.

Overall, civil society actors were largely successful in achieving their demands. The Canadian government's growing interest in the region is reflected in the fact that Latin America's share of Canada's total aid program virtually doubled over this period, from 8.2 per cent of Canada's total bi-lateral ODA in the five year period 1980–81 to 1986–87 to 15.4 per cent in 1990–91 to 1995–96.[17] By 1986, Colombia, Haiti, Honduras, and Peru were listed as countries of concentration for ODA purposes. And the sig-nificance of NGO involvement is underlined by the fact that the percentage of total Canadian ODA delivered through NGOs was by far the highest in this region in 1991, at 24 per cent, compared to 7 per cent for francophone Africa, 11 per cent for anglophone Africa, and 7 per cent for Asia.[18] Grow-ing Canadian assistance thus reflected both increased prioritization of the region in Canadian foreign policy because of geopolitical and humanitar-ian concerns, and increased civil society contestation. The government also responded to many of the specific demands of NGOs related to the Central American conflict, including the temporary suspension of aid to El Salva-dor and Guatemala, and increased assistance to Nicaragua. The Canadian government supported the Contadora and Esquipulas peace initiatives and participated in a UN peace observer mission (ONUCA).[19] Despite the sus-pension of aid to two countries, much of the increase in Canadian develop-ment assistance to Latin America went to Central American countries, as Canadian aid to Central America tripled over the 1981–86 period to $100 million and doubled again in the six-year period 1988–89 to 1994–95.[20]

These decisions were extremely contentious. The Trudeau government had to weigh pressure from NGOs and the White House before choosing to defy US wishes and cut off aid to El Salvador and Guatemala because of the "consistent and massive abuses of human rights" in those countries.[21] However, as documented by Brian Stevenson, in justifying the government's choice, Foreign Minister Allan MacEachen referred to "growing Canadian public interest in Central America" and recognized that public concern "certainly did have influence on government policy."[22] Indeed, this influence persisted. After coming to power in September 1984, Brian Mulroney's Progressive Conservative government, though ideologically closer to the Reagan Administration, maintained many elements of Liberal policy. The new government renewed aid to El Salvador, but continued to support regional peacekeeping efforts and designed aid policies to promote peace and stability.[23] Overall, Canada's role in the hemisphere was more mature and independent, largely because of the productive role played by NGO pressure.

FIGURE 11.2
Surging popular resistance to oppressive dictatorships in several Latin American countries in the early 1980s encouraged an activist response by Canadian civil society. Canadian singers Bruce Cockburn and Nancy White are shown here on their way to deliver Oxfam Canada emergency medical equipment to strife-ridden Nicaragua in February 1983. (Source: Oxfam Canada: Dan O'Connell and Sean Goertz-Gadon/LAC e999920082)

1990s and Early 2000s—New Role for Canada in Latin America?

In the 1990s, Canada's role in the hemisphere entered a new phase as a result of growing economic, political, and social linkages.[24] Canadian aid policy continued to be intertwined with these changing foreign policy dynamics. In 1990, Mulroney's government decided to join the OAS. This sudden decision was a natural extension of the prime minister's continentalist approach, which was expressed most clearly in the signing of the Canada-US Free Trade Agreement.[25] Canadian policy under Mulroney thus rejected some of the Trudeau government's desire for a more independent foreign policy vis-à-vis the United States. Simultaneously, the end of the Cold War provided greater space for Canada to develop a stronger relationship with countries south of the United States, resulting in a new emphasis on democracy and human rights. Yet the debt crisis that broke out across the Latin American region in the early 1980s led to the promotion of structural adjustment policies by Western countries and the International Monetary Fund and World Bank that compromised these aims. The neo-liberal ideas behind these policies, which came to be known as the "Washington consensus," included tariff reductions, cutbacks in social policies, the end of state subsidies for domestic industries, deregulation, privatization, trade liberalization, and other market-friendly policies. The Canadian government stridently supported these policies, while civil society in both Latin America and Canada strongly criticized them for their harsh impact on the poor.

One example of Canada's greater role in promoting human rights and democracy was its support for the creation of a Unit for the Promotion of Democracy in the OAS in 1991. Similarly, Canada, alongside Peru, led the push to create an Inter-American Democratic Charter, which was adopted after the 2001 Summit of the Americas in Quebec City, where it was supported by regional leaders.[26] This emphasis on democracy and human rights had some spinoff effects on Canadian aid policy. CIDA, for instance, created a $1.5 million Democratic Development Fund for Guatemala in 1993. This program reflected many of the demands and values of NGOs in both Canada and Guatemala, as well as CIDA's increased recognition of the importance of the role played by civil society and the Department of Foreign Affairs and International Trade (DFAIT)'s interest in supporting the peace process. It included the promotion of "confidence-building and dialogue between groups, especially between elements of civil society and its formal institutions." The government championed the fund as a means for strengthening "relationships and synergy between Canadian NGOs in Guatemala and between Canadian and local NGOs."[27]

In general, however, the Washington consensus dominated aid policy making in this decade (especially through Canadian support for the IDB, which continued to absorb a significant part of Canada's regional aid budget). The Liberal government of Jean Chrétien became a strong promoter

Laura Macdonald

of the Free Trade Agreement of the Americas (FTAA) initiative (though it eventually failed). It also signed free trade agreements (FTAs) with Chile and Costa Rica, which came into force in 1997 and 2002 respectively, and launched several other FTA negotiations. The Liberal governments of both Chrétien and his successor, Paul Martin, viewed economic integration and liberalization as highly compatible with democratization in the hemisphere. And Canadian and Latin American civil society organizations that opposed these neo-liberal policies were for the most part not effective in promoting alternative policies.

While the Canadian government did have a significant foreign policy interest in Latin America during this period, this interest was not reflected in aid priorities. According to John Cameron, "countries from the Americas were only very rarely in the top 10 list of ODA recipients and clearly were not top priorities for Canadian ODA."[28] Since the mid-1990s, government efforts to improve "aid effectiveness" tended to concentrate Canadian development assistance in a smaller number of states, mostly in Africa, as well as in "failed and fragile states," tilting aid away from relatively prosperous Latin America.[29] CIDA also produced a list of twenty-five "development partners" to whom two-thirds of Canadian development assistance was to be devoted by 2010. Only four of those states—Bolivia, Guyana, Honduras, and Nicaragua—were located in the Americas. They were the lowest-ranked states in the hemisphere based on both per capita Gross National Income and the Human Development Index, apart from Haiti, which was included in the category of "failed and fragile states."

The decision to adopt GNI per capita as the primary criterion for choosing "focus countries" meant that the large number of poor people in relatively wealthier but highly unequal Latin American countries would be overlooked.[30] If the IPS's focus on selection of development "partners" based on poverty had been strictly applied, all Latin American states might have been cut. But bureaucratic inertia as well as Ottawa's desire for diplomatic and commercial influence in the region meant that they could not be cut out altogether.[31] Levels of Canadian ODA to the Americas as a percentage of its total government-to-government ODA had increased from 8.2 per cent in 1980–81 to 1984–85 to 15.4 per cent in 1985–86 to 1989–90. This level of support increased again to a high of 17.8 per cent in 1990–91 to 1994–95, reflecting the factors outlined above. In the next five-year period, under Chrétien, aid to the region fluctuated between a low of 12.4 per cent in 1996–97 and a high of 15.4 per cent in 2000–01.[32] As well, in this period, aid figures for the region began to be dominated by the high levels of assistance that began to flow to Haiti, which was included in the list of failed and fragile states (along with Afghanistan and Iraq). After many years of indecision, the government decided to substantially increase finding to Haiti in July 2004, dedicating more than $180 million over two years.[33] This decision was partly based on the country's poverty (even before the 2010 earthquake), reflecting humanitarian motivations and Canada's interest in promoting "good governance." However, the presence of a Haitian diaspora population in Quebec, concentrated in a few ridings in Montreal, also contributed to making Haiti a top priority for both Liberal and Conservative governments.[34]

Ottawa's optimistic outlook on the Americas waned by the mid-2000s following the failure of the FTAA and the emergence of "new left" governments in the region that rejected the Washington consensus policies that Canada and the United States had promoted heavily. While trade and investment opportunities had increased (particularly in the extractive sector during the early 2000s), overall levels of trade remained minimal. And the Liberal government's shift in aid policy meant that the region no longer represented a major priority, though its share of the aid budget remained more or less constant.[35]

The Harper Era, 2006–15: "Virage" in Aid Motivations and Mechanisms[36]

The coming to power of Stephen Harper in 2006 and his rigid Conservative approach to foreign policy led to a dramatic shift in aid policy toward Latin America. Canadian aid policies were also shaped by changes within the region: the resource boom; the swing to the left by many local governments; the rejection of Washington consensus policies in most countries; the decline of US hegemony; substantial progress in reducing poverty and inequality; and the emergence of non-traditional donors, particularly Brazil and Venezuela. The lurch to the right in Ottawa put Canada out of line with most of its regional counterparts.

Shortly after coming to power, the Harper government announced that Latin America would become a major foreign policy priority. The Americas Strategy, announced in a 2007 speech by Harper in Santiago, Chile, highlighted three objectives: increasing economic prosperity (with a focus on Canadian, not Latin American, economic interests); reinforcing democratic governance; and advancing common security. This strategy reflected a broader shift in Harper's foreign policy away from the emphasis that Liberal governments placed on Africa and poverty reduction toward an emphasis on benefits to Canadian economic interests.[37] In particular, the prominence of Canadian-based mining companies in the Latin American region during the resource boom was a prime driver of the government's approach to the region. While Liberal governments promoted neo-liberal reforms and regional free trade agreements, these economic dimensions were often balanced against broader concerns with human rights and democracy. Under their Conservative successor, however, Canadian policy became more narrowly focused and corporate actors took on new importance in shaping Canadian foreign policy in general and aid policy specifically. The initial "cornerstone" of the Americas Strategy was the "prosperity pillar," under which Canadian trade and investment interests were promoted, assuming that this would bolster the other two early objectives, democracy and security. The strategy's objectives under this pillar included "strengthening the region's enabling environment for economic growth and helping governments and private sector organizations connect to global markets." It also included a focus on "standardizing and harmonizing" investment and taxation, reinforcing regulatory frameworks, and strengthening public financial management, rather than emphasizing support for the poor and marginalized sectors of the population.[38]

Reflecting these commercial motivations, the main outcome of Harper's Americas Strategy was a series of trade agreements with the Americas. FTAs were implemented with Peru (2009), Colombia (2012), Panama (2013), and Honduras (2013), while the government tried to negotiate deals with the Caribbean Community (CARICOM), the Dominican Republic, and Central America.[39] These trade agreements included investment chapters modelled on the North American Free Trade Agreement (NAFTA), giving corporate interests a generous right to sue host countries for actions infringing on their commercial interests.

In addition to the emphasis on signing trade agreements with countries in the Americas, government aid policy was "instrumentalized" in support of the government's commercial objectives.[40] Even though the "prosperity pillar" of the Americas Strategy was expressed in terms of Canadian economic interests, not in terms of poverty reduction or human rights (as was required under the ODA Accountability Act), CIDA played an extremely important role in the Americas Strategy because of the lack of dedicated new resources within DFAIT or other government departments attached to the strategy. Only CIDA received new resources dedicated to the Americas.[41]

In 2009, Development Minister Bev Oda announced a revised list of twenty "countries of concentration," which would receive 80 per cent of Canada's bilateral ODA. The list included only seven African countries, five Asian nations, and six countries from the Americas, up from four on the previous list. The targeted American countries included Peru and Colombia, both upper-middle income developing countries where Canada had important economic interests and strong ideological affinities. Reaction to the list was sharply critical. The government was criticized for selecting focus countries with relatively high levels of economic development (GDP per capita in 2015 in Colombia was over $7,748 and over $6,796 in Peru).[42] There was also a heavy emphasis on promotion of aid toward the private sector under the new strategy. Particularly controversial was the decision to fund NGO partnerships with mining companies, especially in the Andean region. Stephen Brown refers to this support for the Canadian extractive sector through ODA as part of a "recommercialization of aid."[43] In addition, the selection of Honduras as focus country seemed to obey an ideological and political logic,[44] as did the 2014 decision to downgrade Bolivia as a country of concentration[45] despite the fact that the program was strongly praised in an internal evaluation.[46]

The recent increase in Canadian corporate investment abroad (particularly by mining companies) has led some authors to view Canada's behaviour in Latin America as reflecting imperialist motives. Canada has become a particularly important investor in Latin America, where the behaviour of its corporations has resulted in major human rights violations and environmental degradation. The Canadian state has actively supported these companies through its promotion of trade and investment agreements and its aid program.[47] These authors offer an instrumentalist conception of the Canadian state that overlooks the capacity of the state to behave in a relatively autonomous fashion. Yet, as Michael Bueckert argues, it is important to recognize that development assistance is not always functional to capitalist interests and that it can also to some extent (as argued in this chapter) reflect the agency of civil society actors. The Harper government's merger of CIDA with DFATD did reduce this limited autonomy, however, and left less space for civil society contestation.[48]

Despite the predominance of commercial considerations in many aspects of assistance to Latin America under the Harper government, it is important to recognize that other factors were at play. In particular, the extremely poor country of Haiti received a large share of the aid budget to the region as a result of the humanitarian crisis caused by the earthquake of 2010, continued state fragility, and the continued electoral relevance of the Haitian diaspora, especially the large number of NGOs based in the Quebec Haitian community operating in their homeland.[49]

At the same time, the rearticulation of the government's development assistance policies coincided with a closing of dialogue with civil society and the defunding of important interlocutors. For example, the Canadian Foundation for the Americas (FOCAL), created by Mulroney's government to promote policy research and analysis on Canada's role in the Americas, was defunded by Harper and forced to close in 2011, as was the North-South Institute in 2014. Development NGOs historically critical of government policy, including KAIROS, OXFAM, and Inter Pares did not have their CIDA funding renewed and struggled to maintain a presence in the Americas. In other cases, NGO assistance continued to flow, but it was increasingly determined by government priorities, moving away from the old "responsive" framework in which trusted NGOs received government funding for programs they designed themselves, normally in consultation with Southern NGOs.[50] The new funding framework acted to reinforce more technocratic and paternalistic forms of aid and cut off lines of dialogue between state and civil society that had flourished earlier.

Conclusion

This chapter has reviewed the evolution of the program of development assistance to Latin America over the last several decades. The very small initial program has grown and flourished in a way that Spicer could not have foreseen in the mid-1960s when he wrote *A Samaritan State?*. The evolution of Canadian development assistance has been shaped by changes in Canadian foreign policy, which have interacted in different ways with civil society efforts over time. Government support for development efforts in Latin America first increased under Pierre Trudeau, motivated in part by the desire to project a bilingual and bicultural presence in the world and to move away from an earlier emphasis on the British Commonwealth. The Mulroney government increased the weight placed on Latin America in Canadian foreign and development policy, reflecting that government's greater interest in North-South continental ties, as reflected in the signing of the Canada-US Free Trade agreement. In contrast, the Chrétien and Martin governments shifted toward a greater focus on Africa because of their desire to improve aid effectiveness and to concentrate on providing assistance to the poorest countries. Most recently, Harper's government made Latin America a diplomatic priority, but the focus of the foreign policy agenda was constrained, blocking productive dialogue between state and non-business civil society. In its place, corporate interests tended to predominate.

In its first term in office, Prime Minister Justin Trudeau's government has not prioritized Latin America in the same way that Harper did. Minister of International Development Marie-Claude Bibeau's Feminist International Assistance Policy, announced in June 2017, eliminated the practice of identifying a fixed list of countries of concentration. The policy signalled that the government would increase support for "least-developed countries," directing "no less than 50 per cent of its bilateral international development assistance to sub-Saharan African countries by 2021–22." Presumably this will lead to a decline to aid to Latin America.[51] Nevertheless, as we have seen above, there is considerable inertia in regional allocations of development assistance, which means there is unlikely to be a dramatic shift away from aid to Latin America. We are also likely to see the government end its controversial support for partnerships between Canadian NGOs and mining companies. In January 2018 Trade Minister François-Philippe

Champagne announced the creation of an independent Canadian Ombudsperson for Responsible Enterprise (CORE), who will be mandated to investigate independently and monitor compliance with the government's policies around responsible behaviour of Canadian corporations abroad. The ombudsperson will also be empowered to recommend remedies when policies are violated.[52]

It is unlikely, however, that the Trudeau government will move decisively away from an emphasis on the promotion of free trade and neo-liberal policies in the region. More hopefully, the long tradition of North-South civil society engagement, the strength of the women's movement in Latin America, and that region's success in integrating women into the political process means that it is likely that the region will see benefits from the new Feminist International Assistance Policy. In June 2018, the government announced $79.21 million in new development assistance for nine projects in the Americas aimed at empowering women and girls.[53] This is a significant shift away from the move toward commercialization of aid that occurred under the Tories and displays the continued importance of civil society actors in defining relations between Canada and Latin America.

Notes

Thanks to Megan Pickup and Arne Rückert for their assistance with this research. Thanks also to Greg Donaghy and Stephen Brown for their helpful comments on an earlier version of this chapter.

1   Laura Macdonald, "Canada in the Posthegemonic Hemisphere: Evaluating the Harper Government's Americas Strategy," *Studies in Political Economy* 97, no. 1 (2016): 1–17.

2   Cranford Pratt, "Canada: A Limited and Eroding Internationalism," in *Internationalism Under Strain: The North-South Policies of Canada, the Netherlands, Norway, and Sweden*, ed. Cranford Pratt (Toronto: University of Toronto Press, 1989); see also David R. Black, "Humane Internationalism and the Malaise of Canadian Aid Policy," in *Rethinking Canadian Aid*, 2nd ed., ed. Stephen Brown, Molly den Heyer, and David R. Black (Ottawa: University of Ottawa Press, 2016), 17–33.

3   Gabriel C. Goyette, "Charity Begins at Home: The Extractive Sector as an Illustration of Changes and Continuities in the New De Facto Canadian Aid Policy," in Brown, den Heyer, and Black, *Rethinking Canadian Aid*, 259–75.

4   Laura Macdonald, "Unequal Partnerships: The Politics of Canada's Relations with the Third World," *Studies in Political Economy* 47, no. 1 (Summer 1995): 111–41.

5 Peter McKenna, *Canada and the OAS: From Dilettante to Full Partner* (Montreal: McGill-Queen's University Press, 1995), 82–84.

6 Keith Spicer, *A Samaritan State?: External Aid in Canada's Foreign Policy* (Toronto: University of Toronto Press, 1966), 62–63.

7 David Morrison, *Aid and Ebb Tide: A History of CIDA and Canadian Development Assistance* (Waterloo, ON: Wilfrid Laurier University Press), 77.

8 Maurice Demers, *Connected Struggles: Catholics, Nationalists, and Transnational Relations between Mexico and Quebec, 1917–1945* (Montreal: McGill-Queen's University Press, 2014), 3–6.

9 Spicer, *A Samaritan State?*, 61.

10 Morrison, *Aid and Ebb Tide*, 79.

11 James Rochlin, *Discovering the Americas: The Evolution of Canadian Foreign Policy Towards Latin America* (Vancouver: University of British Columbia Press, 1994), 77.

12 Morrison, *Aid and Ebb Tide*, 80, 123.

13 Rochlin, *Discovering the Americas*, 96.

14 Morrison, *Aid and Ebb Tide*, 456–48.

15 François Audet and Judy Meltzer, "L'aide canadienne en Amérique Latine: Une coopération paradoxale," in *L'Aide Canadienne au Développement : Bilan et perspective*, ed. François Audet, Marie-Eve Desrosiers, and Stéphane Roussel (Montréal: Presses de l'Université de Montréal, 2008), 321; Jean-Philippe Thérien, Gordon Mace, and Myriam Roberge, "Le Canada et les Amériques: La difficile construction d'une identité régionale," *Canadian Foreign Policy Journal* 11, no. 3 (2004): 17–37.

16 Laura Macdonald, "Current and Future Directions for Canadian NGOs in Latin America," in *A Dynamic Partnership: Canada's Changing Role in the Americas*, ed. Jerry Haar and Edgar J. Dosman (Piscataway, NJ: Transaction, 1993), 113–28.

17 Morrison, *Aid and Ebb Tide*.

18 Macdonald, "Current and Future Directions," 117.

19 Stephen Baranyi and John W. Foster, "Canada and Central America: Citizen Action And International Policy," in *Canada Looks South: In Search of an Americas Policy*, ed. Peter McKenna (Toronto: University of Toronto Press, 2012), 246.

20 Brian Stevenson, *Canada, Latin America, and the New Internationalism: A Foreign Policy Analysis, 1968–1999* (Montreal: McGill-Queen's University Press, 2000), 6.

21 Ibid., 146.

22 Ibid., 146. See also the discussion by Stephen Baranyi and John Foster of a specific citizens' initiative called Canada Central America Policy Alternatives (CAPA), which carried out research and organized roundtables in Parliament, with the support of sympathetic parliamentarians, to promote a strong Canadian role in fostering peace and social justice in the region. This author also participated in this initiative. See Baranyi and Foster, "Canada and Central America."

23   Stevenson, *Canada, Latin America, and the New Internationalism*, 148.

24   Jean Daudelin and Edgar Dosman, "Canada and Hemispheric Governance: The New Challenges," in *Leadership and Dialogue, Canada Among Nations 1998*, ed. Maureen A. Molot and Fen O. Hampson (Toronto: Oxford University Press, 1998), 212.

25   McKenna, *Canada and the OAS*, 131.

26   Maxwell A. Cameron and Jason Tockman, "Canada and the Democratic Charter: Lessons from the Coup in Honduras," in McKenna, *Canada Looks South*, 90–91.

27   Laura Macdonald, "Changing Directions? Challenges Facing Canadian Non-governmental Organizations in Latin America," in *Beyond Mexico?: Canada in the Americas*, ed. Jean Daudelin and Edgar Dosman (Ottawa: Carleton University Press, 1995), 237–56. See also Baranyi and Foster, "Canada and Central America," 249–51.

28   John Cameron, "CIDA in the Americas: New Directions and Warning Signs for Canadian Development Policy," *Canadian Journal of Development Studies* 28, no. 2 (2007): 234.

29   As noted by Stephen Brown, the other two criteria were the "ability to use aid effectively" and "sufficient Canadian presence to add value." Stephen Brown, "'Creating the World's Best Development Agency?' Confusion and Contradictions and Tensions In CIDA's New Development Blueprint," *Canadian Journal of Development Studies* 28, no. 2 (2007): 220.

30   Laura Macdonald and Arne Rückert, "Continental Shift? Rethinking Canadian Aid to the Americas," in Brown, den Heyer, and Black, *Rethinking Canadian Aid*, 125–42.

31   Cameron, "CIDA in the Americas," 236.

32   Cameron, "CIDA in the Americas," 238–39.

33   François Audet and Judy Meltzer, "L'aide canadienne en Amérique Latine'," 313–41.

34   Yasmine Shamsie, "Canadian Assistance to Haiti: Some Sobering Snags in a Fragile-State Approach," in McKenna, *Canada Looks South*, 184–85.

35   Cameron, "CIDA in the Americas."

36   For more detailed discussion of Canadian aid policy in this period, see Macdonald and Rückert, "Continental Shift."

37   For a discussion of the Americas Strategy, see Laura Macdonald, "Canada in the Posthegemonic Hemisphere: Evaluating the Harper Government's Americas Strategy," *Studies in Political Economy* 97, no. 1 (2016): 1–17.

38   For example, in the 2011 internal then-DFAIT (now Global Affairs Canada) evaluation of the Americas Strategy, all of the achievements mentioned under the strategy are the signing of trade agreements and parallel labour and environmental agreements attached to those FTAs. Global Affairs Canada, "Evaluation of the Americas Strategy," January 2011, http://www.international.gc.ca/gac-amc/publications/evaluation/2011/tas_lsa11.aspx?lang=eng.

39   Macdonald, "Canada in the Posthegemonic Hemisphere."

40 Stephen Brown, "The Instrumentalization of Foreign Aid under the Harper Government," *Studies in Political Economy* 97, no. 1 (2016): 18–36.

41 Global Affairs Canada, "Evaluation of the Americas Strategy."

42 McLeod Group, "Canadian Development Assistance: The Issue of Focus," http://www.mcleodgroup.ca/wp-content/uploads/2014/12/McLeod-Group-briefing-note-3---A-Question-of-Focus.pdf.

43 Stephen Brown, "Undermining Foreign Aid: The Extractive Sector and the Recommercialization of Canadian Development Assistance," in Brown, den Heyer, and Black, *Rethinking Canadian Aid*, 277–95.

44 Macdonald and Rückert, "Continental Shift."

45 Liam Swiss, "New focus countries not about effective aid," blog post, 14 July 2014, http://blog.liamswiss.com/category/aid/page/6/.

46 Department of Foreign Affairs, Trade and Development, "Bolivia Country Program Evaluation – 2005–2010 – Synthesis Report," January 2014, accessed 15 May 2017 from http://www.international.gc.ca/gac-amc/publications/evaluation/2014/bcpe-eppb-2005-2010.aspx?lang=eng.

47 See, for example, Todd Gordon, *Imperialist Canada* (Winnipeg: Arbeiter Ring, 2010); Todd Gordon and Jeffrey R. Webber, "Imperialism and Resistance: Canadian Mining Companies in Latin America," *Third World Quarterly* 29, no. 1 (2008): 64; Jerome Klassen, "Canada and the New Imperialism: The Economics of a Secondary Power," *Studies in Political Economy* 83, no. 1 (2009): 163–90.

48 Michael Bueckert, "CIDA and the Capitalist State: Shifting Structures of Representation under the Harper Government," *Studies in Political Economy* 96, no. 1 (2015): 3–22. For a more extended discussion and critique of the notion of Canada as a new imperialist power, see J. Z. Garrod and Laura Macdonald, "Imperialism or Something Else? Rethinking 'Canadian Mining Imperialism' in Latin America," in *Mining in Latin America: Critical Approaches to the "New Extraction,"* ed. Kalowatie Deonandan and Michael Dougherty (New York: Routledge, 2016), 100–115.

49 Audet and Meltzer, "L'aide canadienne en Amérique Latine," 313–41.

50 Stephen Brown, "CIDA's New Partnership with Canadian NGOs: Modernizing for Greater Effectiveness?," in *Struggling for Effectiveness: CIDA and Canadian Foreign Aid*, ed. Stephen Brown (Montreal: McGill-Queen's University Press, 2012), 289.

51 Government of Canada, "Canada's Feminist International Assistance Policy," http://international.gc.ca/world-monde/issues_development-enjeux_developpement/priorities-priorites/policy-politique.aspx?lang=eng. Bibeau was minister of international development from 2015 to March 2019.

52 Global Affairs Canada, "The Government of Canada brings leadership to responsible business conduct abroad," https://www.canada.ca/en/global-affairs/news/2018/01/the_government_ofcanadabringsleadershiptoresponsiblebusinesscond.html.

53 Global Affairs Canada, "Canada announces $79.21 million in development assistance for Americas," https://www.canada.ca/en/global-affairs/news/2018/06/canada-announces-7921-million-in-development-assistance-for-americas.html.

CIDA and Aid to Africa in the 1990s: A Crisis of Confidence

David Black

> There exists now such a degree of cynicism and despair about CIDA that the situation can fairly be described as having reached a crisis of confidence.
>
> —Patrick Johnston, 2010[1]

The March 2013 announcement in the federal budget that the Canadian International Development Agency (CIDA) would be "merged" with the Department of Foreign Affairs and International Trade (DFAIT) to form an integrated Department of Foreign Affairs, Trade, and Development (now Global Affairs Canada) was both immediately surprising and long anticipated. It was surprising because, true to form, Prime Minister Stephen Harper's Conservative government had engaged in no discernible consultations with the traditional development policy community prior to this abrupt and far-reaching institutional restructuring. It was long anticipated because, for at least a decade, CIDA had been repeatedly portrayed as deeply and probably irredeemably flawed: chronically defensive, risk averse, inefficient, and lacking in clear vision or purpose. By 2013, therefore, it was widely perceived as (in John Stackhouse's phrase) a "dead agency walking."[2]

While much of the commentary on CIDA's weaknesses was arguably overstated, it had become entrenched by the mid-1990s largely because of the absence of robust rebuttals from the agency or its political masters. This, in turn, reflected an institution that had come to think of itself as uncertain, weak and vulnerable, and that lacked powerful advocates and allies among the political and administrative elites of the federal government. In bureaucratic politics terms, its "organizational essence" had become embattled and unclear. In short, it was suffering from a chronic, collective crisis of confidence.[3]

This chapter argues that, while the roots of this condition are long, they were dramatically deepened (and arguably rendered irreversible) by a series of blows over the course of the 1990s, many of them related to CIDA's policies and performance in Africa, where its programming was most heavily concentrated. Together, these blows led to chronic uncertainty and a lack of conviction concerning its organizational essence, making it an easy mark for the many skeptics and critics that beset it.

"Organizational Essence" and the Aid Agency

In an article on "Canada and the Bureaucratic Politics of State Fragility," focusing on DFAIT and the Department of National Defence/Canadian Forces (DND/CF), Marie-Eve Desrosiers and Philippe Lagassé argue that "governmental organisations—agencies, services, or departments—are driven to defend their essences. In basic terms, an organizational essence is an identity that is reproduced through institutional practices, norms, and culture. An organizational essence is that which forms an organisation's *raison d'être*. It is a self-definition of what an agency, service, or department is, what it does, and how it does it, how it relates to other agencies, services, departments, and to the government or the state as a whole."[4] Drawing from the work of former US national security bureaucrats Morton Halperin and Priscilla Clapp,[5] Desrosiers and Lagassé contend that organizational essences are composed of "missions, roles, and capabilities." Like other socio-cultural identities, an organizational essence is not unchanging, nor is it uncontested. Nevertheless, it typically has a high level of stability and durability. Indeed, if it does not, this can be seen as a sign of institutional infirmity.

If we accept that such essences are key determinants of the health and behaviour of public sector institutions, what sort of essence can we ascribe to CIDA? As anyone familiar with the agency will quickly realize, and as the various chapters in this collection make clear, this is not a straightforward question to answer. However, there are a few general points we can make. First, CIDA was (and now forever shall remain) a relatively young organization, certainly compared with its key interlocutors in international policy: Foreign Affairs and International Trade, Defence, and Finance. As a result, it was inevitably beset by a certain level of insecurity and inexperience within the bureaucratic politics of the federal government. Second, it was legislatively, and thus politically, subordinate to DFAIT. Much of its institutional history was therefore spent seeking to protect and, periodically and cautiously, enlarge its relative autonomy. Third, it was self-consciously an institution apart. It was an organization of outsiders, often recruited from non-governmental development organisations, "who brought to the agency a commitment to development and a desire to build a career around it."[6]

In terms of core mission(s), there was some foundational ambiguity. As has been habitually noted, at least since Keith Spicer's path-breaking analysis in 1966 (see Brown's exploration in this collection), the motives underlying development assistance programming are inescapably mixed, including geo-strategic, diplomatic, commercial, and ethical objectives. Whereas the other agencies with significant responsibilities for dispensing portions of Canadian aid, including Finance, DFAIT, and to a lesser degree Defence, were much more attuned to the first several of these motivations, CIDA (by far the largest dispenser of development funds) was indissolubly linked to the objective of "provoking development," in the words of former agency president Marcel Massé.[7] This meant a core commitment to the ethical or moral purpose of aid. In the words of the 1994 Special Joint Parliamentary Committee Reviewing Canadian Foreign Policy, "help for those most in need expresses the basic moral vision of aid and corresponds closely to what the vast majority of Canadians think development assistance is all about."[8] While CIDA personnel clearly understood the need to design their policies and programs in ways that also achieved other, narrower purposes, if only to sustain the support they required from other bureaucratic and political actors, the basic *developmental* purpose of poverty alleviation and, beyond this, progress toward a more just international society was at the core of their organization's self-defined essence.[9] Quite what this meant and how it was to be achieved remained a matter of ongoing contestation.

Finally, in terms of roles and capabilities, by the late 1980s there was a core tension concerning what CIDA could and *should* be doing, and what capabilities it required to fulfill the roles it sought to perform. Historically, CIDA was principally a policy taker rather than a policy maker, with a strong bias toward institutionally (though *not* geographically)[10] decentralized operational capacities aimed at successfully navigating projects through the shoals of local dynamics "in country." The agency's heavy emphasis on applied operational capacity and contextual understanding meant that its capacity for research and reflection was limited.[11] It also meant that it forged particularly close though often fraught relationships with Canadian non-governmental (or civil society) development organizations, resulting in a robust, diverse, and growing complex of state-civil society "partnerships"[12] on which its operational activities relied.

This relatively decentralized structure, within and beyond the agency, ran up against a different kind of imperative in the late 1980s. In the context of debt crises in Africa and Latin America, as well as the rise of neo-liberal thinking, key international financial institutions (notably the International Monetary Fund [IMF] and the World Bank) instituted structural adjustment lending, requiring recipient countries to undertake market-oriented policy reforms as a condition of new development finance. Major bilateral donor agencies increasingly followed suit, supporting structural adjustment "conditionalities" in their development programming. In this policy environment, CIDA's leadership tried to embrace a more macro, country-wide, policy planning and advising orientation toward recipient countries, in line with neo-liberal policy prescriptions. Increasingly, the agency sought to become a locus of expertise on the development *problematique* more broadly, albeit with a narrowly macro-economic emphasis. In this regard, it sought a key role as a policy *player* if not a major policy *maker*, rather than just a taker of big ideas generated elsewhere. By the early 1990s, this had become a source of contestation within the agency, and with its partners in the non-governmental development community, concerning its organizational essence and its bureaucratic relationships with other international policy agencies. The tension between CIDA's claim to specialized capacity in the understanding of project-based operational challenges in developing countries, and its aspiration to become a locus of high-level expertise on the more long-term, structural challenges facing these countries, became a source of intra-agency uncertainty concerning (in Halperin and Clapp's terms) its core missions, roles, and capabilities.

By the early 1980s, CIDA's organizational essence had also become tightly bound up with its practices and performance in its proliferating array of African aid recipients. From 1980 onward, Africa overtook Asia to become, and remain, the largest regional recipient of Canadian aid.[13] It is also the region where poverty and human insecurity were and remain most prevalent, and therefore humanitarian need is greatest; and where aid is proportionately most significant as a source of development finance, and thus most implicated in the results (both positive and negative) of development interventions.[14] Consequently, it became an ongoing testing ground for various, evolving innovations in development assistance, Canadian and global. Finally, African recipients took on a high level of political prominence because the continent's heavy concentration of francophone and anglophone countries, often members of either *la Francophonie* or the Commonwealth, meant that Canada had both a relatively high level of prominence as a donor and a strong identity-based interest in highlighting its continental role.

In the course of the 1990s, each of these aspects of CIDA's "organizational essence" was brought under scrutiny and challenge. It is worth emphasizing that this challenge was bipartisan, unfolding during both the final years of Brian Mulroney's Progressive Conservative government and the early and middle years of Jean Chrétien's Liberal government.

CIDA, Aid Policy, and Africa in the Late Mulroney years

With hindsight, CIDA's fortunes arguably reached their apex in the late 1980s, with the publication of the highly regarded "Winegard Report" (*For Whose Benefit?*) in 1987 and the subsequent release of CIDA's policy document, *Sharing our Future*.[15] The former was seen as a thoughtful and forthright effort to set aid policy on a firmly "humane internationalist" footing.[16] The latter was rightly seen by critics as watering down Winegard's message and prescriptions, but it still carried many of them forward.[17] Of these, the one that, in David Morrison's assessment, "probably had the greatest potential for changing CIDA's organizational thinking and behaviour" was the proposal to decentralize key decision-making and implementation functions away from headquarters in Gatineau to a number of field-based hubs, including Dar es Salaam, Dakar, Abidjan, and Harare in Africa.[18] It was anticipated that this would lead to more efficient and grounded policy and program decision making, with a higher degree of responsiveness to local needs and requirements (what later came to be known as "ownership"). The costs of decentralization were to be underpinned by slow but steady growth of the aid budget, from 0.5 per cent of GDP when *Sharing our Future* was released, to the longstanding target of 0.7 per cent of GDP by 2000.[19] On these premises, CIDA and DFAIT expeditiously initiated a substantial process of decentralization beginning in 1989, more than doubling the number of field-based aid personnel in nine diplomatic posts and a number of satellite offices.

These plans were almost immediately thrown into doubt, however, when the 1989 budget imposed an unexpectedly large cut of $360 million on the CIDA base budget (a 13 per cent cut). A succession of "streamlining" measures were adopted as further cuts ensued, and by the summer of 1992 it became clear that the short-lived experiment with decentralization was dead.[20] Decentralizing steps that, in 1988, had been projected to "significantly improve the quality and efficiency of Canada's assistance, as well as bringing our programs closer to the people we are trying to reach—the poorest"[21] were within four years deemed expendable.

Decentralization was not only a casualty of austerity. In the first years of the 1990s, new leadership at CIDA under the "second coming" of Marcel Massé as president sought to steer the agency away from its more organizationally decentralized emphasis on a policy approach that was "'tailor-made' locally and incrementally,"[22] and toward a more strategic, knowledge-intensive policy leadership role. The reasons for this were several. As noted above, they reflected the new primacy of controversial "policy lending" or structural adjustment programs (SAPs) as the centrepiece of development assistance policies, reflecting the "high neo-liberal" tenor of the times and the intrusive policy approach adopted by the IMF and World Bank in response to the debt crisis of many developing countries, particularly in Africa and Latin America. CIDA had been a relatively late adopter of structural adjustment and was a "policy taker" in the process.[23]

FIGURE 12.1
Marcel Massé
returned to CIDA as
its president in 1989,
attuned to the new
global emphasis on
neo-liberal structural
adjustment programs.
(Source: Global Affairs
Canada/LAC)

Given the controversy surrounding the draconian social impacts of these policies and the sharp opposition to them among many of CIDA's non-governmental "partners" in Canadian civil society, they were undoubtedly a source of controversy within and beyond the agency. CIDA's own role and emphasis in relation to SAPs became one of mitigating their negative social impacts in key "partner" countries such as Ghana and Guyana.[24] SAPs and CIDA's role in enabling them were a jarring challenge to the agency's sense of its core mission as an organization committed to poverty alleviation. But for Massé, fresh from a term as Canada's Executive Director at the IMF and World Bank, they were a matter of intellectual conviction.[25]

SAPs were also part of a strategic vision for the agency that emphasized its role as a policy leader on issues of international development and Canada's role therein. This vision sought to carve out greater autonomy in Ottawa's policy-making process to pursue this goal. Toward this end, *Groupe Sécore* from Montréal was commissioned to undertake a comprehensive Strategic Management Review in 1990–91. Based largely on its recommendations, senior management decided in early 1991 to recommend to the minister of state responsible for international cooperation, Monique Landry, that it adopt "sustainable development" as its overarching framework; that it focus more attention on influencing and supporting the core policy functions of recipient governments; and that it "work 'horizontally' in attempting to influence the areas of Canadian government policy affecting developing countries."[26] By early 1992, CIDA had prepared a recommendation seeking cabinet's approval for the new policy direction.

Given CIDA's historic role as an implementing agency and policy taker, this approach (resting on overarching country programming frameworks and more proactive strategies in support of African regional integration) required the acquiescence of other powerful players in Canadian development cooperation policies, notably DFAIT and Finance.[27] Indeed, University of Toronto political scientist Cranford Pratt interpreted the agency's embrace of structural adjustment as partly a reflection of its desire to earn the trust of these players, committed as they were to a more "realist" view of aid policy. "It was as if CIDA wanted to prove to DFAIT and to cabinet that it could be trusted with decisions that had important commercial and foreign policy dimensions," he wrote.[28] If this was the intention, it failed. DFAIT effectively blocked consideration of CIDA's policy paper at cabinet and, at the behest of Foreign Minister Barbara MacDougall, had an alternative "international assistance policy update paper" prepared by a senior departmental official that outlined a far more forthrightly self-interested vision of Canadian foreign aid as an instrument of key foreign and trade policy priorities. "There could hardly be more dramatic evidence," Pratt summarized, "that DFAIT was far more preoccupied with commercial and foreign policy concerns than with any commitment to reach and help the poorest people and countries."[29] The policy update paper generated a storm of controversy among Canadian development CSO's and sympathetic scholars, and was eventually put on hold. Nevertheless, it clearly signalled DFAIT's opposition to a substantially more autonomous policy role for CIDA.

Finally, and in some respects most shockingly, CIDA responded to a third successive round of budget cuts in 1993 by making an abrupt decision to cut bilateral aid programming to an entire region, central and east Africa, rather than adopt a "lawnmower approach" that would cut programs across the board. The primary upshot was a decision to slash the bilateral program in Tanzania, one of Canada's largest and longest-standing development and Commonwealth "partners." In doing so, CIDA took a strategic decision to prioritize a variety of political and commercial considerations over the obvious and ongoing humanitarian and developmental case for aid to Tanzania.[30] This decision, so clearly at odds with the core of CIDA's organizational mission, demonstrated how shallow and fragile this mission was. Although the specific decision on aid to Tanzania was reversed not long after the defeat of the Progressive Conservative government in the 1993 federal election, it portended more traumas to come, later in the same decade.

By the time the Chrétien Liberals took power in 1993, therefore, CIDA's efforts to reinforce its mission and expand its role had been twice rebuffed, through the dismantling of decentralization and the sidelining of its aspirations for an enlarged policy role. Meanwhile, its "partnerships" with Canadian civil society had been seriously strained by the agency's prioritization of structural adjustment. And it had demonstrated a high degree of sensitivity to more narrowly self-interested political and commercial priorities, in contravention of "humane internationalist" considerations and long-standing bilateral and civil society partnerships, through its program cut to Tanzania. As uncertainties about the direction and viability of its "organizational essence" grew, morale came under unprecedented strain. Yet, there was reason to hope for improved fortunes under the new Liberal government.

CIDA, Africa, and the Chrétien Liberals

The pre-election references to foreign aid in the Liberal Party's platform, expressed in its *Red Book* and *Foreign Policy Handbook*, were not extensive, but they strongly criticized the decision to cut aid to Tanzania and contained relatively clear humane internationalist statements of intent.[31] Once the party was in power, there was further encouragement for those with a humane internationalist bent from the report of the Special Joint

Parliamentary Committee Reviewing Canadian Foreign Policy. While the report was not as authoritative on foreign aid issues as the Winegard Report, the committee made clear its view that "the primary purpose of Canadian Official Development Assistance is to reduce poverty by providing effective assistance to the poorest people, in those countries that most need and can use our help."[32] It then laid out a set of proposed priorities (basic human needs, human rights, good governance and democratic development, the participation of women, private sector development, and public participation) that, though broad and imprecise, were generally consonant with this core purpose.

In contrast, the government's own 1995 White Paper on foreign policy, *Canada in the World*, clearly compromised this clarity of intent, situating aid, first, in the service of Canadian jobs and prosperity; second, as a contribution to global security; and third, as an expression of Canadian values and culture.[33] Moreover, the foreign affairs minister, André Ouellet, while admired within the agency for his energy and efficiency, was primarily concerned with "the Canadian side of the operation, especially in the distribution of work to private-sector suppliers and the use of ODA to promote trade."[34] In the absence of strong political leadership and a confident sense of purpose, the agency was exceptionally vulnerable as, under the leadership of Chrétien and Finance Minister Paul Martin, the government decided to prioritize dramatic budgetary restraint and eliminating the fiscal deficit over all other policy priorities in the mid-1990s.

The hammer fell in a series of devastating budgetary blows, beginning with the 1995 federal budget, which announced a three-year, 20.5 per cent decrease in international assistance spending. Foreign aid became "ground zero" for Martin's deficit cutting project. As the Canadian Council for International Cooperation (CCIC) later noted, "Canadian aid was hit harder by budget cuts than any other federal programme area, falling in real terms by 37 per cent between 1991–92 and 1999–2000, while federal spending as a whole fell by 11 per cent, and defence spending (in the course of what has been characterized as a 'decade of darkness' for the Canadian Forces) was cut by 20 per cent."[35] Nor can it be said that other donors were behaving in a comparably draconian manner. Despite overall declines in aid spending during the 1990s, among OECD Development Assistant Committee (DAC) members only Finland cut more deeply. Thirteen of the then twenty-two

FIGURE 12.2
When Prime Minister Jean Chrétien's Liberal government prioritized tackling Canada's deficit, CIDA and its aid programming were especially vulnerable. Chrétien watches while Finance Minister Paul Martin defends his budget in the House of Commons in February 1995. (Source: The Canadian Press/Tom Hanson)

DAC members actually *increased* their aid spending. As a percentage of GDP, Canadian aid fell from 0.45 per cent in 1991 to 0.25 per cent in 2000, and to a low of 0.22 per cent in 2001—the lowest level since the mid-1960s.

Particularly devastating to CIDA's core sense of mission was that the cuts fell hardest on Sub-Saharan Africa (SSA)—the region where impoverishment and insecurity were most acute. Between 1992–93 and 1997–98, Canadian aid to SSA fell in nominal dollars by 29.1 per cent, compared with the overall rate of decline in ODA of 24.3 per cent, and of all bilateral aid of 23.1 per cent (see Figure 12.3)—this, despite the fact that Africa's relative fortunes and rates of absolute poverty continued to worsen as the continent struggled through a second successive "lost decade."[36]

There were several possible ways of interpreting this trend. All of them profoundly challenged CIDA's organizational essence. One was that the political leadership in Ottawa had lost any real confidence that aid could effectively address the manifold challenges confronting the countries and

FIGURE 12.3

Canadian Aid to Africa versus other regions, 1990–99.

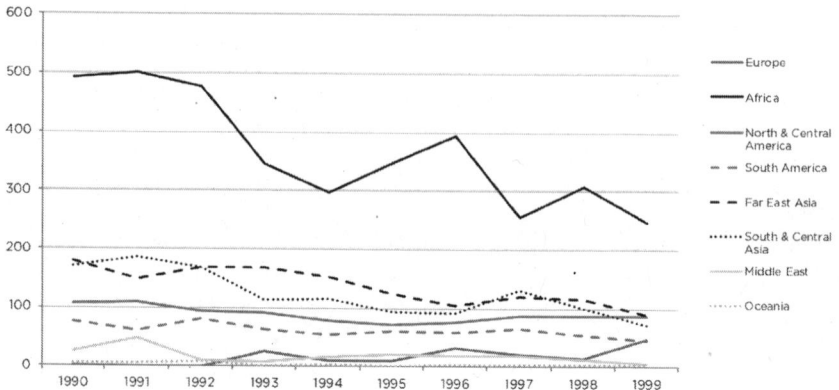

people of Africa. While this was never explicitly acknowledged, such an existential challenge to the core mission of aid would be profoundly discouraging. It was reinforced externally by the emergence of a new round of devastating critiques of aid failures in practice. A striking example was Peter Uvin's study of the role of the "aid system" in unwittingly enabling the genocidal violence in Rwanda.[37] A second interpretation, just as disheartening, was that aid, notwithstanding its obvious challenges and limitations, *could* make a difference in ameliorating the condition of the poorest people and countries, but that the government cared too little about these conditions to act as if they mattered. A third, and related, view was that the government was simply reflecting the concerns of its electorate, which, despite persistently high levels of support for aid in the abstract, saw development assistance as a priority that came after almost *every other* policy priority subject to the government's deficit-cutting scrutiny.[38] Any and all of these interpretations were deeply discomfiting to the agency's sense of collective purpose and morale.

Further eroding CIDA's sense of mission were a series of assaults on its long-standing and mutually supportive ties with Canadian civil society organizations. A budget-linked decision in 1995 abolished the agency's

Public Participation Program (PPP) and cut all funding to the broad network of community-based development education NGOs in Canada. Similarly, CIDA cancelled the Global Education Program, which supported the efforts of teachers' associations to build global education into school curricula and teacher training.[39] A small but vital element of CIDA programming for over twenty years (see Brushett in this collection), PPP and responsive public education funding were likely, and ironically, targeted due to the sharp criticism levelled by many development CSOs against the agency, particularly as it prioritized the unpopular structural adjustment policies of the late 1980s and early 1990s. Nevertheless, these cuts eroded the foundation for CIDA's organizational essence directly and indirectly. Directly, they meant that CIDA lost important voices in Canadian communities advocating engagement with the challenges of global poverty and inequality. Indirectly, the cuts signalled to CIDA that the government was prepared to "ride out" public opposition in this policy domain, judging the development education and advocacy community to be politically marginal. None of this was promising for efforts to defend CIDA's organizational essence in caucus and cabinet, let alone with the Canadian public.

A further challenge to CIDA's organizational essence came from a resurgence of tension with DFAIT, revolving around the ascendant "Human Security Agenda." When Lloyd Axworthy became minister of foreign affairs in 1996, he brought to the portfolio an activist agenda seeking to recast and expand the idea of security as the foundation for a re-energized Canadian foreign policy.[40] Supported bureaucratically by the new Global Issues Bureau within DFAIT, Axworthy undertook an array of initiatives, most of which were concentrated in Africa or bore particularly on the "security-development nexus" there.[41]

Unfortunately for Axworthy, the foreign ministry had insufficient resources to underpin his activism. CIDA, though battered by cuts, still had far more money for programming than DFAIT, which made it a ripe target for what Pratt characterized as a "takeover bid."[42] Though this never became a serious possibility at the time, there were various encroachments on CIDA's budget—for example, the $10 million per year Peacebuilding Fund established within the agency which, though wholly inadequate to the scale of the challenges associated with the new multilateral emphasis on peacebuilding in complex post- or peri-conflict situations, nevertheless reinforced a growing trend toward the "securitization" of Canadian aid.[43] While the need for serious engagement between development and (human) security issues had become increasingly self-evident, particularly in Africa, deploying aid funds to meet security imperatives compelled CIDA to divert resources from the slow and patient work of fostering sustainable development in its broadest sense. This disturbing trend reached its apex with the rapid emergence of Afghanistan as the largest bilateral program in agency history under the Harper government, alongside Canada's costly twelve-year military deployment to the Afghan war.

Conclusion: The Long Demise

Beginning in the early 2000s, CIDA's fortunes experienced a partial revival, as the Chrétien government, in the company of other donors, substantially reinvested in development assistance to support its commitment to the UN Millennium Development Goals as well as the G-8's Africa Action Plan, launched (with energetic leadership by Chrétien) at the Kananaskis Summit in 2002. Over the remainder of the decade, Canada committed to doubling ODA, and to doubling aid to Africa marginally faster. Notwithstanding some controversy over the base from which this growth was to occur, the commitment was formally met, even when the Harper government that took office in 2006 signalled its intention to de-emphasize Africa and prioritize Latin America.[44]

Yet by the end of the decade and the years of re-investment in development aid at a rate of 8 per cent annually, Canadian ODA had reached a mere 0.34 per cent of GDP—well below the 0.45 per cent where it had stood when the Mulroney cuts began in 1991.[45] More to the point of this chapter, even in this relatively expansive and hopeful period, CIDA was routinely maligned by critics and supporters of foreign aid alike. A year after the Harper Conservative government took office, for instance, the Standing Senate Committee on Foreign Affairs and International Trade issued a damning report entitled *Overcoming Forty Years of Failure: A New Road Map for Sub-Saharan Africa*. Though rightly critiqued as "deeply flawed in its assumptions, methodology and argumentation,"[46] its criticisms of the agency as "ineffective, costly and overly bureaucratic" and of Canadian development assistance as "slow, inflexible, and unresponsive to conditions on the ground in recipient countries" typified many other assessments.[47] Its stark conclusion was that "despite the dedication and hard work of CIDA employees over the years, the Government of Canada should undertake an immediate review of whether or not . . . CIDA should be relieved of its duties. The experiment of creating an independent aid agency to strengthen Canadian development assistance has not produced the intended results."[48] While widely panned at the time, this conclusion turned out to be prescient.

The argument in this chapter is that the sense of CIDA as weak, vulnerable, and defensive, and the various procedural and policy pathologies that flowed from it, was rooted in the agency's inability to defend its organizational essence—its core sense of corporate identity—and to adequately articulate and sustain the mission(s), roles, and capabilities on which it was based. Indeed, over time, weakness and vulnerability came to at least partially *define* CIDA's organizational essence. This largely unanswered challenge was strongly and irreversibly advanced by a series of blows inflicted during the 1990s by the leadership of both major political parties. Despite the agency's efforts to adapt, it ended up failing both to expand its autonomy to pursue its core mission(s) in relation to other government departments concerned with international policy and to sustain the vitality of its "partnerships" with Canadian development CSO's.

To be sure, much of this failure was rooted in structural, political, and ideational factors beyond CIDA's control. These included the perennial controversy over the appropriate role(s), utility, and limits of foreign aid, a controversy which, as the chapters in this collection indicate, is as old as the Canadian aid program. Nor does this conclusion diminish the achievements of CIDA personnel, projects, and programs in various times and places over the course of its forty-five years of existence. But it does highlight the importance of carving out a distinctive organizational space whose identity and capacities are firmly linked to addressing the challenges of global poverty and inequality. As Nilima Gulrajani has argued about the architecture of development agencies more broadly, whether this space is lodged within the foreign ministry (as now seems certain for the foreseeable future) or elsewhere is less important than that this institutional home has a distinct identity and a robust political and intellectual foundation.[49] Without it, Canada's ability to address these acute global challenges and the multiple problems arising from them will remain enfeebled.

Notes

1   Patrick Johnston, "*Modernizing Canadian Foreign Aid and Development: Challenges Old And New*" (Toronto: Walter and Gordon Duncan Foundation, 2010), 3.

2   John Stackhouse, "CIDA was long dead. Harper only buried it," *Globe and Mail*, 22 March 2013.

3   It can be argued that this crisis of confidence was three-dimensional, involving: an internal dimension, concerning the agency's capacity to make, defend, and sustain key policy decisions; a prescriptive dimension, reflecting uncertainty and division concerning the best uses of development aid; and an external dimension, entailing a lack of confidence among other international policy institutions in Ottawa concerning CIDA's capacity to succeed in its core mission, and questioning the utility of that mission.

4   Marie-Eve Desrosiers and Philippe Lagassé, "Canada and the Bureaucratic Politics of State Fragility," *Diplomacy and Statecraft* 20, no. 4 (2009): 660.

5   Morton Halperin and Priscilla Clapp, *Bureaucratic Politics and Foreign Policy*, 2nd ed. (Washington, DC: Brookings Institution, 2006).

6   Philip Rawkins, "An Institutional Analysis of CIDA," in *Canadian International Development Assistance Policies: An Appraisal*, ed. Cranford Pratt (Montreal: McGill-Queen's University Press, 1994), 160.

7   Rawkins, "An Institutional Analysis of CIDA," 166.

8   Cited in Cranford Pratt, "Development Assistance and Canadian Foreign Policy: Where We Now Are," *Canadian Foreign Policy Journal* 2, no. 3 (1994): 80.

9   On the persistent centrality of poverty alleviation to the mission of Canadian foreign aid, see Ian Smillie, "Institutional Corruption and Canadian Foreign Aid," *Canadian Foreign Policy Journal* 23, no. 1 (2017): 47–59.

10 CIDA's operations were notoriously heavily concentrated at headquarters in Gatineau, with only very limited decision-making authority decentralized to missions in recipient countries. Geographic decentralization has long been mooted as a key requirement for enhanced responsiveness and effectiveness, but it has never been sustainably implemented.

11 It can also be argued that the decision to establish a dedicated development research institution—the International Development Research Centre—in 1970, shortly after CIDA's own establishment, reinforced the operational and somewhat anti-intellectual bias of the agency. On the decentralized and operational orientation of CIDA, see Rawkins, "An Institutional Analysis of CIDA."

12 See, for example, Betty Plewes and Brian Tomlinson, "Canadian CSOs and Africa: The End of an Era?" in *Canada Among Nations 2013: Canada-Africa Relations – Looking Back, Looking Ahead*, ed. Rohinton Medhora and Yiagadeesen Samy (Waterloo, ON: Centre for International Governance Innovation and Carleton University, 2013), 213–26.

13 See David Morrison, *Aid and Ebb Tide: A History of CIDA and Canadian Development Assistance* (Waterloo, ON: Wilfrid Laurier University Press, 1998), 455; Stephen Brown, "Canadian Aid to Africa," in Medhora and Samy, *Canada Among Nations 2013*, 181.

14 Though the share of aid in external financial flows to Africa has steadily declined, from 62 per cent in 1990 to 22 per cent in 2012. See Amadou Sy, "Africa in Focus: How Finance Flows to Africa," Brookings institution, 20 May 2015, https://www.brookings.edu/blog/africa-in-focus/2015/05/20/how-finance-flows-to-africa/.

15 For a detailed account of this period, see Morrison, *Aid and Ebb Tide*, 277–312.

16 Humane internationalism was defined by Cranford Pratt as "an acceptance by the citizens of the industrialized states that they have ethical obligations towards those beyond their borders and that these in turn impose obligations on their governments." See Pratt, "Humane Internationalism: Its Significance and Variants," in his edited collection *Internationalism Under Strain: The North-South Policies of Canada, the Netherlands, Norway, and Sweden* (Toronto: University of Toronto Press, 1989), 13.

17 Pratt was among the critics. See Pratt, "Canada: A Limited and Eroding Internationalism," in his edited collection *Internationalism Under Strain*, 24–69.

18 Morrison, *Aid and Ebb Tide*, 311.

19 CIDA, *Sharing our Future* (Gatineau: CIDA, 1988), 22.

20 Morrison, *Aid and Ebb Tide*, 311.

21 CIDA, *Sharing Our Future*, 35.

22 Rawkins, "An Institutional Analysis of CIDA," 173; Massé had previously been president in 1980–82.

23 Marcia Burdette, "Structural Adjustment and Canadian Aid Policy," in Pratt, *Canadian International Development Assistance Policies*, 210–39.

24 David Black and Peter McKenna, "Canada and Structural Adjustment in the South: The Significance of the Guyana Case," *Canadian Journal of Development Studies* 16, no. 1 (1995): 55–78.

25 Morrison, *Aid and Ebb Tide*, 313.

26 Rawkins, "An Institutional Analysis of CIDA," 176.

27 CIDA, Africa and the Middle East Branch, *Africa 21: A Vision of Africa in the 21st Century* (October 1991).

28 Pratt, "Development Assistance and Canadian Foreign Policy," 78.

29 Cranford Pratt, "DFAIT's Takeover Bid of CIDA," *Canadian Foreign Policy Journal* 5, no. 2 (1998): 4.

30 See Morrison, *Aid and Ebb Tide*, 373.

31 Morrison, *Aid and Ebb Tide*, 380–81.

32 Pratt, "Development Assistance and Canadian Foreign Policy," 80.

33 Government of Canada, *Canada in the World*, Government statement (1995), 40; Morrison, *Aid and Ebb Tide*, 399–401; Canadian Council for International Cooperation (CCIC), *Canada in the World: A Review and Analysis of the Government's Foreign Policy Statements*, February 1995.

34 Morrison, *Aid and Ebb Tide*, 377.

35 CCIC, "Renewing Canadian Aid: A CCIC/*in common* Fact Sheet," 2000.

36 See CCIC, "Renewing Canadian Aid"; and Larry Elliott, "The lost decade," *Guardian* (Manchester), 9 July 2003, https://www.theguardian.com/world/2003/jul/09/population.aids.

37 See Peter Uvin, *Aiding Violence: The Development Enterprise in Rwanda* (Hartford, CT: Kumarian Press, 1998).

38 For an insightful critique of the proposition that Canadians were supporters of a generous humane internationalist aid program, see Alain Noël, Jean-Philippe Thérien, and Stephane Dallaire, "Divided over Internationalism: The Canadian Public and Development Assistance," *Canadian Public Policy* 30, no. 1 (2004): 29–46.

39 Morrison, *Aid and Ebb Tide*, 416–17.

40 See Lloyd Axworthy, "Canada and Human Security: The Need for Leadership," *International Journal* 52, no. 2 (1997): 183–96; and Greg Donaghy, "All God's Children: Lloyd Axworthy, Human Security and Canadian Foreign Policy, 1996–2000," *Canadian Foreign Policy Journal* 10, no. 2 (2003): 39–58.

41 For examples, see Rob McRae and Don Hubert, eds., *Human Security and the New Diplomacy: Protecting People, Promoting Peace* (Montreal: McGill-Queen's University Press, 2001).

42 See Pratt, "DFAIT's Takeover Bid."

43 See, for example, Stephen Brown and Jörn Grävingholt, eds., *The Securitization of Foreign Aid* (Basingstoke, UK: Palgrave-Macmillan, 2016).

44 For details, see David Black, *Canada and Africa in the New Millennium: The Politics of Consistent Inconsistency* (Waterloo, ON: Wilfrid Laurier University Press, 2015), especially chaps. 2 and 5.

45 And from 2010 onward, ODA experienced another round of deep cuts, as the Harper government, like its Liberal predecessor, leaned disproportionately on foreign aid to bring the budget deficit back toward "balance."

46 Stephen Brown, "CIDA under the Gun," in *Canada Among Nations 2007: What Room for Manoeuvre?*, ed. Jean Daudelin and Daniel Schwanen (Montreal: McGill-Queen's University Press, 2008), 91–107. See also Stephen Brown, "Le rapport du Sénat sur l'aide canadienne à l'Afrique : une analyse à rejeter," *Le Multilatéral* 1, no. 3 (2007): 1, 6–7.

47 The generally sympathetic study by Patrick Johnston of the Walter and Gordon Duncan Foundation noted that "bureaucratic, hidebound, out-of-touch, ineffectual, risk averse, contradictory, vacillating—these and many similar criticisms of CIDA have now become commonplace." See Johnston, "*Modernizing Foreign Aid and Development*," 3.

48 Senate Standing Committee on Foreign Affairs and International Trade, *Overcoming Forty Years of Failure: A New Road Map for Sub-Saharan Africa* (Ottawa, 2007), 96–97.

49 See Nilima Gulrajani, "Bilateral Donors in the 'Beyond Aid' Agenda: The Importance Of Institutional Autonomy For Donor Effectiveness," Global Economic Governance Working Paper 2015/106, August 2015.

13

A *Samaritan State?*, Canadian Foreign Aid, and the Challenges of Policy Coherence for Development

Stephen Brown

In 1966, when Keith Spicer's seminal book, *A Samaritan State? External Aid in Canada's Foreign Policy*, first came out, Canada had been providing foreign aid for fifteen years, with responsibility split between the Department of External Affairs and the Department of Trade and Commerce.[1] Pierre Trudeau's government created the semi-autonomous Canadian International Development Agency (CIDA) only two years later, in 1968. *A Samaritan State?* was the first book ever published on Canadian foreign aid and, in fact, the only one for another one and a half decades.[2] Roughly fifty years on, Spicer's ground-breaking analysis is ripe for revisiting, and for comparison to current perspectives, policies, and practices.

Oddly enough, the book never answered its titular question: Was Canada a "Samaritan State"? In fact, the book never used the term, other than in its title. One can surmise that the expression was adopted after Spicer had completed the manuscript, as part of discussions with the publisher on how to market the book. Ironically, the title's undefined expression has become the book's most lasting legacy.

The term refers to the Biblical parable of the Good Samaritan, told by Jesus to his fellow Jews. In it, a half-dead naked man, presumably Jewish, lies on the ground, after having been beaten by robbers. Two successive men, both also Jews, see him lying there but keep walking. The third person to walk by, a Samaritan, stops to help the severely injured man, nursing his wounds and putting him up at an inn at his own expense, despite the general antipathy between their respective peoples.[3] A Good Samaritan has thus come to mean someone who helps a complete stranger out of the goodness of his or her own heart. Good Samaritanism corresponds to the concept of altruism or humanitarianism in the literature on foreign aid: the idea that a state, like a person, should be generous to complete strangers without any self-interested motive.

A Samaritan State? covered a wide range of topics, conducted several case studies, and provided a lot of empirical data.[4] This chapter focuses on Spicer's views on two key overarching issues that remain extremely relevant today: (1) the goals of Canadian foreign aid; and (2) the optimal relationship between Canada's aid policy and its other international policies. It examines each of these in turn, comparing Spicer's beliefs to Canada's recent policies and practices, mainly under the Conservative government of Prime Minister Stephen Harper. It then examines the short record and current thinking of Prime Minister Justin Trudeau's Liberal government in these two areas. Five decades after the book's publication, there is much to retain, in Spicer's vision for foreign aid and policy coherence for development, that past and present governments seem to have forgotten.

Why Give Foreign Aid?

In his book, Spicer very clearly disapproved of Samaritanism/altruism. He was not interested in morality as a basis of public policy:

> Philanthropy is plainly no more than a fickle and confused policy stimulant, derived from the personal conscience. It is not an objective of government. Love for mankind is a virtue of the human heart, an emotion which can stir only individuals—never bureaucracies or institutions. Governments exist only to promote the public good; and, as a result, they must act purely in the selfish interest of the state they serve. Altruism as foreign policy is a misnomer, even if sometimes

the fruits of policy are incidentally beneficial to foreigners. To talk of humanitarian "aims" in Canadian foreign policy is, in fact, to confuse policy with the ethics of individuals moulding it, to mix government objectives with personal motives.[5]

Though this might seem like realism at its bleakest, completely devoid of compassion, with no place for ethics, Spicer embraced many positions that would make altruists happy. For instance, he recognized the fundamental need to have a peaceful, stable world, as a prerequisite for most other policy goals. He even supported the use of humanitarian rhetoric in order to help generate public support for aid.[6] Indeed, there is much convergence between what he recommended and what altruists advocate. The motive might be different—self-interest versus selflessness—but the result is very often the same, as long as one takes, as Spicer usually did, a long-term perspective based on "enlightened self-interest."[7] In this, his perspective resembled what Alexis de Tocqueville called "*l'intérêt bien entendu*," usually translated as "self-interest rightly understood" or "self-interest properly understood."[8] For Spicer, helping others was good for Canada in the long run, and that was justification enough.

As David Black recently argued, too much emphasis has been placed on labelling the motives underlying Canadian aid and setting them up against each other. For instance, he discusses how the valuable work of the late Cranford Pratt, Canada's top scholar on foreign aid throughout the 1980s and 1990s, analytically opposed "international realists" and "humane internationalists" in ways that were sometimes counterproductive.[9] In a sense, these perspectives do not matter as much as the common ground that can be found between them on policies and practices. Accordingly, it is of lesser import whether something is the right thing to do for purely ethical reasons or because it is in the interest of global peace and prosperity and thus in Canada's long-term interests.

Regardless of whether one agrees with Spicer's perspective or not—and he himself might not hold today some of the views he expressed over fifty years ago—many of his observations remain valid. For instance, he was skeptical of aid's capacity to promote democratization and stability, which have proven much more difficult to achieve than many scholars and policy makers naively believed, for example, in places such as Afghanistan, Iraq, and Libya. It seems to be a lesson repeatedly learnt and then forgotten. Similarly, he warned against expectations that aid would easily engender economic growth, reminding readers that domestic factors matter a lot.

Spicer believed that Canada should provide generous levels of aid spending, in large part because the contact it generates would give Canadians a greater understanding of the Global South and thus help it engage as a "middle power" able to "keep the peace."[10] Still, recognizing that there is no clear correlation between aid and peace and security, Spicer was very supportive of aid as a "*symbol* of Canada's concern,"[11] and seemed less interested in the actual development that should result from aid than in the goodwill that the aid would generate for the Canadian government. He was also concerned that a lack of generosity would generate ill will, which would hamper any Canadian global leadership ambitions. While Spicer acknowledged that results can be mixed, in hindsight it is clear that he placed too much trust in the power of symbols and overestimated recipients' degree of gratitude. For example, he praised the wisdom of the Soviet Union in obtaining Afghans' allegiance by paving the streets of their capital, providing in his words a "paved thoroughfare for the camel-filled metropolis of Kabul."[12] However, the nine-year war against the Soviet occupation in the 1980s demonstrated that providing infrastructure was not a lasting guarantee of Afghan loyalty, though Western countries seem to have forgotten that lesson a couple of decades later.

The book's most interesting case study is of the Warsak dam in Pakistan near the Afghan border. This challenging project, discussed in Ryan Touhey's chapter in this volume, provided electricity and water for irrigation for decades following its inauguration in 1961. Writing soon after its completion, Spicer lauded the project, not least for having employed, albeit only temporarily, some 10,000 Pakistani men (whom he described as "wandering Pathan tribesmen"), which the Pakistan government greatly appreciated.[13] In his account, Pakistani gratitude to Canada was the main goal and measure of success, as documented in local press coverage. Spicer also highlighted the importance of the school and clinic that were set up alongside the dam, primarily to serve expatriate Canadians and their families. In his words, they "probably won for Canada the gratitude of more ordinary foreign nationals than any other single Canadian project. . . .

FIGURE 13.1
Like the Warsak Dam in Pakistan, the Dahla Dam was a 1950s-style Canadian signature project in Afghanistan, drawing regular visits from Ottawa. Prime Minister Stephen Harper, second from right, walks with Canadian Ambassador to Afghanistan Ron Hoffmann, right, Chief of the Defence Staff Walter Natynczyk, second from left, and Chantal Ruel, CIDA's Assistant Deputy Director of Development in Kandahar as they visit the Dahla Dam in May 2009. (Source: The Canadian Press/Sean Kilpatrick)

Through this care, the tribal folk [*sic*] obviously understood in simple human terms the message of international solidarity that the great concrete dam itself was partly intended to convey."[14]

The gratitude that Spicer valued and carefully documented, however, did not last. As he himself noted in passing, Pakistan's goodwill toward Canada all but disappeared when the latter provided military support to India in 1963.[15] Although Spicer obviously could not know how hated the Soviets would become in Afghanistan, he should nonetheless have drawn some conclusions from the ephemerality of Pakistani gratitude that he witnessed.

The parallel with Canada's support for the Dahla Dam across the border in Afghanistan's Kandahar Province in the late 2000s and early 2010s is inescapable. Like the Warsak Dam, the Dahla Dam was a 1950s-style "signature project"—a stand-alone scheme closely identified with the donor. It ignored decades of learning in development assistance that strongly suggested that aid is more effective when integrated with national programs and systems, rather than carried out independently to provide visibility for the donor.

Canadian assistance to the Dahla Dam was plagued with problems from the start, including inflated security costs that drained $10 million out of the dam's $50 million budget to pay for the services of a private security company with ties to an Afghan warlord, in what is best described as a protection racket.[16] Although the Canadian government declared success, it had ignored local Afghan calls for the height of the dam to be raised, severely hampering its utility, and left the dam unfinished when Canadian troops left the province.[17] An evaluation commissioned by the Canadian government recognized that the aid program in Kandahar, where Canadian aid was concentrated, "failed to ensure sustainable, long-term development results." Moreover, it pointed out that Canadian assistance incorrectly assumed that the main local Afghan grievances were economic, which explains why they were not won over by building infrastructure.[18]

For many decades, virtually all critiques of the effectiveness of Canadian aid, including from parliamentary committees, NGOs, and scholars—and of foreign aid more generally, not just Canada's—have emphasized the fact that aid has served many purposes other than fighting poverty, which governments have always presented as aid's primary purpose.[19] The overall confusion of purpose, the mixing of development goals with political and economic ones, is overwhelmingly seen as one of the main reasons why aid has not been more effective in achieving development goals. All too often, it is not meant primarily to serve that purpose. This chapter therefore looks more closely at the relationship between aid policy and other foreign policy objectives.

Aid's Relations with Other Components of Foreign Policy

Spicer strongly believed in the value of a Canadian aid program. In addition to earning gratitude abroad, he believed that it encouraged contact with other countries and improved interaction between Canada and the wider world. Beyond the aid relationship, it also leads to a more enlightened foreign policy, more effective diplomacy, and better participation in the international system. Many of the recommendations in *A Samaritan State?* have in fact been implemented, though not necessarily as a result of the book.

Though Spicer believed in linking aid and non-aid policies, he recognized the need for a dedicated aid program, separate from other areas of foreign policy. He suggested a distinct career stream for government aid officials "because aid administration demands specialized knowledge that cannot be absorbed and usefully exploited by men [sic] whose primary career [is] in trade or diplomacy."[20] The government did, in fact, adopt this practice after creating the semi-autonomous aid agency CIDA in 1968. However, CIDA's absorption into the Department of Foreign Affairs and International Trade (DFAIT) in 2013 has devalued development expertise and otherwise marginalized staff who came to the department from CIDA.[21]

Although he did not frame it in these terms, much of Spicer's vision for aid and trade was based on the concept of self-interest, provided that it was "properly understood" à la Tocqueville to pursue a long-term systemic vision rather than evanescent short-term gains. Thus, letting aid recipients exercise ownership of their development plans and aligning Canadian aid with their strategies would actually benefit Canada in the long run (articulating some of the Paris Principles on Aid Effectiveness almost forty years before they were adopted). He therefore strongly opposed tying aid to the purchase of goods and services in Canada, rather than obtaining them where they were cheapest, even if he considered the practice "inevitable."[22] Though he slightly overstated how hard it would be to eliminate tied aid, it did take until 2012 for Canada to completely phase it out. Even so, a large proportion of aid grants are still channelled through Canadian NGOs and used to hire Canadian consultants, even though there is no formal obligation to do so.

A key quandary in global development today is the appropriate role of the private sector. No other actor has the potential to unleash the trillions of dollars required to reach the Sustainable Development Goals (SDGs) by 2030, however controversial an actor it may be. Spicer, writing in a very different historical context, barely even discussed private investment because, he argued, "It is probably safe to assume . . . in view of Canada's own notorious need of foreign capital, that Canadian private investment in overseas development is now very small and is unlikely soon to become significant."[23]

Clearly, much has changed over the past fifty years. Canadian direct foreign investment in the developing world was worth $295 billion in 2015, which is about sixty years' worth of foreign aid at current spending levels.[24] Moreover, the Canadian government has, for the last few years, begun to promote quite actively the role of the private sector in development, especially the Canadian extractive industry. CIDA's partnerships with mining companies, first announced in 2011, have elicited a fair bit of attention—and criticism.[25] Moreover, it is important to remember that Canadian aid and other mechanisms, such as credit insurer Export Development Canada, have long promoted the Canadian private sector's involvement in developing countries.

Spicer advocated greater coordination of "aid, trade, defence, cultural relations, immigration and classical diplomacy," which is the core of what is now referred to as *policy coherence*, and saw aid as "simply one of several sometimes useful techniques of pursuing national goals abroad."[26] He thus favoured the instrumentalization of aid, not for short-term commercial or electoral gains, which undermine aid effectiveness, but over the long term.[27]

Clearly, greater policy coherence is an old idea, but it has seen a surge of popularity in Ottawa since at least the mid-2000s. It was manifest first in the "3D" approach—diplomacy, defence, and development—adopted by Prime Minister Paul Martin's Liberal government, and later in the broader "whole-of-government" approach championed by the Conservatives. In fact, Minister of International Cooperation Julian Fantino invoked the need for greater policy integration as the main reason for CIDA's abolition and merger with DFAIT, citing twin objectives: "To enhance coordination of international assistance with broader Canadian values and objectives, and to put development on an equal footing with trade and diplomacy."[28]

Most foreign policy and trade analysts applauded the CIDA-DFAIT merger, but many development specialists believed that the move would facilitate the increased subservience of aid to non-development objectives. Spicer might have approved, though, as he saw aid as an instrument of Canadian policy and decried how it had become "a cause in itself, a self-justifying crusade, a powerful Messianic magnet for a generation of liberals hungry for a purpose to fit a uniting world."[29] Spicer would not, however, have endorsed the blatant commercialization of aid envisaged in the 2013 *Global Markets Action Plan*, the first policy statement after the merger, which advocated "leverag[ing] development programming to advance Canada's trade interests."[30] Spicer would have considered such a short-term approach ineffective for promoting Canada's longer-term interests. Indeed, that part of the plan actually appears to contravene Canadian law, which mandates that the primary purpose of Canadian aid is to be poverty reduction.[31]

Advocating a form of policy coherence for development, Spicer presented some concrete steps outside the realm of aid that Canada could take to help developing countries, including ones that provide greater benefits than aid. For instance, he advocated trade concessions, which he recognized as improbable, and greater flows of immigrants, which would increase the amount sent to the developing world in the form of remittances.[32]

Contemporary development-oriented scholars and activists, however, favour policy coherence that will promote the interests of developing countries and reinforce their capacity to fight poverty, which is for them the ultimate goal. Spicer advocated it because it would help developing countries achieve their objectives and thereby gain Canada international praise, as well as increase the chances of long-term peace and stability. Despite their differences, these two perspectives are compatible at the policy level. However, they are not universally shared. Many Canadian politicians and taxpayers want aid to provide clear short-term benefits at home. Conservative Bev Oda, toward the end of her five-year tenure as Minister for International Cooperation, admitted that she did not separate Canada's trade and foreign policy interests from its development goals.[33] The OECD subsequently reminded the Canadian government that "there should be no confusion between development objectives and the promotion of commercial interests."[34] Still, Oda's successor, Julian Fantino, insisted that "Canadians are entitled to derive a benefit" from Canadian development assistance.[35]

If Canada is unwilling to protect the aid piggy bank from being raided by non-development interests, it would be preferable to insulate the aid bureaucracy. A separate aid ministry would be the obvious institutional mechanism, though no guarantee. The United Kingdom and Germany provide good, albeit not perfect, examples of independent ministries that are better able to defend their development mandate. Canada, however, has taken the path in the opposite direction and "de-merging" CIDA does not seem to be on anyone's agenda. Therefore, the role of development within Global Affairs Canada (GAC) is a crucial factor to monitor closely.

One of Spicer's key recommendations on aid was for periodic, independent, evidence-based policy reviews. In fact, he devoted most of the book's conclusion to that topic. This chapter therefore turns to a discussion of the International Assistance Review launched by the Liberal government in 2016 and resulting in a new policy in 2017.

Reviewing Canada's International Assistance Policy

Between May and July 2016, the Canadian government held 300 consultations in Canada and across the world as part of its International Assistance Review. It interacted with over 15,000 people and organizations in 65 countries and received over 10,000 contributions—a massive investment of time and other resources.[36] The consultations in Ottawa, however, were stage-managed around sectoral themes, rather than discussing how to make more fundamental improvements to Canada's aid program, including asking deeper questions on what the weaknesses of Canadian aid have been.[37] One of these underlying problems is the continual shifting of thematic and sectoral priorities, which is disruptive and actually harms aid effectiveness.[38]

Despite some genuflecting before the altar of policy coherence, the review was limited to "international assistance," i.e., aid, with the exception of some activities under the peace and security rubric. This limited approach did not augur well for the new aid policy, especially since no review of broader foreign policy seemed to be in the works, leaving aid without a larger context and the relationship between the two unexamined, *contra* Spicer's recommendations.

GAC subsequently published a web page on "What We Heard," making available to the public a summary of the results of the consultations, an unprecedented and very welcome action.[39] It mentioned the need "to build greater complementarity among Canadian policies and initiatives in the fields of defence, trade, diplomacy, security and development," a form of policy coherence Spicer firmly endorsed. It provided no indication, however, of the nature of this complementary relationship. Would development considerations have an important sway over the other fields, or would aid be subservient to short-term Canadian interests, as has all too often been the

FIGURE 13.2
With its new "feminist international assistance policy," Canadian aid policy headed off in a direction unimagined by Keith Spicer, though its troubling shortage of funds was a familiar part of the story. Two of the policy's leading supporters, Prime Minister Justin Trudeau and International Development Minister Marie-Claude Bibeau, are shown here at the opening of the Nelson Mandela Peace Summit at UN Headquarters in September 2018. (Source: The Canadian Press/Adrian Wyld)

case in the past? In other words, was the Canadian government aspiring to policy coherence *for development* or to policy coherence for other purposes?

The government finally published its new aid policy in June 2017. Billed as "Canada's first feminist international assistance policy," its most notable commitment was that within five years "at least 95 per cent of Canada's bilateral international development assistance investments will either target or integrate gender equality and the empowerment of women and girls,"[40] an area of focus unexamined by Spicer. The new policy was widely applauded for this emphasis, but concerns remained regarding how it would be implemented and what the impact would be on other programming.[41]

The policy makes some references to policy coherence, for instance: "When it comes to gender equality and the empowerment of women and girls, a more integrated approach is needed—one that also includes diplomacy, trade and the expertise of a wide range of Canadian government departments and agencies."[42] However, no detail was provided on how other government institutions would internalize this new priority.

A major flaw in the new aid strategy is that the government, after a decade or more of dismantling its development expertise and cutting its aid budget, is not interested in providing the financial resources required to rebuild the aid program. The Liberals' first three federal budgets (tabled in 2016, 2017, and 2018) provided only modest nominal increases in aid spending, leaving ODA as a percentage of gross national income around 0.26 per cent (see discussion in this volume's introduction). As a result, any new programming in one area will have to come at the expense of programs in others. As Spicer warned, important cutbacks to bilateral programming in certain countries actually generate ill will and can be harmful to Canada's interests.[43] The Conservatives' clumsy cutting of African countries of focus may have contributed to Canada losing its bid to be elected to the UN Security Council in 2010, an important fact for the Liberals to consider as they campaign for a seat in 2021.

Given its own lack of financial contributions, the government places much emphasis instead on contributions from the private sector. The new aid policy reintroduces the use of aid to provide loans (euphemistically referred to as "repayable contributions"), a practice abolished long ago by CIDA, and highlights the creation of a Canadian development finance institute (DFI) under the name FinDev Canada. The latter, originally announced by the Conservative government in 2015, has a budget of $300 million and is housed not at GAC but—tellingly—at Export Development Canada.

Such mechanisms risk repeating the errors of the past, focusing on commercial self-interest, supporting Canadian businesses rather than ones in developing countries, and wasting vast sums of money. Here, the experience of CIDA's long-standing Industrial Cooperation Program (known as CIDA-INC), founded in 1978, is highly relevant. It had a success rate of only 15 per cent and was shut down in 2012 amid fraud investigations.[44]

DFIs in other donor countries have been severely criticized for supporting "big businesses" rather than poverty reduction.[45] Although the government has charged FinDev Canada with empowering women, mitigating climate change, and reducing poverty, it is not clear how such

Stephen Brown

endeavours will be able to generate sufficient short-term profits to make the required loan repayments.

While the "feminist" components of the new aid policy have attracted the lion's share of public attention, the policy and subsequent government pronouncements demonstrate remarkable continuity with the previous government in promoting the role of the private sector in development.[46] Despite all the fanfare, it might be business as usual on that front. The private sector's poor collective record in promoting women's rights and gender equality suggests that there may be an unaddressed fundamental contradiction between the two core characteristics of the new aid policy. Moreover, the potential use of ODA funds in "innovative" mechanisms that are not truly focused on poverty reduction might even break Canadian law again. Spicer, who called for independent, evidence-based reviews, would have been disappointed with the result of Canada's latest iteration.

An additional major limitation of the new aid strategy is that it was designed, as mentioned above, in a foreign policy vacuum. What is actually required is an overarching policy that goes beyond aid, to encompass all dimensions of international policy, and provides clear guidance on the promotion of international development and the needs of poor people in poor countries.[47] Such an integrated approach is the only way countries, not just Canada, can hope to even come close to achieving the SDGs. Canada's aid review may prove to be a lost opportunity in that sense.

Looking Beyond Aid Policy

Spicer clearly considered aid to be part of Canada's broader foreign policy and thought that aid policy should be designed within that context. Similarly, today's scholars should not examine Canadian aid in isolation but rather as part of all of Canada's activities that have an impact on developing countries. John Cameron makes this point very convincingly and reminds us of the basic ethical principle: first, do no harm.[48] For instance, the foreign operations of Canadian mining companies provide benefits to the countries where they operate, including jobs and royalties, often augmented by their corporate social responsibility activities. Yet it is important to weigh the negative effects too. The extractive industry often does a lot of harm, and has been implicated in causing environmental destruction, the abuse of human rights, the creation of health problems, and the displacement of people and the loss of their livelihoods. According to a damning report commissioned by a Canadian extractive industry association but never publicly released, "Canadian companies are far and away the worst offenders."[49] Still, the Canadian government provides considerable support for the mining industry's investments abroad, including practical support through Canadian embassies and by subsidizing their philanthropic activities. As Cameron argues, scholars should therefore not limit the scope of their enquiry to the aid sector while ignoring the others as if the realms were independent of each other, rather than related manifestations of broader government support and policies.

It is not yet clear if the emphasis on Canadian business interests, and those of the extractive sector in particular, will differ considerably under the Trudeau Liberals. Minister of International Development Marie-Claude Bibeau told *Le Devoir*, "My mandate is development . . . not Canadian economic interests."[50] This may mean that the Canadian aid program may distance itself from the promotion of mining, though she did not say that it would. On the contrary, the government specifically affirmed its continued support for the controversial Canadian International Resources and Development Institute, created by CIDA and housed at the University of British Columbia, which receives $5 million in ODA funds annually.[51]

So far, under the Liberal government, one of the biggest failures of policy coherence for development, the feminist foreign policy, and the "do no harm" principle has been the sale of $15 billion in weaponized vehicles to Saudi Arabia, despite the severe human rights abuses in the country and strong reasons to believe that the arms would be used against civilians in Saudi Arabia or in Yemen. The government's justifications were lamentable: that it had "no choice" because the deal had been finalized by the previous government, that jobs in southern Ontario were at stake, and that if Canada did not sell them, someone else would. The first statement was a lie, and the remaining two arguments could be marshalled to justify selling weapons to any regime in the world, no matter how violent and dictatorial. In addition, the government argued that there was no "conclusive evidence" that Saudi Arabia had used Canadian vehicles for human rights violations in the past. In doing so, regardless of the credibility of the claim, the government ignored the fact that the legal criterion is actually the risk of such violations in the future.[52] Though the Federal Court eventually ruled that the minister had the discretionary power to approve the sale, doing so made a mockery of Canadian claims to have a robust process in place that takes into account human rights before approving such sales.[53]

The Trudeau government's aid policy states that it is "committed to strengthening our policy framework to ensure Canadian companies reflect Canadian values, respect human rights and operate responsibly."[54] However, the government will likely, as in the past, invoke human rights mainly when Canada has no other significant interests at play. Together, these practices will not win the plaudits abroad for which Spicer hoped.

Another conundrum in achieving policy coherence for development is how to reconcile the government's commitment to fighting climate change with its promotion and massive subsidization of the petroleum sector, providing over $3.3 billion annually to oil and gas producers and promoting pipelines that will encourage the extraction from the very environmentally destructive oil sands.[55] Policy coherence, and especially policy coherence *for development*, require sacrifices in policy areas that will undermine the short-term interests of some Canadian sectors and actors. To live up to commitments for such policy coherence requires not only a clear overarching vision to provide a cogent rationale but also the political will to implement it.

Conclusion

Many lessons that Spicer drew in his study over fifty years ago are crucial to recall today. Though Spicer was misguided in his quest for gratitude from aid recipients, his Tocquevillian emphasis on self-interest in the long run, which requires a peaceful, prosperous world, is a valuable reminder not to be distracted by short-term political or economic considerations. Seeking quick gains by supporting Canadian commercial interests, for instance, a key concern of the Harper government, makes for ineffective development policy and will not be of lasting benefit to Canada or developing countries. Spicer concluded, rightly, that ambitious global goals cannot be met by aid alone but require the coordination of all of Canada's international policies and better coordination with other international actors, a fact too often forgotten when faced with the desire to fly the flag. It remains to be seen to what extent the Trudeau government will be able or even willing to adopt a long time horizon and seek systemic benefits, such as global peace and prosperity.

Spicer's presumed rejection of the Samaritan State can be embraced to a certain extent, not, like him, out of contempt for the Good Samaritan's altruism, which can be a useful motivation, but in recognition that aid and other means of promoting development are not simply charitable activities, despite the way they are often portrayed for fundraising purposes. Rather, supporting development is part of a shared imperative to create a more equitable, peaceful, and environmentally sustainable world.

Notes

For generous support, the author thanks the Stellenbosch Institute for Advanced Study (STIAS), Wallenberg Research Centre at Stellenbosch University, Stellenbosch 7600, South Africa, where he was Fellow at the time of writing this chapter. He is also grateful for funding from the Social Sciences and Humanities Research Council of Canada.

1   Keith Spicer, *A Samaritan State? External Aid in Canada's Foreign Policy* (Toronto: University of Toronto Press), 1966.

2   At which time two very different critical books appeared: Robert Carty, Virginia Smith, and the Latin American Working Group, *Perpetuating Poverty: The Political Economy of Canadian Foreign Aid* (Toronto: Between the Lines, 1981); and Paul Fromm and James P. Hull, *Down the Drain? A Critical Re-examination of Canadian Foreign Aid* (Toronto: Griffin House, 1981).

3   Luke 10:25–37.

4   For a more complete overview of the book, see Stephen Brown, "Canada's Foreign Aid before and after CIDA: Not a Samaritan State," *International Journal* 68, no. 3 (2013): 501–12.

5   Spicer, *Samaritan State*, 11.

6   Spicer, *Samaritan State*, 12.

7   Ibid.

8   Alexis de Tocqueville, *De la démocratie en Amérique* (Paris: Pagnerre, 1850), published in English as Alexis de Tocqueville, *Democracy in America* (New York: The Century Co., 1898). Self-interest properly understood is often invoked in the McLeod Group's recommendations for Canadian development policy—see www.mcleodgroup.ca.

9   David R. Black, "Humane Internationalism and the Malaise of Canadian Aid Policy," in *Rethinking Canadian Aid*, 2nd ed., ed. Stephen Brown, Molly den Heyer, and David R. Black (Ottawa: University of Ottawa Press, 2016), 17–33.

10   Spicer, *Samaritan State*, 52.

11 Ibid., 21. Emphasis mine.

12 Ibid., 36.

13 Ibid., 127.

14 Ibid., 137.

15 Ibid., 36 and 142.

16 Jessica McDiarmid, "Canada spent $10 million for security at Afghan dam project," *Toronto Star*, 13 March 2013, https://www.thestar.com/news/canada/2013/03/13/ afghanistan_dam_project_9_million_set_aside_for_security_contractors_including_ those_in_armed_standoff.html.

17 David Pugliese, "More problems for the Dahla Dam—one of Canada's Afghan signature projects," *Ottawa Citizen*, 26 February 2016, http://ottawacitizen.com/news/national/ defence-watch/more-problems-for-the-dahla-dam-one-of-canadas-signature-project-in-afghanistan.

18 Canada, Department of Foreign Affairs, Trade and Development, *Synthesis Report – Summative Evaluation of Canada's Afghanistan Development Program, Fiscal Year 2004-2005 to 2012-2013* (Gatineau: Foreign Affairs, Trade and Development Canada, 2015), 48 and 41–42. For a more in-depth discussion of Canadian aid to Afghanistan, see Stephen Brown, "From Ottawa to Kandahar and Back: The Securitization of Canadian Foreign Aid," in *The Securitization of Foreign Aid*, ed. Stephen Brown and Jörn Grävingholt (Basingstoke, UK: Palgrave Macmillan, 2016), 113–37.

19 Ian Smillie, "Institutional Corruption and Canadian Foreign Aid," *Canadian Foreign Policy Journal* 23, no. 1 (2017): 45–46.

20 Spicer, *Samaritan State*, 115.

21 Jamey Essex and Logan Carmichael, "Restructuring Development Expertise and Labour in the CIDA-DFAIT Merger," *Canadian Geographer* 61, no. 2 (2017): 266–78.

22 Spicer, *Samaritan State*, 79.

23 Spicer, *Samaritan State*, 210.

24 I calculated this amount from Global Affairs Canada, Table 6-6, "Canadian Direct Investment Abroad: Stock by Region," *Canada's State of Trade: Trade and Investment Update 2016* (Ottawa: Public Works and Government Services Canada, 2016), 79. I included Canadian investment stock in all countries except for Australia, Japan, South Korea, the United States, and those located in Europe.

25 See, for instance, Stephen Brown, "Undermining Foreign Aid: The Extractive Sector and the Recommercialization of Canadian Development Assistance," in Brown, den Heyer, and Black, *Rethinking Canadian Aid*, 277–95; Ruby Dagher, "The Canadian International Development Agency: Trade, Mining and the Role of Orthodoxy in the Harper Era," in *How Ottawa Spends, 2014-2015: The Harper Government - Good to Go?*, ed. G. Bruce Doern and Christopher Stoney (Montreal: McGill-Queen's University Press, 2014), 192–204.

26 Spicer, *Samaritan State*, 244.

27 For a contrast with the Conservative government, see Stephen Brown, "The Instrumentalization of Canadian Foreign Aid under the Harper Government," *Studies in Political Economy* 97, no. 1 (2016): 18–36.

28 Julian Fantino, "Today, the Honourable Julian Fantino, Minister of International Cooperation issued a statement following the release of Economic Action Plan 2013," 21 March 2013, Global Affairs Canada website, https://www.canada.ca/en/news/archive/2013/03/today-honourable-julian-fantino-minister-international-cooperation-issued-statement-following-release-economic-action-plan-2013.html.

29 Spicer, *Samaritan State*, 244.

30 Foreign Affairs, Trade and Development Canada, *Global Markets Action Plan*, 12 September 2014, accessed 24 January 2017 from http://international.gc.ca/global-markets-marches-mondiaux/plan.aspx?lang=eng.

31 Official Development Assistance Accountability Act, SC 2008, c. 17, http://laws-lois.justice.gc.ca/eng/acts/O-2.8/FullText.html.

32 Spicer, *Samaritan State*, 246.

33 Elizabeth Payne, "Private Sector becomes key player in Canada's overseas aid," *Ottawa Citizen*, 26 January 2012.

34 OECD, *Canada: Development Assistance Committee (DAC) Peer Review 2012* (Paris: OECD/DAC, 2012), 11.

35 Cited in Kim Mackrael, "Fantino defends CIDA's corporate shift," *Globe and Mail*, 3 December 2012, http://www.theglobeandmail.com/news/politics/fantino-defends-cidas-corporate-shift/article5950443/.

36 Government of Canada, "2016 International Assistance Review: What We Heard," December 2016, https://international.gc.ca/world-monde/issues_development-enjeux_developpement/priorities-priorites/what_we_heard-que_nous_entendu.aspx?lang=eng.

37 See discussion in "Canada's International Assistance Review: Opportunities and Red Herrings," McLeod Group Blog, 20 May 2016, http://www.mcleodgroup.ca/2016/05/20/canadas-international-assistance-review-opportunities-and-red-herrings/.

38 Stephen Brown, "Aid Effectiveness and the Framing of New Canadian Aid Initiatives," in *Readings in Canadian Foreign Policy: Classic Debates and New Ideas*, 3rd ed., ed. Duane Bratt and Christopher J. Kukucha (Don Mills, ON: Oxford University Press, 2015), 470–71.

39 Government of Canada, "What We Heard," https://international.gc.ca/world-monde/issues_development-enjeux_developpement/priorities-priorites/what_we_heard-que_nous_entendu.aspx?lang=eng.

40 Government of Canada, "Canada's Feminist International Assistance Policy," June 2017, http://international.gc.ca/world-monde/issues_development-enjeux_developpement/priorities-priorites/policy-politique.aspx?lang=eng.

41 See Stephen Brown and Liam Swiss, "Canada's Feminist International Assistance Policy: Game Changer or Fig Leaf?," in *How Ottawa Spends, 2017–2018*, ed. Katherine A. H. Graham and Allan M. Maslove (Ottawa: Carleton University School of Public Policy and Administration, 2017), 117–31.

42   Government of Canada, "Canada's Feminist International Assistance Policy."

43   Spicer, *Samaritan State*, 38.

44   See "A Backgrounder on Canada's Development Finance Initiative," McLeod Group Policy Brief, 15 May 2016, http://www.mcleodgroup.ca/wp-content/uploads/2016/05/ REVISED-McLeod-Group-Policy-Brief-16-DFI-UPDATED.pdf.

45   Claire Provost, "British aid money invested in gated communities and shopping centres," *Guardian* (Manchester) online, 2 May 2014, https://www.theguardian.com/ global-development/2014/may/02/british-aid-money-gated-communities-shopping-centres-cdc-poverty. For a more systematic critique of nine countries' DFIs, see Javier Pereira, *The Development Effectiveness of Supporting the Private Sector with ODA Funds* (Brussels: Trade Union Development Cooperation Network and CSO Partnership for Development Effectiveness, 2016).

46   In fact, the differences in the aid program under Conservatives and Liberals are more a question of framing than of substance. See Stephen Brown, "All About That Base? Branding and the Domestic Politics of Canadian Foreign Aid," *Canadian Foreign Policy Journal* 24, no. 2 (2018): 145–64.

47   Anni-Claudine Bülles and Shannon Kindornay, *Beyond Aid: A Plan for Canada's International Cooperation* (Ottawa: North-South Institute, 2013).

48   John D. Cameron, "Revisiting the Ethical Foundations of Aid and Development Policy from a Cosmopolitan Perspective," in Brown, den Heyer, and Black, *Rethinking Canadian Aid*, 51–65.

49   Les Whittington, "Canadian mining firms worst for environment, rights: Report," *Toronto Star*, 19 October 2010, https://www.thestar.com/news/canada/2010/10/19/ canadian_mining_firms_worst_for_environment_rights_report.html.

50   Marie Vastel, "Les priorités économiques ne dicteront plus l'aide internationale," *Le Devoir*, 12 May 2016, http://www.ledevoir.com/politique/canada/470693/les-priorites-economiques-ne-dicteront-plus-l-aide-internationale. My translation. Bibeau was minister of international development from November 2015 to March 2019.

51   For in-depth analysis and critiques of the institute, see the Stop the Institute website, http://stoptheinstitute.ca/.

52   Murray Brewster, "No evidence Canadian vehicles involved in Saudi crackdown on civilians, says federal report," CBC News, 7 May 2018, http://www.cbc.ca/news/politics/ saudi-lavs-freeland-report-1.4652614.

53   César Jaramillo, "Despite ruling, many questions on Saudi arms deal linger," *Globe and Mail*, 25 January 2017, http://www.theglobeandmail.com/opinion/despite-ruling-many-questions-on-saudi-arms-deal-linger/article33742260/.

54   Government of Canada, "Canada's Feminist International Assistance Policy."

55   Oliver Milman, "Canada gives $3.3bn subsidies to fossil fuel producers despite climate pledge," *Guardian* (Manchester), 15 November 2016, https://www.theguardian.com/ world/2016/nov/15/climate-change-canada-fossil-fuel-subsidies-carbon-trudeau. This figure does not include the $4.5 billion purchase of the Kinder Morgan pipeline, announced in May 2018.

CONCLUSION

Concluding Reflections: Beyond Aid

Dominique Marshall

The symposium that gave rise to this volume was perhaps the first in Canada to focus on the evolution of Canadian official development assistance as its centre of historical inquiry. The two-day gathering, which brought together over 200 scholars, aid workers, and policy makers from Canada and abroad, uncovered a surprising variety of policy expertise, drawn from different traditions and generations.[1] The conference and this collection are welcome witness to the intellectual energy and openness of this emerging field of study in Canada, and are an encouragement to pursue, in history, what Stephen Brown demands of Canadian ODA: an "integrated approach . . . beyond aid, to encompass all dimensions of international policy."[2]

One possible avenue for integration is suggested by the work of the United Kingdom's Overseas Development Institute (ODI), whose project for a global history of humanitarianism promotes "the use of history in the practice and policy-making of humanitarian action."[3] Over the past decade, the ODI has held historical symposia across the Global South, helping to develop complementary but asymmetrical shared histories of donors and recipients. The initiative recalls the ideals of partnership and "humane internationalism" held by Canadian aid workers during the 1970s and discussed by Kevin Brushett and Asa McKercher in this volume. Many Canadian historians are going further, and starting to chart the movements of influences between Indigenous and development aid policies, as well as between recipients and distributors, in a similar intellectual endeavour.[4]

Shared intellectual endeavour marks this collection. Histories of British and American postwar development assistance have been, by force of circumstance, directly informed by critiques of colonialism and the self-interested policies of cold war superpowers. Several authors in this collection apply critical Anglo-American concepts and perspectives to tackling the history of Canadian development aid. Jill Campbell-Miller, for instance, examines India through the modernization lens developed by David Ekbladh, while Stefano Tijerina use the notion of a "promotional state" to account for the evolution of aid to Colombia.[5] Similarly, as Greg Donaghy and David Webster note in their introduction to this volume, the historiography of Canadian development assistance, aid from an intermediary state, mirrors the history of its foreign relations; it shows the country "neither as heroic do-gooder nor as imperialist exploiter, [but rather in] a more ambiguous position that has both reflected and shaped global trends in development thought and practice."[6]

The transnational "turn"—away from national toward global paradigms of understanding—invites further questions about the impact of aid's history in the Global South on other histories, especially in the Northern Hemisphere.[7] David Webster's study of Hugh Keenleyside, for example, explores how Canadian aid workers and bureaucrats worked with ideas about the role of the state that were closely associated with Canadian domestic traditions, playing the resulting UN consensus back to Ottawa to extract more aid. Reciprocal influence is a theme pursued by Campbell-Miller as well. Indeed, Keith Spicer, the author of the original *A Samaritan State?*, noted a parallel leitmotif in recalling the impact of the Colombo Plan on his subsequent career as a Canadian public servant: "the Colombo Plan, which was a Commonwealth program . . . was my point of entry, and the discovery of French Canadians working abroad with English Canadians, impressed me very much. . . . English and French Canadians working together overseas, . . . wasn't this a marvelous thing, why can't we do it at home?"[8]

The history of Canadian foreign aid has recently come into its own for many reasons. Urgent among them is the age of the first generation of CIDA workers, whose papers and testimonies are in danger of disappearing. From another direction, from Canadians who are children of diasporas, comes a renewed and different curiosity about development aid. The questions that Nassisse Solomon asks about Canada's response to the Ethiopian famine

Dominique Marshall

represents one such history, as do the public histories of Canadian aid told by former Chilean refugees and their allies.[9] The historiographical movement echoes Nik Cavell's sense that the changing nature of Canada's population would eventually call for different international relations (and different histories). This is certainly implied in Kevin Brushett's study of CIDA's Malaysian-born bureaucratic entrepreneur, Lewis Perinbam. His cosmopolitan outlook and transnational roots seemed to lead inexorably toward "aiding" the people of the region of his origins. Coming full circle, Canadian University Service Overseas successfully targets "second-generation" Canadians wishing to work where their parents were born.[10] Laura MacDonald and David Black write in this collection of Canadian aid's effect in Africa and Latin America. Both regions may also be affecting Canada, as Asia already has.

Historians of development assistance emerge from several professional traditions. While most in this collection are rooted in government and the universities, others come from NGOs, churches, and human rights organizations. Retired aid workers and NGO veterans, often trained in critical and scholarly inquiry, are busy writing parts of the story. This is true, for instance, of former Oxfam Canada secretary general Lawrence Cumming, who is currently composing a complex story of reciprocal influence and dependency, and of John Foster, who is coordinating a commemorative project on the solidarity work of the Latin American Working Group (LAWG). [11]

At times, mutual state-NGO trust and cooperation helped consolidate Canadian efforts, increasing aid's legitimacy within Canadian communities and educating them to the realities of the Global South. Much of the material for a bottom-up history of aid, which will complement Ted Cogan's top-down history of government public relations, can be gathered from such reflections. Occasions such as the conference that led to this book go a long way toward consolidating the mutual trust required to record recollections and archive personal papers.[12]

NGO archives, which document multiple interactions with Canada's official development assistance program, reveal traces of unexpected encounters. These range from inventive appeals by humanitarian workers for charitable status to tenacious attempts to secure visas for their workers to the collaborative work of Canadian politicians, artists, and philanthropists traveling abroad in awareness-raising delegations. The archives of Canadian

NGOs are rich with information on the activities of publicly funded development workers in the Global South, and writing about their activities opens wider horizons for the history of Canada's foreign relations.[13]

Former aid workers and civil servants want their stories recorded and shared. The conference on "The Samaritan State Revisited" provided the occasion of doing more history than these pages attest: I returned to Spicer's papers, interviewed him, and, with the help of research assistant Tyler Owens, organized his pictures and postcards into an online exhibit.[14] Yet, too often, the resources to document our aid history are still lacking. The uncertain fate of CIDA's extensive photo library, studied in this collection by Sonya de Laat, speaks to the "devaluation of development expertise," described elsewhere in this volume by Stephen Brown.[15] The politics of scholarly research, with the multiplication of programs competing for limited funding, has long created similar difficulties for "thick" research into the history of aid.

Happily, the future of aid archives has taken a turn for the better. The conference provided a platform for a group of concerned historians to engage Global Affairs Canada, convincing it to curate CIDA's historical photo collection and make it available to researchers.[16] More important, after a hiatus of two decades, Library and Archives Canada has resumed its practice of collecting NGO archives.[17] Moreover, LAC employees joined historians of all stripes in a pre-conference workshop on the "Archives of Foreign Aid" to disentangle the world of development aid records, from their inception to their archiving, and to make sense of the strange filing systems left by "the often informal administrative procedures" described in Donaghy's contribution.[18]

Those reading these pages will have seen that the borders of the history of development aid seem more fluid than ever: what is aid, and who aids whom? What of the role of private insurance companies? of security companies? of environmental agencies? What of the religious influences on official development aid during the last 30 years? Historians of all kinds are only starting to explore these topics. We hope that the wealth of material uncovered by this book will inspire the many recollections, reflections, archival rescues, and public displays required to build a dynamic and clear-sighted history of Canadians' changing sense of the wider world.

Dominique Marshall

Notes

1   Julie Van Drie, "When Historians Meet Aid Workers and Policy Makers," CNHH Blog post, 30 March 2017, http://aidhistory.ca/when-historians-meet-aid-workers-and-policy-makers/.

2   Brown, chapter 13 in this volume.

3   See https://www.odi.org/projects/2547-global-history-modern-humanitarian-action-moving-forward-hpg.

4   See Dominique Marshall with Julia Sterparn, "Oxfam Aid to Canada's First Nations, 1962–1975: Eating Lynx, Starving for Jobs, and Flying a Talking Bird," *Journal of the Canadian Historical Association* 22, no. 2 (2012): 298–343, https://www.erudit.org/fr/revues/jcha/2012-v23-n2-jcha0589/1015796ar/; see also David Meren's unfolding project on "First Nations, Third World: A Reconnaissance of the Origins of Canadian Foreign Aid"; Jill Campbell-Miller's post-doctoral project on "Settler Colonialism and Development: Experiences from Canada and India, 1953–58"; and the chapters by Henry Yu, Whitney Lackenbauer, and David Webster in *Dominion of Race: Rethinking Canada's International History*, ed. Laura Madokoro, Francine McKenzie, and David Meren (Vancouver: University of British Colombia Press, 2017).

5   On the distinct nature of the history of aid from countries on the periphery, see Kevin O'Sullivan, "History and the Development Aid Debate in the Republic of Ireland," *Policy and Practice* 12 (Spring 2011): 110–23, https://www.developmenteducationreview.com/issue/issue-12/history-and-development-aid-debate-republic-ireland; and Ann Nehlin, "Exporting Visions and Saving Children: The Swedish Save the Children Fund," *Linköping Studies in Arts and Sciences*, no. 494, Linköping University, 2009, http://www.diva-portal.org/smash/get/diva2:240412/FULLTEXT02.pdf.

6   Donaghy and Webster chapters, this volume.

7   Pierre-Yves Saunier, *Transnational History* (New York: Palgrave Macmillan, 2013); Akira Iriye and Pierre-Yves Saunier, eds., *The Palgrave Dictionary of Transnational History* (New York: Palgrave Macmillan. 2009).

8   Author interview with Keith Spicer, 30 November 2017. On community work methods brought to Canada from the Global South, see also Joy Parr, "Local Water Diversely Known: Walkerton, Ontario 2000 and After," *Environment and Planning D: Society and Space* 23, no. 2 (2005): 251–71; Jessica Haynes also discovered how Canadian nurses working in family planning in India brought back to Canada's first feminist clinics their knowledge about contraception. "The Legacy of Scientific Motherhood: Doctors and Child-Rearing Advice in the 1960s and 1970s in English Canada" (PhD diss., Carleton University, 2007).

9   "Carleton University Celebrates 45 Years with the Chilean Diaspora: Jose Venturelli Eade, Muralist," 4 December 2017, CNHH, http://aidhistory.ca/event/carleton-university-celebrates-45-years-with-the-chilean-diaspora/. Archives and Research Collections, Carleton University (ARC) uncovered archives of a 2000 application by the development consultants Latin America Development Projects led by the curator of the

exhibit and refugee of the first hour, Leonor Leon, to Match International, toward the building of a community centre in the small town of San José de Maipo, in Chile.

10   See chapter 7 in this volume.

11   LAWG: Hay Camino History Project, accessed December 2017 from https://lawghaycamino.wordpress.com/. See also the LAWG archives, deposited at York University's CERLAC: http://cerlac.info.yorku.ca/resources/collections/latin-american-working-group-lawg-library.

12   I would like thank the three successive heads of Oxfam Canada from the mid-1970s to the mid-1990s, whom I interviewed in 2016: Meyer Brownstone, Lawrence Cumming, and John Foster. The papers, slides, and audio archives of Brownstone and Foster are now at ARC: https://archie.library.carleton.ca/index.php/meyer-brownstone-oxfam-international-fonds; and https://archie.library.carleton.ca/index.php/john-foster-fonds. Partly as a result of the symposium that gave rise to this volume, Hunter McGill and Ian Smillie have established a partnership with ARC toward a "Development Assistance and Humanitarian Archives Rescue Project." Handout in possession of the author, December 2017.

13   See the archives of Match International Women's Fund, recently acquired by ARC, https://archie.library.carleton.ca/index.php/match-international-womens-fund-fonds; Victoria Hawkins, "Creche for the Children of Hospital Workers in Lusaka, 1980–1981," CNHH Blog post, 7 November 2016, http://aidhistory.ca/creche-for-the-children-of-hospital-workers-in-lusaka-zambia-1980-1981/; and the archives of Oxfam UK, acquired in 2013 by the Bodleian Library of Oxford University, https://www.bodleian.ox.ac.uk/weston/our-work/projects/saving-oxford-medicine/cataloguing-the-oxfam-archive. See also the citation by the Canadian Journalists for Free Expression, who awarded Bob Thomson, a CIDA officer who leaked confidential telegrams from the Canadian embassy in Santiago on the brutalities of General Augusto Pinochet's right-wing coup in Chile, the Integrity Award in 2013: http://www.cjfe.org/resources/features/2013-integrity-award-winner-bob-thomson.

14   Tyler Owens and Dominique Marshall, "Keith Spicer: Illustrated Maps of Humanitarian Travels in Asia, 1960," CNHH Blog post, 21 April 2017, http://aidhistory.ca/keith-spicer-illustrated-maps-of-humanitarian-travels-in-asia-1960/.

15   Brown, chapter 13 in this volume.

16   Meeting and correspondence of the author with Ralph Duchesne, 25 October 2017.

17   The social justice section readily accepted the papers of the Canadian Hunger Foundation after its closing in 2015. Will Tait, "Virtual Visit to the Offices of the Canadian Hunger Foundation on the Eve of its Closing, August 2015," CNHH Blog post, 22 September 2015, http://aidhistory.ca/virtual-visit-to-the-offices-of-the-canadian-hunger-foundation-on-the-eve-of-its-closing-august-2015/. The papers of many closed or diminished institutions of development research await archiving, such as those of the diminished North-South Institute. Blair Crawford, "North South Institute, Ottawa-based think tank, to close," Ottawa Citizen, 10 September 2014, http://ottawacitizen.com/news/local-news/north-south-institute-ottawa-based-think-tank-to-close.

18 Tyler Owens, "Archives of Foreign Aid, A Workshop Summary," CNHH Blog post, 6 February 2016, http://aidhistory.ca/archives-and-foreign-aid-a-workshop-summary/. David Webster noted that Hugh Keenleyside recalled that the UN's technical assistance work was measurably hampered in the 1950s by the organization's "absurd registry and filing system." Staff could often not find crucial documentation because dozens of files had identical titles. Correspondence with the author.

BIBLIOGRAPHY

Archival Sources

DIEFENBAKER CANADA CENTRE, Saskatoon
John G. Diefenbaker Papers

LIBRARY AND ARCHIVES CANADA
Andrew Brewin Papers

Canada Foundation Papers

Canadian Council of Churches Records

Canadian Council on International Co-operation Records

CUSO Papers

Gordon Churchill Papers

Walter Herbert Papers

Douglas LePan Papers

Hugh Keenleyside Papers

W. L. Mackenzie King Papers

David MacDonald Papers

Paul Joseph James Martin Papers

Oxfam Canada Papers

L. B. Pearson Papers

Privy Council Office Records

A. E. Ritchie Papers

L. S. St. Laurent Papers

NATIONAL ARCHIVES OF INDIA

Indian Ministry of External Affairs Records

TRINITY COLLEGE ARCHIVES, Toronto

John W. Holmes Papers

ARCHIVES AND RESEARCH COLLECTIONS, CARLETON UNIVERSITY

Lawrence Cumming Papers

John Foster Papers

Match International Women's Fund Archives

UNITED NATIONS

United Nations Archives and Records Administration

NEWSPAPERS AND PERIODICALS

Chili-Québec Informations

CIDA Contact

Cooperation Canada

El Tiempo (Colombia)

Evening Telegram (St. John's)

Globe and Mail

Guardian (Manchester)

Halifax Chronicle Herald

Last Post

Le Devoir

Le Droit

Lethbridge Herald

London Free Press

Maclean's

Montreal Gazette

Montreal Star

New York Times

Ottawa Citizen

Ottawa Journal

Quebec Chronicle Telegraph

Saturday Night

Toronto Star

Toronto Sun

University World News

Vancouver Province

Windsor Star

Winnipeg Free Press

Government and Institutional Publications

CANADA

Barry, Donald, ed. *Documents on Canadian External Relations*, vol. 19: *1953*.

Canadian International Development Agency (CIDA). *Annual Review 1972–1973*. Ottawa: Information Canada, 1973.

———. *Annual Review 1973–1974*. Ottawa: Information Canada, 1974.

———. *Annual Review 1979–1980*. Ottawa: Minister of Supply and Services, 1980.

———. *Canada and the Developing World: CIDA Annual Review 1970–1971*. Ottawa: Information Canada, 1971.

———. *Development: CIDA's Photographic Library*. Ottawa: Government of Canada, 1987.

———. *Report to CIDA: Public Attitudes Toward International Development Assistance*. Ottawa: Minister of Supply and Services Canada, 1988.

———. *Sharing our Future*. Gatineau: CIDA, 1988.

———. *Strategy for International Development Cooperation, 1975–1980*. Ottawa: Information Canada, 1975.

CIDA, Africa and the Middle East Branch. *Africa 21: A Vision of Africa in the 21st Century*. October 1991.

Department of External Affairs. Consultative Group on International Agricultural Research. "Summary of Proceedings: Third meeting of the Consultative Group on International Agricultural Research."

———. *Foreign Policy for Canadians.* Ottawa: Queen's Printer, 1970.

———. *Foreign Policy for Canadians: International Development.* Ottawa: Queen's Printer, 1970.

———. *Foreign Policy for Canadians: Latin America.* Ottawa: Queen's Printer, 1970.

———. *Preliminary Report of the Ministerial Mission to Latin America, October 27–November 27, 1968.* Ottawa: DEA, 1969.

———. *Report of the Department of External Affairs 1953.* Ottawa: Queen's Printer, 1954.

———. *Statements and Speeches.*

Department of External Affairs, External Aid Office. *A Report on Canada's External Aid Programmes 1965–66.* Ottawa, 1966.

———. *Annual Review: 1966–1967.* Ottawa, 1967.

Department of Foreign Affairs, Trade and Development. *Synthesis Report – Summative Evaluation of Canada's Afghanistan Development Program, Fiscal Year 2004–2005 to 2012–2013.* Gatineau: Foreign Affairs, Trade and Development Canada, 2015.

Department of Finance. *Public Accounts of Canada for the Fiscal Year Ended March 31, 1951 and Report of the Auditor General.* Ottawa: King's Printer, 1951.

———. *Public Accounts of Canada for the Fiscal Year Ended March 31, 1957.* Ottawa: Queen's Printer, 1957.

———. *Public Accounts of Canada, 1978.* Ottawa: Minister of Supply and Services, 1978.

———. *Public Accounts of Canada, 1979.* Ottawa: Minister of Supply and Services, 1979.

———. *Public Accounts of Canada, 1980.* Ottawa: Minister of Supply and Services, 1980.

Department of Trade and Commerce. *Annual Reports, 1950–1958.* Ottawa: Queen's Printer, 1951–59.

———. *Postwar Trade Reviews: Colombia and Venezuela.* Ottawa: King's Printer, 1946.

Donaghy, Greg, ed. *Documents on Canadian External Relations,* vol. 16: *1950.* Ottawa: Canada Communications Group, 1995.

———, ed. *Documents on Canadian External Relations,* vol. 17:*1951.* Ottawa: Canadian Government Publishing, 1996.

———, ed. *Documents on Canadian External Relations,* vol. 23: *1956–57, pt. 2.* Ottawa: Canadian Government Publishing, 2002.

Global Affairs Canada. *Canada's State of Trade: Trade and Investment Update 2016.* Ottawa: Public Works and Government Services Canada, 2016.

House of Commons. *Debates.*

International Development Research Centre (IDRC). *IDRC at 40: A Brief History.* Ottawa: IDRC, 2010.

——. *International Development Research Centre Projects 1970–1981*. Ottawa: IDRC, 1982.

MacDonald, David. Canadian Emergency Coordinator. *The African Famine and Canada's Response: For The Period From November 1984–March 1985*. Ottawa: Secretary of State, 1985.

Mackenzie, Hector, ed. *Documents on Canadian External Relations*, vol. 15: *1949*. Ottawa: Canada Communications Group, 1995.

Office of the Auditor General. *Report of the Auditor General to the House of Commons (Fiscal Year Ended 31 March 1976)*. Ottawa: Minister of Supply and Services, 1976.

——. *Report of the Auditor General to the House of Commons (Fiscal Year Ended 31 March 1979)*. Ottawa: Minister of Supply and Services, 1979.

Perinbam, Lewis. *Embracing Change in the Federal Public Service*. Ottawa: Treasury Board, 2000.

Public Service Commission of Canada. *Annual Reports, 1962–1977*.

Senate Standing Committee on Foreign Affairs and International Trade. *Overcoming Forty Years of Failure: A New Road Map for Sub-Saharan Africa*. Ottawa, 2007.

COLOMBIA

República de Colombia. Departamento Nacional de Planeación. *Las Cuatro Estrategias*, ed. Departamento Nacional de Planeación. Bogotá, 1972.

COLUMBO PLAN

Consultative Committee. *The Colombo Plan for Co-operative Economic Development in South and South-East Asia, Progress Report*. New Delhi: October 1953.

——. *Second Annual Report of the Consultative Committee, The Colombo Plan for Co-operative Economic Development in South and South-East Asia*. New Delhi: October 1953.

——. *Tenth Annual Report of the Consultative Committee of The Colombo Plan for Co-operative Economic Development in South and South-East Asia*. Commemorative Issue to mark the Tenth Anniversary of the Colombo Plan. Kuala Lumpur: November 1961.

INDIA

Ministry of Finance. *External Assistance, 1967–68*. New Delhi: Government of India, 1968.

National Planning Commission. *Second Five Year Plan*. New Delhi, 1956.

ONTARIO

Department of Economics and Development. Applied Economic Branch, Office of the Chief Economist. *Colombia: A Market for Canadian Products*. Toronto, 2 December 1968.

ORGANISATION FOR ECONOMIC CO-OPERATION AND DEVELOPMENT

Canada: *Development Assistance Committee (DAC) Peer Review 2012*. Paris: OECD/DAC, 2012.

UNITED NATIONS

Complete Oral History Transcripts from UN Voices. CD-ROM. New York: United Nations Intellectual History Project, 2007.

I Saw Technical Assistance Change Lives. New York: United Nations, 1952.

Partners in Development. Report of the Commission on International Development chaired by Lester Pearson. New York: United Nations, 1969.

Public Papers of the Secretaries-General of the United Nations, vol. 1: *Trygve Lie, 1946–1953*. New York: Columbia University Press, 1969.

Books, Articles, and Dissertations

Adas, Michael. *Dominance by Design: Technological Imperatives and America's Civilizing Mission*. Cambridge, MA: Harvard University Press, 2006.

Adeleke, Ademola. "Ties Without Strings? The Colombo Plan and the Geopolitics of International Aid, 1950–1980." PhD diss., University of Toronto, 1996.

Alexander, Robert J. *The Bolivian National Revolution*. Westport CT: Greenwood Press, 1958.

Amrith, Sunil, and Glenda Sluga. "New Histories of the United Nations." *Journal of World History* 19, no. 3 (2008): 251–74.

Amrith, Sunil. *Decolonizing International Health: India and Southeast Asia, 1930–65*. London: Palgrave Macmillan, 2006.

Armstrong-Reid, Susan, and David Murray. *Armies of Peace: Canada and the UNRRA Years*. Toronto: University of Toronto Press, 2008.

Arndt, H. W. *Economic Development: The History of an Idea*. Chicago: University of Chicago Press, 1987.

Audet, François, and Judy Meltzer. "L'aide canadienne en Amérique Latine : une coopération paradoxale." In *L'Aide Canadienne au Développement : Bilan et perspective*, edited by François Audet, Marie-Eve Desrosiers, and Stéphane Roussel, 313–41. Montréal: Presses de l'Université de Montréal, 2008.

Ault, Orville. *My Way*. Ottawa: privately published, 1991.

Avromovic, Dragoslav, ed. *Economic Growth of Colombia: Problems and Prospects; Report of a Mission Sent to Colombia in 1970 by the World Bank*. Baltimore, MD: Johns Hopkins University Press, 1970.

Axworthy, Lloyd. "Canada and Human Security: The Need for Leadership." *International Journal* 52, no. 2 (1997): 183–96.

Azoulay, Ariella. *Civil Imagination: A Political Ontology of Photography*. London: Verso, 2012.

Azzi, Stephen. *Walter Gordon and the Rise of Canadian Nationalism*. Montreal: McGill-Queen's University Press, 1999.

Bangarth, Stephanie. "The Politics of African Intervention: Canada and Biafra, 1967–1970." In *From Kinshasa to Kandahar: Canada and Fragile States in Historical Perspective*, edited by Michael K. Carroll and Greg Donaghy, 53–72. Calgary: University of Calgary Press, 2016.

———. "'Vocal but not Particularly Strong?': Air Canada's Ill-fated Vacation Package to Rhodesia and South Africa and the Anti-Apartheid Movement in Canada." *International Journal* 71, no. 3 (2016): 488–97.

Baranyi, Stephen, and John W. Foster. "Canada and Central America: Citizen Action And International Policy." In McKenna, *Canada Looks South*, 240–64.

Barnett, Michael. *Empire of Humanity: A History of Humanitarianism*. Ithaca, NY: Cornell University Press, 2011.

Barry-Shaw, Nikolas, and Dru Oja-Jay. *Paved With Good Intentions: Canada's Development NGOs From Idealism to Imperialism*. Halifax: Fernwood, 2012.

Benthall, Jeremy. *Disasters, Relief and the Media*. London: I.B. Tauris, 1993.

Berger, Carl. *The Sense Of Power: Studies in the Ideas of Canadian Imperialism*. Toronto: University of Toronto Press, 1970.

Berquist, Charles. *Café y Conflicto en Colombia (1886–1910); La Guerra de los Mil Días, sus Antecedentes y Consecuencias*. Bogotá: Ancora Editores, 1981.

Bingham, Jonathan B. *Shirt-Sleeve Diplomacy: Point 4 in Action*. New York: John Day, 1953.

Black, David. *Canada and Africa in the New Millennium: The Politics of Consistent Inconsistency*. Waterloo, ON: Wilfrid Laurier University Press, 2015.

———. "Humane Internationalism and the Malaise of Canadian Aid Policy." In *Rethinking Canadian Aid*, 2nd ed., edited by Stephen Brown, Molly den Heyer, and David R. Black, 17–33. Ottawa: University of Ottawa Press, 2016.

Black, David, and Peter McKenna. "Canada and Structural Adjustment in the South: The Significance of the Guyana Case." *Canadian Journal of Development Studies* 16, no. 1 (1995): 55–78.

Bourdieu, Pierre. *Photography: A Middle-Brow Art.* Translated by Shaun Whiteside. Stanford, CA: Stanford University Press, 1990.

Bratt, Duane. *The Politics of Candu Exports.* Toronto: University of Toronto Press, 2006.

Brégent-Heald, Dominique. "Vacationland: Film, Tourism, and Selling Canada, 1934–1948." *Canadian Journal of Film Studies* 21, no. 2 (2012): 27–48.

Brennan, Patrick H. "'A Good Man for the Middle Innings': Lester Pearson and the Media, 1963–1968." In *Pearson: The Unlikely Gladiator,* edited by Norman Hillmer, 117–30. Montreal: McGill-Queen's University Press, 1999.

———. *Reporting the Nation's Business: Press-Government Relations During the Liberal Years, 1935–1957.* Toronto: University of Toronto Press, 1994.

Brewin, Andrew. "Canadian Economic Assistance to Under-Developed Areas." *International Journal* 5, no. 4 (1950): 304–14.

Brodhead, Tim, Brent Herbert-Copley, and Anne-Marie Lambert. *Bridges of Hope?: Canadian Voluntary Agencies and the Third World.* Ottawa: North-South Institute, 1988.

Brodhead, Tim, and Cranford Pratt. "Paying the Piper: CIDA and Canadian NGOs." In Pratt, *Canadian International Development Assistance Policies,* 87–119.

Brouwer, Ruth Compton. *Canada's Global Villagers: CUSO in Development, 1961–86.* Vancouver: University of British Columbia Press, 2013.

———. *Modern Women Modernizing Men: The Changing Missions of Three Professional Women in Asia and Africa, 1902–69.* Vancouver: University of British Columbia Press, 2002.

———. "When Missions Became Development: Ironies of 'NGOization' in Mainstream Canadian Churches in the 1960s." *Canadian Historical Review* 91, no. 4 (Dec. 2010): 661–93.

Brown, Stephen. "Aid Effectiveness and the Framing of New Canadian Aid Initiatives." In *Readings in Canadian Foreign Policy: Classic Debates and New Ideas,* 3rd ed., edited by Duane Bratt and Christopher J. Kukucha, 467–81. Don Mills, ON: Oxford University Press, 2015.

———. "All About That Base? Branding and the Domestic Politics of Canadian Foreign Aid." *Canadian Foreign Policy Journal* 24, no. 2 (2018): 145–64.

———. "Canada's Foreign Aid before and after CIDA: Not a Samaritan State." *International Journal* 68, no. 3 (2013): 501–12.

———. "Canadian Aid To Africa." In *Canada-Africa Relations: Looking Back, Looking Ahead,* edited by Rohinton Medhora and Yigadeesen Samy, 181–94. Waterloo, ON: Centre for International Governance Innovation and Carleton University, 2013.

———. "CIDA under the Gun." In *Canada Among Nations 2007: What Room for Manoeuvre?*, edited by Jean Daudelin and Daniel Schwanen, 91–107. Montreal: McGill-Queen's University Press, 2008.

———. "CIDA's New Partnership with Canadian NGOs: Modernizing for Greater Effectiveness?." In Brown, *Struggling for Effectiveness*, 287–304.

———. "'Creating the World's Best Development Agency?' Confusion and Contradictions and Tensions In CIDA's New Development Blueprint." *Canadian Journal of Development Studies* 28, no. 2 (2007): 213–28.

———. "From Ottawa to Kandahar and Back: The Securitization of Canadian Foreign Aid." In Brown and Grävingholt, *The Securitization of Foreign Aid*, 113–37.

———. "The Instrumentalization of Canadian Foreign Aid under the Harper Government." *Studies in Political Economy* 97, no. 1 (2016): 18–36.

———. "Le rapport du Sénat sur l'aide canadienne à l'Afrique : une analyse à rejeter." *Le Multilatéral* 1, no. 3 (2007): 1, 6–7.

———, ed. *Struggling for Effectiveness: CIDA and Canadian Foreign Aid.* Montreal: McGill-Queen's University Press, 2012.

———. "Undermining Foreign Aid: The Extractive Sector and the Recommercialization of Canadian Development Assistance." In Brown, den Heyer, and Black, *Rethinking Canadian Aid*, 277–95.

Brown, Stephen, Molly den Heyer, and David Black, eds. *Rethinking Canadian Aid.* Ottawa: University of Ottawa Press, 2014.

Brown, Stephen, and Jörn Grävingholt, eds. *The Securitization of Foreign Aid.* Basingstoke, UK: Palgrave-Macmillan, 2016.

Brown, Stephen, and Liam Swiss. "Canada's Feminist International Assistance Policy: Game Changer or Fig Leaf?" In *How Ottawa Spends, 2017–2018*, edited by Katherine A.H. Graham and Allan M. Maslove, 117–31. Ottawa: Carleton University School of Public Policy and Administration, 2017.

Brushett, Kevin. "Partners in Development? Robert McNamara, Lester Pearson, and the Commission on International Development, 1967–1973." *Diplomacy and Statecraft* 26, no. 1 (2015): 84–102.

Bryce, Robert B. *Canada and the Cost of World War II: The International Operations of Canada's Department of Finance, 1939–1947.* Edited by Matthew J. Bellamy. Montreal: McGill-Queen's University Press, 2005.

Buckner, Phillip A., ed. *Canada and the End of Empire.* Vancouver: University of British Columbia Press, 2005.

Bueckert, Michael. "CIDA and the Capitalist State: Shifting Structures of Representation Under the Harper Government." *Studies in Political Economy* 96, no. 1 (2015): 3–22.

Bülles, Anni-Claudine, and Shannon Kindornay. *Beyond Aid: A Plan for Canada's International Cooperation.* Ottawa: North-South Institute, 2013.

Burdette, Marcia. "Structural Adjustment and Canadian Aid Policy." In Pratt, *Canadian International Development Assistance Policies,* 210–39.

Butler, Judith. "Torture and the Ethics of Photography: Thinking with Sontag." In *Frames of War: When Is Life Grievable?,* edited by Judith Butler, 63–100. London: Verso, 2009.

Cameron, John. "CIDA in the Americas: New Directions and Warning Signs for Canadian Development Policy." *Canadian Journal of Development Studies* 28, no. 2 (2007): 229–49.

——. "Revisiting the Ethical Foundations of Aid and Development Policy from a Cosmopolitan Perspective." In Brown, den Heyer, and Black, *Rethinking Canadian Aid,* 51–65.

Cameron, Maxwell A., and Jason Tockman. "Canada and the Democratic Charter: Lessons from the Coup in Honduras." In McKenna, *Canada Looks South,* 87–116.

Campbell-Miller, Jill. "The Mind of Modernity: Canadian Bilateral Foreign Assistance to India, 1950-60." PhD diss., University of Waterloo, 2014.

Cardwell, Curt. *NSC 68 and the Political Economy of the Early Cold War.* New York: Cambridge University Press, 2011.

Carty, Robert. "Giving For Gain: Foreign Aid and CIDA." In Swift and Clarke, *Ties that Bind,* 149–211.

Carty, Robert, Virginia Smith, and Latin American Working Group. *Perpetuating Poverty: The Political Economy of Canadian Foreign Aid.* Toronto: Between the Lines, 1981.

Champion, C. P. *The Strange Demise of British Canada: The Liberals and Canadian Nationalism, 1964-68.* Montreal: McGill-Queen's University Press, 2010.

Chapnick, Adam. "Canada's Aid Program: Still Struggling After Sixty Years." *Behind the Headlines* 65, no. 3 (May 2008): 1–28.

——. "The Politics of Reforming Canada's Foreign Aid Policy." In Brown, *Struggling for Effectiveness,* 305–26.

Charlton, Mark. *The Making of Canadian Food Aid Policy.* Montreal: McGill-Queen's University Press, 1992.

Chin, Carol. "Beneficent Imperialists: American Women Missionaries in China at the Turn of the Century." *Diplomatic History* 27, no. 3 (2003): 327–52.

Constantine, Stephen. *The Making of British Colonial Development Policy, 1914-1940.* London: Frank Cass, 1984.

Cowen, M. P., and R. W. Shenton. *Doctrines of Development.* London: Routledge, 1996.

Cross, Philip, and Philippe Bergevin. *Turning Points: Business Cycles in Canada since 1926.* Toronto: C.D. Howe Institute, 2012.

Cullather, Nick. "Development? It's History." *Diplomatic History* 24, no. 4 (October 2000): 641–53.

———. "Modernization Theory." In *Explaining the History of American Foreign Relations,* 2nd ed., edited by Michael J. Hogan and Thomas G. Paterson, 212–20. Cambridge: Cambridge University Press, 2004.

Currie, Lauchlin Bernard, ed. *The Basis of a Development Program for Colombia.* Washington: World Bank, 1950.

Curtis, Heather D. "Picturing Pain: Evangelicals and the Politics of Pictorial Humanitarianism in an Imperial Age." In Fehrenbach and Rodogno, *Humanitarian Photography,* 22–46.

Dagher, Ruby. "The Canadian International Development Agency: Trade, Mining and the Role of Orthodoxy in the Harper Era." In *How Ottawa Spends, 2014-2015: The Harper Government - Good to Go?,* edited by G. Bruce Doern and Christopher Stoney, 192–204. Montreal: McGill-Queen's University Press, 2014.

Daudelin, Jean, and Edgar Dosman. "Canada and Hemispheric Governance: The New Challenges." In *Canada Among Nations 1998: Leadership and Dialogue,* edited by Maureen A. Molot and Fen O. Hampson, 211–38. Toronto: Oxford University Press, 1998.

Demers, Maurice. *Connected Struggles: Catholics, Nationalists, and Transnational Relations between Mexico and Quebec, 1917-1945.* Montreal: McGill-Queen's University Press, 2014.

———. "Promoting a Different Type of North-South Interactions: Quebécois Cultural and Religious Paradiplomacy with Latin America." *American Review of Canadian Studies* 46, no. 2 (2016): 196–216.

Desmules, Martin. « Histoire du volontariat international au Québec : Le cas du service universitaire canadien outre-mer – SUCO. » Maitrise en histoire, Université du Québec à Montréal, 2009.

Desrosiers, Marie-Eve, and Philippe Lagassé. "Canada and the Bureaucratic Politics of State Fragility." *Diplomacy and Statecraft* 20, no. 4 (2009): 659–78.

Diefenbaker, John G. *One Canada: Memoirs of the Right Hon. John G. Diefenbaker.* Toronto: Macmillan, 1976.

Dogra, Nandita. "'Reading NGOs Visually'—Implications of Visual Images for NGO Management." *Journal of International Development* 19, no. 2 (2007): 161–71.

———. *Representations of Global Poverty: Aid, Development and International NGOs.* New York: I.B. Tauris, 2014.

Donaghy, Greg. "All God's Children: Lloyd Axworthy, Human Security and Canadian Foreign Policy, 1996-2000." *Canadian Foreign Policy Journal* 10, no. 2 (2003): 39–58.

———. *Grit: The Life and Politics of Paul Martin Sr.* Vancouver: University of British Columbia Press, 2015.

———. "A Wasted Opportunity Canada and the New International Economic Order, 1974–82." In Wright and Wylie, *Canada and the United Nations: Legacies, Limits, Prospects*, edited by Robert Teigrob and Colin McCullough, 183–207. Montreal: McGill-Queen's University Press, 2017.

Donaghy, Greg, and Mary Halloran. "*Viva el pueblo Cubano*: Pierre Trudeau's Distant Cuba, 1968–78." In *Our Place in the Sun: Canada and Cuba in the Castro Era*, edited by Robert Wright and Lana Wylie, 143–62. Toronto: University of Toronto Press, 2009.

Dorn, Glenn J. "Pushing Tin: U.S.-Bolivian Relations and the Coming of the National Revolution." *Diplomatic History* 35, no. 2 (April 2011): 203–28.

Drake, Earl. *A Stubble-Jumper in Striped Pants*. Toronto: University of Toronto Press, 1999.

Duffield, Mark. *Global Governance and the New Wars: The Merging of Development and Security*. 2nd ed. London: Zed Books, 2014.

Duffield, Mark, and Vernon Hewitt. *Empire, Development and Colonialism: The Past in the Present*. Suffolk, UK: Boydell and Brewer, 2009.

Easterly, William. *The Elusive Quest for Growth: Economists' Adventures and Misadventures in the Tropics*. Cambridge, MA: MIT Press, 2001.

———. *The White Man's Burden: Why the West's Efforts to Aid the Rest Have Done So Much Ill and So Little Good*. New York: Penguin, 2006.

Ekbladh, David. *The Great American Mission: Modernization and the Construction of an American World Order, 1914 to the Present*. Princeton, NJ: Princeton University Press, 2010.

Engerman, David. "Development Politics and the Cold War." *Diplomatic History* 41, no. 1 (Jan. 2017): 14–19.

Escobar, Arturo. *Encountering Development: The Making and Unmaking of the Third World*. Princeton, NJ: Princeton University Press, 2012 [1995].

———. "Planning." In Sachs, *The Development Dictionary*, 145–60.

Essex Jamey, and Logan Carmichael. "Restructuring Development Expertise and Labour in the CIDA-DFAIT Merger." *Canadian Geographer* 61, no. 2 (2017): 266–78.

Fehrenbach, Heide, and Davide Rodogno, eds. *Humanitarian Photography: A History*. Cambridge: Cambridge University Press, 2015.

Ferguson, James. *The Anti-Politics Machine: Depoliticization and Bureaucratic Power in Lesotho*. Minneapolis: University of Minnesota Press, 1994.

Fisher, Robert C. "'We'll Get our Own': Canada and the Oil Shipping Crisis of 1942." *The Northern Mariner* 3, no. 2 (April 1993): 33–39.

Fluharty, Vernon Lee. *Dance of the Millions: Military Rule and the Social Revolution in Colombia*. Pittsburgh: University of Pittsburgh Press, 1957.

Franks, Suzanne. *Reporting Disasters: Famine, Aid, Politics and the Media.* Oxford: Oxford University Press, 2014.

Frey, Marc, Sönke Kunkel, and Corinna R. Unger, eds. *International Organizations and Development, 1945-1990.* London: Palgrave Macmillan, 2014.

Fromm, Paul, and James P. Hull. *Down the Drain? A Critical Re-examination of Canadian Foreign Aid.* Toronto: Griffin House, 1981.

Garrod, J. Z., and Laura Macdonald. "Imperialism or Something Else? Rethinking 'Canadian Mining Imperialism' in Latin America." In *Mining in Latin America: Critical Approaches to the "New Extraction,"* edited by Kalowatie Deonandan and Michael Dougherty, 100-115. New York: Routledge, 2016.

Gendron, Robin. *Towards a Francophone Community: Canada's Relations with France and French Africa, 1945-1968.* Montreal: McGill-Queen's University Press, 2006.

Glazov, Jamie. *Canadian Policy Toward Khrushchev's Soviet Union.* Montreal: McGill-Queen's University Press, 2002.

Gordon, Todd. *Imperialist Canada.* Winnipeg: Arbeiter Ring, 2010.

Gordon, Todd, and Jeffery R. Webber. *Blood of Extraction: Canadian Imperialism in Latin America.* Halifax: Fernwood, 2016.

———. "Imperialism and Resistance: Canadian Mining Companies in Latin America." *Third World Quarterly* 29, no. 1 (2008): 63-87.

Gorin, Valérie. "Looking Back over 150 Years of Humanitarian Action: The Photographic Archives of the ICRC." *International Review of the Red Cross* 94, no. 888 (2012): 1349-79.

———. "'Millions of Children in Deadly Peril': Utilisation des d'enfants affamés par Save the Children pendant l'entre-deux guerres." *Revue Suisse D'histoire* 37: Special Issue on Media And Famines (2014): 95-112.

Gorman, Dan. "Race, the Commonwealth, and the United Nations: From Imperialism to Internationalism in Canada, 1940 to 1960." In Madokoro, McKenzie, and Meren, *Dominion of Race: Rethinking Canada's International History,* 196-225.

Goyette, Gabriel C. "Charity Begins at Home: The Extractive Sector as an Illustration of Changes and Continuities in the New De Facto Canadian Aid Policy." In Brown, den Heyer, and Black, *Rethinking Canadian Aid,* 259-75.

Granatstein J. L., and Robert Bothwell. *Pirouette: Pierre Trudeau and Canadian Foreign Policy.* Toronto: University of Toronto Press, 1990.

Grant, Kevin. "Christian Critics of Empire: Missionaries, Lantern Lectures, and the Congo Reform Campaign in Britain." *Journal of Imperial and Commonwealth History* 29, no. 2 (2001): 27-58.

Grant, Shelagh. "Hugh Llewellyn Keenleyside: Commissioner of the Northwest Territories, 1947-1950." *Arctic Profiles* 43, no. 1 (1990): 80-82.

Hale, Geoffrey. *Uneasy Partnership: The Politics of Business and Government in Canada.* 2nd ed. Toronto: University of Toronto Press, 2018.

Halperin, Morton, and Priscilla Clapp. *Bureaucratic Politics and Foreign Policy.* 2nd ed. Washington: Brookings Institution, 2006.

Halttunen, Karen. "Humanitarianism and the Pornography of Pain in Anglo-American Culture." *American Historical Review* 100, no. 2 (1995): 303–34.

Hanson, A. H. *The Process of Planning: A Study of India's Five-Year Plans, 1950–1964.* London: Oxford University Press, 1966.

Hardt, Michael, and Antonio Negri. *Empire.* Cambridge, MA: Harvard University Press, 2000.

Haslam, Jonathan. *The Nixon Administration and the Death of Allende's Chile: A Case of Assisted Suicide.* London: Verso, 2005.

Haynes, Jessica. "The Legacy of Scientific Motherhood: Doctors and Child-Rearing Advice in the 1960s and 1970s in English Canada." PhD diss., Carleton University, 2007.

Hayter, Teresa. *Aid as Imperialism.* Baltimore: Penguin, 1971.

Head, Ivan L., and Pierre Elliott Trudeau. *The Canadian Way: Shaping Canada's Foreign Policy, 1968–1984.* Toronto: McClelland and Stewart, 1995.

Henderson, James. *Modernization in Colombia: The Laureano Gómez Years, 1889–1965.* Gainesville: University Press of Florida, 2001.

Herren, Madeleine. "Towards a Global History of International Organizations." In *Networking the International System: Global Histories of International Organizations,* edited by Madeleine Herren, 1–12. Heidelberg: Cham, 2014.

Heryanto, Ariel. "The Development of 'Development.'" *Indonesia* no. 46 (1988): 1–24.

Higgins, Benjamin. *All the Difference: A Development Economist's Quest.* Montreal: McGill-Queen's University Press, 1992.

———. *Economic Development.* New York: W. W. Norton, 1968.

Hill, O. Mary. *Canada's Salesmen to the World: The Department of Trade and Commerce, 1892–1939.* Montreal: McGill-Queen's University Press, 1977.

Hilliker, John, and Donald Barry. *Canada's Department of External Affairs,* vol. 2: *Coming of Age, 1946–68.* Montreal: McGill-Queen's University Press, 1995.

Hilliker, John, Mary Halloran, and Greg Donaghy. *Canada's Department of External Affairs,* vol. 3: *Innovation and Adaptation, 1968–1984.* Toronto: University of Toronto Press, 2017.

Hodge, Joseph. *The Triumph of the Expert: Agrarian Doctrines of Development and the Legacies of British Colonialism.* Athens: Ohio University Press, 2007.

———. "Writing the History of Development (Part 1: The First Wave)." *Humanity* 6, no. 3 (2016): 429–63.

———. "Writing the History of Development (Part 2: Longer, Deeper, Wider)." *Humanity* 7, no. 1 (2016): 125–74.

Huebner, Stefan. *Pan-Asian Sports and the Emergence of Modern Asia, 1913–1974.* Singapore: NUS Press, 2016.

Igartua, José Eduardo. *The Other Quiet Revolution: National Identities in English Canada, 1945–71.* Vancouver: University of British Columbia Press, 2006.

Iriye, Akira, and Pierre-Yves Saunier, eds. *The Palgrave Dictionary of Transnational History.* New York: Palgrave Macmillan. 2009.

Johnston, Patrick. *Modernizing Canadian Foreign Aid and Development: Challenges Old And New.* Toronto: Walter and Gordon Duncan Foundation, 2010.

Keck, J. M. "Making Work: Federal Job Creation Policy In The 1970s." PhD diss., University of Toronto, 1995.

Keenleyside, Hugh. *International Aid: A Summary, with Special Reference to the Programmes of the United Nations.* Toronto: McClelland and Stewart, 1966.

———. *Memoirs of Hugh Keenleyside,* vol. 1: *Hammer the Golden Day.* Toronto: McClelland and Stewart, 1981.

———. *Memoirs of Hugh Keenleyside,* vol. 2: *On the Bridge of Time.* Toronto: McClelland and Stewart, 1982.

Kennedy, Dennis. "Selling the Distant Other: Humanitarianism and Imagery – Ethical Dilemmas of Humanitarian Action." *Journal of Humanitarian Assistance* 28 (Feb. 2009): 1–25.

Klassen, Jerome. "Canada and the New Imperialism: The Economics of a Secondary Power." *Studies in Political Economy* 83, no. 1 (2009): 163–90.

———. *Joining Empire: The Political Economy of the New Canadian Foreign Policy.* Toronto: University of Toronto Press, 2014.

Kleinman, Arthur, and Joan Kleinman. "The Appeal Of Experience; The Dismay of Images: Cultural Appropriations of Suffering in our Times." *Daedalus* 125, no. 1 (1996): 1–23.

Lackenbauer, P. Whitney, ed. *An Inside Look at External Affairs during the Trudeau Years: The Memoirs of Mark MacGuigan.* Calgary: University of Calgary Press, 2002.

Lancaster, Carol. *Foreign Aid: Diplomacy, Development, Domestic Politics.* Chicago: University of Chicago Press, 2007.

———. *Transforming Foreign Aid: United States Assistance in the 21st Century.* Washington, DC: Peterson Institute, 2000.

Langlois, Suzanne. "'Neighbours Half the World Away': The National Film Board of Canada at Work for UNRRA (1944–47)." In *Canada and the United Nations: Legacies, Limits, Prospects,* edited by Colin McCullough and Robert Teigrob, 44–81. Montreal: McGill-Queen's University Press, 2016.

Laqueur, Thomas W. "Bodies, Details, and the Humanitarian Narrative." In *The New Cultural History*, edited by L. A. Hunt, 176–204. Ann Arbour: MPublishing, University of Michigan Library, 1989.

Latham, Michael. *Modernization as Ideology: American Social Science and "Nation-Building" in the Kennedy Era*. Chapel Hill: University of North Carolina Press, 2000.

Latin American Working Group. *Canadian Aid: Whose Priorities? A Study of the Relationship between Non-Governmental Organizations, Business, and the Needs of Latin America*. Toronto: Latin American Working Group, 1973.

Lavergne, Réal. "Determinants of Canadian Aid Policy." In *Western Middle Powers and Global Poverty: The Determinants of the Aid Policies of Canada, Denmark, the Netherlands, Norway and Sweden*, edited by Olav Stokke, 33–89. Uppsala, Sweden: Scandinavian Institute of African Studies, 1989.

Lenette, Caroline. "Writing with Light: An Iconographic-Iconologic Approach to Refugee Photography." *Forum Qualitative Sozialforschung* 17, no. 2 (2016). http://dx.doi.org/10.17169/fqs-17.2.2436.

Lidchi, Henrietta. "Finding the Right Image: British Development NGOs and the Regulation of Imagery." In *Culture and Global Change*, edited by T. Skelton and T. Allen, 275–96. London: Routledge, 1999.

Lissner, Jorgen. "Merchants of Misery." *New Internationalist* 6, no. 1 (1981): 1–11.

———. *The Politics of Altruism: A Study of the Political Behaviour of Voluntary Development Agencies.* Geneva: Lutheran World Foundation, 1977.

Lloyd, Trevor. *Canada in World Affairs 1957–1959*. Toronto: Oxford University Press, 1968.

Lyon, Peyton V., R. B. Byers, and D. Leyton-Brown. "How Official Ottawa Views the Third World." *International Perspectives* (Jan.–Feb. 1979): 11–16.

Macdonald, Laura. "Canada in the Posthegemonic Hemisphere: Evaluating the Harper Government's Americas Strategy." *Studies in Political Economy* 97, no. 1 (2016): 1–17.

———. "Changing Directions? Challenges Facing Canadian Non-governmental Organizations in Latin America." In *Beyond Mexico?: Canada in the Americas*, edited by Jean Daudelin and Edgar Dosman, 237–56. Ottawa: Carleton University Press, 1995.

———. "Current and Future Directions for Canadian NGOs in Latin America." In *A Dynamic Partnership: Canada's Changing Role in the Americas*, edited by Jerry Haar and Edgar J. Dosman, 113–28. Piscataway, NJ: Transaction, 1993.

———. "Unequal Partnerships: The Politics of Canada's Relations with the Third World." *Studies in Political Economy* 47, no. 1 (Summer 1995): 111–41.

Macdonald, Laura, and Arne Rückert. "Continental Shift? Rethinking Canadian Aid to the Americas." In Brown, den Heyer, and Black, *Rethinking Canadian Aid*, 125–42.

Mace, Gordon, and Gérard Hervouet. "Canada's Third Option: A Complete Failure?" *Canadian Public Policy* 15, no. 4 (Dec. 1989): 387–404.

Mackenzie, Hector. "The Path to Temptation: The Negotiation of Canada's Reconstruction Loan to Britain in 1946." *Historical Papers/Communications historiques* 17, no. 1 (1982): 196–220.

———. "Sinews of War and Peace: The Politics of Economic Aid to Britain, 1939–1945." *International Journal* 54, no. 4 (Autumn 1999): 648–70.

Madokoro, Laura, Francine McKenzie, and David Meren, eds. *Dominion of Race: Rethinking Canada's International History.* Vancouver: University of British Columbia Press, 2017.

Magdoff, Harry. *The Age of Imperialism: The Economics of U.S. Foreign Policy.* New York: New York University Press, 1969.

Mallon, Richard R. *The New Missionaries: Memoirs of a Foreign Advisor in Less-Developed Countries.* Cambridge, MA: Harvard Institute for International Development, 2000.

Marshall, Dominique, with Julia Sterparn. "Oxfam Aid to Canada's First Nations, 1962–1975: Eating Lynx, Starving for Jobs, and Flying a Talking Bird." *Journal of the Canadian Historical Association* 22, no. 2 (2012): 298–343.

McCullough, Colin, and Robert Teigrob, eds. *Canada and the United Nations: Legacies, Limits, Prospects.* Montreal: McGill-Queen's University Press, 2016.

McGill, Allan S. *My Life As I Remember It.* Abbotsford: Granville Island Publishing, 2004.

McKenna, Peter. *Canada and the OAS: From Dilettante to Full Partner.* Montreal: McGill-Queen's University Press, 1995.

———, ed. *Canada Looks South: In Search of an Americas Policy.* Toronto: University of Toronto Press, 2012.

McKenzie, Richard B. "Was It a Decade of Greed?" *The Public Interest* 106 (Winter 1992): 91–96.

McRae, Rob, and Don Hubert, eds. *Human Security and the New Diplomacy: Protecting People, Promoting Peace.* Montreal: McGill-Queen's University Press, 2001.

Meehan, John. *The Dominion and the Rising Sun: Canada Encounters Japan, 1929–41.* Vancouver: University of British Columbia Press, 2004.

Meren, David. "The Tragedies of Canadian International History." *Canadian Historical Review* 96, no. 4 (Winter 2015): 534–66.

Michaud, Nelson, and Kim Richard Nossal. "The Conservative Era in Canadian Foreign Policy, 1984–93." In Michaud and Nossal, *Diplomatic Departures*, 3–24.

———, eds. *Diplomatic Departures: The Conservative Era in Canadian Foreign Policy, 1984–93.* Vancouver: University of British Columbia Press, 2001.

Millikan, Max F. "An Introductory Essay." In Richard N. Gardner and Max F. Millikan, eds., "The Global Partnership: International Agencies and Economic Development." *International Organization* 22, no. 1 (Winter 1968): 1–15.

Mills, Sean. "Popular Internationalism: Grassroots Exchange and Social Movements." In *Canada and the Third World: Overlapping Histories*, edited by Karen Dubinsky, Sean Mills, and Scott Rutherford, 246–66. Toronto: University of Toronto Press, 2016.

Minden, Karen. *Canadian Development Assistance: The Medical Missionary Model in West China, 1910–1952*. Toronto: Joint Centre for Asia Pacific Studies, 1989.

Moeller, Susan. *Compassion Fatigue: How the Media Sell Disease, Famine, War and Death*. New York: Routledge, 1999.

Morrison, David. *Aid and Ebb Tide: A History of CIDA and Canadian Development Assistance*. Waterloo, ON: Wilfrid Laurier University Press, 1998.

Mosse, David. "The Anthropology of International Development." *Annual Review of Anthropology* 42 (2013): 227–46.

Muirhead, Bruce. "From Dreams to Reality: The Evolution of Anglo-Canadian Trade During the Diefenbaker Era." *Journal of the Canadian Historical Association* 9, no. 1 (1998): 243–66.

Muirhead, Bruce, and Ronald N. Harpelle. *IDRC: 40 Years of Ideas, Innovation, and Impact*. Waterloo, ON: Wilfrid Laurier University Press, 2010.

Muller, Tanja R. "'The Ethiopian Famine' Revisited: Band Aid and The Antipolitics of Celebrity Humanitarian Action." *Disasters* 37, no. 1 (2013): 61–79.

Mulroney, Brian. *Memoirs, 1939–93*. Toronto: McClelland and Stewart, 2007.

Murray, D. R. "Canada's First Diplomatic Missions in Latin America." *Journal of Interamerican Studies* 16, no. 2 (May 1974): 153–72.

Muschik, Eva-Maria. "Managing the World: The United Nations, Decolonisation and the Strange Triumph of State Sovereignty in the 1950s and 1960s." *Journal of Global History* 12, no. 1 (March 2018): 122–44.

Myers, Tamara. "Blistered and Bleeding, Tired and Determined: Visual Representations of Children and Youth in the Miles for Millions Walkathon," *Journal of the Canadian Historical Association* 22, no. 1 (2011): 245–75.

———. "Local Action and Global Imagining: Youth, International Development, and the Walkathon Phenomenon in Sixties' and Seventies' Canada." *Diplomatic History* 38 (2014): 282–93.

Naik, J. V. "Forerunners of Dadabhai Naoroji's Drain Theory." *Economic and Political Weekly* 36, nos. 46/47 (2001): 4428–32.

Nakazato, Nariaki. "The Transfer of Economic Power in India: Indian Big Business, the British Raj and Development Planning, 1930–1948." In *The Unfinished Agenda: Nation-Building in South Asia*, edited by Mushirul Hasan and Nariaki Nakazato, 247–307. New Delhi: Manohar, 2001.

Nerbas, Don. *Dominion of Capital: The Politics of Big Business and the Crisis of the Canadian Bourgeoisie, 1914-1947.* Toronto: University of Toronto Press, 2013.

Noël, Alain, Jean-Philippe Thérien, and Stephane Dallaire. "Divided over Internationalism: The Canadian Public and Development Assistance." *Canadian Public Policy* 30, no. 1 (2004): 29–46.

Nossal, Kim Richard. "Mixed Motives Revisited: Canada's Interest in Development Assistance." *Canadian Journal of Political Science* 21, no. 1 (1988): 35–56.

———. "Opening Up the Policy Preference: Does Party Make A Difference?." In Michaud and Nossal, *Diplomatic Departures,* 276–89.

Nossal, Kim Richard, Stéphane Roussel, and Stéphane Paquin. *The Politics of Canadian Foreign Policy.* 4th ed. Montreal: McGill-Queen's University Press, 2015.

Oakman, Daniel. *Facing Asia: A History of the Colombo Plan.* Canberra: Pandanus Books, 2004.

O'Sullivan, Kevin. "History and the Development Aid Debate in the Republic of Ireland." *Policy and Practice* 12 (Spring 2011): 110–23.

Owen, David. "The United Nations Expanded Program of Technical Assistance – A Multilateral Approach." *Annals of the American Academy of Political and Social Science* 323 (1959): 25–32.

Panitch, Leo, ed. *The Canadian State: Political Economy and Political Power.* Toronto: University of Toronto Press, 1977.

Paragg, Ralph R. "Canadian Aid in the Commonwealth Caribbean: Neo-Colonialism or Development?" *Canadian Public Policy* 6, no. 4 (Autumn 1980): 628–41.

Parr, Joy. "Local Water Diversely Known: Walkerton, Ontario 2000 and After." *Environment and Planning D: Society and Space* 23, no. 2 (2005): 251–71.

Payne, Carol. "'You Hear It in Their Voice': Photographs and Cultural Consolidation among Inuit Youths and Elders." In *Image and Memory: Oral History and Photography,* edited by Alexander Freund and Alistair Thomson, 97–114. London: Palgrave, 2011.

Pearson, Lester B. *Mike: The Memoirs of the Right Honourable Lester B. Pearson,* vol. 2: *1948-1957.* Edited by John A. Munro and Alex I. Inglis. Toronto: University of Toronto Press, 1973.

Pereira, Javier. *The Development Effectiveness of Supporting the Private Sector with ODA Funds.* Brussels: Trade Union Development Cooperation Network and CSO Partnership for Development Effectiveness, 2016.

Pernet, Corinne A., and Amalia Ribi Forclaz. "Revisiting the Food and Agriculture Organization (FAO): International Histories of Agriculture, Nutrition, and Development." *International History Review* (2018). https://doi.org/10.1080/070753 32.2018.1460386.

Petras, James, and Henry Veltmeyer. "Age of Reverse-Aid: Neoliberalism as a Catalyst of Regression." *Development and Change* 33, no. 2 (2002): 281–93.

Plewes, Betty, and Brian Tomlinson. "Canadian CSOs and Africa: The End of an Era?" In *Canada Among Nations 2013: Canada-Africa Relations – Looking Back, Looking Ahead*, edited by Rohinton Medhora and Yiagadeesen Samy, 213–26. Waterloo, ON: Centre for International Governance Innovation and Carleton University, 2013.

Poster, Alexander. "The Gentle War: Famine Relief, Politics, and Privatization in Ethiopia, 1983–1986." *Diplomatic History* 36, no. 2 (April 2012): 399–425.

Pratt, Cranford. "Canada: A Limited and Eroding Internationalism." In Pratt, *Internationalism Under Strain*, 24–69.

———. "Canadian Development Assistance: A Profile." In Pratt, *Canadian International Development Assistance Policies*, 3–24.

———, ed. *Canadian International Development Assistance Policies: An Appraisal.* Montreal: McGill-Queen's University Press, 1994.

———. "Development Assistance and Canadian Foreign Policy: Where We Now Are." *Canadian Foreign Policy Journal* 2, no. 3 (1994): 77–85.

———. "DFAIT's Takeover Bid of CID." *Canadian Foreign Policy Journal* 5, no. 2 (1998): 1–13.

———. "Dominant Class Theory and Canadian Foreign Policy: The Case of the Counter-Consensus." *International Journal* 39, no. 1 (Winter 1983/1984): 99–135.

———. "Ethics and Foreign Policy: The Case of Canada's Development Assistance." *International Journal* 43, no. 2 (1988): 264–301.

———. "Humane Internationalism and Canadian Development Assistance Policies." In Pratt, *Canadian International Development Assistance Policies*, 334–70.

———. "Humane Internationalism: Its Significance and Variants." In Pratt, *Internationalism Under Strain*, 3–23.

———, ed. *Internationalism Under Strain: The North-South Policies of Canada, the Netherlands, Norway, and Sweden.* Toronto, ON: University of Toronto Press, 1989.

———, ed. "Middle Power Internationalism and Global Poverty." In Pratt, *Middle Power Internationalism*, 3–24.

———. *Middle Power Internationalism: The North-South Dimension.* Montreal: McGill-Queen's University Press, 1990.

Protheroe, David. "Canada's Multilateral Aid and Diplomacy." In Pratt, *Canadian International Development Assistance Policies*, 25–54.

Quiring, David. *CCF Colonialism in Northern Saskatchewan: Battling Parish Priests, Bootleggers, and Fur Sharks.* Vancouver: University of British Columbia Press, 2004.

Rawkins, Philip. "An Institutional Analysis of CIDA." In Pratt, *Canadian International Development Assistance Policies*, 156–85.

Rea, K. J., and Nelson Wiseman, eds. *Government and Enterprise in Canada*. Agincourt, ON: Methuen, 1985.

Reid, Escott. "Canadian Foreign Policy, 1967–1977: A Second Golden Decade?" *International Journal* 22, no. 2 (1967): 171–81.

Reinisch, Jessica. "'Auntie UNRRA' at the Crossroads." *Past and Present* 218, Issue supp. 8 (2013): 70–97.

———. "Introduction: Relief in the Aftermath of War." *Journal of Contemporary History* 43, no. 3 (2008): 371–404.

Relin, David Oliver. "When Greed Was Good: The 1980s Will Go Down in History as a Decade of Excess." *Scholastic Update* 123, no. 12 (1991): 14.

Reuber, Grant L. "The Trade-Offs among the Objectives of Canadian Foreign Aid." *International Journal* 25, no. 1 (1969): 129–41.

Rist, Gilbert. *The History of Development: From Western Origins to Global Faith*. 2nd ed. London: Zed Books, 2002.

———. *The History of Development: From Western Origins to Global Faith*. 4th ed. London: Zed Books, 2014.

Roberts, Lance W. *Recent Social Trends in Canada, 1960–2000*. Montreal: McGill-Queen's University Press, 2005.

Robinson, H. Basil. *Diefenbaker's World: A Populist in Foreign Affairs*. Toronto: University of Toronto Press, 1989.

Roche, Douglas. *Justice not Charity: A New Global Ethic for Canada*. Toronto: McClelland and Stewart, 1976.

———. "Toward a Foreign Policy for Canada in the 1980s." *International Perspectives* (May/June, July/August 1979): 3–8.

Rochlin, James. *Discovering the Americas: The Evolution of Canadian Foreign Policy Towards Latin America*. Vancouver: University of British Columbia Press, 1994.

Rodney, Walter. *How Europe Underdeveloped Africa*. London: Bogle-L'Ouverture Publications, 1972.

Rodogno, Davide, and Thomas David. "All the World Loves a Picture: The World Health Organization's Visual Politics, 1948–1973." In Fehrenbach and Rodogno, *Humanitarian Photography*, 223–48.

Rosenberg, Emily S. *Spreading the American Dream: American Economic and Cultural Expansion, 1890–1945*. New York: Hill and Wang, 1982.

Rostow, Walt W. *The Stages of Economic Growth: A Non-Communist Manifesto*. Cambridge: Cambridge University Press, 1960.

Rozario, Kevin. "'Delicious Horrors': Mass Culture, The Red Cross, and the Appeal of Modem American Humanitarianism." *American Quarterly* 55 no. 3 (2003): 417–55.

Rubinstein, Alvin Z. *Soviets in International Organizations: Changing Policy toward Developing Countries, 1953–1963*. Princeton, NJ: Princeton University Press, 2015.

Rutherford, Paul. *When Television Was Young: Primetime Canada 1952–1967.* Toronto: University of Toronto Press, 1990.

Sachs, Wolfgang, ed. *The Development Dictionary: A Guide to Knowledge as Power.* London: Zed Books, 1992, 2010.

Sanger, Clive. *Half a Loaf: Canada's Semi Role Among Developing Countries.* Toronto: Ryerson Press, 1969.

Saunier, Pierre-Yves. *Transnational History.* New York: Palgrave Macmillan, 2013.

Scott, James C. *Seeing Like a State: How Certain Schemes to Improve the Human Condition have Failed.* New Haven, CT: Yale University Press, 1998.

Sekula, Allan. *Photography Against the Grain: Essays and Photo-Works 1973–1983.* Halifax: Press of the Nova Scotia College of Art and Design, 1984.

Sexton, Jack. *Monenco: The First 75 Years.* Montreal: Monenco, 1982.

Shamsie, Yasmine. "Canadian Assistance to Haiti: Some Sobering Snags in a Fragile-State Approach." In McKenna, *Canada Looks South*, 180–211.

Simon, David, ed. *Fifty Key Thinkers on Development.* New York: Routledge, 2005.

Sliwinski, Sharon. *Human Rights in Camera.* Chicago: University of Chicago Press, 2011.

Small, John. "From Pakistan to Bangladesh 1969–1972: Perspective of a Canadian Envoy." In *Special Trust and Confidence: Envoy Essays in Canadian Diplomacy,* edited by David Reece, 209–38. Ottawa: Carleton University Press, 1996.

Smillie, Ian. *The Alms Bazaar: Altruism Under Fire – Non-Profit Organisations And International Development.* London: Intermediate Technology, 1995.

———. "Institutional Corruption and Canadian Foreign Aid." *Canadian Foreign Policy Journal* 23, no. 1 (2017): 47–59.

———. *The Land of Lost Content: A History of CUSO.* Toronto: Deneau, 1985.

Smillie, Ian, and Henny Helmich (in collaboration with Tony German and Judith Randel), eds. *Public Attitudes and International Development Co-operation.* Paris: OECD, 1998.

Smith, Arnold. *Stitches in Time: The Commonwealth in World Politics.* Don Mills, ON: General Publishing, 1981.

Smith, Denis. *Rogue Tory: The Life and Legend of John G. Diefenbaker.* Toronto: Macfarlane Walter and Ross, 1995.

Sontag, Susan. *Regarding the Pain of Others.* New York: Picador, 2003.

Sorensen, John. "Mass Media and Discourse on Famine in the Horn of Africa." *Discourse and Society* 2, no. 2 (April 1991): 223–42.

Spicer, Keith. "Clubmanship Upstaged: Canada's Twenty Years in the Colombo Plan." *International Journal* 25, no. 1 (Winter 1969–70): 23–33.

———. *A Samaritan State? External Aid in Canada's Foreign Policy.* Toronto: University of Toronto Press, 1966.

Spooner, Kevin. *Canada, the Congo Crisis, and UN Peacekeeping, 1960–64.* Vancouver: University of British Columbia Press, 2009.

Stevenson, Brian. *Canada, Latin America, and the New Internationalism: A Foreign Policy Analysis, 1968–1999.* Montreal: McGill-Queen's University Press, 2000.

Stokke, Olav. *The UN and Development: From Aid to Cooperation.* Bloomington: Indiana University Press, 2009.

Swift, Jamie, and Brian Tomlinson, eds. *Conflicts of Interest: Canada and the Third World.* Toronto: Between the Lines, 1991.

Swift, Richard, and Robert Clarke, eds. *Ties that Bind: Canada and the Third World.* Toronto: Between the Lines, 1982.

Tagg, John. *The Disciplinary Frame: Photographic Truths and the Capture of Meaning.* Minneapolis: University of Minnesota Press, 2009.

Thérien, Jean-Philippe, Gordon Mace, and Myriam Roberge. "Le Canada et les Amériques: La difficile construction d'une identité régionale." *Canadian Foreign Policy Journal* 11, no. 3 (2004): 17–37.

Tiessen, Rebecca. "Gender Equality and the 'Two CIDAs': Successes and Setbacks, 1976–2013." In Brown, den Heyer, and Black, *Rethinking Canadian Aid*, 195–210.

Tijerina, Stefano. "Ahora o Nunca: La Misión Ministerial Canadiense a América Latina de 1968 y su Impacto en las Relaciones Bilaterales con Colombia." *Perspectivas Colombo-Canadienses* 2 (2009): 10–29.

———. "Canadian Official Development Aid to Latin America: The Struggle Over the Humanitarian Agenda, 1963–1977." *Journal of Canadian Studies* 51, no. 1 (Winter 2017): 217–44.

———. "A 'Clearcut Line': Canada and Colombia, 1892–1979." PhD diss., University of Maine, 2011.

Tocqueville, Alexis de. *Democracy in America.* New York: The Century Co., 1898.

Tomlinson, B. R. "The Weapons of the Weakened: British Power, Sterling Balances, and the Origins of the Colombo Plan." In *The Transformation of the International Order of Asia: Decolonization, the Cold War, and the Colombo Plan*, edited by Shigeru Akita, Gerold Krozewski, and Shoichi Watanabe, 34–49. London: Routledge, 2015.

Touhey, Ryan. "Commonwealth Conundrums: Canada and South Asia During the Pearson Era." In *Mike: Lester Pearson, Pearsonianism, and Canadian Foreign Policy,* edited by Asa McKercher and Galen Perras, 251–74. Vancouver: University of British Columbia Press, 2017.

————. *Conflicting Visions: Canada and India in the Cold War World*. Vancouver: University of British Columbia Press, 2015.

————. "Dealing in Black and White: The Diefenbaker Government and the Cold War in South Asia 1957–1963." *Canadian Historical Review* 92, no. 3 (Sept. 2011): 429–54.

Tucker, Michael. *Canadian Foreign Policy: Contemporary Issues and Themes*. Toronto: McGraw-Hill Ryerson, 1980.

Uvin, Peter. *Aiding Violence: The Development Enterprise in Rwanda*. Hartford, CT: Kumarian Press, 1998.

Walinsky, Louis J. *The Planning and Execution of Economic Development*. New York: McGraw-Hill, 1963.

Walmsley, Norma. *Canadian Universities and International Development*. Ottawa: Association of Universities and Colleges of Canada, 1970.

Warrington, S., and J. Crombie. *The People in the Pictures: Vital Perspectives on Save the Children's Image Making*. London: Save the Children UK, 2017.

Wolf, Charles Jr. *Foreign Aid: Theory and Practice in Southern Asia*. Princeton, NJ: Princeton University Press, 1960.

Wright, Robert. *Three Nights in Havana: Pierre Trudeau, Fidel Castro and the Cold War World*. Toronto: HarperCollins, 2007.

Wright, Robert, and Lana Wylie. *Our Place in the Sun: Canada and Cuba in the Castro Era*. Toronto: University of Toronto Press, 2009.

Wyse, Peter. *Canadian Foreign Aid in the 1970s: An Organizational Audit*. Montreal: Centre for Developing Area Studies, McGill University, 1983.

Young, Mary M., and Susan J. Henders. "'Other Diplomacies' and World Order: Historical Insights from Canadian–Asian Relations." *Hague Journal of Diplomacy* 11 (2016): 351–82.

Young, Roger. "Canadian Foreign Aid: Facing a Crisis of its Own?" *Journal of Canadian Studies* 19, no. 4 (1985): 28–41.

CONTRIBUTORS

DAVID BLACK is the Lester B. Pearson Professor of International Development Studies and the chair of the Political Science Department at Dalhousie University.

STEPHEN BROWN is a professor of political science at the School of Political Studies at the University of Ottawa.

KEVIN BRUSHETT is an assistant professor of history and chair of the Military and Strategic Studies Programme at the Royal Military College of Canada.

JILL CAMPBELL-MILLER is a SSHRC postdoctoral fellow in the Department of History at Carleton University

TED COGAN completed his PhD in history at the University of Guelph in 2017.

SONYA DE LAAT completed her PhD in the Faculty of Information and Media Studies at Western University in 2017.

GREG DONAGHY is head of the Historical Section at Global Affairs Canada.

LAURA MACDONALD is a professor in the Department of Political Science and the Institute of Political Economy at Carleton University.

Dominique Marshall is chair of the History Department at Carleton University.

Asa McKercher teaches history of the Royal Military College of Canada.

Nassisse Solomon is a PhD candidate in the Collaborative Graduate Program in Migration and Ethnic Relations at Western University.

Stefano Tijerina teaches history, international relations, and business at the University of Maine.

Ryan Touhey is an associate professor and chair of the History Department at St. Jerome's University.

David Webster is a professor of history at Bishop's University.

INDEX

A

A Samaritan State?, 1–2, 11, 14, 27, 94, 125, 138, 145, 164, 178, 246, 271–72, 288, 295, 334; contemporary relevance, 119, 311–12, 317–23, 325

Abbott, Douglas (Canadian politician), 33, 44, 73, 195

Afghanistan, 14, 272, 306, 314; as fragile state, 284; and Dahla Dam, 315

Africa 2000, 258

Africa: relations with, 1, 91, 190; and cold war, 155, 157, 233; as aid recipient, 5, 13–16, 136, 246, 273–75, 283, 285–86, 288, 335; and former French colonies, 145, 148, 202, 280; 293–94; in Mulroney era, 297–301; in Chrétien era, 301–6. *See also* Botswana; Biafra; Nigeria; Ethiopia

African Recovery Fund, 255

Alcan, 137

Allende, Salvador (Chilean politician), 149, 278

Alliance for Progress, 133, 135

Amagoalik, John (Inuit leader), 253

Angola, 262

Anstee, Margaret (UN aid advisor), 82

Argentina, 133, 146, 149

Asia: relations with, 1, 24, 55, 58; as aid recipient, 4–6, 8 13, 16, 24, 32–33, 35, 39, 44, 60, 62, 65; 73, 123, 146; and cold war, 60–61, 88, 91, 93, 105, 132, 194, 233, 275, 280, 286, 297, 335. *See also* India; Pakistan

Atomic Energy of Canada Limited (AECL), 44, 113

Atomic power. *See* nuclear cooperation

Ault, Orville (Canadian public servant), 23, 54, 68; career, 65–66; dismissal, 67–68; plans for growth, 65–66

Axworthy, Lloyd (Canadian politician), 305

B

Baird, Irene (Canadian public servant), 56

Balkans, as aid recipient, 231

Ban Ki-Moon (UN Secretary-General), 261

Banerjee, P.K. (Indian diplomat), 37

Bangladesh, 106, 115, 117, 118, 230, 238

Barbour, David (Canadian photographer), 228, 231

Bartlett, David W. (Canadian public servant), 63, 64, 67

Batchelor, Sheila (CIDA employee), 172, 173

Belize, as aid recipient, 279

Bergbusch, Eric (Canadian diplomat), 152, 178

Bhutto, Zulfikar Ali (Pakistani politician), 108–10, 116

Biafra, 211, 247, 250

Bibeau, Marie-Claude (Canadian politician), 288, 324

Bill and Melinda Gates Foundation, 23

Blaikie, Bill (Canadian politician), 257

Bolivia: as aid recipient, 82, 89, 283, 286; UN mission to, 77–81

Borg, Roberta (CIDA employee), 241n13

Botswana, 230, 235, 238, 239

Bow, Malcolm (Canadian diplomat), 154

Bramley, Mary (CIDA employee), 241, 241n17
Brazil, 126, 146, 149, 284; as aid recipient, 136, 150, 154
British West Indies, 65. *See also* Commonwealth Caribbean
Brook, Tom J. (Canadian trade commissioner), 23, 54, 68; career, 55–56
Brown, Ken (Canadian diplomat), 153–54
Bull, Fred (Canadian public servant), 58, 60
Burma, 4, 57, 65, 83; as recipient of technical assistance, 89
business sector: as beneficiary of aid, 8–9, 29, 41, 44, 123–34, 137–38, 151, 285–86, 302, 318, 322–24; and Ethiopian famine relief, 253; influence on aid policy, 271–72, 285, 319, 322–23; and Latin America, 149, 278; relations with CIDA, 149, 171, 210, 254, 288; as stakeholder, 192, 203, 207; view of aid recipients, 43. *See also* promotional state

C

Cadbury, George (Canadian economist), 83
Cadieux, Marcel (Canadian diplomat), 111, 153
Canada in the World, 302
Canadair, 130
Canadian Association for Latin America (CALA), 149
Canadian Catholic Organization for Development and Peace (CCODP), 173
Canadian Commercial Corporation, 34
Canadian Congress of Labour, 86
Canadian Council for International Cooperation (CCIC), 13, 169–70, 207, 209, 302
Canadian Council of Churches, 152
Canadian Executive Service Overseas (CESO), 168
Canadian Institute of International Affairs (CIIA), 57
Canadian Institute of Public Affairs, 57
Canadian International Development Agency (CIDA), 2, 7, 8, 10, 12, 189; and aid to Africa, 14, 250, 254–55, 259, 294,
297, 300; and aid to Chile, 148–52; and aid to Colombia, 137–38; and aid to Cuba, 153–57; and aid to India, 117; and Latin America, 136, 147–49, 277, 282–83, 286; and aid to Pakistan, 117; budget cuts in the 1990s, 12, 213, 271, 298, 301–2; Business and Industry Program, 171; Communications Branch, 206; criticism for financial mismanagement at, 157, 164, 169, 182n25, 212, 255–56, 306; creation of, 7–8, 45, 103, 167–68, 206, 225, 311, 317; culture and identity, 14, 168–69, 213, 272, 294–97, 301, 303–4, 307; Democratic Development Fund for Guatemala, 282; Development Education Program, 207; Development Information Program, 231; Educational Institutions Program, 210; and embrace of structural adjustment programs, 12, 271–72; Global Education Program, 305; Industrial Cooperation Program, 210, 322; Information Division, 206; International NGO Program, 176; Management for Change Program, 171; merger with Department of Foreign Affairs, 13–14, 271, 287, 293, 305, 317–18; NGO Division, 164, 168–70, 172, 174–76, 210, 335; and programming for women, 173; Public Affairs Branch, 226; Public Participation Program, 13, 177–78, 305; relations with civil society, 9–10, 13, 206–13, 271–72, 282, 300, 304–5, 307; relations with CUSO, 169, 170, 172, 178, 207, 211; relations with the Department of External Affairs/Foreign Affairs, 167–68, 173–75, 282, 295, 300, 305; relations with Department of Trade and Commerce, 9, 13; relations with NGOs, 9, 168–70, 172–74, 178, 207, 210–11, 287, 296, 311; Special Programs Branch (CIDA), 9, 164, 168, 178, 255. *See also* International Development Photo Library; Margaret Catley-Carlson; Michel Dupuy; Paul Gérin-Lajoie; Marcel Massé; Lewis Perinbam; Maurice Strong

Canadian International Development Board (CIDB), 173, 176, 178

Canadian International Resources Development Institute, 324

Canadian national identity: and aid projects, 10, 37, 39, 59, 70n29, 83, 189–90, 192, 198, 199, 201, 205–6, 213, 273, 276; and citizenship, 258; and Commonwealth, 197, 297; and the role of photographs, 240

Canadian Ombudsperson for Responsible Enterprise, 289

Canadian University Services Overseas (CUSO), 1, 154, 157, 209; origins, 166, 168–69, 203, 335; relations with CIDA, 169, 170, 172, 178, 207, 211; returned volunteers, 172

Canadian Wheat Board (CWB), 128–29

CARE, 171

Caribbean: relations with, 1, 145; aid for, 5, 123–24, 146, 174–75, 202, 275. *See also* British West Indies

CARICOM, 285

Castro, Fidel (Cuban revolutionary and politician), 152, 154, 156, 277

Catley-Carlson, Margaret (Canadian public servant), 11, 169

Cavell, R. G "Nik" (Canadian public servant), 5, 23, 34, 37, 54, 66, 68, 189, 272, 335; early career, 56–59, 61; expansion ambitions, 64–65; management style, 62, 84; nomination to Sri Lanka, 65; public relations skills, 196; relations with Department of External Affairs, 62–63; views on aid, 60

Centennial International Development Program, 168, 203

Central America, relations with, 13; as aid recipient, 136, 272, 280; and cold war crises in, 279; trade agreement with, 285

Ceylon. *See* Sri Lanka

Champagne, François-Philippe (Canadian politician), 289

Chile, 9, 133, 278, 335; and 1973 coup, 104, 278; as aid recipient, 146, 149–52, 155, 157–58, 176, 278; free trade with, 283

China, People's Republic, 13, 194; and aid to Pakistan 111–12; war with India, 109–10, 112

Chrétien, Jean (Canadian prime minister): and aid budget cuts, 13, 271, 297, 302–3; on Ethiopian famine, 247–48; and G-8 Action Plan, 306; and interest in Latin America, 282–84, 288

Christian Action for Development in the Caribbean (CADEC), 174

churches in Canada, 1, 12, 173, 174–75, 178, 192, 335; and Latin America 152, 276, 278; as pressure group, 84, 211, 247, 249, 253; relations with CIDA, 13, 207, 209. *See also* Canadian Council of Churches; Inter-Church Committee on Human Rights in Latin America; Inter-Church Fund for International Development; Taskforce on Churches and Corporate Responsibility

Churchill, Gordon (Canadian politician), 66, 67

Citizens for Foreign Aid Reform (C-FAR), 212

CITY TV, 252

Civil Service Commission, 56, 60, 66

civil society: in aid recipient countries, 11, 282; in Canada, 9, 10, 11, 14–13, 23, 24, 146, 288; influence on aid policy, 9, 15, 104, 146, 191, 193, 211, 271–72, 274, 283, 287; interest in Latin America, 13–14, 104, 276, 278–80; relations with CIDA, 103, 169–70, 282, 296, 299, 300–301, 304, 307; renewed interest in, under Justin Trudeau, 16, 274

Clark, Joe (Canadian prime minister): and Ethiopian famine relief, 245–48, 250, 254, 256

Claxton, Brooke (Canadian politician), 57, 73

Clay, Lucius (American general), 200

Cockburn, Bruce (Canadian entertainer), 281

Cold War: and aid, 12, 16, 33, 60–1, 74, 95, 275, 233; in Asia, 118, 194–95; in Bolivia 78; end of, 282; and Ethiopian

Colombia, 126, 129–30; and Economic and Technical Assistance Branch, 66, 67; and External Aid Office, 67–68, 103, 311; International Economic and Technical Cooperation Division, 5, 58, 66, 68; relations with CIDA, 173, 210; relations with Department of External Affairs, 33, 53, 55–56, 65, 67–68, 311; and Technical Cooperation Service, 87, 94. *See also* Ault, Orville; Brooke, T.J.; Bull, Fred; Cavell, R.G.; Department of Industry, Trade and Commerce; International Economic and Technical Cooperation Division

Development Education Animateur Programme (DEAP), 207, 209, 211

development education, 305

development planning, 88

Diefenbaker, John G. (Canadian prime minister), 6, 45, 65, 196; and aid for Pakistan 106–8; and relations with Perinbam, 166

Dominican Republic, 285

Douglas, Tommy (Canadian politician), 83

Dupuy, Michel (Canadian public servant), 9

E

Eberts, Christopher (Canadian diplomat), 109

Ecuador, 150

Edwards, Jim (Canadian politician), 249

Eggleton, Art (Canadian politician), 252

Egypt, 228

El Salvador, 151, 279, 280

Emergency Coordinator for African Relief, 250

English, John (Canadian public servant), 67, 68

environment, 286

Eritrea, 257

Ethiopia, 11, 190, 231; famine relief in the 1980s, 245–67, 271, 334

Export Development Canada, 318, 322

Export Development Corporation (EDC), 151–52, 155

Exports Credits Insurance Corporation, 135

External Aid Office (EAO), 6, 7, 45, 103; creation of, 53, 67–68, 103, 311; and CUSO, 203; and photography in, 225; transformation into CIDA, 7–8, 45, 103, 167–68, 206, 225, 311, 317. *See also* Herb Moran

F

Fantino, Julian (Canadian politician), 318–19

FinDev Canada: creation of, 322

food aid: as a weapon, 259, 261. *See also* Canadian Wheat Board; wheat

Food and Agriculture Organization (FAO), 92

For Whose Benefit? (Winegard Report), 11, 297, 302

Ford, Robert (Canadian diplomat), 55

Foreign Policy for Canadians, 8, 134, 136, 147, 205–6, 210, 276

Foundation for the Americas (FOCAL), 287

fragile states, 283, 284

Francophonie (La): as aid recipient, 14, 202, 297

G

Garrett, Nancy (CUSO volunteer), 166

GATT-Fly, 178, 211

Gedolf, Bob (British entertainer), 260

Gérin-Lajoie, Paul (Canadian public servant), 7, 9, 148, 154, 167, 176; interest in Latin America, 277

Germany, 319

Ghana, 66, 299

Glazebrook, George (Canadian diplomat and historian), 66

Global Affairs Canada, 231, 293, 320; and International Assistance Review, 320–23

Global Market Action Plan, 319

Gode, Ethiopia, 252

Godfrey, John (Canadian politician), 251

Goldschlag, Klaus (Canadian diplomat), 153

Gomez, Laureano (Colombia politician), 129

Gordon, Walter (Canadian politician), 200

Grandy, J. F. (Canadian diplomat), 134

Green, Howard (Canadian politician), 67
Gregg, Allan (Canadian pollster), 249
gross domestic product: aid as percentage
of, 7, 8, 9, 11, 17, 202, 265n63, 298, 303,
306, 322
Guatemala, 147, 151, 279, 280
Guelph African Relief Network (GAFRN),
252, 253
Guyana, 283, 299
Gwyn, Sandra (Canadian journalist), 164

H

Haiti, 16, 123, 173, 212, 273, 280, 284;
electoral importance, 284; as failed
state, 283, 287
Harper, Stephen (Canadian prime
minister), 13, 14, 16, 34, 138, 284; and
instrumentalization of aid, 274, 286;
interest in Latin America, 285, 287, 306;
merger of DFAIT and CIDA, 293, 318;
and record on aid, 312, 325
Head, Ivan (Canadian public servant), 212
Heasman, George (Canadian diplomat), 54
Heeney, Arnold (Canadian public servant),
55
Hellyer, Paul (Canadian politician), 155
Herbert, W. H. (Canadian cultural activist),
57
Herman, Lloyd (UN expert), 93
Higgins, Benjamin (Canadian development
economist), 6
high modernism, 28, 29, 46–47
Hobart, J. T. (Canadian public servant), 64
Holmes, John (Canadian diplomat), 56
Honduras, 279, 280, 283; country of focus,
286; and trade agreement, 285
Howe, C. D. (Canadian politician), 34, 58,
76, 154, 212; goodwill trade mission to
Colombia, 124–29; sale of jet fighters to
Colombia, 130–31
human rights, 324–25, 335; in Central
America, 280, 282; in Chile, 150–52;
in Cuba, 155–58; as influence on aid,
9, 146, 149, 178, 274, 278, 282, 285–86,
302; as factor in Ethiopian famine
relief, 255–56; in Haiti, 173; in Saudi
Arabia, 324–25

humane internationalism, 9, 170, 176, 249,
273, 297, 301, 313, 333
humanitarianism: as motive for aid, 8–9, 23,
31, 33, 60, 104, 116, 125, 134, 138, 165,
178, 196, 199, 231–32, 252, 280, 312

I

India, 4, 8, 24, 27–52, 60, 64, 75, 196, 271;
and Colombo Plan aid, 36–41; and
development planning, 35–36; and food
aid, 38, 41–42; Kundah hydro-eclectic
project, 44; and nuclear cooperation,
38, 41, 42, 43–44, 110; Mayurakshi
Dam (Canada Dam), 39, 43, 44; as
military aid recipient, 109, 112, 315;
and modernization, 28–31; and origins
of Colombo Plan aid, 31–35; and
Umtru Dam, 37, 44; and World Bank
consortium, 42
Indian National Congress, 36
Indigenous peoples, 30, 37, 76, 78, 333. *See
also* Inuit
Indonesia, 13, 65, 79, 83
Inter Pares, 172, 287
Inter-American Development Bank (IDB),
124, 133, 137, 146, 147, 148, 150, 152;
Canadian contribution to, 275, 278, 282
Inter-American Institute of Agricultural
Sciences, 147
Inter-Church Committee on Human Rights
in Latin America, 278
Inter-Church Fund for International
Development, 178
International Development Association, 103
International Development Photo Library
(Photothèque), (CIDA) 223–40; history,
225–31; contents, 232–35; significance,
236–39, 336
International Development Research Centre
(IDRC), 7, 136–37, 209
International Monetary Fund (IMF), 12, 271,
272, 282, 296, 298
Inuit, 244n45, 253
Iraq, 314; as failed state, 284
Israel, 66

372

INDEX

Peterson, David (Canadian politician), 252
Philippines, 229
Pinilla, Rojas (Colombian general), 129, 132
Pinochet, Augusto (Chilean dictator), 150, 152, 278
Plumptre, Wynne (Canadian public servant), 56, 57, 66, 73
Posgate, Dale (CIDA employee), 172
Pratt, Cranford (Canadian political scientist), 2, 15, 124, 170, 193, 249, 300, 305, 313
Pratt, Frank (Canadian public servant), 64
Privy Council Office, 66
promotional state, 113, 123–24, 129, 139, 189
Protheroe, David (Canadian consultant), 165
public engagement: as aid priority, 302; and CIDA, 9–10, 13, 155, 167, 169, 177, 224, 226, 232, 234, 237, 271, 305; and criticism of foreign aid, 150–51, 155, 174, 205–13; and Diefenbaker, 197–200; with Ethiopian famine relief, 11, 246–55, 262; with Latin American issues, 276, 280; and Lester B. Pearson, 201–05; and St. Laurent, 193–97; and support for foreign aid; 1, 30, 37, 58, 86, 189, 213, 313; and Pierre Elliott Trudeau, 205–13; and UN, 24, 84, 94. *See also* civil society; non-governmental organizations

R

Reagan, Ronald (American president), 259, 279, 280
Reid, Escott (Canadian diplomat), 54, 60, 203
Ritchie, A. E. "Ed" (Canadian diplomat), 62–63, 67; and aid to Cuba, 154–55
Roberts, James (Canadian businessman and public servant), 67
Robertson, Norman (Canadian diplomat), 67, 110
Robinson, H. Basil (Canadian diplomat), 108
Roche, Douglas (Canadian politician), 155, 157–58
Ronning, Chester (Canadian politician and diplomat), 44
Rosenthal, W. (Canadian public servant), 63

Rostow, Walt, (American economist) 6, 90
Royal Canadian Air Force (RCAF), 110, 131
Rwanda, 231, 235, 239

S

Somalia, 262
Saudi Arabia: arms sales to, 15, 324
Scott, Frank (Canadian scholar), 83
Second World War, 6, 54, 65, 76, 125, 189, 232; influence on postwar aid, 31, 36, 46, 194, 233
securitization, of aid, 306
Sharing our Future, 297
Sharp, Mitchell (Canadian politician): as trade official, 132; as secretary of state for external affairs from 1968-74, 117, 134, and aid to Cuba, 153, 154
Shastri, Lal Bahadur (Indian prime minister), 110
signature projects, 316. *See also* Afghanistan—Dahla Dam; India; Warsak hydro-electric project
Sims, David (Canadian public servant), 62
Sinclair, James (Canadian politician), 34
Šlezić, Lana (Canadian photographer), 231
Small, John (Canadian diplomat), 116, 117, 118
Smillie, Ian (Canadian development activist), 169
Smith, L. A. H. "Larry" (Canadian diplomat), 174–75, 176
Smith, Sidney (Canadian politician), 197
South America: *See* Latin America; individual country names
Southeast Asia, 65
Soviet Union: and aid to Afghanistan, 314; and aid to Pakistan, 111–12; and UN technical assistance, 91–92
Special Fund for Africa, 255
Special Joint Parliamentary Committee Reviewing Canadian Foreign Policy, 295, 302
Spender, Percy (Australian politician), 33
Spicer, Keith (Canadian public servant), 1–2, 14, 27, 39, 125, 138, 145

United Nations Conference on Human Settlements (Habitat), 225
United Nations Conference on Trade and Development (UNCTAD), 103, 178
United Nations Development Programme (UNDP), 7, 23, 83, 103
United Nations Educational, Scientific and Cultural Organization (UNESCO), 166
United Nations Expanded Programme of Technical Assistance, 23, 28, 54
United Nations Relief and Rehabilitation Agency (UNRRA), 3, 32
United Nations Technical Assistance Administration (TAA), 28; in Bolivia 74-75, 78, 82; Canadian contribution to, 84-87; experts by country, 89; and modernization theory, 89-90; and resident representatives, 82, 83, 91; and Soviet Union, 91-93; and UN specialized agencies, 92
United States Agency for International Development (USAID), 7, 103, 279
United States, 59, 75, 128, 259, 276; Canadian relations with, 1, 12, 65, 86, 147, 189, 199-200, 276-77, 279-80, 282, 284; foreign aid, 7, 24, 31-33, 43, 55, 60, 84, 89, 91, 94, 106, 200; foreign policy, 13, 15, 31, 89, 91, 116, 333; and Latin America, 104, 129, 131-32, 134, 136, 145, 149-50, 153, 275-76, 279; and technical assistance, 74-75, 79, 84, 86, 91-93, 95
universities, 37, 84, 137, 201, 203, 251, 253, 324; as aid recipients, 150, 154, 324; as aid stakeholders, 175, 192, 207, 209-10. *See also* Canadian University Service Overseas; World University Service of Canada
Uruguay, 149

V

Venezuela, 147

W

Wanzell, Grant (CUSO volunteer), 170
Warsak hydro-electric and irrigation project, 61, 107, 112, 198, 314-15
Washington consensus. *See* structural adjustment programs
Weld, John (Canadian diplomat), 111, 114, 115
Wershof, Max (Canadian diplomat), 63
wheat: as aid, 41-42, 65, 114. *See also* Canadian Wheat Board
White, Nancy (Canadian entertainer), 281
Wilgress, Dana (Canadian diplomat), 32
Winegard, William (Canadian politician), 11, 297, 302
Winters, Robert (Canadian politician), 77
Women in Development (WID), 173
women, 11, 15, 16, 173, 231, 259, 302; Justin Trudeau and, 274, 288, 289, 320-24
World Bank, 5, 12, 65, 103, 166; and Aid India Consortium, 42, 45; and Bolivia 82; in Chile, 152; and Colombia 128, 135; and structural adjustment programs, 271, 272, 282, 296, 298
World Conference on Women (1995), 231
World Food Conference, 177
World Food Programme, 45, 262
World Health Organization (WHO), 92
World University Service of Canada (WUSC), 165, 166; and Ethiopian famine relief, 251-52
WWII. *See* Second World War

Y

Yemen, 324